JUN 2 5 2010

EAST MEADOW PUBLIC LIBRARY

3 1299 00830 9453

D0628931

East Meadow Public Library
1886 Front Street
East Meadow, NY 11554
(516) 794-2570
www.eastmeadow.info

MASTERS

OF THE GAME

ALSO BY KIM EISLER

SHARK TANK:
*Greed, Politics, and the Collapse of Finley Kumble,
One of America's Largest Law Firms* (1990)

THE LAST LIBERAL:
*Justice William J. Brennan, Jr. and the Decisions
That Transformed America* (1997)

REVENGE OF THE PEQUOTS:
*How a Small Native American Tribe
Created the World's Most Profitable Casino* (2002)

MASTERS
OF THE GAME

INSIDE THE WORLD'S

MOST POWERFUL

LAW FIRM

KIM EISLER

THOMAS DUNNE BOOKS
ST. MARTIN'S PRESS
NEW YORK

THOMAS DUNNE BOOKS.
An imprint of St. Martin's Press.

MASTERS OF THE GAME. Copyright © 2010 by Kim Eisler. All rights reserved. Printed in the United States of America. For information, address St. Martin's Press, 175 Fifth Avenue, New York, N.Y. 10010.

www.thomasdunnebooks.com
www.stmartins.com

Library of Congress Cataloging-in-Publication Data

Eisler, Kim Isaac.
    Masters of the game : inside the world's most powerful law firm / Kim Eisler.—1st ed.
      p. cm.
    Includes bibliographical references and index.
    ISBN 978-0-312-55424-8
    1. Williams & Connolly—History.   2. Law firms—Washington (D.C.)—Biography.
I. Title.
    KF355.W27E38 2010
    340.06'0753—dc22

2009047580

First Edition: June 2010

10 9 8 7 6 5 4 3 2 1

For Judy

CONTENTS

———◼———

ACKNOWLEDGMENTS..ix

INTRODUCTION: The Firm That Runs the World...........................1

1. Roots, Build, Grow, Branch...7

2. Hollywood on the Potomac..14

3. The Passed-Over Partner...34

4. War Department Meets State Department.............................43

5. Where Is Captain Sullivan Tonight?................................50

6. "Sully" Sacks a Veep..58

7. Craig's Gist...67

8. The Little Generalist...72

9. Another Day, Another Dollar.......................................80

10. The Stage Manager..86

11. The Elevator Operator's Son......................................91

12. The Courtesy Man..103

13. The High Watermark..106

14. Cigars with Castro, Flowers for Ferraro.........................111

15. Non-Hodgkin's Strikes Out.......................................118

Contents

16. The Potted Plant 124

17. No Apple for the Teacher 144

18. St. Gabriel's Cemetery 150

19. Spying on the Birds 157

20. The *Enquirer* Meets the Renaissance. 163

21. Swank Hillary 175

22. The Husky Football Star: Not! 180

23. The Fabulous Bennett Brothers. 188

24. Hillary: The First Client 202

25. A Summitt and a Tragedy 208

26. Pricked by a Hatpin 216

27. Elián 231

28. Pardon Us 240

29. Goldin Parachutes 246

30. Book Sport in D.C. 263

31. Barack Atah Illinois 270

32. Dueling Hotheads. 277

33. Half-Baked Alaska 285

34. Afterword 300

BIBLIOGRAPHY 303

INDEX 313

ACKNOWLEDGMENTS

———■———

This is my second book for Thomas Dunne, who started me on the path to popular writing about lawyers and law firms with the publication of *Shark Tank* in 1990. I am indebted to him for reaching into his memory bank to recall our glory days and to want to make it happen again. I am also extremely grateful to my never-say-die agent, Jane Dystel, who was willing to forget a few awkward moments in our professional relationship and help me restart my career writing books. In both cases, it has been a fulfilling reunion.

I had no idea at the time I broached this proposal to Jane that she would end up being a character in the book. This naturally caused me a little discomfort and uncertainty about how to deal with her part, and while I feel confident my account is accurate, I hope I have not offended either Jane, or her sometime competitor Robert Barnett, with whom I have had good professional relationships. I have attempted to deal with their conflicted involvement in Barack Obama's autobiography in a neutral fashion.

For over two decades, I covered Williams & Connolly as a law beat reporter, first for *The American Lawyer* magazine, then *Legal Times*, and later for *Washingtonian* magazine. Some years ago, I wrote a story for *Washingtonian* about the amazing web of clients that Williams & Connolly represent, on all sides of the political spectrum. In our office we called such stories "octopus," since the long arms of the firm seemed to shoot out in all directions. This particular octopus was rarely harpooned.

In the course of reporting on the firm for those twenty years, I became one of the few reporters in the country to win access to Brendan Sullivan, Larry Lucchino, David Kendall, and Bob Barnett, and at various times had written profiles of all of them.

Acknowledgments

Gregory Craig I had interviewed on the phone, from time to time, but did not know as well. In the world of Washington lawyers, they stood head and shoulders above any other attorneys I have ever encountered as interesting and iconoclastic subjects. Washington law is populated with a great deal of self-important, self-promoting individuals and clearly the culture at Williams & Connolly, in the post–Edward Bennett Williams era, was not typical. The notion that a firm that was now famous for representing a president had also represented the man who shot a president was just the tip of the iceberg when it came to irony or coincidence. It seemed that there was hardly an event on the world stage in which Williams & Connolly wasn't always in the background, if not front and center.

At various times, each of the principal partners had told me that they would never write a book about their cases. Brendan Sullivan, in particular, delighted in saying that just as Supreme Court Justice Hugo Black used to boast, he would burn his papers and take his secrets to the grave.

Following the publication of my article on Williams & Connolly in *Washingtonian,* entitled "The Firm That Runs the World," it occurred to me the firm's web of relationships would make for an interesting and revealing book about who really pulls the strings in Washington law, media, politics, and, to a degree, even business.

I was still uncertain how to proceed because I knew that each of the partners would probably not be cooperative once the word "book," was mentioned, although each of them had always been helpful and cooperative when I was simply writing stories or asking them questions, a happenstance that many of my colleagues found rather amazing.

A breakthrough in my thinking came when the normally reticent Brendan Sullivan called me one morning and asked if I would meet him for lunch. I can't say what the topic was that prompted the invitation, but it was a unique event. There was a question that he wanted to ask me and we ended up having a delightful conversation in a quiet Italian restaurant. During the course of that lunch, Sullivan said that he thought it was worthy of my noting, in future articles, how many Williams & Connolly alumni had gone on to bigger and maybe better things outside of the field of law. Few Williams & Connolly partners leave to join another firm, but quite a few, like Jeffrey Kindler, the CEO of Pfizer Corporation, have gone on to become titans of business, industry, and, in the case of Larry Lucchino, sports.

I had never heard Sullivan make a story suggestion before, so I attached some significance to it, and concluded that if I were to write a book about Williams & Connolly, as the "firm that runs the world," Brendan wouldn't necessarily come to my house and strangle me.

Subsequently I had another lunch with Brendan Sullivan at Washington's Metropolitan Club, where I learned that I was only the second reporter he had invited to lunch in the past ten years, which I took as a badge of honor, especially since I had now had lunch with him twice. I subsequently met with David Kendall, who had forgotten my e-mail telling him about the book, and seemed genuinely stricken when he was reminded of it later. He seemed, however, to overcome his natural shyness and cooperated, providing me with the details of his colorful life before joining Williams & Connolly. Nevertheless, he never discussed any of his cases, nor did he make any comments about his involvement with Hillary Clinton or the Senate trial of her husband, President Bill Clinton. The closest he came to mentioning her name was relating how he had had a car accident while campaigning for her during the Iowa caucuses in 2008.

Eventually I went to Ft. Myers, Florida, where the Red Sox have spring training, to interview Larry Lucchino, who I had written about many times over the years since first meeting him in 1987, when he was a young Williams & Connolly partner. We had our interview in the bleachers at the Ft. Myers' spring training facility.

Perhaps I had known Bob Barnett the best of the five over the years. In my early days of covering lawyers, he was the person who dealt most often with press inquiries, since the firm had no spokesperson or PR department.

Shortly after determining that I was going to write a book about these five disciples of Edward Bennett Williams, my editor at *Washingtonian* read a story in *The Wall Street Journal* about Barnett's representation of former British prime minister Tony Blair. He asked if I would write a profile on Barnett for the magazine. Some of the biographical material in this book on Barnett appeared in my *Washingtonian* profile of him. Some of the other bits and pieces about Washington lawyers and their foibles, for lack of a better word, have also appeared in my columns over the years.

In short, I am indebted to all the past and present partners at Williams & Connolly whom I interviewed, but particularly the principals. I tried to walk the fine line between being honest and forthright, while not violating any confidences that the partners had placed in me. Even before writing the book, they knew I was a reporter. Occasionally something would come up where one of them asked me not to write something. I have tried to honor that, although in a couple of cases I discovered that what they asked me not to write, they had already said to someone else. One example was some comments by Lucchino about his former boss Eli Jacobs. It turned out what he had asked me not to use was almost exactly what he had said previously in a published oral history of the Orioles.

Over my twenty years as a legal reporter, I have been fortunate to work with and learn from some of the best journalists in the business: Steven Brill, Hodding Carter III, David Beckwith, Jill Abramson, Aaron Freiwald, Jim Lyons, Eleanor Kerlow, Mary Billard, Joe Registrato, Chuck Conconi, Rob Boynton, John Henry, Glenn Garvin, Milt Policzer, and numerous others. At *Washingtonian*, my sounding board for many of my story ideas was Ken DeCell, the best editor in the business. I am also indebted to John Limpert, who, until I left *Washingtonian* in August 2009, showed great latitude in giving me time and space to complete this project. I am always indebted to my friends Edward Nelson, Joel Chineson, Edward Klein, Alan Fisch, Nona Edelson, Ken Adams, and all the members of the gang from Lynchburg.

I also want to thank India Cooper for her enormously helpful suggestions and changes; also at St. Martin's Press, Henry Kaufman, Bob Berkel, John Schoenfelder, Margaret Smith, and Rob Kirkpatrick.

Most of all I thank my wife, former *Washington Post* editor Judy Sarasohn, and our daughter, Sara Sophie Eisler, now a budding marine biologist at the University of North Carolina-Wilmington.

MASTERS

OF THE GAME

INTRODUCTION

THE FIRM THAT RUNS THE WORLD

———■———

It was April 7, 2009, yet another in a series of uncharacteristically cool and windy spring days in Washington that year, when a crowded white van pulled up outside the downtown offices of Williams & Connolly. There was no uniformed concierge at the curb; Washington is anything but a doorman town.

From the shotgun, the front right seat by the driver, a slight, angular man with dark glasses and puffy white hair, his jaw locked tightly in a serious but satisfied grip, jumped out and slid open the vehicle's middle door. Out spilled newly exonerated Alaska senator, Ted Stevens, his wife, Catherine, two daughters, and several attorneys, mostly toting thick briefcases and giant smiles. All except Stevens's principal attorney, still standing stoically by the door he had just released, a scowl on his face. He was, in his own words, in a "silent rage."

Brendan V. Sullivan Jr., who had turned sixty-seven just three weeks earlier on March 11, 2009, had never been a young-looking man. His high school classmates back at Providence Country Day School most often used the word "fearsome" to describe the boy whom the yearbook editors called "our esteemed leader." Their nickname for Sullivan was "George Sully," the George in honor of the country's first president, who was also known for his stony countenance and historic leadership skills.

For the last thirty-five years, with only one exception, the mention of which could send Sullivan into high-pitched paroxysms of anger, there had not been a single guilty verdict for one of his clients that he had not been able to undo or finesse. In all that time, only one of Sullivan's clients had ever seen the inside of a prison, despite the fact that, by Sullivan's own admission, "by the time someone comes to me, they are pretty far up the creek."

Even after Stevens had been convicted of multiple felonies by a federal jury in Washington some weeks earlier, Sullivan had never doubted for a moment that the conviction would be overturned and Stevens would never spend a day in jail.

Admittedly disappointed by the jury verdict, it was only a question, he had assured Stevens, of when and how that verdict would be overturned. As it happened, by the modern molasses-like measures of criminal justice, the reversal had taken a remarkably short period of time. Even so, Brendan Sullivan was not the type to dance in the end zone. "I don't do high fives," he would dourly grumble after his biggest courtroom successes. After Attorney General Eric Holder had announced a week earlier that the U.S. Department of Justice could no longer go forward with the prosecution of Stevens, it had been a foregone conclusion that Judge Emmet Sullivan (no relation to Brendan), would dismiss the case and effectively void the jury's unanimous verdict. Not only had Sullivan won the dismissal of the case against his client, it had happened in a way the government could not even appeal. It was one of the cleanest and most decisive victories in his career. For years there had been a myth about Sullivan. It went like this: In any case Brendan Sullivan tries, there is a greater chance the federal or state prosecutor will go to jail than his client. On the surface such a notion seemed totally counterintuitive, a lawyerly exaggeration. Yet in this case, the aphorism had hit 100 on the truth-o-meter. While Stevens was going free, the prosecutors on the team that had brought the massive resources of the federal government against the wily forty-year Senate veteran—apparently for not revealing he had been given a chair, a barbecue grill, some Christmas lights, and home repairs as gifts—were themselves headed for investigation of their allegedly "unethical" prosecutorial conduct.

As Sullivan clambered onto the sidewalk, he silently pondered one of his most satisfying courthouse victories. For Williams & Connolly, the firm with which he had been associated for more than forty years, it was simply another day in the life of Washington's most powerful and influential partnership. Sullivan was not so crass as to say it, but many years earlier, after winning a not-guilty verdict for a man who had shot the president of the United States in front of a national television audience, one of Sullivan's partners had crowed, "Another day, another dollar." It was an unofficial firm motto the more discreet Sullivan preferred not to advertise.

Upstairs in this downtown Washington office building, Sullivan had old phone messages from client Dick Grasso, the former head of the New York Stock Exchange, from dozens of fellow attorneys being sued for malpractice, from CEOs of giant corporations, and from mischievous tech titans under scrutiny and prosecution by the Securities and Exchange Commission. He was, in simple terms, the most highly sought-after criminal defense attorney in the United States. It was a reputation he had worked hard to build, and while he was not the sort to toot his own horn, or even to put out a news release, it was richly satisfying. Although he never sought press coverage when attention came to him, as it had in the Stevens case, he was not averse or immune to what it meant to his reputation or to his ability to attract clients. Walking into the grand lobby of the building where Williams & Connolly maintains its one and only office, Sullivan often contemplated the power and glory shooting outward from this place, an influence not just geographic but crossing disciplines from politics to business to sports and, naturally, to law. He had watched both himself and many of his partners, one-by-one, land the biggest cases and achieve the greatest glory. By the spring of 2009, their power and mystique had never been greater. Although books could be written about the power of the nine justices of the Supreme Court, the real-life day-to-day influence of the members of the current High Court paled in comparison to the dozen or so top past and present partners at Williams & Connolly who spent their time picking those Supreme Court judges, counseling U.S. presidents and foreign leaders, arranging media and press personalities like pieces on a game board, and even winning World Series games in baseball. The "nine" of the conservative and slow-moving Supreme Court might hope to have that much impact on American life and law, but not since the Warren Court in the 1950s and 1960s could they even make a good argument for actually having it. The power center of Washington law had shifted from the magnificent "Marble Palace" to this almost architecturally obscure structure in the middle of the downtown business district. Even if one acknowledged the ultimate power the Court did have, if exercised, to change life in the United States, even the path to the court now went through Wiliams & Connolly's partners.

Less than a mile to the west of where Sullivan and Stevens now stood, the lawyer's right arm draped comfortably on the senator's back, one of the most powerful offices in Washington, the White House counsel's job, was, at the time, still filled by Gregory Craig, who up until his appointment by

President Barack Obama had been Sullivan's partner at Williams & Connolly. Craig was busy considering who he might recommend as the next justice for the Supreme Court, a monumental decision upon which his views would have as much impact as anyone's. Among the top candidates, a few blocks to the south, was Elena Kagan, the new solicitor general of the United States. She was no doubt busy preparing to decide what cases the United States would support during the current term of the Supreme Court. The SG is not only the most prestigious legal job in the country and a historic stepping-stone to a seat on the High Court, it is certainly one of the most important in terms of shaping American law itself. Like Craig, Kagan was a former lawyer at Williams & Connolly. Another possibility, a fellow graduate of Yale Law School named Sonia Sotomayor, also figured in Craig's calculations. As it turned out, Sotomayor won the nomination this time around, but most figure Kagan's turn will eventually come.

To Sullivan's north just a few blocks sat the offices of the *Washington Post*. For several decades this most important influential daily newspaper had been a client of Williams & Connolly. Now, however, the firm's connections to the *Post* amounted to more than mere libel defense and vetting of controversial stories: The paper's new publisher, Katharine Weymouth, like Kagan, was a former lawyer from Williams & Connolly, herself imbued with the history, traditions, and unique mental makeup that came with the job. As the trademarks and nameplates of corporate America flashed in front of Sullivan's van on the ride back from the courthouse, so also did the names of other former partners who were connected with the biggest of them. Richard Hoffman was a vice president at Marriott. Judith Miller was the general counsel of Bechtel. Nicole Seligman was now high up in the corporate boardroom of Sony. Sven Holmes was the public face of controversial accounting giant KPMG. Jeff Kindler was the chairman and CEO of Pfizer, the world's largest drug company, the keeper of both Lipitor and Viagra. On the side of a bus was an advertisement for Washington's Major League Baseball team. Baseball's hottest executive, Boston Red Sox president Larry Lucchino, had been a Williams & Connolly partner for three decades, using karma and acquired mental discipline to climb up the standings of the sports world, doing magic with baseball's unluckiest— some say cursed—team.

The most powerful of them all were just feet away, still working in the building. Up above on the eleventh floor, partner Robert Barnett paced his own corner office. He had impressive clients to contemplate. Former British prime minister Tony Blair had come to America to teach a class and deliver lectures; Laura Bush could be on the phone any minute. Sarah Palin, then still the governor of Alaska, was calling about a book that might partially fund her presidential run in 2012 and keep her in the spotlight until then. Barnett would have to put her on hold if former president George W. Bush called about a memoir as he might at any time. The television in his office was turned to mute, but, over time, he could see the faces of more clients: Wolf Blitzer, Katie Couric, Chris Wallace, George Will, Bob Woodward, and Alan Greenspan. Tim Russert, the host of *Meet the Press*, had been both a client and a close friend before his death. The politicians, the elite press corps, cabinet officers both leaving an administration and entering it—all seemed to want to check with Barnett before they made any kind of a career move or even a speech.

Not far from Barnett's office a floor below, was the sanctum of David Kendall. As the principal attorney for Hillary and Bill Clinton, this reclusive midwesterner perhaps kept more secrets about the powerful presidential couple than anyone else. He was the lawyer for dozens of other attorneys and the chief counsel to the family of Mohamed Al Fayed, whose son had been killed in the crash with Princess Diana. Kendall was one of the preeminent media lawyers in the world, often knowing before anyone else what would be in papers as varied as the *Washington Post* and the *National Enquirer*, advising not just the executives who ran those publications but often the colorful personalities about whom they wrote.

Sullivan had always imagined the offices of Williams & Connolly as a Marine Corps barracks. A recent cover of the *American Lawyer* magazine had depicted them with turrets instead of windows and cannons instead of curtains. Sullivan, steeped in his litigator persona, loved the imagery, and the courtroom was his personal Antietam. He once wrote "like the marines, we fight with all our energy and skill to defend our clients. This is the way it should be; zealously, as the Rules of Professional Conduct require." In fact, with field officers like Greg Craig then in control at the White House, and Barnett upstairs, one could quickly get the sense that this centrally located building was more than just barracks—it was a command center. What were they commanding? Everything, some only half-joked, from Pfizer to Fenway.

With no battalion of PR men and women to promote them, on most days their efforts were revealed to others only on a need-to-know basis. Now the highly publicized Stevens trial had put them in a rare and almost uncomfortable spotlight. Outside of the courthouse or the lawyer-loaded Metropolitan Club, most people had no idea what Sullivan, Craig, or Barnett even looked like. Even in Washington, some of the most avid political junkies couldn't recognize any of them. Nevertheless, if Americans wanted to understand who was really running the Washington game, they needed to figuratively look no further than the starting lineup of Sullivan, Barnett, Craig, and Kendall. When it came to Larry Lucchino, the baseball allusion was literal. The "nine" is the important number in American legal life—but the "five" may well have them beat.

I

ROOTS, BUILD, GROW, BRANCH

———————— ■ ————————

Many American cities are defined by the names on their tallest build-ings: the banks of Charlotte, the insurance companies of Hartford or Jacksonville, the retail world of Chicago with its Willis (formerly Sears) Tower and Wrigley Building. In Washington, the city where I live and went to college, there are just short squat buildings, hundreds of them. In anthropomorphic terms, they are more reminiscent of Sam Rayburn or Theodore Bilbo than of Abraham Lincoln. No building in Washington can be more than thirteen stories tall. Reacting to the construction of a perceived ugly fourteen-story building in the late 1890s, Congress passed the Height of Buildings Act, which effectively mandated that no structure in Wash-ington could be higher than the U.S. Capitol dome. Since then, the law on tall buildings has been amended, but the bottom line is that D.C. is not a city of skyscrapers.

However, if you walk around Williams & Connolly's world in down-town Washington and happen to be familiar with an arcane lawyer's refer-ence book called the Martindale-Hubbell Law Directory, you would notice that the names on the squattest but most substantial buildings are those of powerful national law firms: Venable, DLA Piper, Winston & Strawn, O'Melveny & Myers, Hogan & Hartson. Maybe the names don't sound immediately familiar, but each is the name of a giant law firm with hun-dreds, even thousands, of lawyers. Very few are doing anything as interest-ing as what you see on television dramas. Flamboyant personalities are frowned upon. One of the dirty little truths about Washington-style law is that lawyers here largely believe that once you have gone to court, you and your client have already lost. In one of the most famous comments ever made on the prosecution of a Washington insider, former secretary of labor Raymond Donovan once asked, after his acquittal on fraud charges, "Where do I go to get my reputation back?"

According to Bar Association records, there are some one hundred thousand lawyers around this city. A good many of them deal in regulatory work. They are the lawyers who practice at federal agencies known only by initials: ICC, FCC, FEC, FERC, FDA, OTS, and USDA. You come up with the initials, lawyers will appear there. The cheery agriculture lawyers practice at the USDA; the pessimists prefer to call it the DOA. If there is no agency yet with your initials, just wait; there will be soon. Be sure a band of so-called experts in that alphabetic field will be waiting to break in.

Washington has more than its share of regulatory lawyers, banking lawyers, Food and Drug Administration lawyers (thousands of whom are in the employ of drug companies), real estate lawyers, contentious divorce lawyers (a small but busy band), labor lawyers, employment lawyers, trade advisers, and, of course, noisy white-collar defense lawyers, the guys you call when the FBI or the IRS is going through your trash. Not everyone can practice with Brendan Sullivan at Williams & Connolly, but the milieu surrounding them is both rich and often inbred, and the paths between Williams & Connolly and everyone else often cross.

There are the lawyers who lobby Congress, although many lobbyists are not lawyers at all but former congressional staffers. Some have law school training, others don't. It isn't unique to Washington, but naturally there is a good-sized number of slip-and-fall guys—even big shots can fall off a podium while giving a speech. You can drill down to some unique specialties. Nothing illustrates this more than the one lawyer in Washington who specializes in representing accused spies or beautiful dames, or a beautiful dame who happens to be a spy. That would be the ultimate client for Plato Cacheris, a son of Greek immigrants, who has represented some fairly famous people over the years. During the Iran-Contra scandal, Plato represented Fawn Hall, the attractive secretary of U.S. Marine Lt. Col. Oliver North, the most famous of Brendan Sullivan's clients. When North was trying to get secret documents out of the White House in advance of federal investigators, they were allegedly smuggled out in Fawn's skirt and bra. Plato is over eighty now but still looks fabulous and totally in his element with a beautiful female client on his arm.

During the Clinton years, Plato represented Monica Lewinsky—not that she seemed as attractive as Fawn Hall, although apparently she was alluring to a certain U.S. president who had grown up in Arkansas. More to the point, Plato is still the guy to call if you are a busted spy, like CIA traitor Aldrich Ames or Robert Hanssen, the turncoat FBI agent about whom the movie *Breach* was made. Plato probably wouldn't have his own television show, however. He almost always cuts a deal for his client. If the client faces death, Plato gets him life. If he faces life, Plato can get him out in forty years. Back in his day, spectators drove hundreds of miles to see Plato Cacheris perform in court, but he rarely, if ever, participates in actual trials anymore.

Cacheris is a charming old-schooler. He is warm, courteous, friendly with the press, easy to like. He sends thank-you notes when reporters write something nice about him. Espionage gamers keep his number in their Rolodex. When he was taken to federal prison in Alexandria to meet double agent Aldrich Ames for the first time, Cacheris stretched out his hand to introduce himself. "Plato Cacheris," he said.

The prisoner looked at him with awe and glee. "I was wondering what I was going to do for a lawyer," he exclaimed proudly, "and I get Plato Cacheris!"

Plato looks like a fearsome Washington power player in $1,500 Tasmanian fine merino wool suits that he buys from London's Denman & Goddard. On the surface one might look at him and say "Washington establishment," but despite the trappings, he's a bit of a nonconformist. Plato can't work in a big law firm. Corporate firms keep trying to hire him. Every five years or so the deal is so good that he accepts, plunging from his sole practitioner's office into the bowels of a hectic, sock-'em-in-six-minute-intervals law firm. He never lasts long. Plato can't fill out billing records. He can't bear to force clients to pay, and he's embarrassed telling them that firm bean counters are expecting him to charge nearly $1,000 an hour. He won't double bill, an unethical practice not unusual in Washington. If a lawyer can talk to two clients in the same five-minute period, he can charge both of them his minimum billing rate, which is six minutes' worth. Associates can use this as a way to slip ahead of their fellows on the partnership track, and it's how unscrupulous lawyers manage to bill more hours than exist in a week, thanks in large part to the legal profession's greatest profit-enhancing device, the BlackBerry. Technology is a two-edged sword, of course. The problem is so pervasive that clients now hire companies whose sole job is to uncover unethical billing practices and profit by split-ting the refunds with the client. Another neat law firm trick is to charge clients excessively for office services, especially photocopying. When one young associate arrived at Fried, Frank, Harris, Shriver & Jacobson, a powerful New York City–based firm largely representing banks and finan-cial institutions, he was told to charge clients twenty-five cents per page. The lawyer was surprised and calculated the actual cost to be only nine cents at most, including labor. When he brought it up to senior manage-ment, he was told photocopying was a firm "profit center."

Plato hates tedious meetings, he has no inclination for bullshit, and nobody has ever seen his thumbs rolling over an electronic device. He has no BlackBerry, he can't do paperwork, and he won't cheat. The green-eyeshade types ask for his billing sheets; he usually doesn't fill them out. This most corporate-looking attorney in Washington is totally not corpo-rate. After a few months in the Orwellian prison of the modern megalaw firm, Plato is back practicing by himself again, and the cycle begins anew. You can't always tell as much as you think just by looking at someone. That's the lesson—not the myth—of this modern day Plato.

The center of downtown Washington, around Thirteenth and F streets, was once a no-man's-land. In the early 1970s, I had a job requiring me to carry a film-filled red mesh fruit sack from the offices of *Time* magazine at Sixteenth and I streets, two blocks from the White House and next to the elegant Hay-Adams Hotel, to the bus station about five blocks away. Even-tually the rolls of valuable film would be loaded on a bus, sent to New York, and picked up at the Port Authority station in midtown to be taken to the *Time* photo editor in the Time-Life Building in Rockefeller Center.

Time would happily have paid for my cab fare, but I was a hungry college student. Well, the hunger was taken care of, since *Time* paid the dinner ex-penses each night for anyone who had to work after 8:00 P.M., which meant me. Cabdrivers did not exactly welcome a seventy-five-cent fare (yes, that's what it was then) when on the other floors of our building were the distin-guished lawyers from Washington's most elite old-line law firm, Covington & Burling. So I stashed the cab fare from petty cash in my pocket and walked to the bus station. One of Covington's best-known partners was Dean Acheson, who had been secretary of state in the Truman administra-tion. He was the epitome of what a diplomat should look like, from the bowler to the white bushy eyebrows. I felt lucky when I realized I lived and worked in a place where I could just catch a glimpse of such a great man. One afternoon I found myself in the elevator with him. With us was a knot of chattering, complaining secretaries, returning from lunch. They got out, but I kept going, just so I could be alone in the elevator with a historic figure. It was a good move on my part. No sooner had they exited than he looked over at me and wiggled the eyebrows. "Trouble is the water we swim in," Acheson instructed me. That was Washington in a nutshell.

Nonetheless, I worried my billing *Time* for cabs I never took might one day disqualify me from holding Acheson's position. Perhaps that made me, like the lawyers, a double biller? I prefer to think of the petty cash allotment as a combat zone bonus. People thought I was nuts for walking into that area in those years. Suicidal might be a better word, In the 1960s and early 1970s, you simply didn't cross Fifteenth Street in the eastward direction of the U.S. Capitol. Dozens of rats scampered openly across the sidewalks, heading for big blue bins of trash. You learned to look straight ahead walking the dangerous streets of Washington. Hookers lined the sidewalks of L and K streets like spectators at the inauguration parade. You never made eye contact with strangers. That was way too dangerous. People yelled, you kept going. I was never robbed and never shot, but I knew some who were.

The route taken by this small-town teenager to the bus station is not scary anymore. The porn stores and wall-to-wall hookers are long gone. The old Greyhound station itself, a protected neoclassic design that cannot be legally torn down, was rebuilt into a fancy office building. The old bus ticket counter is now a fancy reception area. There is a faux boarding bay in the lobby that still tells the story of the once busy bus station that used to be here. The reality of the Greyhound station was not nearly so glamorous as the nostalgic bus display makes it seem. Come to think of it, riding on a crowded intercity bus wasn't really all that much fun. The rest of the building is now filled with lawyers. There are some who would probably say, "Bring back the rats."

The best-known firm that was located inside the renovated bus station was a personal injury law practice headed by Michael Hausfeld, who had made millions suing companies and Swiss banks that aided or financed the Holocaust. He filed antismoking suits against tobacco companies and took on Exxon on behalf of local fishermen after the 1989 *Exxon Valdez* oil spill damaged the fishing areas of native Alaskans. Time and distance had no importance to Hausfeld. He would sue anybody, anywhere. Descendants of people who aided the Inquisition could not consider themselves safe. He devised a grand plan—in the middle of the 2008 recession—to put offices all over the world to satisfy his dreams of global legal conquest. One day in 2008, when he was out of the country, his partners decided Hausfeld was too ambitious and his cases simply too expensive to pursue. So they voted him out of his own firm and taped a notice to that effect on his office chair.

When Hausfeld got to his office and found the note, he was perturbed. He told his partners that they were "cold" for putting the note on the chair, and he announced his intention to pursue what one could only assume was the logical end of his career: He hired attorneys to sue his partners. It was a fitting end to the firm he had cofounded some two decades earlier. They took umbrage that anyone would suggest there was anything unusual about work-chair notification. The managing partner of the firm told me, "As is the case with virtually any partnership, changes in status require formal written notification. Finding him out of the office, we left the documents in Michael's office in a place where he was certain to see them—on his office chair, as well as informing him by e-mail." So, silly me. It was apparently the most routine method of firing there is. I just didn't know.

A few blocks west of the Greyhound station is a building that takes up about 80 percent of its block. It's striking because in the back of the building, near Twelfth and F streets, there are trees and an open area with tables and chairs. Because of Washington's height restrictions on buildings, it is unusual for architects to leave much open space at ground level. Because the architects can't go up, they feel like they have to use every inch. The height restrictions supposedly preserve the view of the Capitol and the Washington Monument, although trying to spot either of them from downtown is like finding Mount Rainier from downtown Seattle on a cloudy day. In fact, under the law of unintended consequences, the building rules just make Washington even hotter and stuffier than it is already. Not that the summer heat isn't oppressively stuffy in Washington anyway. Of course, that isn't the fault of the buildings, though they probably don't help.

On the ground floor of this particular building is a Così coffee shop and a random Plaza Café. A bunch of scrawny, mostly leafless trees grow out of the concrete, and several art pieces stand in the middle of it all. The artist is identified as Richard Hunt. The sculpture was dedicated in 1992. The official description of it reads *Build-Grow, Branching Column, Four Growth Columns, Swan Column Fountain,* 1992. I can't disagree with any of that, though none of those choices might have comprised my first guess as to what was being depicted.

Behind the Hunt artwork is the 302,000-square-foot, twelve-story office building. A five-level parking garage underneath has room for 324 cars. The builders claim that the structure "projects the classical strength of Washington's monumental stone buildings." As you can discern, bullshit is not the exclusive province of bureaucrats, members of Congress, or their spokespeople.

Inside the giant lobby are Italian marble floors, mahogany walls, and moldings of bird's-eye maple. The name over the door reads EDWARD BENNETT WILLIAMS BUILDING. Next to the entrance is a small plaque with the name of the major tenant that occupies the 250,000 square feet of usable nonretail office space, the Washington law firm Williams & Connolly.

If there was one lawyer who dazzled and epitomized Washington legal practice for the half century between 1938 and 1988, it was Edward Bennett Williams. Already there have been at least two major biographies written about him. One of them, *The Man to See,* by *Newsweek* editor Evan Thomas, is held in high esteem by the partners at the firm. The other one, entitled *Edward Bennett Williams for the Defense,* by Robert Pack, is more critical and thus held in lesser regard, as evidenced by the fact that the Evan Thomas book is mentioned on the firm's official Web site. Mention the Robert Pack book to a firm partner, and you might get escorted to the tall glass door, though probably not thrown through it. Life at the firm has its oddities, but it is probably not as overtly violent as the movie of the John Grisham thriller *The Firm,* starring Tom Cruise. It may be dramatic in subtle ways, but there are a lot more people thrown through plate glass in reel life than in real life.

The fact that Williams & Connolly even has a Web site is rather remarkable. One of the distinguishing characteristics of the lawyers who work in this building is that for the most part they do not talk to reporters, even though they represent virtually every important network anchor and news media celebrity in the country and are ostensibly some of the biggest advocates for the freedom to say anything, true or false. Keep in mind one of their largest clients has been the *National Enquirer.* Still, they themselves don't generally communicate with reporters. There was a time when that was considered proper for lawyers. Today, *not* bragging about yourself is considered quaint.

2.

HOLLYWOOD ON THE POTOMAC

———————■———————

Needless to say, in the blocks that surround the Edward Bennett Williams Building are numerous other large law firms. Most of them couldn't be more different from Williams & Connolly, but their history and practices provide a good illustration of how Washington law had come to operate in the twenty-first century and what Williams & Connolly's differences would be.

Around the corner on F Street, for example, is the Washington office of the Los Angeles–based law firm Latham & Watkins. A mighty center of power in Washington, Latham is not the only influential import from the West Coast. Los Angeles has generated three large important national law firms of which Latham is the largest, the most profitable, and the least identifiable in political terms. The other two are the historically Republican Gibson, Dunn & Crutcher and the once more Democratic and liberal O'Melveny & Myers.

Gibson, Dunn & Crutcher had close ties to Ronald Reagan. It started building a big and important Washington practice in 1980 when one of its senior partners, William French Smith, was named Reagan's first attorney general. Among the famous lawyers who have worked there is Kenneth Starr, who would later become the inquisitorial Whitewater prosecutor during the Clinton administration. Now, the best-known conservative "movement partner" is Theodore Olson, who served in powerful positions in the administrations of both Reagan and George W. Bush but has often been more influential out of public office than when he has been in it.

Born in Chicago on September 11, 1940, Olson was nineteen days old when his father, a United Airlines ground service engineer, moved the family to New York City. At the end of World War II, the Olsons literally landed in Cheyenne, Wyoming, then moved to California, living in San

Francisco and Redwood City, before arriving in Los Altos, where Olson went to high school. At the University of the Pacific in Stockton, he became a fearsome member of the championship debate team. "Somehow," he says, "I always knew I wanted to be a lawyer." After law school at the University of California, Olson took a job at staid, conservative Gibson, Dunn & Crutcher in 1965. Right-wing is really an apt expression for this firm in the 1960s and 1970s. Morgan Chu, who later would become one of the nation's top five high-tech patent litigators, once told me that after he graduated from Harvard Law School in 1976, he went to Gibson Dunn for an interview. Before knowing anything about him, the interviewer declared that Chu should know right off the bat that there were firm partners who belonged to clubs that excluded Asians, and not to expect that things would change.

"Okay," Chu thought, "I don't think this is the place for me."

For Olson, though, it was perfect. There were no firm members who belonged to clubs that excluded Norwegians, so Olson's ancestry was okay. He became a favorite of firm chairman William French Smith, who had spent most of his career defending helpless electric, steel, and railroad companies. Smith was a charter member of the Reagan "kitchen cabinet," which funded and masterminded the former actor's political career, from getting him elected governor of California in 1966 to president of the United States in 1980.

When Smith went to the Justice Department, he named Olson to be head of his Office of Legal Counsel, a job that is akin to being the lawyer for the attorney general. Starr was named Smith's chief of staff. After his term in government ended with Smith going back home to California, Olson returned to Gibson Dunn. He became a darling of the ideological right and has argued numerous landmark cases at the Supreme Court. One of his most noteworthy, though unsuccessful, efforts was trying to keep would-be women cadets out of the Virginia Military Institute.

Starr went on to become a federal judge, then the solicitor general of the United States, and ultimately would gain notoriety, in the worst sense of the word, as President Clinton's "Inspector Javert" in the Monica Lewinsky affair. Before he was run over by Williams & Connolly during the Clinton impeachment episode, Starr owed everything that he had accomplished in law, which had led him right up to the brink of a seat on the U.S. Supreme Court, to Olson and Smith, who had hired him after Starr's double-length clerkship with Chief Justice Warren Burger had ended. Starr's ties to the powerful chief justice were tight. Burger considered him the best clerk the Court ever had, and he was the only clerk that Burger ever invited back for a second year. After George H. W. Bush became president in 1988, Starr was the leading contender for a vacancy on the Supreme Court. Everything about his career seemed on the fast track. He was only thirty-seven in 1983 when Burger interceded to make him the youngest lawyer, up to that time, ever appointed to the U.S. Circuit Court of Appeals. Starr then gave up that position to become solicitor general at the tender age of forty-three. The solicitor general argues cases for the United States in the Supreme Court, and the job is often a stepping-stone for a seat on the High Court itself. Legal journals called Starr "the man with the golden résumé." His elevation to the highest court in the land seemed just a matter of timing.

When Justice William J. Brennan Jr. retired from the Court in 1990, inside Washington viewed a Starr appointment as a certainty, but a couple of things conspired against him. As a federal judge, Starr had written the ruling in an important libel case that pitted the *Washington Post* against the Mobil Oil Company. Starr had ruled in favor of the *Post*, which was represented in the case by the erudite, quiet-spoken Williams & Connolly partner David Kendall, who specializes in media law.

The fact that Starr had sided with the *Post* and the First Amendment rather than with a GOP-friendly oil company executive made his true conservative credentials suspect in certain crowds. President Bush and his top legal adviser, Boyden Gray, fretted that Starr as a Supreme Court justice might take a dangerous turn to the left. Gray's worries were exacerbated when Starr admitted that back in 1968 he had voted for liberal Democrat Hubert Humphrey for president. Philosophical changes after arriving on the bench had happened with a number of previous GOP Supreme Court appointments, notably Earl Warren and William Brennan, two of the five Eisenhower appointees in the 1950s. Together they became a pair of the most liberal and influential justices in the history of the Court, revolutionizing American law, society, and culture in complex ways that conservatives have still not been able to untangle fifty years later.

Two important Bush friends and advisers from New Hampshire—his White House chief of staff, John Sununu, and Senator Warren Rudman—urged Bush to pick instead their mutual friend David Souter, a supposedly

conservative judge who had made a name on the New H⟨a⟩
preme Court before being appointed to the federal bench. It⟨
cidence that at that time one of the country's smallest state⟨
influential figures in Washington politics.

Thus it was that Starr, who had coveted the position for his entire professional career, lost his best chance for a Supreme Court appointment.
Until his resignation in 2009, David Souter, one of the most conservative
individuals that anyone could encounter, turned out to be a reliable member of the High Court's liberal bloc, and sure enough—for all of Bush's effort to the contrary—became known as the latest incarnation of a man
who switched from conservative to liberal once he arrived on the Court.
Eisenhower was always said to have muttered that Chief Justice Earl Warren and William Brennan were the two biggest mistakes he ever made. The
first President Bush ended up having to say that about Souter. They had
tried so hard, too. It was reminiscent of the day jockey Willie Shoemaker
misjudged the finish line aboard Gallant Man in the 1957 Kentucky Derby,
after being specifically warned not to. Some things are just inevitable.

Starr's consolation prize was a million-dollar-a-year partnership at the
Washington office of Kirkland & Ellis, which many years ago did most of
the legal work for AT&T and other telecommunications giants. There he
built one of the most successful private practices in the United States,
representing companies with cases at the Supreme Court. In 1996, he was
selected by a three-judge court panel to be the special counsel in the investigation of President Bill Clinton's Whitewater land dealings. This would
eventually lead to the impeachment of President Clinton, where Starr's
chief legal foe was the very same David Kendall to whom he had handed
what turned out to be a Pyrrhic decision (for Starr) in the *Washington Post–
Mobil Oil* case. As legendary Washington columnist Drew Pearson once
observed, the Washington merry-go-round never stops. It would be hard
to predict how the mercurial Starr would have performed as a justice. He
ultimately took a job as dean of Pepperdine University Law School and
moved to beautiful Malibu, California, where one of his first acts was to
institute the prestigious annual William French Smith Memorial Lecture.
In a way, Reagan's attorney general was a funny person to name a lecture
after. He was one of the quietest public officials Washington had ever
seen and seldom spoke in public. The first three speakers to receive the
all-expenses-paid honor of delivering the lecture were all justices on the

Supreme Court, where Starr still argued cases. One of the prime donors that takes care of the justices' speech expenses is Gibson, Dunn & Crutcher. So the Smith Lecture is good business for both Starr and Olson.

At Pepperdine, when he wasn't busy being dean, Starr took up the defense of death row inmates and argued the free speech rights of an elementary school student with a political message on a T-shirt. On the other hand, he has been steadfastly opposed to gay marriage in California. He is a complicated man.

Once I had a conversation with Ken Starr about his marriage and religion. It was intriguing to me that Starr was the son of very conservative fundamentalist parents from rural Texas. He enrolled at fundamentalist Harding College (now University) in Arkansas. Starr was one of the few members of the campus Young Democrats, and he wrote a much heralded article for the conservative college paper defending the right of antiwar protestors to speak on campus. "We often forget the value of listening to the other side," he wrote in 1965. "Some, in short, have condemned those who, though disagreeing with our views, may in actuality be performing a vital service to society."

Eventually, Starr found his outsized intellect was a little too large for such a small college in such a tiny Arkansas town. To this day fellow Harding students say that Starr was asked to leave the school after writing an article in his own personal paper, *Starrdust*, objecting to the harsh way the university dealt with people caught drinking on campus.

He ended up at my own alma mater, George Washington University, and then took some classes at Brown University. He was taking a language course at Harvard when he met a Skidmore undergrad, Alice Jean Mendell, whom he would marry. Alice was Jewish when they met, and Starr's father did not come to his wedding. After their marriage, Alice and Ken became members of a Methodist Church in McLean, Virginia. When Alice learned that I was going to mention in a magazine article that they were attending Methodist services, she called and asked if I could remove that detail from the story. She said that Ken hoped to send the article to his Baptist mother to read, but that if it revealed he had become a Methodist, he would not want to send it to her.

Starr's cross-country movements and his relentless ambition were symptomatic of a symbiotic Washington-to-California axis that never seems to end.

After Latham and Gibson Dunn, the third influential Los Angeles–based firm in Washington is O'Melveny & Myers. Its leader for many years was Warren Christopher, a Democratic Party power, who later would become President Clinton's first secretary of state. One of Christopher's protégés was a young lawyer named Ron Klain. When he was just thirty-five, *Washingtonian* magazine named him, of all the lawyers in Washington, the most powerful one in town who was not yet forty. He served as chief of staff for Vice President Al Gore, and if Gore had won the presidency in 2000, Klain would likely have gotten a top job in the Gore White House, probably chief of staff. Instead Klain got to be played by a too-old-looking Kevin Spacey in *Recount*, a made-for-TV HBO movie about the "stolen" 2000 presidential election. Klain's Democratic Party side lost the battle, but he was memorialized in the film. Ted Olson, George W. Bush's lawyer, argued the winning side of the landmark Supreme Court case, although his character hardly shows up in the movie at all. So it goes in Washington and Hollywood. To the extent that lawyers become famous, it is usually as individuals, and not as parts of the giant, powerful, multiheaded institutions from which they spring and to which they are beholden.

Although the firms themselves eschew being labeled in ideological terms, it is hard to avoid the generalization that Olson's Gibson Dunn is a home to conservative Republican lawyers, while Christopher's O'Melveny historically housed more liberal Democrat types. That's how it seemed, at least, but reality is not quite that simple when it comes to right versus left, not in Washington. People unfamiliar with the ways of Washington think that the U.S. capital is polarized into two warring camps, as it is often simplistically portrayed on Fox Cable News or MSNBC. Washington politicians and lobbyists may *seem* to be divided into camps, but inside the Beltway, they are more often in cahoots than they are at war. Most of the "division" in the nation's capital only occurs when dividing up the spoils.

For example, one of the biggest Washington insiders over the last three decades is the former senator from Tennessee, Howard Baker Jr. He has been out of the headlines for the last few years, but during the Watergate hearings of the early 1970s, the ranking Republican member of the Senate Watergate Committee came off as a small-town country lawyer as he interrogated witnesses about the excesses of the Richard Nixon White House. "What did the president know and when did he know it?" he would ask Nixon's men in his slight Central Tennessee twang.

Baker played Watergate as skillfully as any Republican politician possibly could in defending a president of his own party. His political dexterity thrust him into the presidential spotlight, but the timing for his own presidential ambitions was never quite right. He lost two primaries in the 1980 election cycle and then withdrew from the running. By 1984, his wife, Joy, was suffering from cancer, and he decided to leave the Senate and join the Washington office of Vinson & Elkins, a large Houston-based law firm that represented a lot of oil and gas clients with business at the alphanumeric federal agencies of Washington. Baker had decided to make another bid for the presidency and had convinced himself that he could not successfully run for president while being a sitting senator.

At Baker's side, also becoming a partner at Vinson, was his former chief legislative aide from Tennessee, a man who inside the hallways of the U.S. Capitol was almost as influential as the boss. His name was Arthur B. Culvahouse Jr., and he was the son of a mailman from the small southeastern Tennessee town of Ten Mile. After law school he was hired onto Baker's staff, where his loyalty to his senator turned into a power base.

It was well known that if you wanted something from Baker, you went to Culvahouse. Your savvy as a Washington insider could be judged by what you called the up-and-coming University of Tennessee grad. Pity the poor fool who picked up the phone and asked for "Arthur." You'd be better off calling famous Las Vegas mobster Benjamin Siegel "Bugsy." Or, more closely analogous, it was like calling Washington's premier lobbyist, Thomas Hale Boggs Jr., "Tommy." When he was little, all the congressmen fawned over little Tommy, the son of House Majority Leader Hale Boggs, but when Tommy grew up, he vowed to ice anybody who ever called him by that little boy's nickname. As an adult, to anyone who wanted to get anywhere in town, he was "Tom." Similarly, if you didn't know enough to ask for "A. B.," you weren't going to last long in Washington. Culvahouse's father was also called A. B., and if you called *him* "Arthur," there was a good chance you risked not getting your mail that day.

A. B. stayed with Senator Baker formally for only three years, from 1973 to 1976. He then became an associate at O'Melveny & Myers, though he admits that he never really left Baker, even though he was ostensibly on his own. "Even though I was no longer on his staff, I continued to be his counsel," Culvahouse told me. He acknowledged a twinge of regret that he was so closely identified as someone else's person, rather than being his own man. Still, there were benefits. As the close associate of Baker, Culva-house could now bill the equivalent of a year's salary from the government just about every month in private practice.

When Baker decided not to run for reelection to the Senate in 1984, O'Melveny partners badly wanted Culvahouse to persuade him to join them as well. It would have been a great feather in their cap. However, Baker had other ideas. One of the conditions he insisted on was that he be allowed to be a dual partner of his new law firm and his Tennessee-based family firm. The only law firm that would agree to that condition was Vinson & Elkins. They agreed to Baker's second demand, too: that A. B. also be admitted as a full-fledged partner. Nearly nine years after Culvahouse had left Baker's em-ploy, he was really still in it. Wherever they were going, they were going to go together. So A. B. had to reluctantly leave O'Melveny so he could stay with his mentor. "My firm tried to recruit him to join us," Culvahouse still bemoans, "but he turned the tables on us and recruited me to go with him."

Although Baker's presidential aspirations had gone off track, he was probably just as influential outside of government as in. The private sector was certainly more profitable. In 1986, Baker made $1.2 million a year at Vinson & Elkins, largely through work done on behalf of Memphis-based Federal Express. His mission for FedEx was to win additional landing spots and routes at Japanese airports. He was probably a powerful enough sena-tor and politician to have accomplished that in public office—but then he wouldn't have legally made $1.2 million.

From his separate partnership in his family's Nashville law firm, Baker Donelson, he earned another $300,000 per year. Baker recorded another $121,000 from speeches and appearances. Few politicians leave Washing-ton after their terms are over, especially those who criticize the nation's beautiful capital the most. Now you know why. A lot of people think that public office holders are on the take. Maybe a few are, but it's when politi-cians *leave* office that the payoff really begins.

Baker and Culvahouse remained at Vinson & Elkins for less than three years. When the Iran-Contra scandal erupted in 1987, Reagan sought out Baker as the Washington "wise hand" who could save his presidency from collapsing the way Nixon's had. Hiring lawyers was not something easy for Reagan. As one who frequently repeated the same jokes over and over, Reagan often asked Culvahouse, "What do you have when you have a law-yer up to his neck in sand?"

"I don't know," A. B. would say politely.

"Not enough sand," Reagan would say. No matter how many times A. B. heard the joke, he laughed heartily. He knew how to behave and thrive in Washington.

If nothing else, Baker was an expert on all the mistakes that Nixon and his not-so-merry men had made to propel their administration into oblivion. So Baker left Vinson & Elkins to become Reagan's chief of staff in 1987. Before he agreed, though, Baker got an ironclad promise that A. B. would also have a job.

Baker placed him in the West Wing as White House counsel. He didn't bother to even ask Culvahouse if he wanted to come along; he told the managers at Vinson & Elkins that both he and A. B were leaving. Then he callously told his protégé, "Now that you are out of a job, I hope you will take the one that's been offered."

When A. B asked what their job would be, Baker replied, "You don't want to be the first White House counsel in history to have his client convicted in an impeachment trial." Baker then added, "And we are going to elect another Republican president in 1988." In Baker's mind the two goals were not mutually exclusive.

In that extremely powerful position, Culvahouse was put in charge of vetting and approving all of Reagan's appointments to the federal bench, including that of ill-fated Supreme Court nominee Robert Bork. Culvahouse would later take some of the blame for Bork's disastrous appearance before Senator Joe Biden's Judiciary Committee. Ordinarily he would have arranged a full dress rehearsal for the Bork nomination hearings. Not much is left to chance in Washington. Appearances before congressional committees are pretty much as scripted as a ten–minute appearance on Jay Leno, where guest politicians are almost always handed their jokes in advance. Bork, however, refused to be coached. He was more than just a bit on the arrogant side, even Culvahouse had to later conclude. Bork brushed up a little on some cases he might get asked about, but practicing deference to the committee, or shaving his scraggly beard to look better on television, seemed unnecessary to him. Culvahouse would later admit that all Bork's brilliance did not prepare him for a "political knife fight."

Bork convinced Culvahouse and Baker that he would simply overwhelm the committee with brainpower, but raw intellect was ultimately overcome by Bork's scruffy appearance and his condescending arrogance. It is traditional at Senate hearings that nominees spend most of the time telling the senators how brilliant *they* are, and what a perceptive and intelligent question each questioning senator has just constructed. Bork only wanted to argue philosophy with Biden's Judiciary Committee and have the senators recognize how smart *he* was. He didn't understand one of Washington's fundamental guiding principals: Senators don't like anyone who brazenly appears to be smarter than they are.

Culvahouse and political consultant Tom Korologos pleaded with Bork to dumb it down and stop arguing with the equally arrogant Republican senator, Arlen Specter, the ranking member of Bork's party on the committee. "Stop arguing with him," they pleaded. "Just say, 'That's a fascinating point you have made, I had not quite thought of it in those terms.'" Korologos tried to explain the "80-20" rule to Bork: In congressional hearings the senator talks for 80 percent of the time, while the witness talks for only 20 percent of the time. Bork, he complained, continued to believe that the hearings should be 50-50. In the end, Bork didn't have it in him to be a suck-up, and he lost both Specter's vote and the seat on the Supreme Court.

Rejected as a nominee for the Supreme Court, Bork joined a think tank and embarked on a career as one of the most outspoken opponents of frivolous slip-and-fall lawsuits. Nothing, in fact, infuriated this conservative jurist more than irresponsible people who tried to blame others for their injuries. In 1995, Bork coauthored an article with Ted Olson bemoaning the fact that courts have become "meccas for every conceivable unanswered grievance or perceived injury." Such suits, they wrote, were symptomatic of the runaway liability system that endangered the country. That was the mantra of "tort reform" that became a quadrennial staple of both the Republican Party platform and presidential nomination acceptance speeches. Now that he would never make chief justice, Bork became the nation's high priest of tort reform. Olson, with a pleasing resonant baritone that would have gotten him a wonderful television or radio career, had argued many of the landmark Supreme Court cases attempting to reverse excessive damage awards in product liability cases, or better yet contending that manufacturers of dangerous products couldn't be sued at all.

On June 6, 2006, Bork slipped and fell while mounting a dais to deliver a speech at the Yale Club in New York City. Exactly one year later, he filed suit in federal court demanding $1 million in damages from the club for failing to have a handrail up to the speaker's platform. Bork hired the New York office of Olson's law firm to press the one slip-and-fall case in the history of the law that apparently was *not* frivolous. The case was settled for an undisclosed sum.

When Reagan's term ended, Baker and Culvahouse finally parted ways. Baker tried to run for president again in 1988 but didn't make it. He would become the ambassador to Japan for four years, from 2001 to 2005, where he continued his efforts to gain Far-Eastern landing slots for American-based carriers, including FedEx.

By now Culvahouse's work and title at the White House had finally made him marketable in his own right, though he was always aware and worried that he would never be seen as a Washington power player. In 1990, with George Herbert Walker Bush in the White House, O'Melveny & Myers needed to shore up its Republican credentials, and it rehired A. B. as a partner and installed him on the management committee.

If there was one easily identifiable trend of Washington law and lobbying firms in the 1980s, it was the desire to be bipartisan. This was ironic in a sense, because it was a response to the actual politics of the city becoming more partisan. In the forties, fifties, and sixties, a political operator could move easily back and forth, simply speaking the language of money. Now you needed Republicans to deal with Republicans and Democrats to deal with Democrats. This sometimes made things less than smooth with the law and lobbying firms, where opponents had to coexist, although two powerful partners in the same Washington office, Culvahouse and Klain, had an ironclad understanding never to talk politics with each other, and they never did.

When the Democrats had controlled the House and the Senate, almost without interruption between 1948 and 1994, public policy firms in Washington were very comfortable hiring the aides or children of powerful Democrats like Louisianian Thomas Hale Boggs Jr. of Patton Boggs. In a sense these old-time aides were the last vestiges of Washington's seniority system, when powerful long-serving southerners ruled Congress. In most cases the committee chairmen for whom they had worked were long gone, but as ex-staffers, the most savvy of them had continued to thrive. These Washington survivors were the masters of the backroom political system, experts in appropriations, and skillful in knowing how to write or kill a bill on behalf of their Fortune 500 or defense industry clients. When Clinton beat Bush for the presidency in 1992, O'Melveny's managing partner, Warren Christopher, was put in charge of Clinton's transition team, arguably the most important job in Washington when there is a change in power. Transitions are all about jobs. The man in charge of jobs took the best and most romantic cabinet position, secretary of state, for himself. O'Melveny, which had a large number of lawyers who advised clients on international trade issues, and which was among the first of the American law firms to open its own China office, was in the catbird seat as trade grew between the two countries under Christopher.

Even while Christopher covered the bases at the White House, though, there was concern about the increasing power of the Republicans in Congress. The largely Democratic partners at O'Melveny needed a hedge against a national swing to the right.

Culvahouse, Reagan's former White House counsel, was their insurance policy. If the Republicans came into town, O'Melveny would be covered. Of course, in 1994, that was exactly what happened. The Republicans seized control of both houses of Congress. To commemorate this new reality, Culvahouse was elevated to O'Melveny's national executive committee and became head of the mighty Washington office.

On June 5, 2000, just five months after Republican George W. Bush replaced Bill Clinton as president, O'Melveny & Myers partners voted to make Culvahouse their national chairman. There had only been nine, and he was the first not to come from O'Melveny's home office in Los Angeles. The long arm of the new Republican administration was reaching into one of the most Democratic of Washington institutions. Political opportunism was surpassing all other measures in deciding who would run and control these far-reaching legal institutions.

Culvahouse oversaw the hiring of more conservative attorneys, some of whom came to be the attorneys for corrupt Republican officials caught up in the Jack Abramoff lobbying scandal. The move to the right alarmed longtime O'Melveny partners, some of whom, like Klain, headed for the exit. Klain became the general counsel for one of the firm's clients, Steve Case, the billionaire cofounder of America Online. The staff director for the vice president, who claimed to have invented the Internet, went to work for the man who in a very practical sense arguably did invent the modern Internet. Maybe Gore's aide fed the right line to the wrong guy?

———

Ron Klain had been one documentable Democrat who had been neutral in the primary campaign, but after the 2008 general election, Klain left Steve Case and became chief of staff for Vice President Joe Biden. Professionally speaking, Klain is in a bit of a career rut. The talented former Gore aide can't seem to rise above the vice-presidential level.

Some at O'Melveny claimed that Culvahouse's conservative slant, and the loss of its more liberal but productive partners, sent the firm temporarily into a modest downturn in the only way that firms now judge themselves, profits per partner. O'Melveny partners slipped to third in the rankings of Los Angeles–based practices, behind Gibson Dunn and Latham & Watkins.

None of this stopped Republican presidential candidate John McCain from asking the Baker protégé to lead his search for a vice-presidential running mate. In June of 2008, Culvahouse made a secret trip to Juneau to interview and vet Alaska governor Sarah Palin. Culvahouse was impressed with the peppy forty-four-year-old governor. "She is a person who can fill a room," A. B. told me. He acknowledged that he had been enthralled with her and continued to believe after the 2008 campaign that the problem was not with his recommendation but with how she was handled by McCain staffers.

The fact that she was not even remotely qualified to be president of the United States did not concern him. A lot of vice-presidential picks had fit—or not fit—that bill, including Nixon's choice, Spiro Agnew, in 1968, and Barry Goldwater's selection of obscure congressman William Miller in 1964. "Besides," he said, "it was hard to find anyone else that John liked. That was tough."

Palin was supposed to have been an expert on energy issues. "What people forget," Culvahouse said afterward, "was that when we picked her, gasoline was four dollars a gallon." He still claims her Republican ticket was doomed because the price of gasoline took a precipitous nosedive, taking the drilling issue off the table. Palin and her crowds continued to chant, "Drill, Baby, Drill," but when the average price for a gallon of gasoline went below two dollars toward Election Day, not that many people outside her immediate retinue really cared.

Palin blamed her problems with the news media and CBS anchor Katie Couric, in particular, on the fact that she was a Republican, not a Democrat, but she was oblivious to the history of onetime Democratic vice presidential candidate Geraldine Ferraro. Shortly after Culvahouse and McCain settled on Palin, McCain called Ferraro, an old friend from the days when they served in the House of Representatives together. Ferraro got the message at her law firm and called back. After Ferraro told Mc-Cain to wish good luck to Palin, the candidate said, "Wait, she's right here, you tell her." The Republican presidential candidate then put Palin on the line to talk to her. Palin said little and gave no evidence of recognition of the horrible press travails that Ferraro, a liberal Democrat, had endured, a terrifying experience that made Palin's media experience, by comparison, a walk through the park, albeit maybe a rugged Alaskan park. "You try to stand in front of two hundred bloodthirsty reporters shouting questions about your husband and family finances at you," Ferraro recalled.

After just a few seconds, Palin quickly handed the phone back to McCain who ended the conversation. (Eighteen months later, Palin wrote her book *Going Rogue*, about her campaign experiences. She claims that Ferraro initiated a call to her campaign bus to let her know that she was grateful to Palin for showing the proper appreciation for Ferraro's historic 1984 vice-presidential bid. Palin claims the call came in response to a campaign "shout-out," where she gave Ferraro credit as a feminist trailblazer. Ferraro told me that she didn't even know Palin had said any such thing and was just returning McCain's call.) Despite their political and memory differences both Palin and Ferraro would come to share the same Washington lawyer and adviser, Williams & Connolly's Bob Barnett.

When Palin was nominated as McCain's running mate, questions were raised about just how efficient a vetting job Culvahouse had done. Curiously, after she was picked, and people began thinking that maybe she would be a good choice, Palin immediately began to declare that she would change Washington, the very same Washington that Culvahouse had come in his years at O'Melveny to epitomize. Given that she had been selected by an ultimate Washington insider, Palin's pro-maverick, anti-Washington attitude seemed to be rude at best. After all, veteran UPI reporter Helen Thomas had once written of Culvahouse, "He is the sage of what Ralph Nader famously dubbed Washington's permanent government. Elected officials came and went but their aides stayed, earning their stripes as lobbyists or consultants or joining the city's leading law firms, some of which become as influential as the real pillars of government."

McCain's decision to have Culvahouse do the so-called vetting of Palin irritated Ted Olson, who would have been more than happy to do the same job, and who most figured would have done it much better. Olson was a major player in McCain's campaign committee, after originally supporting Rudolph Giuliani.

Privately, Olson found the Palin selection baffling from both a political and a personal perspective. As befuddling as the Palin pick was for many in politics, in Washington it was the Culvahouse-over-Olson pick that political pros found hard to understand. Olson had no idea why Culvahouse and not he was brought in to do the vetting. "I don't know why I wasn't asked," Olson said, when I questioned him about it. "Not that I am offended at all, but I do know a lot about the vetting process and what questions need to be asked and how to get the answers. This VP thing is certainly peculiar, and the pregnancy of Palin's daughter certainly was handled in the most awkward way possible."

After the election, the often excessively partisan Olson was not displeased that the Democrats had won. "We ran a horrible campaign and deserved to lose," Olson said, maybe miffed at a notion making the rounds that had McCain been elected, A. B., and not Ted, would have been named attorney general. Eventually Palin would end up in the embracing lawyer arms not of Culvahouse or Olson but of Robert Barnett at Williams & Connolly.

As for Vinson & Elkins, Baker's firm ended up paying $30 million in a court-approved settlement to make up for giving green-light approvals on Enron's most questionable business deals in that famous case of corporate fraud. Firm lawyers privately said the deal had been more than a wash. They had made $40 million in revenue from Enron, so the firm's partners still made out with a $10 million profit—and none of them went to jail, a nice bonus. The firm they hired to represent them against suits that were spawned by the controversy was Williams & Connolly. When Miami's Greenberg Traurig got into trouble for the illegal lobbying activities of its lawyer Jack Abramoff, it, too, turned to Williams & Connolly.

Former Enron executive Jeffrey Skilling, however, was indicted and tried separately from the corporation. He became a client of O'Melveny and was acquitted on nine of the ten serious insider trading counts against him. Still, Skilling received a stiff sentence of twenty-four years on the one count for which he was convicted. According to the June 16, 2006, edition of the *Washington Post*, O'Melveny & Myers lost $25 million on the case in unpaid fees and expenses. the *Post's* Carrie Johnson labeled O'Melveny "Enron's last victim." Culvahouse admitted to me, "I can't find anything in her article that was wrong."

On the other hand, the government's leading prosecutors in the Enron case, Sean Berkowitz and Assistant Attorney General Alice Fisher, didn't make out too badly. Both ended up being offered prized partnerships at Latham & Watkins. As a member of the Enron Prosecution Task Force, Berkowitz was making just over $100,000. When the trial concluded, he was enticed to join Latham, where the average sum made by each partner was approximately $2.1 million a year, some $400,000 higher than the average partner draw even at O'Melveny. Alice Fisher followed along at the end of 2008, when government officials began leaving the Bush administration.

In the course of a few years, Latham had taken several of the best federal prosecutors in the country and positioned them to represent Wall Street cheats *against* the government. Many of the clients that Berkowitz and Fisher would represent would face allegations and charges brought by the Enforcement Division of the Securities and Exchange Commission (SEC). At Williams & Connolly, that would be viewed as letting the pirates run the ship. It doesn't happen.

The SEC, though, was no longer the strict enforcement machine it had been in past administrations. Many of its prosecutions seemed weak and ineffective, and they put the Latham partners in a position to beat back the government and look even better to their clients.

The chairman of the SEC, who had done so much to damage the once glittering image of the institution, was a Harvard-trained lawyer, Christopher Cox. He had been named to head the once proud agency in 2005 by President George W. Bush, after Bush's first pick for the job, Harvey Pitt, had been forced to resign after the Enron scandal in 2003, and a replacement, William Donaldson stepped down in 2005.

Be that as it may, Cox began steering the SEC toward disaster in just his first year. Forty-five enforcement positions were quickly eliminated, prosecutions declined by nearly 10 percent, and fines for corporations engaged in mischief were often reduced to mere slaps on the wrist.

Seven months before the collapse of Bear Stearns, Cox said the brokerage companies were in good shape. When clues appeared about the demise of a $50 billion fund run by former NASDAQ chief Bernard Madoff, Cox's SEC simply ignored it. Rules that aid short sellers were implemented at the expense of longer-term investors. When the dust settled at the SEC in late 2008, it became clear that Cox's mismanagement of the agency bore the major responsibility for the subprime housing crisis and the subsequent economic turmoil. In one of the most remarkable displays of government chutzpah ever, Cox called a news conference to declare that he would not rest until he found out why the SEC had failed to uncover the Madoff Ponzi scheme before it was too late. Cox would have been the last to realize it, but he sounded an awful lot like O. J. Simpson announcing he was going to search for the real killer.

In the last days of the 2008 presidential campaign, John McCain would demand Cox's resignation, accuse him of "betraying the public trust," and put the blame for much of the economic crisis, which helped cost McCain the presidency, on Cox's inept reign as chairman. On that, McCain was right on target.

What was rarely mentioned was that before becoming head of the SEC, Cox had been a partner for eight years at, yes, Latham & Watkins. Before moving east, he had been the partner in charge of the corporate department in California's Orange County. During the Reagan administration, Cox had worked in the White House counsel's office and helped Olson and Starr cull through Supreme Court possibilities. When Culvahouse came over in 1987, Chris Cox was the one person that Nancy Reagan said couldn't be fired. Cox stayed on to deal with matters relating to securities laws. He went back to California to run for Congress.

In December 1994, Orange County became the largest local government in the United States ever to file for bankruptcy. Perhaps it was a coincidence. Maybe trouble just follows him. Once in Congress, Cox was named chairman of the House of Representatives Task Force on Capital Markets. As a leading advocate of securities industry deregulation both at the White House and in the House of Representatives, Cox had helped gut the SEC before he even arrived there.

Perhaps as much as any other firm in the country, Latham & Watkins is a tireless self-promoter. It employs an army of public relations experts to get its name out front every time one of its lawyers pushes open the courthouse door. The firm hires numerous "inside" public relations and "business development" people, and for big jobs hires large outside public relations giants to hide its warts. The intrusive PR people demand to know what you are writing about them before they will even provide a photo of one of their partners. Their effort to push good news and avoid the bad is relentless and clumsy at the same time.

When the firm hires a Supreme Court clerk, it pays him, in addition to the generous third-year associate's salary, a signing bonus of $250,000.

Williams & Connolly, by contrast, does have a Web site, although a few of its partners refuse to give out any personal information about themselves. True, the firm does mint money by the barrel, paying lawyers every bit as much as Latham and sometimes more. Unlike at Latham & Watkins, though, you will find no battalion of PR people pimping for the Williams & Connolly partners. For sure, it is the last and greatest large law firm in America that does not employ public relations experts, and if it ever hired an outside PR firm to promote something it had done, that would be a rare or recent event. Williams & Connolly partners aren't really in the game of throwing big parties or making splashy media announcements. The firm's annual Christmas party is not even open to spouses. If you were to ask anyone in Washington what the most distinctive trait of Williams & Connolly attorneys is, it would be that they officially don't talk to reporters. They don't talk about their cases. They take pride in telling people that they don't talk, they don't self-promote, not even off the record.

Brendan Sullivan delights in calling reporters back at night just to tell them that he won't talk to them. Once, I asked Sullivan for a clip from a major magazine about one of his most illustrious cases. "As you might have guessed, I don't keep clipping files," he said curtly. He is slowly realizing that he is an anachronism, possibly one of only a handful of lawyers who don't court the press or even keep a personal scrapbook.

When Sullivan was defending Ted Stevens, the Alaskan U.S. senator accused of lying on required financial disclosure statements, he refused to acknowledge reporters he had known for decades. "I'm concentrating," he said to several who thought they might at least get a handshake or maybe a nod. Any other criminal defense lawyer in the world would be handing out his card and creating a receiving line for the press, but not Sullivan. When Neil Lewis of the *New York Times* approached him during the trial, Sullivan appeared not to notice him. He was too busy concentrating, he repeated. Still, even Sullivan can see the changes that have taken place around him. "I'm not going to change," he once told me, "but I do wonder sometimes when I see the prosecutors talk, talk, talking to the reporters in the hall during the break, am I doing the right thing?" Sullivan actually did show some signs after the Stevens trial that he is flexible, holding a three-minute-long "live statement" to, in his words, "clarify the record about government misconduct." That was a first in his four-decade-long career.

Nor does Williams & Connolly, like the Los Angeles firms, have offices in dozens of cities all over the globe. It is, in fact, the most prominent law firm in the United States not to have any offices anywhere but in Washington. "Who needs them?" Sullivan asked me. "Too many offices just breed contempt."

One other thing that makes Williams & Connolly unusual, if not old-fashioned, is that the firm does not accept "lateral" partners. In the big-money lawyer world of today, attorneys move around like free-agent baseball players whose contracts have expired. No matter that you have spent the first twenty years of your life in an institution that gave you a chance, nurtured you, showered money and benefits on you. That's all so yesterday, except at Williams & Connolly. There is hardly a single partner at this firm who has ever worked for any substantial period of time at a rival. There is no lawyer, except perhaps one tax specialist who arrived to represent Leona Helmsley, who has been wooed away from another prominent firm with the obvious intent of capturing that firm's business. Make no mistake about it. Some of the most valuable lateral movers in the legal profession are pompous jerks you don't want to have to talk to at your firm's annual retreat, but most firms—if the attorney has enough business, and they think the firm can play off it and make more money for their partners—will embrace a lateral. Of course, it's a bit like getting engaged to a guy who has been married three times before. Like a fourth wife, law firm managers are often so egotistical and cocksure of themselves that they always think the star will never leave *them* in the lurch. After a while, though, the partner might move on yet again, taking his business and his associates, and often leaving a lawsuit between partner and firm over who owes who what. As if there weren't enough money to go around, the millionaires fight for each and every scrap.

Williams & Connolly never has that problem. The lawyers who run the firm today were all hired out of top law schools or taken from a prominent government agency or a military posting. Once they arrive, they often stay for life. It is worth noting that while Williams & Connolly does not take laterals or engage in the business of bidding for an established lawyer's services, as sports teams do, two of its prominent partners, Lon Babby and Jim Tanner, specialize in representing athletes—especially National Basketball Association stars—who are often trying to get out of a contract so they can sign a more lucrative deal with a different team. Then there is Bob Barnett, who runs an employment practice that does for everyone else what would never happen at his own firm. He takes already wealthy lawyers from a firm where they feel they are "unappreciated" to another where they might hang around for a while, until a better offer comes along. Loyalty to a place or a long-standing institution is no longer part of a lawyer's lexicon, but Barnett himself would never leave or even think of leaving Williams & Connollly, where loyalty is still its most highly regarded value.

The old-fashioned people at Williams & Connolly seem to be the last to still believe that if you really have talent, you don't have to tell people about it. You show it, and people will come to recognize it. That's not necessarily the ethic of a Washington that is consumed with shameless and obvious self-promotion. Williams & Connolly doesn't really have to hire PR or market-ing agencies or put out press releases or try to seduce reporters with expensive dinners and lunches. Inside the walls of this secretive legal monument, the decisions that shape politics, business, and law in America are being made. From what books you read to what teams make the World Series or the NBA Championships to who has control of the nation's Viagra supply to the sale of helicopters for Iraq to the selection of presidential candidates to the develop-ment of online music to what you watch on television news every day, a part-ner at Williams & Connolly, or someone who was trained there, is in the background, like that wizard back in Oz, pulling the levers.

Williams & Connolly is without question the most powerful legal insti-tution on the planet. Latham & Watkins, Gibson Dunn, O'Melveny & Myers, even Vinson & Elkins are all immensely powerful, influential, and wealthy—and they spend literally millions of dollars to make sure every-one knows it. A PR person would have a field day publicizing just a small amount of what goes on at Williams & Connolly, but superdiscreet part-ners like defense lawyer Brendan Sullivan or reclusive former presidential lawyer David Kendall are just as happy not to have anyone know whose hands those are dangling the strings of Washington's puppets.

3.

THE PASSED-OVER PARTNER

———————— ■ ————————

The founder of this enigmatic law firm, Edward Bennett Williams, died on August 13, 1988. His death came after a twenty-year battle against cancer told in great and accurate detail in the Evan Thomas–authored book *The Man to See*. In the days before his death, Williams's son Tony had showed him a copy of a magazine article touting him as one of the most powerful men in Washington. Thomas relates that Williams replied, "They don't know what true power is. I'm about to see true power."

Edward Bennett Williams was born in Hartford, Connecticut, on May 31, 1920. His father had lost his department store job in the Depression, but Williams won a scholarship to Holy Cross College in Worcester, Massachusetts. In 1941, he came to Washington to attend Georgetown University Law School, but his studies were interrupted by the Japanese attack on Pearl Harbor on December 7, 1941. He enlisted in the Army Air Corps and was assigned to a base in Alabama. Five months after joining the army, however, Williams was discharged. According to military records, he was deemed "a source of danger to his own life as well as the lives of others." Humiliated, Williams told his friends and family that he had been injured in a crash. He returned to law school, graduating in 1944.

His first job out of college was at Hogan & Hartson. In those days of mostly solo practitioners or two-man partnerships, a ten-lawyer firm like this one was considered a megafirm. There Williams studied under legendary Washington lawyer Frank Hogan. The most illustrious lawyer of his own generation, Hogan hobnobbed with movie stars of the age, like Helen Hayes and Lillian Gish, and was a close friend and adviser to President Theodore Roosevelt. For a period in the late 1920s, when the Harding administration's Teapot Dome scandal broke, Hogan became, after Clarence Darrow, the most famous criminal lawyer in the country. He was the attorney for Edward L. Doheny, the businessman accused of paying bribes to Harding's interior secretary, Albert Fall, for an oil lease at the Elk Hills Petroleum Reserve near Taft, California. After his surprising acquittal in 1930, Doheny wrote Hogan a thank-you check for $1 million and had a Rolls-Royce delivered to Hogan's driveway on Massachusetts Avenue in Washington. "The jury has declared you to be what we know you are," Hogan announced on the courtroom steps after the trial, "an honest man and an honest patriotic citizen."

Even so, the question that Raymond Donovan would ask in 1987—*where do I go to get my reputation back?*—was as relevant and frustrating in 1930 as it would be four decades later. The pursuit of that goal—to restore his name and reputation—was expensive for Doheny. He subsequently gave millions of dollars to charity, much of it to the University of Southern California, where the university library is named after his son, but the ordeal of the trial was not something from which he ever recovered. He died in 1935, and the last three years of his life he was confined to bed.

Frank Hogan was more than merely Ed Williams's role model. Williams had apparently cemented his future at Hogan & Hartson by marrying Hogan's granddaughter Dorothy in 1946. He adopted Hogan's creed that you never walk into court without knowing everything about the facts, the client, the opponent, the judge, and especially the opponent's attorneys. With the facts and knowledge of the case as his ammunition belt, Williams's strategy was always to be the aggressor. Even when he was defending a client, there would be little that was defensive about it.

In the first case he tried as a young lawyer, Williams was asked to defend a bicyclist who had knocked down and injured a pedestrian. Williams's successful strategy was to accuse the pedestrian—the person who was actually hurt—of failing to get out of the way. That, in a nutshell, demonstrated what would be the Williams way for the next seventy years.

Whether he was defending an accused criminal or representing someone who was being sued, Edward Bennett Williams simply did not entertain the idea of defeat. Even when a client's insurance company wanted to give up and agree to a settlement, he would have none of it, insisting on taking every case to its ultimate conclusion. By 1949, Williams had decided that he had earned a partnership at Hogan. He was the best lawyer there, and he had married the boss's granddaughter. What more could he do? Williams wondered. In life, as for a trial, he had covered all the bases.

In terms of status, however, Williams up to that point had been one of the lesser tier of lawyers that firms still, as in those days, call "associates." Associates are basically salaried junior lawyers. Their time, though, might be billed out to clients at double their pay rate, the difference between their salary and the income generated by them becoming the profit for the firm partners. For example, if an associate were to bill two thousand hours at $300 per hour—about half what a modern-day partner charges—he would have brought $600,000 into the firm. The associate's cost might be as high as $300,000, but probably not much more. If a firm has one partner and can generate enough work for fifty associates, that partner could make $15 million and never do anything but bring in the clients and supervise his subordinates. The ratio of associates to partners is referred to in the profession as leverage. The higher the number of associates billing at the highest possible rate divided by the fewest possible partners (owners) equals the highest possible profit.

In the 1940s and 1950s, law firm partners had nice lives. They could spend a great amount of time at the Metropolitan Club just north of the White House having lunch and dispensing wisdom while the associates did all of the real hourly labor. Once you became a partner at a prestigious firm like Covington & Burling or Hogan & Hartson, you were pretty much set for life. The only thing that could upset the applecart would be productive but impatient associates suddenly demanding their fair share of what they were producing. In that regard, Edward Bennett Williams was light-years ahead of his time.

By 1949, Williams had only been at Hogan & Hartson for five years. The partnership track was a minimum of seven years. Often an associate wasn't made partner until his eighth year at a firm. Rather than make an exception and give Williams the position, Hogan & Hartson's ruling partners brought in a veteran criminal defense attorney named John Sirica to head its criminal practice. In the parlance of the legal trade, Sirica would be known as a lateral partner. Sirica had no years of experience at Hogan & Hartson, five fewer than Williams, but he had practiced on his own for more than seven years and thus jumped all the firm's associates to become a partner. Hiring a lateral was generally a slap in the face to a firm's associates, stripping away a coveted partnership. Already, in a "class" of ten associates, only two or three might be expected to make partner. When a lateral takes one of the partnerships, that reduces it to one or two—and doesn't endear them to those left behind, who had been there first.

Clearly it would have been fairer to give Williams the job, but the message that would send, that someone could become partner after less than seven years, threatened the entire economic structure of the legal world. If that became the norm, what was to stop a lawyer from getting paid for all his work, rather than having some of his income spent by the partners in membership dues at the Congressional Country Club? There were two or three more years that partners could profit off of Williams before he started to profit off someone else. Hogan & Hartson didn't want to give up those years.

When the firm's partners hired Sirica rather than promote their ambitious associate, Williams walked out of Hogan & Hartson. Not even for a grandson-in-law could the legal establishment sidestep one of its hidebound traditions. Half a century later, the firm that Williams would establish would be the only major law firm in America to still have a rarely violated credo of no lateral hires. It is safe to say that Edward Bennett Williams had a long memory, one that he passed along to his protégés.

Williams, still just twenty-nine years old, initially formed a partnership with an established Washington lawyer named Nicholas Chase, and together they moved into an office on the tenth floor of the Hill Building in downtown Washington, just a few blocks northwest of the White House.

Now on his own, Williams began representing gamblers and bottle club owners against alleged liquor law violations, particularly one called the Atlas Club. Williams began spending as much time hanging out at the club as he did defending it in court. Among the people he met drinking at the Atlas Club was Ben Bradlee, a young reporter from the *Washington Post*. Evan Thomas writes, "As they poured down the booze at the Atlas Club, they loudly teased each other and silently plotted the careers that would cross many times in the years ahead." Williams's nocturnal activities jeopardized his relationship with the more conservative-minded and less flamboyant Chase, who wanted respectability and felt that Williams was just in law for the glory.

In 1950, Williams appeared at the office and announced to Chase that they had been hired to get deported gangster Charles "Lucky" Luciano back into the United States from his forced Sicilian exile. Chase was skeptical that they could win the argument. Williams figured the publicity would be terrific either way, whether he won or not. It certainly appeared that, just as Chase had believed, Williams was basing his decisions not on sound business calculations but rather on the publicity value of the cases that presented themselves. This was a perfect example. Chase said he didn't want to represent "skunks" and expressed concern that he would have to answer to his children for the type of people he represented. By the summer of 1950, Williams and Chase dissolved their partnership. Their primary interaction from then on would be spending a great deal of their time trying to keep one another out of the same clubs.

Over the years that followed, Williams's representation of lowlife gamblers and tax evaders successfully evolved into a higher-class practice that centered around labor union goons and Mafia figures such as Sam Giancana and Frank Costello. Sometimes they were the same.

Just as he had become fascinated by the perpetually dark Atlas Club, Williams became enamored with the even blacker underworld. Petty criminal cases had led him to the defense of some of the most famous Mafia figures in the land. That, in turn, invariably brought Williams into contact with Washington politicians. He would often meet senators or representatives, some of them crooked, through a congressional hearing in which he was the lawyer for the suspected Communist or the suspected mobster. Later, as happens in Washington, it would be the politician who would need the lawyer, and Williams would be the first that most would think of. In a sense, he had already auditioned before them.

The most colorful and famous senator with whom Williams would become associated was Wisconsin's Joseph McCarthy. In 1950, McCarthy was linked in a series of Drew Pearson newspaper columns to various financial improprieties. McCarthy responded by calling Pearson "a Moscow-directed character assassin" in a thirty-seven-page speech, and Pearson then sued McCarthy for $5 million.

There are various accounts of how Williams came to represent McCarthy, and both men are now dead. Popular lawyer lore is that Williams audaciously walked into McCarthy's office and solicited him as a client; McCarthy made some calls around town and was satisfied with Williams's reputation. McCarthy would eventually become one of Williams's most identifiable and steady clients. McCarthy was constantly in trouble with the IRS; this was very good news for Williams, but he was not averse to stretching this profitable relationship in another direction.

Because of his closeness to McCarthy, Williams sensed an opportunity in representing suspected Communists who were being called up to testify on Capitol Hill, especially at the House Un-American Activities Committee, infamously known at the time as HUAC. Williams had the best "in" for representing suspected "pinkos" before Red-hunters at congressional hearings. After all, he was Joe McCarthy's lawyer. His mere presence next to someone suspected of having Communist sympathies was calming. If you wanted to get off the blacklist, who better to call than McCarthy's friend? Williams became very popular with liberal Hollywood directors and producers. Often, as part of his fee, he would offer to take 10 percent of a producer's next film. It was an interesting gamble on Williams's part, sort of a contingency fee on steroids. One of the movies he turned down was *Marty*, with Ernest Borgnine. In a 1983 TV movie about Washington politics called *Blood Feud*, J. Edgar Hoover was played by Ernest Borgnine. Williams was played by José Ferrer. Williams was not happy. "He's seventy-four and Cuban," Williams protested. *Marty* ended up making a lot of money, which showed that Williams knew more about law than about Hollywood. Instead he took a 10 percent stake in a 1956 overbudget epic called *Alexander the Great*. It turned into one of Richard Burton's most memorable flops, and Williams got no return on his paper investment.

In 1954, Williams was at McCarthy's side when the Senate commenced hearings to censure him for his witchhunting conduct. Thomas describes Williams's defense tactic as "tu quoque" (you're another), basically the aggressive defense for which Williams was known, accusing the accusers. Though Williams lost the effort to beat the McCarthy censure, 67–22, the publicity did wonders for the attorney's growing reputation. He had never gotten Lucky Luciano back from Italy, either, but Williams had learned that no one would remember whether he had won or lost a particular case, only that when there was a front-page trial in the newspapers, Williams was the name that would be in thick black headlines.

In 1957, Williams was hired to defend Teamsters president Jimmy Hoffa, after the union leader allegedly tried to bribe a lawyer in exchange for passing him confidential documents from a congressional committee chaired by Senator John L. McClellan that was investigating corruption and mob influence in the truckers union. Robert Kennedy, who was the chief counsel to the McClellan Committee, believed the case was "a slam dunk," as writer Steven Brill describes it in his book *The Teamsters*. Kennedy had photos of the lawyer handing over documents to Hoffa for cash. The prosecutors had both the photographs and the testimony of the attorney. Case closed.

The jury panel at the Hoffa trial, which began in the summer of 1957, was comprised of eight black and four white panelists. Williams's primary strategy was to portray the attorney, who was the chief prosecution witness, as a racist bigot who sat around in his spare time trying to investigate civil rights heroes and stop federal attempts at integration. Another Williams tactic involved the unexpected cameo appearance of boxing hero Joe Louis at the trial. In full view of the jury, the Brown Bomber walked up to Hoffa, hugged him, declared their long friendship, and wished him well. In fact, they barely knew each other, and all of Louis's expenses were paid for by Hoffa's friends.

Four days after the hug, the jury acquitted Hoffa following barely an hour of deliberation. Remembering that Bobby Kennedy had said he would jump off a tall building if Hoffa slipped through this "airtight case," Williams sent him a note offering the use of a parachute. Kennedy was not amused. Ultimately the government would win a conviction against Hoffa, but that was years later.

The Joe McCarthy case and the Hoffa trial had made Williams the most famous and successful trial lawyer in America. He had reached the status that Frank Hogan had occupied, as the living embodiment of Clarence Darrow on the East Coast. Invariably, Williams had achieved his victories by ignoring the case against his client and by attacking the prosecutors, the police, or even the court.

Evan Thomas wrote of Williams, "No matter how guilty his clients, Williams was usually able to find some way to attack the prosecution for violating the defendant's rights." As the Hoffa case showed, if that didn't work, he had other tricks up his sleeve.

Williams originated what would become the trademark of his law firm for the next fifty years—finding outrageous arguments to make when all else failed. There was one case when a prospective client was unable to suggest a single exculpatory or mitigating fact; Williams, for a rare moment, seemed uncertain what to argue in defense. "If I had a defense I wouldn't need *you*," the client blurted.

Williams lost that case after falling back on an argument that his client was insane because of chronic narrow veins that caused "mental deterioration." It was all he could think of. Not even the jury bought that one, and it became that rare time when Williams lost a case.

It would become a mantra of the Williams & Connolly lawyers that they were only brought into a case when it was so far gone that nobody else could help. "If the case was winnable, they wouldn't hire us," Williams would say. "They could hire a Slobodkin." In a sense, just hiring a lawyer from Williams & Connolly is an admission that someone under investigation or indictment is pretty much doomed, or would be with any other lawyer or firm. It could be a two-edged sword, but the reality is that virtually no ordinary juror would have any way of knowing that. When he went into trial, Williams would go into a self-proclaimed "monastic" existence. He totally immersed himself in his cases, refusing to see or acknowledge old friends, including the bottle, and even refusing to eat. His goal, he would say, was to use every second to learn every piece of a case. The old lawyer's adage that you never ask a question that you don't know the answer to was never more true than when Ed Williams went into a trial.

Among Williams's more upscale personal clients, scattered among the riffraff, were Philip and Katharine Graham, the publisher of the *Washington Post* newspaper and his heiress wife, whose father had built the paper. The paper itself was not represented by Williams & Connolly, although Williams dreamed that one day it would be. For most of its corporate work, the *Post* used either Covington & Burling or Rogers & Wells, a very serious law firm whose "Rogers" was the onetime Republican attorney general, later secretary of state, William P. Rogers. On a personal basis, Ed and Phil met at Burning Tree Country Club in 1957 and became fast friends. They shared a few things in common. Graham had married the boss's daughter, just as Williams had married his boss's eldest granddaughter. Williams's marriage hadn't had quite the pull that he had expected, while Graham had been more successful—he had married into the family of Washington's most powerful newspaper, and when the *Washington Post* became a publicly traded company in the late 1940s, Graham ended up with most of the stock in the company in his own name. As Evan Thomas astutely noted, the most important thing about their relationship was that while Williams often referred to himself in psychological terms as a manic-depressive, Phil Graham was certifiably bipolar, in the worst possible way.

By 1962, Graham had become ostentatiously involved in an affair with a twenty-seven-year-old Australian, Robin Webb. At large parties Graham would grandiosely announce to a stunned audience that he was divorcing Kay to marry young Robin. Graham wanted Edward Bennett Williams to handle what would be a complicated divorce from his then forty-five-year-old wife. How could he get rid of Kay but keep her father's newspaper? It would have been tricky.

Behind the scenes, Williams maneuvered not to destroy the Grahams' marriage but to save it, constantly putting Graham's desires on hold, telling him it was a bad time, that he would have to sober up and curb the public outbursts. Then one day while Williams was traveling, Graham came into the office and demanded that he get a new will, one that cut Katharine out completely and gave one third of her family's newspaper to Miss Webb. This was a rather heartless predicament for Mrs. Graham, since her husband had only come to own the paper through his father-in-law. Katharine had resolved not to give Phil a divorce until he transferred the majority of the company's voting shares to her. Wrote Mrs. Graham later, "I am not sure how I came to this conclusion but I do know that my determination was total. I was not going to lose my husband *and* the paper."

When Williams returned to Washington, he added a note to the file that Graham was not competent to make or amend a will and that the law firm had drawn the will only under duress with the intent of keeping Phil Graham from harming himself. In 1963, protecting Phil Graham became a full-time job as his mental illness spiraled out of control. Williams said at one point, "Any will lawyer would have been horrified by the way I handled this, but if you just operate from your instincts you do better."

After Williams persuaded Robin Webb to go home to Australia and to stop haunting the publisher, he then tore up all the wills that had left Graham's fortune to her. Two months later the now lonely publisher killed himself at his weekend house in Virginia. When Katharine became aware of the extraordinary efforts Williams had taken to prevent her husband's divorcing her, she was surprised and exceedingly and forever grateful. He had both preserved her fortune and kept the *Washington Post* newspaper in her hands. It didn't take long before his new best friend and client was the new publisher of the *Washington Post*, Katharine Graham. She was more than eager to show her gratitude by using her influence and the paper's power to make Ed Williams the mayor of Washington.

4.

WAR DEPARTMENT MEETS STATE DEPARTMENT

————■————

In 1967, President Lyndon B. Johnson persuaded Congress to reorganize District of Columbia government in such a way that he, the president, could name the mayor of the city. Up until that time, Washington was officially run by an appointed three-member commission, but in real life, Washington was controlled by the House District Committee, which in turn was controlled by a band of segregationists, eager to use their power to "keep the blacks in check," to use the parlance of the times.

The chairman of that committee for many years was a Democratic congressman from South Carolina, John L. McMillan, but it was often the ranking Republican, a segregationist from northern Virginia, Joel Broyhill, who held sway. His goal was to ensure that his mostly white suburban constituents could get home at night as quickly and safely as possible. That largely meant appropriating money for wide bridges across the Potomac River. Oddly enough, there was no expressway out of town to the Maryland suburbs, where most liberals lived. They had to slog through city traffic to get home. Broyhill and McMillan made sure that as little money as possible was spent on schools or social services, and that people who lived in Virginia but worked in the District only had to pay state income taxes in Virginia, not in Washington, D.C.

Until LBJ came along and began the process of changing the racial realities of America, Washington was very much a segregated southern enclave, more representative of the side that had lost the Civil War than of the Union armies that had won it. The commissioners, who on paper had influence, in reality had no power whatsoever. One called being a District commissioner "the most frustrating position in the world." Another said, "You have tremendous responsibility and no authority."

The White House lawyer who was put in charge of fixing this mess and handling the appointment of a mayor for the president was the Washington "whiz kid" of that political era, Joseph A. Califano.

A height-challenged half-Italian, half-Irish native of Brooklyn, Califano was the son of a well-to-do IBM executive. He was born in 1931, just two weeks after the Empire State Building opened. Califano attended a Jesuit High School in New York before enrolling at Holy Cross College in Worcester, Massachusetts. In 1955, Califano graduated from Harvard Law School, then served in the U.S. Navy, and in 1958 he was rewarded with a job at the prestigious New York firm of Dewey Ballantine, whose senior partner was Thomas E. Dewey, the former governor of New York and two-time Republican presidential candidate. In those days it was rare for a Catholic to be admitted to a firm like Dewey Ballantine.

Califano hated Dewey Ballantine from the beginning. "I thought I would love it, but in short order I was bored to death. There I was making money for people who already had more money than they could ever spend in their entire life."

Although his family had been Republican, Califano was stirred by John F. Kennedy's campaign for president in 1960. As Califano would later write in his memoir, *Inside*, "I identified with Kennedy as a vehemently anti-communist Catholic, the kind of tried and true cold warrior committed to battle the atheist world power of the Soviet Union."

Califano volunteered to work for JFK in the 1960 campaign, creating an awkward exchange with Dewey, who called Califano into his office to ask him if he would volunteer for Richard Nixon. Told that Califano had already committed to working on the Kennedy campaign, Dewey responded dourly, "I'm disappointed about your choice of candidate." Like Dean Acheson, Dewey often spoke in brief but instantly meaningful expressions.

Disappointed as Dewey might have been, Califano had landed with the winner. After Kennedy's election, he ran into a law school friend who was working at a rival New York City firm, Simpson, Thacher & Bartlett. The friend mentioned that one of the firm's most dynamic partners, Cyrus Vance, then forty-three, was going to Washington to be general counsel to the Defense Department. About the same age as Kennedy, Vance was the adopted son of the 1924 Democratic presidential candidate, James W. Davis. A 1942 graduate of Yale Law School, Vance had served four years as a gunnery officer aboard the USS *Hale*, one of the key ships that was being prepared to support an invasion of Japan when the surrender came.

Califano wrote Vance a letter asking for a job. After a two-hour interview, Vance took him in to meet Secretary of Defense Robert McNamara and offered him one. Califano was told that the efficiency-minded McNamara wanted to reorganize the Pentagon and that Califano's primary job would be "to do the legal work for that effort."

The pay was $9,500 per year, considerably less than the nervous lawyer had been making at Dewey Ballantine, but Vance assured him that "we all have to make sacrifices for the New Frontier."

Califano was torn about leaving New York, and while he couldn't wait to get out of a job he wasn't enjoying, he worried about a pay cut. Dewey, the patriarch of Dewey Ballantine, who had run for president in 1944 against FDR, and then in 1948 against Harry Truman, again pulled his young associate aside.

"Go down there for a while. It will make you a better lawyer," Dewey advised. Califano was still not completely convinced, and he couldn't have been sure that Dewey didn't just want to get rid of the renegade Democrat, but ultimately the tug of Kennedy's Catholicism was decisive. "I was so proud that a Catholic had won the presidency," Califano recalls, "and I wanted to contribute . . . [When he said] 'The torch has been passed to a new generation of Americans,' I knew he was talking about me."

On April 10, 1961, Califano's career in Washington literally began with a walk from his car to the Pentagon's River Entrance. As he entered the massive five-sided structure, its design chosen in 1941 to evoke the memory of similarly shaped Fort Sumter, where the first shots of the Civil War were fired, Califano didn't give a passing thought to the fact that there was not so much as a single security guard posted at the entrance. It was a different time.

Cailfano was honoring a well-honed Washington tradition when he hitched his star to Vance, who would ultimately rise to be secretary of state in the Jimmy Carter administration. Like A. B. Culvahouse after him, he found that one of the best ways for ambitious denizens of Washington to get ahead was to attach themselves to a mentor. Califano also attached himself to a Pentagon junior officer who was assigned to work with him on a task force dealing with the aftermath of the disastrous Bay of Pigs invasion. Later-to-be General Alexander Haig would become Califano's lifetime friend—and often a client.

Sure enough, when President Kennedy named Vance to become secretary of the army, Vance asked the restless Califano to stay with him as his top aide and special assistant. In early 1963, Vance named Califano the general counsel of the army, making him the youngest top legal officer in the army's history. Califano's first assignment in the new position was to direct the army's responsibilities in connection with Dr. Martin Luther King's March on Washington. Califano directed the placement of four thousand U.S. Army troops around the Lincoln Memorial and the National Mall.

On the day that President John F. Kennedy was killed in Dallas, November 22, 1963, Califano was in West Virginia inspecting a dam that was being built by the Army Corps of Engineers. He rushed back to Washington to tell Vance that he was going home to New York, he'd had enough. Vance urged him not to act hastily. "Things are going to move," Vance told him. Before Califano could make a decision on his future, McNamara called and assigned him to handle the legal arrangements for the Kennedy plot at Arlington National Cemetery. It was Califano who would accompany Robert Kennedy on a tour of the grounds and pick the precise location for the eternal flame that marked JFK's grave.

In April 1965, President Johnson invited Califano to come to the LBJ Ranch in Texas for an interview for a job at the White House. When he arrived, Lady Bird encouraged him to eat first. "You better eat something, because you never know when the next meal is coming with Lyndon," she said. Califano was then invited into the swimming pool, where Johnson was standing in the deep section. Johnson was about five inches taller than Califano and could stand on the bottom of the pool with his giant head and ears comfortably in dry air. Califano had to alternately tread water or bounce off the bottom to pay attention to LBJ's big ambitions. "I want to create a Transportation Department," Johnson said. "It's a mess. I want to show we can rebuild the cities of America. I want a Fair Housing Bill. Can you do all this? Can you do all this for your president?"

"Yes, Mr. President," Califano gurgled.

Califano thus became Johnson's most powerful special assistant and domestic policy aide and a particular LBJ favorite. As David Halberstam reported in his book *The Best and the Brightest*, when other staff members complained about Califano's management style, particularly that he co-opted their work as his own, Johnson reacted "almost fiercely," saying, "Don't you criticize Califano. There's never been a man around me who wrote so many memos."

In 1967, Congress passed legislation that for the first time gave Washington the right to have a mayor and a deputy mayor. They were not to be elected, however. That would be carrying democracy a little too far in a city that was then about 70 percent African American. Although Congress was reluctant to put the city of Washington in the hands of an *elected* black leader, Lyndon Johnson was determined that the nation's capital would have an appointed one. The legislation creating this prequel to home rule in Washington left it up to President Johnson to select the new mayor.

For Katharine Graham, there was no doubt in her mind that the one man who had come to epitomize Washington should get the honor. That man was Ed Williams. No person or institution had lobbied harder to get this governmental restructuring for the District of Columbia than Mrs. Graham, the publisher of the *Washington Post*. Williams was now like a god to her. She believed that his actions had saved her from losing the paper after Phil committed suicide. She was determined that the whole city of Washington repay him for his extraordinary actions.

Her request put LBJ in a bind. Johnson had no intention of naming a white person, especially not anyone as independent-minded as Ed Williams, to the mayor's chair. On the other hand, he didn't want to come right out and tell Mrs. Graham how inappropriate, and frankly dumb, her idea was. As Califano related it in his memoir, "LBJ had other ideas and told me to tell her—'Nicely but firmly; we need her to keep her paper with us'—that Williams was out of the question."

What made her suggestion even more implausible was that Ed Williams was at the time representing a former LBJ aide, Bobby Baker, who had been indicted on charges of influence peddling. What a tone-deaf Mrs. Graham was suggesting would be repaying the lawyer for Baker with a favor, after defending him on allegations he had taken favors. It wasn't very likely.

Even trying to be nice proved to be difficult. In Califano's version of events, he carefully explained to Mrs. Graham that the president "wants to appoint the first *Negro* mayor of any major city."

Mrs. Graham replied, "Do *you know* Ed Williams?" Califano felt her attitude was "huffy," but he acknowledged that he had never met the man, as far as he could remember.

"I don't quite see how you can dismiss him out of hand without ever having met him," she replied. Thereafter, Califano recalls, every time Mrs. Graham had one of her Georgetown dinner parties, he was seated next to Williams. After LBJ left the White House in 1969, Mrs. Graham, apparently now on a crusade, persisted in her efforts, even though the history-making job had long ago gone to D.C. civic leader Walter Washington. Along with the publisher of Washington's other major newspaper of the time, the *Washington Evening Star*, she had organized a committee to fight crime, which was quite bad in the District of Columbia in the late 1960s. She asked both Williams and Califano to serve on the committee. Eventually, after years of being squeezed together in the same pen like a couple of the endangered white tigers at the National Zoo, the two men finally hit it off and became close friends. It seemed inevitable, as they had much in common.

Both Califano and Williams had attended Holy Cross College. They both had young sons at the same Washington Catholic school. Eventually, they began a regular pattern of having lunch on Saturdays. When Nixon replaced LBJ in the White House, Califano had taken a job at Arnold & Porter, the firm that had been cofounded by LBJ's friend Abe Fortas. Fortas had left the firm in 1965 to replace Arthur Goldberg on the U.S. Supreme Court but still wielded influence, both in politics and with his old firm. Some say Fortas never really left his firm. His wife, Carolyn Agger, continued to be paid by it. Fortas, despite being a justice, never ceased to be one of Johnson's most trusted political advisers.

In 1968, after a bungled attempt by LBJ to make him the chief justice of the United States, Fortas became enmeshed in a scandal over financial improprieties amid his inexcusable dual political role as both a Supreme Court justice and a presidential adviser. He had written part of LBJ's 1966 State of the Union message while he was receiving $20,000 a year in pay from a former client that had a record of fines from and problems with the Securities and Exchange Commission. His once excellent reputation was so tattered, the very firm he had created—and where his wife still worked—didn't want him back. Nice. Intermediaries began to intervene, asking if Williams might consider taking on Fortas as a partner. The firm would have become Williams & Fortas, presumably, but just determining the order of the two legendary legal names illustrated the ugly potential in such a merger of heavyweights. Could you really put the name of a powerful Supreme Court justice last? Fortas had been forced off the Supreme Court because of a financial relationship that had raised questions. In exploring the possibility of Williams taking him on as a partner, Mrs. Graham once again intervened, suggesting that a potentially less volatile match might be the still not yet forty-year-old Califano.

His appetite whetted for a raid on Arnold & Porter, Williams relented. He would agree to take Califano, as well as a just-hired young protégé named Gregory Craig, who was scheduled to start at Arnold & Porter after his Yale Law School graduation in 1972.

At first Califano resisted all of Williams's entreaties. The law firm was known for its litigation work, and Califano did not see himself as a trial lawyer or even as a legal scholar. Williams assured him not to worry. "We'll be the War Department and you'll be the State Department. Together we'll be more powerful than we are apart," he said.

What was really behind the deal, from Williams's point of view, was that Mrs. Graham had hinted strongly that if Califano came to Williams & Connolly, she would reward their new partnership with all the major legal work of the *Washington Post*. They'd "have a real shot to get the *Washington Post* as a client," Williams said. "I'll give you a free hand to build the firm, bring in all the young talent we need. And your name will go in the firm."

It was quite a heady offer, even for a fast-rising, extremely ambitious Washington star like Joe Califano.

Mrs. Graham's machinations and her involvement in building the careers of Califano and Williams are not included her excellent memoir, *Personal History*, which was later sold to publisher Alfred A. Knopf by Williams & Connolly partner Robert Barnett.

In any event, on April 22, 1971, Califano, Williams, and the other name partner, Paul Connolly, agreed to the deal in a three-way handshake at the Rive Gauche restaurant in Georgetown. Williams & Connnolly became Williams, Connolly & Califano. That was how the deal was done, a handshake. Not a single piece of paper was signed.

5.

WHERE IS CAPTAIN SULLIVAN TONIGHT?

———————■———————

When Califano arrived at the Williams firm, he was surprised by the informality of the place. There were no records. There was no budget, no hiring committee, "no administration, no nothing," he would say. The firm's billing practices were totally idiosyncratic. Often attorneys charged "by the task"—a set fee would be arranged, and it was the attorney's responsibility to complete the task, no matter how long it took. "Everything was done on the back of an envelope," Califano told me. He noticed that except for Williams and the very talented twenty-nine-year-old phenom Brendan Sullivan, hardly anyone else at the firm was originating any business. Califano brought in the legal business of the Democratic National Committee. With Paul Connolly as his ally, as Nicholas Chase was unable to do years earlier, Califano convinced Williams of the need to start billing by the hour—and to make the hourly rate the highest in town. He also told Williams that the firm's low-grade Mafia clients had to go if they wanted to attract a higher quality of corporate criminal. Williams had always hired lawyers on impulse. He might meet someone at a party, like him, offer him a job. Sometimes his hires would last as little as two days before they either sobered up or realized the work was too intense. He also was susceptible to hiring the sons of friends. He gave LBJ's son-in-law Chuck Robb a job, as well as Bill Graham, Katharine's son. Neither stayed long at the firm; one really had to have the stomach for it. Many times, though, his instinctive hires worked out. In 1971, Williams became impressed by Aubrey M. Daniel III, the young army lawyer who prosecuted William Calley. A native of Moncks Corner, South Carolina, Daniel was the son of a coal-mine operator in southern Virginia. He was twenty-nine when he was named by the army to handle the court-martial of Calley, who had overseen the slaughter of four hundred innocent civilians at

My Lai on March 16, 1968. After *New York Times* reporter Seymour Hersh discovered the outrage and turned it into a transformative front-page article, the "My Lai Massacre" helped mobilize the country against the Vietnam War. At the end of the court-martial proceeding, Daniel delivered a devastating three-hour closing argument. At the heart of it was Daniel's certain belief that Calley was not being made a scapegoat and that the army did not—at any level—countenance or endorse civilian massacres. He pointed to the evidence that Calley had deliberately murdered 102 people including an elderly monk and a two-year-old child trying to flee the fighting. "By this slaughter of innocent civilians," Daniel declared, "Calley prostituted all the humanitarian principles for which this country stands . . . When a man wears a soldier's uniform, he is still required to think, to make moral decisions, to know what is right and wrong."

It was an argument that would become legendary in law school and political science classes as debate raged over the responsibility and conduct of soldiers in war. The jury of six officers, five of them Vietnam veterans, sentenced Calley to life imprisonment, but before Calley could serve the sentence, President Richard M. Nixon commuted his punishment to simple house arrest. Some three years later, Calley's conviction was overturned by a federal judge and he never saw the inside of a federal or military prison, not even for a day.

Daniel was so outraged by the aftermath of the case that in April 1970 he risked his entire military career by sending Nixon an angry and personal letter of protest. Williams read about it, and it was this, not the quality of Daniel's trial skills or his argument, that had gotten Williams's attention.

"How shocking it is if so many people across the nation have failed to see the moral issue which was involved in the trial of Lieutenant Calley—that it is unlawful for an American soldier to summarily execute unarmed and unresisting men, women, children and babies," Daniel wrote the president. "But how much more appalling it is to see so many of the political leaders of the nation who have failed to see the moral issue, or, having seen it, to compromise it for political motive in the face of apparent public displeasure with the verdict."

He continued, "I have been particularly shocked and dismayed at your decision to intervene in these proceedings in the midst of the public clamor . . . Your intervention has, in my opinion, damaged the military judicial system and lessened any respect it may have gained as a result of the proceedings . . . Not only has respect for the legal process been weakened . . . the image of Lieutenant Calley, a man convicted of the premeditated murder of at least 22 unarmed and unresisting people, as a national hero, has been enhanced." Daniel concluded, "The greatest tragedy of all will be if political expediency dictates the compromise of such a fundamental moral principle as the inherent unlawfulness of the murder of innocent persons, making the action and the courage of six honorable men [the jurors] who served their country so well meaningless."

Now that was the kind of passion in a lawyer that Williams was looking for. Although Daniel was a graduate of the University of Richmond School of Law, humble in those days and not so top-tier now, he was offered a job. Daniel would remain with Williams & Connolly, as one of its cornerstone attorneys, for the next thirty years. His representation of agriculture giant Archer Daniels Midland would become the focus of a 2009 Matt Damon movie called *The Informant!* True to the nature of Williams & Connolly, the movie depicts how Daniel transferred the emphasis in the case from ADM's conduct to potential wrongdoing by the whistleblower (Damon) and the two FBI agents trying to make the antitrust case against ADM.

Both Daniel and Brendan Sullivan were army captains who made their names fighting the army establishment. In Daniel's case it was My Lai. In Sullivan's it was his aggressive defense of anti–Vietnam War sit-in protesters at the Presidio army base in San Francisco.

Sullivan, who joined the firm in 1970 at the age of twenty-eight, however, would turn into that one in a million, as natural a lawyer as Ted Williams was a baseball player.

Along with a brother and two sisters, Brendan had grown up outside Providence, Rhode Island, and attended Providence Country Day School. Sullivan's father was the general manager for sales and distribution at Philipp Brothers Chemicals and served four years as one of the police commissioners in Warwick, Rhode Island. He was an active member of the Rhode Island Democratic Party, the political identity that he passed on to his son, who, as his career evolved, would later often be wrongly identified as a Republican.

Brendan had been an All-Prep League linebacker, captain of the rifle squad, and the school's clear choice for student body president. In his prep school yearbook, fellow students made it clear what kind of a person he was: "Sully, our esteemed and occasionally fearsome leader. He has completely revamped the Honor system from no system at all to an all-powerful political machine designed to give the individual student virtual autonomy." Sullivan was not voted most likely to succeed; rather he was listed as "Most Ambitious."

Sullivan narrowed his college choices down to Georgetown University or Virginia's Washington and Lee. The choice became obvious when he received a letter from a dean at W&L that began, "Dear Brenda: We do not accept women." Brendan was not the type to be amused.

At Georgetown, Sullivan again gravitated to campus politics. He was elected president of his senior class. Classmates used the words "militaristic" and "procedure freak" to describe him. Before Christmas vacation, Sullivan offered fellow New Englanders the opportunity to apply for a ride home in his immacutely kept eight-cylinder 1950 Packard. He required applications and other paperwork before deciding who would get the ride. "I was a little officious," Sullivan recalls.

He would graduate in 1964, before antiwar attitudes began to emerge even at conservative, Jesuit Georgetown. Sullivan was eyeing a career in business. He enjoyed the notoriety of holding office, and he was, if anything, a born leader. With no desire to leave Georgetown, he decided to enroll in law school, exiting at the worst possible time to be out of school, 1967. Rather than wait to be drafted, he joined the army ROTC.

A year after his graduation, Sullivan was as far from the tony offices of corporate America, or a corporate law firm, as a Providence Country Day grad could have ever imagined. He was commissioned through ROTC as a captain in the Transportation Corps and assigned to be a supply officer at the Fort Mason army base in San Francisco. Sullivan directed units that organized and shipped supplies to bases in South Vietnam. "My assignment was to fight the Vietnam War from San Francisco," Sullivan said.

His roommate at Fort Mason was also a young lawyer and had been assigned the job of defending an escapee from the Presidio stockade nearby. The roommate didn't want to get involved with the case and asked if Sullivan would mind stepping into the breach. On the morning of the hearing for the arrested escapee, Sullivan drove over to the austere military courtroom and was just introducing himself to his client when the judicial officer entered the room and took his seat on the bench.

"They told us at law school that when somebody has been languishing in jail, you file a motion for unreasonable delay," Sullivan recalled. His Georgetown education paid off. He filed a motion for dismissal on those grounds, and it was promptly granted, to everyone's surprise, especially Sullivan's.

The prisoner, Richard Lee Gentile, was returned to the stockade with no additional charges. A few days later, twenty-seven inmates of the facility staged a sit-down strike to protest crowded conditions and the Vietnam War in general. Word began to circulate through the prison that there was this young miracle worker who had amazingly gotten one of their colleagues off the hook, which struck all who heard the story as almost unprecedented. Acquittals were not the order of the day in military justice.

One by one, the stockade inmates requested that Captain Sullivan be assigned to their defense. With annoying persistence, Sullivan filed motion after motion for a change of venue, for suppression of evidence, for the admission of expert testimony. As each motion was denied by the base judge, Sullivan's anger burned brighter and deeper. He didn't like to lose. Had his law education just been a waste of time? Was the real world that far removed from what he had learned in class?

The military brass couldn't understand why Sullivan, like the other military defense lawyers, wasn't simply going through the motions. Didn't the young lawyer know that the result was preordained, that the hearing was just a show? Remembered Sullivan, "Well, the defendant had told me that if I didn't get him off, he was 'going to come looking for me.'"

Sullivan had documentation in law for every request. He couldn't understand the basis on which his motions were denied. The military, he thought, went by the book. Sullivan had the book and was demanding that the military stick by it and give his clients their rights, but it wasn't happening that way. Instead, military prosecutors tried to stop Sullivan through intimidation. "It is my job to see that your stay here is quiet," he was told by one fellow officer during a visit to the Presidio. "I've got men that can look through a keyhole with both eyes at the same time."

The editor of a progressive alternative weekly paper called *Hard Times* was among the first to see what the experience was doing to Sullivan. "He didn't start out with any kind of radical outlook," said reporter Fred Gardner, who covered the trial, "but the Presidio 27 trial opened his eyes to a lot of things."

"Am I a crusader?" Sullivan commented at the time. "Only if you believe it is wrong for a nineteen-year-old to go to prison. Then I am a crusader. I'm just Irish enough not to take that baloney."

Sullivan's actions on behalf of his clients were nonetheless beginning to brand him as some sort of radical. "This did not make me comfortable," he said. He was in his apartment, still working on the trial, when the phone rang. It was the commanding officer of his unit. Sullivan was informed that he was being shipped off to South Vietnam by July 2. In its eagerness to prove to the young military lawyer who was really in charge, the army sidestepped a rule that soldiers with less than six months of active duty remaining could not be sent to Vietnam. Sullivan had been due to be released from army service on January 2 of the following year.

The decision to stop Sullivan by sending him overseas found itself the subject of a news segment of the universally watched *CBS Evening News with Walter Cronkite*. His parents back in Rhode Island cringed as their strait-laced son weirdly became a favorite of the antiwar movement.

"It was a little surreal," Sullivan recalled. "I was on Walter Cronkite every night, and he would start the segment asking, 'Where is Captain Sullivan tonight?'" Sullivan added sarcastically, "My mother loved that." The *New York Times* wrote a front-page story about the case, although it referred to the twenty-seven-year-old officer as "Brandon" Sullivan. Sullivan's father observed, "I am sure it is not true. The army doesn't work that way."

"I wasn't even against the war," Sullivan said. "I thought I was just doing my job as a lawyer." Sullivan might not have taken their strong antiwar stance, but senators Charles Goodell of New York and Alan Cranston of California issued a statement that "assignment to a war zone must not be used as retaliation against those who voice unpopular views or champion unpopular causes." Sullivan himself said, "I have never known of a case where one has only six months of active duty remaining to be shipped to Vietnam." He also noted that the assignment came with only a week's notice. "Usually you get ninety days," he said, "but I have to presume good faith. Maybe I am in the vanguard of a new group." In fact, it was the beginning of a long career in which that "good faith" would steadily dissipate over the decades.

Finally, on the eve of Sullivan's scheduled departure for Saigon, Secretary of the Army Stanley Resor canceled the serviceman's orders. "I'm probably the only lawyer in America who owes his life to the press," Sullivan, who almost never ever speaks to the press, said with a grin.

By 1969, his two-year tour was over. However, as an attorney whom Cronkite had made to seem like some sort of antiwar "radical," Sullivan had burned his bridges to the large corporate firms for which he once seemed destined. Despondent, he called one of his old Georgetown law professors, Richard Alan Gordon.

"What do I do now, Coach?" Sullivan asked. He told Gordon that his experiences in the courtroom in San Francisco had been the most exhilarating, adrenaline-filled time he had ever experienced. Gordon brought up the idea of going to work for Edward Bennett Williams but presented it to Sullivan as a long shot.

"Edward Bennett Williams only takes the top two percent of the class from Harvard and Yale," Gordon said with a small amount of exaggeration. In fact, Williams hired numerous lawyers from Georgetown, as well as a few from Washington and Lee and the University of Virginia.

Sullivan may not have been at the top of his Georgetown class—he had not even made law review—but he was both ambitious and driven. His high school classmates hadn't been wrong. Despite how far-fetched it seemed, he asked Gordon to call Williams and set up an interview.

Williams happened to be in a grumpy mood when Gordon's call arrived.

"Why would I want to talk to *this* kid?" he replied.

Said Gordon, "I just thought you might be interested in somebody who has the fighting spirit and tenacity you *once* had."

Williams was furious, and there was dead silence on the line for several minutes. Finally, Williams decided to talk to Gordon again, though he was not happy. "Tell him the door to my office will be open Saturday night. He can come in."

When Sullivan arrived, it was hard not to see the qualities that Gordon had highlighted. Both were native New Englanders, both were Irish Catholics, and when Sullivan described his emotional feelings about the Presidio trials, Williams felt he might indeed be perceiving a younger version of himself. He told Sullivan he could take an office near his, to learn from him. Sullivan called Gordon to tell him of his hiring.

"You haven't been hired," Gordon said disdainfully. "That has to go through a committee."

"No, I'm hired," Sullivan insisted. "Mr. Williams said that if it doesn't work out, he will blame you."

Two years later, Williams saw Gordon at a Bar Association dinner. "I want to thank you for Brendan," he said. "He is the finest young lawyer we have ever hired."

To make sure the young lawyer didn't get too cocky, though, Williams would never call him by his correct name. For the rest of their time together, fearsome Sully would be known to his boss simply as "Solomon."

6.

"SULLY" SACKS A VEEP

———————■———————

Sullivan was not a Califano hire. You could tell because he had never been a big-time Supreme Court clerk, or anything close to it. Like Daniel, he was hired because Edward Bennett Williams recognized his passion and love for lawyering and his willingness, as demonstrated by the Presidio cases, to do whatever it took to win.

Califano, however, had to acknowledge from the start that Sullivan was something special. Some lawyers just miraculously bring in the business; it is a phenomenon of law that is hard to quantify. Some have it, and some don't. Sullivan just had it.

When he was a mere thirty years old, and Califano was just establishing himself in what amounted to a new firm, Sullivan, a boater, got a call from an engineering company executive in Baltimore named Allen I. Green. Sullivan's name had come to Green from friends who had sailboats docked near his in the Annapolis harbor. On July 14, 1972, Green came to Sullivan's office just a few blocks from the White House to describe some trouble in which he might be involved. According to the initial call it seemed like it had something to do with "contracts in Maryland."

Federal prosecutors in Maryland were already investigating allegations that the vice president and former governor of Maryland, Spiro Agnew, had taken bribes from state contractors while sitting as governor. One informant claimed that the payments had continued after Agnew became vice president in 1968, but the prosecutors had not been able to confirm it.

Green, who had handed sacks of cash to Agnew, would be the corroboration federal prosecuors had been looking for.

The following day, afraid that the Nixon administration had bugged their offices, Sullivan asked Califano to meet him aboard his Annapolis-based boat, the *Mistrial*. With Califano's two sons, Mark and Joe, steering them through the Chesapeake Bay, Sullivan related the story Green had told. Not only had Green paid off Agnew while he was a state official, but also while he was the vice president. Green claimed that over six years, he had probably delivered more than $50,000 in cash to Agnew.

On July 23, with what he believed to be a promise of leniency for Green's cooperation, Sullivan met with Agnew's prosecutor, Barney Skolnik. From Green's testimony, the prosecutors received an enormous amount of information and leads. Green corroborated the testimony of others that Skolnik had interviewed him about Agnew's interest in state contracts. Agnew, who received a salary of only $25,000 a year from the state, had mastered the art of turning a governorship into an ATM machine. In one conversation with Agnew that Green related, the newly elected vice president complained that while he would be making a more respectable $62,500 per year as Richard Nixon's number two, the demands of national office would put more pressure on his personal funds. As Richard Cohen and Jules Witcover would note in *A Heartbeat Away: The Investigation and Resignation of Vice President Spiro T. Agnew*, "Thus it was that Green continued to pay Agnew off personally, delivering $2,000 three or four times a year to the vice president in the Old Executive Office Building or to Agnew's apartment at the Sheraton Park."

It was characteristic of Williams & Connolly that in addition to representing Allen Green, the firm also represented two *Washington Post* reporters who were fighting attempts by Agnew's lawyers to subpoena their notes. Califano was in charge of the *Post* account, aided by his two most loyal "State Department" protégés, Richard Cooper and Greg Craig.

On October 10, 1973, Califano and his "boys" went to the federal courthouse in Baltimore, assuming that they were going to discuss the legal privilege of the *Post* reporters' notes. Instead they were witnesses to history, as Agnew unexpectedly agreed to give up the vice presidency in exchange for a sentence of three years' unsupervised probation and a $10,000 fine. After acknowledging that he had accepted cash bribes as vice president of the United States, Agnew received a letter from President Nixon, which read in part, "I hope that you and your family will be sustained in the days ahead by a well-justified pride in all that you have contributed to the Nation by your years of service as Vice President."

When Sullivan had embarked on his representation of Green, the federal prosecutors, Skolnik and his boss, U.S. Attorney George Beall, had promised that in exchange for Green's testimony and a guilty plea for offering bribes, they would recommend that he not be sentenced to any jail time. Now, Agnew's unexpected deal had swept the legal rug right out from under Green. When the case finally came up for sentencing in November 1973, a special three-judge sentencing panel ignored the promises of the prosecutors and sentenced Green to twelve months in prison.

Agnew, the villain, had basically walked out with a commendation from the president, and the man who had done the most to expose his crimes would go to jail. Sullivan was livid. For the rest of his life, he would complain that it was one of the most unfair sentences anyone was compelled to serve. Sullivan felt that the judges in the case had double-crossed him. He vowed that Green would be his last client to ever serve jail time—for the next thirty-eight years, that would pretty much be true—and he would never, never trust the government again. The Agnew case would always be a reminder of what Sullivan had learned in the army: The government could not be trusted to honor its deals. Sullivan would spend the rest of his career paying them back. "After that experience," said Sullivan, "I vowed never to plead a client guilty, and with only a couple of ironclad exceptions, when I knew a plea would hold, I never did."

Green's call to Brendan Sullivan had come almost a year after five burglars had been arrested trying to break into the offices of the Democratic National Committee, Califano's client. The federal trial judge originally assigned to the cases of the burglars, as well as their minders, G. Gordon Liddy and James McCord, was John Sirica, the very same man whose hiring at Hogan & Hartson had launched Edward Bennett Williams and his great career. The newspaper that would break the most significant revelations in the Watergate burglary, and bring the evidence right to the door of the Oval Office, was the *Washington Post*, also by now a client of Williams, Connolly & Califano. Bob Woodward, the intrepid *Washington Post* reporter most responsible for the demise of Nixon, would be a client of the firm for the rest of his life and be represented by it throughout his famed book-writing career. In the phase of the investigation that dealt with the receipt of illegal campaign contributions, Williams represented shipowner George Steinbrenner, who had just come to national attention in 1973 by buying the New York Yankees. Humorist Art Buchwald seemed to accurately reflect the mood of Washington in 1972–73 when he wrote in his syndicated column, "Thanks to the Watergate fallout every law firm in this city is now on a 24-hour, seven-day-a-week schedule. Whereas most law offices were sedate, quiet places, they now resemble brokerage offices with everyone screaming into the phones."

Throughout 1972 and early 1973, as the footsteps of Watergate came closer and closer to the Oval Office, it had seemed that the one thing protecting Nixon from impeachment was Agnew. As long as Agnew was vice president, there was real concern in Washington about having Nixon removed from office. He was Nixon's safety net. Now the actions of Allen Green, as frustrating as they turned out to be for Brendan Sullivan, had done more than remove a vice president; they had cleared the way to exile a president, for the first time in American history.

As tangled as Williams and Califano were in the various phases of the Watergate scandal, they kept getting more deeply involved. In the summer of 1973, Congress prepared to hold its televised hearings on the burglary highlighted by the appealing personalities of Sam Ervin, the folksy chairman of the committee, and the ranking Republican, Howard Baker. Sitting directly behind Baker as the committee hearings took place was his new staff aide, A. B. Culvahouse. A. B. did not play a large role in the hearings, though he was occasionally asked to do some research on issues of executive privilege, but Baker told him it was as good a place as any to get familiar with the landscape of the Senate. So A. B's job during his first week in Washington was simply to be present at one of the most historic committee hearings of all time.

When Nixon official Alexander Butterfield was subpoenaed to testify at the Senate committee investigating Watergate in July 1973, he, too, called Califano. Butterfield was a presidential aide who had such mundane duties as overseeing the visitors' tours of the White House, but as a former air force officer with some technical skills, he was the one who had been asked to install a taping system in the White House, so that all conversations held there would be recorded.

Butterfield needed some advice. He was trying to figure out how he could avoid volunteering information about the taping system, without at the same time lying to the Ervin Committee. A career serviceman, Butterfield had until then lived a totally honorable life and had no intention of committing perjury.

At that point, even Califano had to acknowledge that Butterfield would make one client too many. Still, Califano couldn't resist giving Butterfield some advice. He told him to tell the truth—and get a "damn good haircut. They're going to take a lot of pictures of you today." Califano added, "Since you have nothing to hide, I suggest you testify without counsel. It'll make a much better impression on the committee."

Califano was also in constant communication with General Alexander Haig, who had risen through the ranks to become Nixon's chief of staff and was as adamant as Butterfield about not getting dragged into the scandal. "I wanted to see the tapes destroyed," Haig said later, but he didn't order them destroyed because Califano specifically had warned him that he would go to jail if that happened.

Butterfield and Haig couldn't have sought advice from a more knowledgeable person about the White House taping system. When President Johnson had left office, it was Califano who pointed out the taping mechanism to Nixon aide Robert Finch during the presidential transition process. Finch would later recall that Califano said to him, "You should see this, because you have to decide whether you want to take it out or leave it in."

Nixon's initial reaction was "I don't want the damn thing in there." Unfortunately for his presidency, Chief of Staff Bob Haldeman convinced him that the tapes would be part of history and that no one would ever listen to them until they were both gone.

It was Butterfield's subsequent testimony on July 13, 1973, about the existence of the White House taping system that launched the biggest legal battle of the Watergate period, the fight for the Watergate tapes, a pitched legal battle between Congress, independent counsel Archibald Cox, and the president that would eventually be decided by the Supreme Court.

That was not, of course, before the third-ranking official in the Nixon Justice Department, Robert Bork, fired Cox, and Nixon was compelled by public pressure to replace him with Leon Jaworski, a modest man who insisted that everyone call him "Colonel."

Butterfield amazingly had followed Califano's counsel, and in doing so had changed American political history. There would be years of speculation about why Butterfield made the revelation. Eventually Butterfield would acknowledge that he simply did what Califano had advised: "I just answered the questions that came up and let the chips fall where they may."

Ultimately the Supreme Court would side with Congress to force the release of the tapes, and on August 9, 1974, Nixon became the first president to resign the presidency. Before he did, though, Califano recalls, an intermediary from the president called to see if Edward Bennett Williams would represent him. That one, Califano said, "was out of the question."

During Watergate, Senate committee chairman Sam Ervin became a national hero, questioning members of the Nixon administration with a southern simplicity and charm. Grandfatherly, seemingly, but not really befuddled, Sam Ervin was not running for office, of course, but his folksy example did show image makers how if he had been younger and more personally ambitious at that stage of his life, he could have parlayed his Watergate exposure into national office.

Williams & Connolly's main client during Watergate had been the *Washington Post*. The firm had also represented the Democratic National Committee, of which Edward Bennett Williams had once been treasurer. Ervin's committee and the threat to impeach the president drove Nixon from office in 1974, but the legal battles that stemmed from Watergate and the tapes were not over.

In 1975, Edward Bennett Williams was summoned by Nixon's secretary of the treasury John Connally to represent him against charges he had accepted bribes from milk industry lobbyists. Williams agreed to represent Connally for a flat fee of $400,000. Conflicts were rampant. One of the reasons occasionally cited for Connally's hiring of Williams was that he assumed it would halt leaks about his case to the *Washington Post*. To an outsider, such a thing might seem logical, but that isn't how newspaper reporters and editors operate, especially in the roiling journalistic furor that was Watergate. It was more likely that Connally hired Williams because he knew that Williams provided his best chance of staying out of jail, which is exactly what did happen. The case involved a claim by a milk industry lobbyist from Texas that he had given Connally two $5,000 payments as a thank-you for helping to bring about higher milk prices. Connally denied the allegations and claimed that the lobbyist, Jake Jacobsen, was lying. Connally's situation became intertwined with Watergate because it was the Watergate special prosecutor who discovered the tape of a conversation between Connally and President Nixon in which Connally suggested to Nixon that if he raised milk price supports, it would lead to greater generosity during campaign season. Two days after the conversation, the administration changed its policy to the benefit of the producers, and contrary to the best interest of consumers.

Because Connally told a federal grand jury that he had not taken any bribes and that his position was not inconsistent with what he had always believed, the special prosecutor slapped a charge of perjury and obstruction of justice on him as well. By the time these charges were brought to court, Connally was a lawyer at Vinson & Elkins, the same firm that Senator Howard Baker and A. B. Culvahouse would later go to. He was fifty-eight years old at the time, and the residue of ill will from the entire unpopular Nixon presidency did not figure to serve him well with a jury. He was doomed. Among reporters who followed the case, Connally's conviction was a foregone conclusion, regardless of the facts.

When Connally's case came to trial, Williams made the argument that Jacobsen had been given money to bribe Connally but that the former Texas governor, who was in the motorcade and took a bullet when President Kennedy was shot, had refused the bribe. At that point, Williams argued, Jacobsen had just kept the money.

Williams then paraded an all-star lineup of character witnesses, one of his trademark tactics, to show that the Texas politician was a man of integrity. Williams did not believe that a defendant should ever take the stand in his own defense. The last witness Williams was able to place before the jury was the Rev. Billy Graham. "What do you do for a living?" Williams asked Graham.

Billy Graham replied, "I preach the gospel of Jesus Christ across the face of the earth."

Graham was never supposed to be the final character witness for Connally. Former LBJ aide and chatty Washington insider Jack Valenti was waiting in the courthouse version of the greenroom. Always a publicity hound, Valenti was piqued at being left in the witness room and never called to testify. When he was released by the marshal, he went to Williams and demanded to know why he and his testimony had been forgotten.

Williams replied that while Billy Graham testified, "I heard two jurors whisper, 'Amen.' One of them was an elderly black lady who carried a Bible every day with her to the courtroom. Jack, at that point I knew we didn't need any more character witnesses."

Williams considered the idea of client conflicts to be relatively quaint, not to say naive. If anyone dared ask him about it, Williams would say that the firm would recognize a conflict when two lawyers from the firm appeared in the courtroom on opposite sides. Otherwise, everything was okay.

The 1976 election-year defeat of the Republican party had an unforeseeable consequence: It signaled the end of Williams's partnership with Califano. Califano's hitch-your-wagon-to-a-star theory of life took a dramatic turn when Cyrus Vance was named to be Jimmy Carter's secretary of state. Vance saw to it that Califano would become his ally in the cabinet, as secretary of health, education, and welfare (HEW). His meteoric rise had left many in its wake, as he now would leave his partners at what was again Williams & Connolly behind. Well, he didn't leave them all behind. Some, like food and drug law expert Richard M. Cooper as well as a promising attorney, Ben Heineman, Califano took with him to the administration. Heineman became an assistant secretary at HEW. Cooper, a Rhodes Scholar before graduating from Harvard Law School, then became a law clerk to Justice William J. Brennan Jr., helping Brennan write one of the most liberal and controversial rulings ever handed down by the nation's highest court. In that case, styled *Goldberg v. Kelly*, Brennan had declared that welfare recipients had the right to due process before bureaucrats arbitrarily cut off their benefits. Conservatives were furious over the ruling, figuring that if you got welfare, you should be thankful, not demanding. Califano had Cooper selected as chief counsel of the Food and Drug Administration (FDA).

In fact, Califano was threatening to sneak off with more partners from the firm when Williams confronted him and told him to knock it off. It didn't help that the following year, in 1977, Paul Connolly died of a heart attack.

Califano's career at HEW (he was the last secretary at the department before it was divided into separate cabinet departments, one for health and one for education) reversed what until then had been an uninterrupted rise to the top of the Washington food chain. Two and a half years into the Carter administration, the peanut-and-tobacco president from Georgia fired Califano. On a policy basis, one could say that Califano was dismissed because the onetime smoker had turned zealously against smoking in 1975 when his son, now a surgeon at Johns Hopkins, asked him to stop smoking as a birthday present. Carter knew he would need tobacco-growing states to win reelection in 1980, and Califano's arrogant air bred too many enemies for him to survive in government, where backstabbing is second only to baseball as the national pastime. Califano acknowledged much of this in his memoir, where he observed that many of his antismoking edicts, like banning the practice in government buildings, "were taken with little, often last-minute, notice to the White House, or none at all."

To the relief of his former partners, many of whom didn't really care for him and prayed that he wouldn't request to return, Califano did not retreat to Williams & Connolly after his abrupt departure from government. Instead, he finally did the only thing that made sense for a man with his brimming self-assurance. From his office in downtown Washington's Hill Building he had a bird's-eye view of the People's Drugstore just across Seventeenth Street and eleven stories below. Every day at noon, Clark Clifford, Washington's most respected "wise man," dressed to the nines, would sit down at the counter and order a tuna sandwich. The fight for seats at the counter next to Clifford was on. Everyone wanted to ask his advice, about careers, about how to handle public relations problems, whether to take the country to war or negotiate a peace. Califano wanted to be what Clifford was. So instead of joining yet another established law firm, he started his own, Califano, Ross & Heineman. His self-stated goal was to dispense "wisdom" to Washington's leaders and become a trusted, but expensive, adviser to presidents, senators, and cabinet members. They were all "eager for the help I could provide," he would say. Califano's new firm would fulfill none of the goals he had espoused, and it broke up in fairly short order, with the three main partners going their separate ways.

Califano did leave something—make that somebody—very important behind at what was again Williams & Connolly. That was the young man he had brought with him from Arnold & Porter, Gregory Craig.

7.

CRAIG'S GIST

———————■———————

Gregory Craig was born in Norfolk, Virginia, at a military hospital where his father, Bill, a navy lieutenant, was on assignment at the end of World War II. The family had hailed from Vermont for several generations. "I grew up in many places," Greg would say, "but Ripton, Vermont, was always home base."

After the war, the elder Craig studied psychology at the University of Minnesota, then education at Harvard University, and eventually became dean of men at Stanford University in Palo Alto, California, where Greg spent much of his youth. He became involved with the Peace Corps as training director and by 1966 was working for John Gardner, one of Califano's predecessors, as secretary of the HEW under LBJ. He later moved back to Vermont, where he became chancellor of the Vermont State College system and ran unsuccessfully for governor.

"Unsuccessfully" may be too generous a term. With son Greg as his campaign manager, Bill Craig got only 28 percent of the vote; Richard Snelling, his Republican primary opponent, received 72 percent. That was it for both politics and Vermont. Bill Craig subsequently moved back to California to lead the 104-campus California community college system.

One of five children, Greg was sent to Phillips Exeter Academy in New Hampshire. He graduated from Harvard in 1967 in the same class as actor John Lithgow. During the summers, Craig worked on civil rights issues in Mississippi, taught in Harlem, and became Harvard's most widely quoted student leader in opposition to the Vietnam War. He participated in a campus debate with United Nations Ambassador Arthur Goldberg. In the course of it, Craig decried students who had shouted down LBJ's defense secretary, Robert McNamara, during a campus speech. Antiwar activist and New York congressman Allard Lowenstein, who had also come to know both Greg and Bill Clinton well, was said to have commented, "One of them will become president of the United States. I just don't know which one."

Craig then enrolled in Yale Law School, where he befriended a bespectacled fellow antiwar activist from Chicago named Hillary Rodham.

Califano had first met Craig in connection with the student's anti–Vietnam War activities. In 1969, after Califano had left the White House and joined Williams, Connolly & Califano, he had been asked by Kingman Brewster, the president of Yale, to meet two law students who wanted to organize a lobbying effort against American involvement in Vietnam. Califano would later describe both men, Craig and Steve Cohen, as "clean-cut, decidedly mainstream and presentable. They bore none of the deliberately sloppy, offensive, shabby-clothing or in your face attitude of protesters that turned off many Americans."

Brewster told Califano that the antiwar movement "needed refining to make it more realistic," and he felt Califano could offer the Yale students suggestions about "constructive outlets" for antiwar activity. Brewster worried that the more radical antiwar activists would lead students into violence. In contrast, Craig's role model was Lowenstein, who believed the war could be stopped by working inside the system. At Harvard, Craig had been active in antiwar moratoriums, often standing for pragmatism against the more radical elements of the Students for a Democratic Society, the SDS, which favored more disruptive actions to stop the war. The SDS scared Brewster, who told Califano, "I fear that the students will destroy some of our major universities if offered no constructive outlets."

Califano says he decided to introduce Craig and Cohen to John Gardner, who was now in the process of organizing Common Cause, which would become a left-of-center grassroots lobbying campaign. Of course, it seems more likely that Craig needed no introduction, since his father was Gardner's friend and colleague at HEW. Be that as it may, Craig wanted to explore ways that public pressure could force Congress to cut off funds for the war. Califano was skeptical that this was a realistic goal, believing Congress would never do so while troops were already in the field. Califano suggested that Craig restrict his campaign to getting funds cut off for any defense spending in Cambodia, where there was not yet officially a war and where no American troops were supposed to be. Craig felt that was too narrow; to get students off the streets and into an organized but civil lobbying effort, he said, they would have to target the whole war, not just a part of it. Califano and Gardner decided to go ahead with the project, which they named Project Purse Strings. Califano accepted Craig's argument about using the whole war to attract bodies to their cause, but privately he continued to feel that a successful result would be to stop the expansion into Cambodia.

Their cause latched itself onto the proposed Cooper-Church Amendment, named after antiwar senators John Sherman Cooper, a Republican from Kentucky, and Frank Church, a liberal Democrat from conservative Idaho. The act would severely curtail the amount of money President Nixon could spend on the Vietnam War effort and stop the war from expanding into Cambodia. Califano pitched the Project Purse Strings campaign to business leaders as an outlet that would "nourish" the student movement but at the same time keep it operating within the system. On June 30, 1969, the Senate passed the Cooper-Church Amendment, thanks in part to the millions of corporate dollars raised to support student lobbying on its behalf, 58–37. The amendment to the defense appropriations bill made it unlawful for the United States to spend any funds for military action in Cambodia, on the ground or in the air.

Craig would not be the only Yale law student with whom Califano would have a memorable encounter. While still at Arnold & Porter, in 1970, Califano had been hired by Coca-Cola to defend its Minute Maid orange juice subsidiary against allegations that the company abused migrant laborers. On July 24, 1970, Califano appeared at a hearing called by Minnesota Democrat Walter Mondale to explain Coca-Cola's position, and in Califano's view to give Coca-Cola an opportunity to say that it had no objection to migrant workers getting protection under the National Labor Relations Act.

It was a sign of the acrimony of the times. Califano says that he had hardly begun to speak when "a young woman with dark hair and thick-rimmed glasses abruptly came in front of me and said, 'You sold out, you motherfucker, you sold out!'" Califano was rather appalled by the encounter but proceeded with making the best case he could that Coke's orange juice subsidiary didn't mistreat migrant workers.

Like many in his generation, Craig had considered claiming conscientious objector status to avoid military service, but he ultimately reported to his draft board in Exeter, New Hampshire. "I thought it was the only honorable thing to do," he says. Nonetheless, Craig received a medical deferment for a damaged shoulder—the result of a prep-school lacrosse injury.

In the fall of 1971, Craig sublet his New Haven apartment at 21 Edgewood Avenue to classmate Hillary Rodham and her boyfriend, some guy from Arkansas named Bill, for seventy-five dollars a month. In those days, that got Hillary and Bill a living room with a fireplace, a bedroom, a tiny bathroom, a kitchen of sorts, and a study/dining area. "We shopped for furniture at the Goodwill and the Salvation Army stores and were quite proud of our student décor," Hillary observed in her memoir, *Living History*.

Shortly after the unpleasant Coca-Cola hearings, Califano began negotiating with Edward Bennett Williams to join the Williams firm and leave Arnold & Porter. Califano had already promised to hire Craig at Arnold & Porter, but he was so impressed with him that he decided to take him to what was now called Williams, Connolly & Califano.

During the summer of 1973, Craig became serious with Derry Noyes, the blue-blooded daughter of Eliot Noyes, one of America's most famous and successful industrial designers and architects. The Noyeses were descended from one of New England's oldest families and owned a summer house in picturesque Menemsha on Martha's Vineyard, where Noyes had personally designed many of the area's most imaginative homes. Derry's house was fifty years old and had been built by her father in just two weeks. He was perhaps best known as the visionary who produced the revolutionary look of the original IBM Selectric typewriter, which came out on July 31, 1961. As longtime island residents, the Noyeses were longtime close friends of the Kennedys, and their next-door neighbor on the island was artist Alexander Calder. In 1973, Derry invited Greg to the Vineyard for the summer. On July 27, 1974, Greg and Derry were married there.

In early 1973, Califano also promised to interview Craig's sublettor and law school classmate, Hillary Rodham. Rodham was scheduled for law school graduation in the spring of 1973, and she knew Washington well, having worked there for the summer with an organization that worked on behalf of children's issues. Her ambitious boyfriend, Bill Clinton, had already decided to go home to Arkansas and get involved in politics, but Hillary declined an invitation to get married and join him down south.

"I was desperately in love with him," she would write in her memoir, "but utterly confused about my life and future, so I said, 'No, not now.' What I meant was give me time."

On March 19, 1973, in the midst of her career and personal indecision, she pushed the polished gold elevator button in downtown Washington's Hill Building for her interview with Greg's boss, the intimidating Joe Califano. She prayed he wouldn't remember—but no sooner did she walk into the office than Califano started laughing to himself. She was unmistakable. Hillary Rodham was the girl who had gotten in his face and called him an m-f!

Califano said nothing that would cause her to remember that he remembered, and when the interview ended, Hillary breathed a giant sigh of relief.

Califano had to admit, this was exactly the kind of chutzpah that really epitomized the spirit of Williams, Connolly & Califano. So in spite of their previous little run-in, he offered her a job anyway. Califano recalls that Hillary later declined the offer, saying she had decided to go to Arkansas with her boyfriend after all. Perhaps that was just that day. Hillary hung around Washington for the next couple of years, not helped in her job hunting by the fact that she had failed the District of Columbia bar examination. She wrote, "I had taken both the Arkansas and Washington, D.C., bar exams during the summer, but my heart was pulling me toward Arkansas. When I learned that I had passed in Arkansas but failed in D.C., I thought that maybe my test scores were telling me something."

The following year, she took a job as a staff member on the U.S. House of Representatives Impeachment Inquiry, where she coincidentally became a colleague of another one of Craig's good friends and Yale classmates, Larry Lucchino.

8.

THE LITTLE GENERALIST

———■———

Larry Lucchino was born and raised in Pittsburgh. He had an older brother, Frank Lucchino, who would later become a Pennsylvania state court judge. Their father, Dominic, owned a small grocery store called the Skyview Superette. It was within walking distance of historic Forbes Field, where the baseball Pirates had played since 1909 and where the football Steelers had joined them in 1933. During the winters, Larry's mother, Rose, always had Sunday dinner ready and served at precisely the moment the first half of the Steelers games ended. The timing was such that when the second half started, everyone was done and back in their chairs.

On his Taylor Allderdice High School basketball team, Larry Lucchino was a scrappy five-foot ten-inch guard, as well as the star middle infielder on the baseball team. Winter Saturdays, Larry could be found at the University of Pittsburgh's parking lot, buying and selling tickets for Pitt football games. On that memorable day in Pittsburgh, October 13, 1960, when Bill Mazeroski hit the home run that dethroned the mighty New York Yankees, Lucchino spent the day at school with a transistor radio stuck to his ear. For many Pittsburgh sports fans, that was a World Series that created a new legion of Yankee haters, the Lucchino brothers among them. Larry was the last person to think of himself as an Ivy Leaguer, but a school guidance counselor encouraged him to apply to Princeton and helped pay for Larry's first commercial airline flight. The money was well spent. Larry was accepted on scholarship and agreed to play on the basketball team.

At Princeton, Lucchino became a reserve point guard on the Bill Bradley–led team that made it to the 1965 NCAA semifinals before being beaten in Portland, Oregon, by the University of Michigan, 93–76. "Larry wasn't as quick as our other guards," Bradley said, "but he always worked hard, he never slacked off." Pressed about how good a player Larry was, Bradley acknowledged, "He was a good passer." It was a distinguished college team. One member became a United States senator, another the treasurer of the World Bank; there was also an architect, two attorneys (including Larry), three investment executives, two presidents of self-owned companies, and two educators.

Dominic and Rose Lucchino were determined that their erudite sons not get "too big for their britches." During summers, Larry and Frank were told to get jobs at the steel mill, where some of their high school friends would spend the rest of their lives. Dominic thought it was exposure to hard work that would keep Larry working hard at college. By his own admission, Larry wasn't always the most fun to be around. He recalls that Rose often borrowed a line from the Jimmy Stewart movie *Harvey*, telling him, "Elwood, in this world you must be oh so clever, or oh so pleasant."

"For forty years I tried clever," Lucchino admitted many years later, echoing Elwood P. Dowd. "I recommend pleasant."

After graduation, Lucchino went to teach for a year in Beirut, Lebanon. Still uncertain about what to do with his life, he entered Yale Law School because he had heard that Yale was the "last stronghold of the generalist." He wasn't, however, prepared for the quality of the intellectual firepower he would find at Yale. Lucchino befriended one of his classmates from his contracts class, the quiet, seemingly shy Indianan David Kendall. When Lucchino was up to about page 30 in the contracts book, he asked Kendall how far along he was, hoping to find somebody else who was finding the going just as tough. Kendall replied that he was on page 700, and that basically once he started reading any book, he just kept at it until he was done. "That's when I realized what league I was in," Lucchino said.

Kendall and Greg Craig met at Yale, too, during a moot court exercise. Kendall played a prosecutor, and Craig was the criminal defendant. They were two roles that, Kendall acknowledged, "we have never been able to assume in our later lives."

Along with Craig, Lucchino graduated law school in 1972, one year ahead of Bill and Hillary Clinton, who were in the law school class of 1973. Kendall graduated in 1971.

Lucchino then accepted a job at a corporate law firm in San Francisco. Craig also found a job in California, and they initially shared an apartment in the Castro district. Soon, however, the lure of the political upheaval that was happening back in Washington in 1973 proved too tempting to resist. The Watergate scandal was in full bloom, and President Nixon's possible impeachment was the political story of the times. So Lucchino quit the law firm and signed on with the House Judiciary Committee's special impeachment inquiry. For nine months, Lucchino's job was to listen carefully to the Oval Office tapes of Richard Nixon, transcribing conversations and doing other factual research on the Watergate burglary and cover-up. Hillary was in charge of researching the history and standards of impeachment, a role that later would become most useful to her. Both worked hard, Lucchino remembered, but nobody on the staff was in earlier, or worked later, than Hillary. Both reported to a brusque New York securities attorney, Bernard Nussbaum, the staff director of the House committee. Because of the press of impeachment work, neither invitee was able to make Greg and Derry's wedding on Martha's Vineyard that summer.

With bushy hair and those thick black glasses, Hillary got along mostly on her talent. "I wasn't exactly your beauty pageant type," she admitted in her memoir. Mississippi congressman Trent Lott, who sat on the House impeachment committee, remembered her for her bad looks and aggressive demeanor. Okay, what Lott actually said to me was that Hillary was "butt ugly." This was after Lott was already in a jam for saying at Strom Thurmond's birthday party that the South Carolina senator, who once railed in favor of white supremacy, should have been president. Of course, that was before Lott discovered Thurmond had fathered a child with the daughter of his family's black housekeeper, which might have changed Lott's mind.

Later, when both Hillary Clinton and Trent Lott were senators, their offices would end up next to each other. Lott, always the southern gentleman, allowed, "She looks a lot better now."

On August 5, 1974—as a result of Butterfield's revelations and the subsequent unanimous Supreme Court ruling giving the special prosecutor access to White House recordings—Nixon was forced to release the so-called smoking-gun tape, which showed how deeply he was involved in the Watergate crimes, which ran the gamut from burglaries to obstruction of justice. Four days later, Nixon resigned from office, leaving Lucchino and Hillary Rodham looking for something new to do. Neither had expected that result quite so abruptly. Lucchino contemplated going to work for the

U.S. attorney's office as a career prosecutor. Lawyers with competitive, even combative temperaments are often very satisfied working as prosecutors, and Lucchino wasn't sure he really wanted to work as hard as a corporate firm demanded. His job in San Francisco had bored him. Greg Craig had already signed on with Williams, Connolly & Califano, so Lucchino was considering applying there as well. John Doar, a Princeton man, who was the chief counsel at the House impeachment committee and had been the Justice Department's head prosecutor in the civil rights case against the Mississippians who had murdered three civil rights workers in a much heralded federal civil rights prosecution, suggested that Lucchino give Edward Bennett Williams a shot. "It's different from any other place," Doar said mysteriously.

His interest piqued, Lucchino followed up the comment. Although he didn't have the stellar credentials, like a Supreme Court clerkship, of Califano's other hires that year, Califano decided to take a chance on him, and Lucchino accepted.

Hillary also pondered her future. Williams, Connolly & Califano was that rare corporate-style law firm where personalities like hers—and Larry's—could thrive. However, staying in Washington would mean having to retake the District of Columbia bar exam. On the other hand, she could take Bill up on his offer to get married. She had already passed the bar in Arkansas, so on a professional level that seemed simpler. Though she didn't really know anything yet, Hillary got a job teaching law at the University of Arkansas. As she would later write, "I decided to give our relationship a chance." With that, Hillary left Washington and moved to Arkansas, although it turned out not to be forever.

On the first day that Lucchino came to work, he was getting settled in his office when Edward Bennett Williams walked in to greet him.

Williams at the time was the operating trustee for the Washington Redskins. The majority ownership of the team was actually in the hands of Jack Kent Cooke, a cable television billionaire, but NFL rules prohibited owners from operating teams in rival leagues, and Cooke also owned the Los Angeles Forum venue, the Los Angeles Lakers basketball team, and a professional hockey team, the Los Angeles Kings. In order to allow him to own the Redskins, the league had requested that his ownership be put into a trust that was controlled by Ed Williams, a minority shareholder in the team.

Williams slouched into a chair and began asking Lucchino what he thought about the Redskins quarterback situation. Should they be playing the popular Sonny Jurgensen, or perhaps give more time to scrappy Billy Kilmer, whom coach George Allen had brought to the team from the Saints? The Sonny-Billy controversy was the second most fervent debate in Washington in the 1970s, after the Vietnam War; there was hardly a car in town that didn't sport a bumper sticker that declared either SONNY or BILLY.

The fact that a brand-new associate was approached in this way by Williams was considered astounding by other young associates at the firm. One recalled that Williams almost never engaged new lawyers in conversation, and that his secretary kept on her desk one of those metal indicators that used to be above the elevator to show what floor the cars were on. Periodically she changed the pointer on it from 1 to 12, to designate Williams's mood and indicate whether he should be approached or not. Lawyers referred to the device as Williams's "mood-o-meter." If the meter was anything above a 4, no associate would dare get near him. Lucchino was the only one who didn't have to worry about it. He could always go in, and his presence always brought Williams down a few "floors."

Lucchino had lived out on the West Coast for a year, so he could converse pretty well about Allen and the former West Coast players like Kilmer, who had started his career as a 49er. After about an hour, Williams left to do other things. Lucchino muttered, "Man, I think I made the right decision."

In the beginning he was paired on some cases with former *Harvard Law Review* president Richard Cooper, by all accounts the most seriously intellectual partner that Califano had hired. Just as Lucchino had been intimidated by Kendall in law school, now he felt the same way about Cooper. It was obvious that while Lucchino may have lacked some of the intellectual firepower of his colleagues, he was all "War Department" in his temperament. While personable and interesting most of the time, Lucchino had a Williams-like hair-trigger temper. Lucchino's dance between the two mentors was solved in 1977, two years after he was hired, when Califano left. Califano may have taken some of his supposed aces—like Cooper—with him to the Carter administration, but Lucchino was more than happy to be left behind with the more like-minded Williams and Sullivan.

He quickly proved his bona fides as a lawyer to the firm's lead attorney in a case in which the government indicted a chemical company for making false statements to investigators from the Environmental Protection Agency. True to the philosophy of Williams & Connolly, Lucchino responded to the charges against his client with a full-scale assault on the prosecutors, alleging massive abuse of the grand jury process. His performance impressed the boss, who then asked Lucchino if he wanted to help with contract negotiations for the Washington Redskins.

Lucchino worked on two cases, one involving defensive back Mike Bass, who had suffered a practice injury but still wanted to be paid for the full season. Then Williams asked Lucchino if he would handle the legal aspects of the firing of Coach Allen. He then participated with Williams in the hiring of new Redskins general manager Bobby Beathard. The negotiations were hampered by a dispute over what Beathard's title would be. Lucchino was reluctant to name him general manager, afraid that the title would unnecessarily provoke resentment from others already in the organization who coveted it, though not necessarily all the headaches that went with it. He expected a battle from Beathard, assuming that if he was going to have all the duties of the general manager, he would want the title as well. Lucchino was prepared to dig down and battle Beathard over the issue when Beathard declared the title meant nothing to him. They could call him whatever they wanted.

When Lucchino reported this to Williams, he thought it was now a matter of finding a substitute title, but Williams said to give the general manager's office—and the title—to Beathard. "That's the kind of guy you want. Somebody who doesn't care about his title. All we need to care about is that Beathard knows where the bodies are buried," Williams said. So Beathard got the title and became the greatest Redskins executive ever, building a team that would make four Super Bowl appearances. Lucchino learned a key lesson in personnel management. "After that," he said, "I always looked for the guy who knew where the bodies were buried."

Both the players and their agents could be pretty tough. Williams wanted someone with as much pugnacity as they had handling the work, and Lucchino fit the bill perfectly. He was more than satisfied with Lucchino's performance, and the following year he put Lucchino on the board of the Redskins. In 1979, Larry was made a partner in the firm, despite the fact that he had been an associate for less than five years. Lucchino also inherited the title of general counsel of the Redskins, a post he held even after Williams sold his 14 percent stake in the Redskins to Jack Kent Cooke and bought the Baltimore Orioles baseball team in August that same year.

Williams purchased the Orioles from the Jerold Hoffberger family, which had manufactured Baltimore's National Bohemian beer, paying $11.8 million for the franchise. During negotiations, Hoffberger hadn't wanted to see the team sold to someone from Washington at all, and he suspected that Williams's true agenda was to steal the Orioles away to Washington. While other bidders for the Orioles, notably former Nixon treasury secretary William Simon, attacked Hoffberger for being unreasonable, Williams sat back and said little. One of Williams's central philosophies of life was that when in doubt, one should say and do nothing.

After an exasperated Simon lost interest in the team, Williams and Lucchino took Hoffberger aside. They assured the beer magnate that he would always be the heart and soul of the Orioles, which they pledged would never leave Baltimore. Williams only came up with $500,000. The rest of the money he borrowed from Jack Kent Cooke, using some real estate he had accumulated as his collateral.

Despite public statements that he would not take the "birds" out of Baltimore, Williams ordered Lucchino to drive up and down Interstate 95, scouting for new stadium sites. Lucchino did him one better, renting a helicopter on the day after the deal closed. No one in Baltimore or Washington believed for one minute that Williams was telling the truth about keeping the Orioles in Baltimore or that Hoffberger would have any continuing role with the team. It would have been counter to a lawyer's DNA for Williams to do so. Lucchino says that what Williams actually said to Hoffberger was that he would never move them as long as they had fan support in Baltimore, which, Lucchino pointed out to me, would always be considered a matter of opinion.

The pressure on the avid baseball fans of Baltimore was great. With a team that included a number of homegrown stars, like Jim Palmer and Brooks Robinson, the team set record or near-record attendance figures nearly every season. The Orioles would come to be considered one of the most valuable franchises in baseball, partly because of their brilliant young Maryland-born shortstop, Rookie of the Year the previous season, Cal Ripken Jr. Ultimately Ripken set the record for most consecutive games ever played, and he would become a nearly unanimous selection to baseball's Hall of Fame, one of baseball's true immortals.

So, instead of the Orioles moving to Washington, Washingtonians moved to Baltimore in droves. The percentage of seats sold to people from Washington and the suburbs of Maryland jumped from 10 to 25 percent. The team's success in those years put the move to the suburbs on hold for the moment, and in both 1979 and 1983 the Orioles made the World Series.

While Lucchino gravitated toward Williams and a law practice that danced around sports law, Greg Craig, the preppy lacrosse guy, was headed in a different direction, toward becoming heavily involved in what some would call the trial of the century. It started with Craig's leaving Washington and returning to Connecticut.

Shortly after coming to Williams, Connolly & Califano, Craig took a leave of absence and became an assistant public defender in Connecticut while Derry got a master's degree in fine arts from Yale. It was a pattern of coming and going that would uniquely characterize Craig's relationship with Williams & Connolly over the years. After Derry graduated, they both returned to Washington in 1976. She set up a graphics design business, which, among other things, designed postage stamps. Lucchino asked if she would frame a plaque that had one of his favorite sayings on it, from *New Yorker* writer Brendan Gill: "Not a shred of evidence exists in favor of the idea that life is serious, though it is often hard and even terrible. And saying that, I am prompted to add what follows out of it; that since everything ends badly for us, in the inescapable catastrophe of death, it seems obvious that the first rule of life is to have a good time; and that the second rule of life is to hurt as few people as possible in the course of doing so. There is no third rule."

Lucchino inserted the words into Derry's home-made frame and kept it proudly on his wall, as a statement of his own personal philosophy of life, which he admitted tended toward hedonism. "For years I did not doubt this quotation," Lucchino admits now. "I have since grasped how limited and misleading that clever passage really is."

9.

ANOTHER DAY, ANOTHER DOLLAR

———————————— ■ ————————————

Although Califano had by now set up his own new firm, Craig decided to stay behind at Williams & Connolly. He had already worked on a case where a Washington businessman, who owned a number of parking lots, had been accused of conspiracy and fraud. It wasn't the biggest case in the United States that year. But the most glamorous case that Craig landed was the representation of Russian novelist Alexsandr Solzhenitsyn, who had moved to Cavendish, Vermont, in 1976 to await the downfall of the Soviet Union. When he was sued for libel by his translator, Olga Carlisle, in 1978, Solzhenitsyn was steered by Vermont senator Patrick Leahy to Craig. Leahy was the first Democrat ever elected to the Senate from Vermont, in 1974, and Greg had actively supported his campaign. Leahy had an aunt who was best friends and neighbors with Craig's mother, Lois, in Shelburne, Vermont. A friend and supporter of Bill Craig's career, he would be a quiet promoter of Greg's as well.

The Solzhenitsyn case was precisely the kind of trial experience that causes young lawyers to go to Williams & Connolly. At many firms, when a case gets ready for trial, the young lawyer who has done all the research and preparation for the case gets bumped for an old-timer who is more familiar with the courtroom and sometimes is a fellow club member of the judge. Craig worked closely on Solzhenitsyn for several years until the case was dismissed by Federal District Judge William Schwarzer in July 1981.

The defeat of President Carter in 1980 was not universally bemoaned in Washington. Outsiders who think that Washington simply loves Democrats and hates Republicans really have no understanding of the culture in the nation's capital. If anything, Carter was more than a bit too self-righteous, and most Washingtonians found him insufferable in every respect. Carter's presidency, unlike his successful postpresidency, would be judged as one of the more dismal in American history. Although Ronald Reagan was an arch-conservative, most Washingtonians, especially Democratic House Speaker Tip O'Neill, welcomed the change, if it meant sending the infuriating Carter out of town. Presidents are usually the only officeholders who do actually leave when they lose office; ex-senators and ex-representatives tend to stay around forever.

Reagan took office on January 20, 1981. When his choice for secretary of state, Alexander Haig, figured to need some advice at his Senate confirmation hearings, the general asked his close friend from his Pentagon days, Joe Califano—now at his own wise-man firm—to guide him through the sometimes thorny process. Califano ultimately charged the Republican Party Transition Office some $86,047 for the advice he would give to Haig about how to answer the committee's questions. In his autobiography *Inside*, Califano notes that his fee for his representation of Haig was "less than half our usual rates." Haig didn't mind. Hardly anyone in Washington picks up his own tab. His bill was covered by funds raised by the Republican National Committee.

Just two months later, only sixty-nine days into his term, on March 30, 1981, as Reagan was exiting the Washington Hilton Hotel after a speech, a gunman jumped out of the press gaggle and began firing shots with a $47 West German–made revolver. Wounded in the attack were President Reagan, his press secretary, James Brady, Secret Service officer Tim McCarthy, and policeman Thomas Delahanty. The shot that struck the president ricocheted off the presidential limousine, hitting Reagan as he was being pushed into the car. None of the victims of the attack died, although Brady, who was the most severely injured, would remain permanently impaired with brain damage and later become the symbol of the legislative movement to restrict the unfettered sales of handguns.

The twenty-five-year-old suspect, John W. Hinckley Jr., was quickly apprehended. The entire attack was captured on multiple television and newsreel cameras. The vice president was on a plane halfway over the Pacific. In the leadership void, Haig rushed to the White House and noisily declared, "I am in charge." The country wasn't sure it wanted that, nor that such a declaration from a general was really calming.

Hinckley was taken to District headquarters at 2:40 P.M. Hardly your typical assassin, he was the son of a wealthy Colorado businessman, who was acquainted with Vice President Bush. While he was in custody,

Hinckley sanguinely requested that he be allowed to talk to Joe Bates, his father's attorney.

By 5:15 P.M. Hinckley had been taken to the FBI Washington Field Office and charged with violation of the federal presidential assassination statute. He was also informed that police had found the lawyer in Texas that he had requested and that the lawyer told him to retain Vincent Fuller, a longtime protégé of Edward Bennett Williams at Williams & Connolly and Williams's co-counsel in the Jimmy Hoffa case. More apropos to this case, Bates and Fuller had been law school classmates at Georgetown.

Fuller was not immediately available, and while the police waited to hear back from him, they asked Hinckley if he had a girlfriend. Hinckley replied that he was in a one-sided relationship and produced the Yale dormitory number for eighteen-year-old actress Jodie Foster. Hinckley said he had talked to Foster two or three times and that tapes of the calls were in his suitcase at his hotel.

Eventually Fuller got the message that Hinckley's family had sought him out. Fuller, the firm's most senior lawyer after Williams, wasn't sure this was a case that Ed Williams would want him to take. His instincts were correct—Williams was not enthusiastic. Reagan had just been elected. The last thing Ed wanted to do, as he bluntly told Fuller, was to "piss off" Nancy Reagan. Even so, he couldn't bring himself to tell Hinckley's father that the firm couldn't represent him. After all, the Hinckleys were the rarest of commodities in a murder case, criminal defendants with plenty of money. He told the senior Hinckley that he understood the disappointments of fatherhood, and he told Fuller to go ahead and represent Hinckley. "This is what the firm was built on," Williams said. "That's what we are all about."

To be Fuller's co-counsel on the case, Williams personally assigned Craig, who seemed well suited for the job because of those two years in Connecticut as a public defender. Williams also wanted to use Craig to keep an independent eye on the case.

Fuller readily admitted that he had never worked with this kind of defendant before, but Craig had. With the facts barely in dispute, and actual television footage of Hinckley firing the shots, Craig felt their options were limited. The only way to go, he decided, was for Hinckley to plead insanity. Ironically, Craig had seen the same insanity defense used in the case of another white, middle-class assassin, Dennis Sweeney. On March 14, 1980, close to a year to the day before Hinckley shot James Brady and President Reagan, Sweeney had murdered Craig's idol, Allard Lowenstein, in his Manhattan office. Sweeney enjoyed a fairly relaxed confinement for most of his sentence, until being released from custody entirely in 2000.

Fuller would later write, "The case was challenging because it was so bizarre. A wealthy young man of Republican heritage, Hinckley tried to kill Ronald Reagan because he was in love with Jodie Foster." Craig and Fuller went out and took Foster's deposition. Under law going back centuries, the rule had been that to prove that a defendant was insane, the defendant's lawyers had to prove that the "insane" person could not tell the difference between right and wrong. However, Craig's research revealed that under an antiquated District of Columbia law, the prosecution had the burden of showing that an assailant was *not* insane. The law stated that a defendant could not be held criminally responsible for his acts if at the time of the commission of the crime he could not, due to mental incapacity, "appreciate the wrongfulness of his act."

Although Fuller wrote articles in the aftermath of the case taking credit for developing the plan, he never completely believed it would work. At the beginning he had no confidence that there was standing for an insanity plea. Fuller wanted Hinckley to plead guilty to the charges. He asked Assistant Attorney General Rudolph Giuliani if the government would accept a plea agreement, with the proviso that Hinckley be eligible for parole after ten years.

Giuliani scoffed. "We don't negotiate with assassins," he said with an air of total finality.

Giuliani's snap decision solved one of the defense team's biggest problems. The natural urge of Fuller was to win his client's freedom, and that was the usual attitude of the firm. However, Craig and Williams believed that a better result would be to pursue an insanity defense and Hinckley's parents agreed.

Craig began developing the strategy to prove that Hinckley could not appreciate that what he was doing was wrong. They decided to humanize Hinckley through his voluminous writings, which included a letter written on the morning of the shooting to Jodie Foster. Craig hoped the letter would show that Hinckley was utterly detached from reality and had no emotional appreciation of it.

Fuller and Craig were able to present a young man to the jury who was friendless, had a terrible sense of hopelessness, and was totally without the requisite mental capacity to appreciate the wrongfulness of his conduct. Still, by the standards of most people, he wasn't totally insane. Hinckley had gotten through two years of college at Texas Tech, where he read books, played the guitar, and enjoyed music. He dropped out in the spring of 1976 and went to Hollywood, where he played the guitar and hoped to break into show business as a songwriter. It was there that he first saw the film *Taxi Driver*, with Robert De Niro and Jodie Foster. Hinckley became obsessed with the movie, acting, dressing, and thinking like Travis Bickle, De Niro's character. Bickle plans a political assassination to win the love of a presidential campaign worker. After that does not succeed, he turns his attention to the Jodie Foster character, whom he rescues from prostitution after a fatal shootout with her pimp.

In the spring of 1977, Hinckley was still sane enough to return to Texas Tech. He then went to Yale to enroll in writing classes and to win the heart of Jodie Foster, who had just enrolled there as a freshman. Hinckley left Foster several letters and poems that were unanswered. Finally, to win her attention and love, he decided to shoot a president. It could have just as easily been a Democrat as a Republican. He bought some guns and stalked Jimmy Carter for a while in 1979, then on March 30, 1981, shot President Reagan.

It's safe to assume that had Hinckley been a black student from Texas Tech, nobody would have bought Craig's story of his being crazy. In no other country in the world, probably not even France, could a person brazenly step before the television cameras and shoot the president of the United States, two law enforcement officers, and a presidential aide, and be found not guilty. Then again, no other country had a law firm like Williams & Connolly operating in it.

The story of the American system of justice is that if you have enough money and can afford a clever enough lawyer, anything is possible. Thus it was that on June 21, 1982, a District of Columbia jury found Hinckley not guilty of the shooting by reason of insanity. He was sentenced to what has been a lifetime spent at St. Elizabeth's Hospital. Among those who seemed to agree with the verdict was President Reagan himself. He told television host Larry King that he forgave Hinckley and had "added him to my prayers." Reagan said he decided Hinckley could use some divine inspiration because "it was clear he wasn't thinking on all cylinders."

Asked for comment when he left the courthouse, Fuller, in a rare moment of attorney candor, reflected his and many of his colleagues' view of the law. "Another day, another dollar," he said. Fuller died of lung cancer at age seventy-five in 2006. Jodie Foster would later win an Academy Award for playing an FBI agent who prosecutes an insane cannibalistic killer, Hannibal Lecter, in *Silence of the Lambs*. Lecter, who seems a lot nuttier than Hinckley, never made an insanity claim. In the movie, he seems to have no attorney at all, much less someone as clever as Craig.

One month after the Hinckley insanity verdict, Califano's client Alexander Haig was fired from his post as secretary of state. Washington humorist Art Buchwald, Califano's close friend, frequently joked that it was "wise man" Califano who had given Haig the memorable line "I'm in control here" and advised Haig to "get over to the White House, right away."

That such a newly minted attorney like Craig could walk in and so quickly become so involved in the trial of the decade was a lesson not lost on other Califano protégés, least of all on bookish Bob Barnett.

10

THE STAGE MANAGER

———■———

Robert Bruce Barnett was born in Waukegan, Illinois, on August 26, 1946. His father, Bernard Barnett, ran the Waukegan office of the federal Social Security Administration and was one of the agency's leading experts on the intricate details of Social Security coverage. The son of a Russian-Jewish immigrant who adopted the name Robert Barnett after arriving in America in 1890, Bernard would literally go door to door to explain to people what their benefits would be. Barnett also hosted a call-in radio program on WKRS that was one of the most listened-to broadcasts in northeastern Illinois. The show began each time with the playing of "Rule, Britannia," but no one was ever sure why.

Fellow Illinois native Bob Woodward, who would later become one of Bob Barnett's most successful clients, says that their common midwestern background makes them both "low-key and straightforward." As a teenager Barnett was drawn to intellectual pursuits, though not solitary ones. He collected stamps and baseball cards, but he was just as active in debate and theater. As a ten-year-old, Barnett once walked into the dry-cleaning store owned by the town's mayor and found the door open but nobody there. He reported it to his father, who called the mayor, who was extremely impressed with young Bob's seriousness when it came to keeping one's shop locked. The mayor, Robert Sabonjian, told Bobby, "From this moment on, you have a future in politics."

He made it more than a platitude, enlisting Barnett up until his teenage years as a campaign aide on bumper sticker duty and leaflet patrol. Bob also was awarded a summer job as "deputy superintendent" of the mayor's mosquito patrol.

His classmates say that in the forty-five or so years since graduating from Waukegan High School in 1964, Barnett has rarely missed even a five-year class reunion. "Waukegan was a real microcosm of American culture," Barnett has said. "There was a real sense of ethnic diversity in which one learned to be tolerant and considerate." Barnett was a runaway selection as senior class president, and he left no one disappointed. He ran on the platform that he would bring the gold-record folk group the Chad Mitchell Trio to Waukegan High. Barnett's class needed to come up with $10,000 up front and then sell out their two-thousand-seat high school auditorium. By the time Barnett was through with his ticket drive, with the help of the mayor, of course, he had sold all two thousand seats, plus another three hundred "premium" seats up on the stage behind the singers.

Barnett loved musical comedies but couldn't sing that well; he was the type who would get cast in straight dramas or the nonsinging roles of musicals. His role of the Stage Manager in Thornton Wilder's *Our Town* is one of the most daunting in all of high school theater, with long uninterrupted speeches to memorize. That was nothing for Barnett, though, who has the kind of mind and memory that allows for that kind of memorization and mimicry. His other major scholastic activity was forensics, and he was a tri-state debate champion for Illinois, Wisconsin, and Indiana. After graduation, Barnett headed for the University of Wisconsin at Madison, only about ninety miles from his home. Barnett, while blessed with natural scholastic brilliance, couldn't work the dorm room washing machine and still liked to take his laundry home on weekends.

Barnett was a member of Pi Lambda Phi Fraternity. A frat brother of his, Steve Zacharias, would go on to write the screenplays for *Revenge of the Nerds* and *The Whoopee Boys*. *Nerds* is loosely based on Pi Lambda Phi's greatest exploits, but Bob's extracurricular activities did not include the usual time-wasting events common to living in the frat house. He was an evening regular at the massive UW library, definitely not a party animal, according to fraternity brother Larry Weiner, then living in Las Vegas. "I would never think somebody from our fraternity could end up being so respectable in that kind of a milieu," he mused.

The fraternity always gave first choice of room to the top student, and nobody could ever wrest that from Bob. Finding him at night was the easiest thing in the world. Everyone on campus knew exactly where to look: in the library. At the same time, he played intramural sports and had a great sense of humor. His fraternity mates couldn't understand why a Pi Lambda

Phi was so serious about school, but that was an eccentricity that made everyone like him.

By the time he was a senior, Barnett had still failed to find a steady girlfriend, and time was running out when a housemate suggested he might like the company of a brainy blond sophomore from Silver Spring, Maryland, who was into Irish literature and Shakespeare, adored painters Vincent van Gogh and Paul Gauguin, but majored, like Bob, in political science.

Barnett was thus introduced to Rita Braver. For their first meeting, he invited her to meet him at the library for a "study date." Barnett was impressed. After walking her back to the dorm that very night, he asked her if she would marry him. She politely declined. "He didn't bring it up again for five years," Rita said.

Barnett insists that he was dead serious about his offer and was devastated when she said no. He was not so crushed as to give up on her, and they continued to date. Barnett had decided to attend law school at that point. He applied and was accepted to several of the top Ivy League schools but enrolled at the University of Chicago, so as not to be too far away from Rita—not that the University of Chicago Law School is any slouch. Rita was flattered to think that Bob had made such a momentous personal decision because of her, but privately she suspected that the real reason was to stay close to his mother's washing machine.

His frat brothers were amazed at their relatively quiet but apparently impulsive buddy. To the nerds, he had struck it rich. Rita was a popular and attractive girl on campus, says one. She wasn't a cheerleader, but to a Pi Lambda Phi, she seemed a catch nonetheless. "Boy, did they click. She was just as focused as he was, two people who knew what they wanted," said another frat brother.

In 1970, while Bob was in law school, Bernard Barnett died of a heart attack. The man who knew more about Social Security than virtually anyone else would never have the chance to apply his knowledge to his own life. The Midwest's leading expert on how to financially survive old age was just fifty-seven at the time of his death.

When Bob was done with law school and Rita was finished at Wisconsin, he landed a clerk's position with New Orleans–based federal judge John Minor Wisdom, a legendary and progressive southern judge of the era. The clerkship with Judge Wisdom was one of the most coveted in the country, and Bob approached the prospect with laserlike intensity, not even noticing the Deep South landscape as he drove through in his 1970 blue Buick Opel, the very same year and model as the car Bill Clinton owned, albeit the future president's was orange.

They took an apartment out on St. Charles Avenue off the trolley line near Tulane. Rita, who was set on a career in journalism, got an entry-level job at the CBS affiliate in New Orleans, WWL, after being turned down for several newspaper jobs. Journalism was then a profession where enthusiasm and enterprise were rewarded, and in just a couple of months she was producing the station's 10:00 P.M. news broadcast.

Barnett proudly directed their expeditions to more than a hundred New Orleans restaurants, which he marked off in a guidebook called *The New Orleans Underground Gourmet* as they went. They spent most Saturday mornings lunching on brabant potatoes with the judge and his wife, Bonnie, at Galatoire's, the famous no-reservations restaurant in the French Quarter. Unlike tourists, the judge and other prominent locals were rarely forced to stand in line for very long.

Clerking suited Barnett well. His take on Judge Wisdom would later sound as close as one might get to Barnett's own self-analysis. "He was brilliant without being arrogant, he was courtly without ever being condescending," Barnett would write after Wisdom's death in 1999. They were character traits that Barnett, although they weren't framed on his wall, pledged to emulate.

It did not surprise anyone that Barnett made a decision to try for a clerkship at the U.S. Supreme Court. He was telling Rita about his new ambition one day when, as she recounts, "he suddenly pulled over and asked me to marry him. Yes, while we were seated in our Opel. This time I accepted on the spot."

The marriage took place at Judge Wisdom's Garden District New Orleans home on April 10, 1972, attended by just fifteen close friends and family members including both their mothers. Louisiana's Napoleonic Code did not allow for a federal judge to conduct the marriage. Despite his organizational and intellectual skills, Barnett has Mr. Magoo–like propensities. He claims, for example, not to have any recollection of driving through Mississippi on his way to New Orleans from Chicago. Nor, when I asked, did he have any recollection of who performed the wedding ceremony, other than it being a state justice of the peace.

They moved to Washington later in 1972, after Bob was offered a job with Supreme Court Justice Byron White. Rita signed on as a young correspondent with CBS News in Washington, where she would often be confused with another up-and-comer, Lesley Stahl. They took an apartment at 4000 Massachusetts Avenue, in an area they would live in for the rest of their lives in Washington, as perennial luxury apartment dwellers.

II.

THE ELEVATOR OPERATOR'S SON

——————■——————

Barnett's immediate predecessor as a clerk for Justice White was Larry Lucchino's friend from contracts class, David Kendall. He had taken a much more committed and circuitous path to Washington.

Born at Camp Atterbury, Indiana, Kendall was the son of a grain elevator operator who had a farm outside of Indianapolis. Kendall would joke that when he told people he was from Sheridan (pop. 2,691), they thought he was just trying to brag about being from a big city. He once had to break up with a sophisticated eastern girlfriend who told her disapproving parents that Kendall's father was an "elevator operator." Kendall decided that under the circumstances, it wasn't worth explaining.

He attended Wabash College, an exclusive, nine-hundred-student, all-men's liberal arts college in Crawfordsville, Indiana, with every intention of going on to medical school and becoming a doctor, which in towns like Sheridan was the highest and most respectable professional calling.

As a junior at Wabash, during the summer of 1964, Kendall took time off to register black voters in Mississippi, one of legions of committed northerners who went south to support the civil rights movement and to enroll black voters in the political process. His roommate for the 1964 Mississippi Summer Project training sessions in Oxford, Ohio, was a more veteran activist in the movement, Andrew Goodman. They took an instinctive liking to each other.

"Andy and I talked a lot about what we thought Mississippi would be like," Kendall later recalled. "Everyone was scared, everyone knew we would be in harm's way, but I think each of us thought in our heart of hearts that we would come through OK."

Almost exactly a week after Kendall and Goodman bunked together in training sessions, Goodman set off to investigate the burning of black

Mt. Zion Church outside of Philadelphia, Mississippi, the county seat of Neshoba County. Kendall was originally assigned to work in McComb, a place that was considered even more dangerous for the civil rights workers than Philadelphia. Before he could leave, however, organizers discerned that Kendall's smooth speaking skills might work better trying to lobby congressmen and senators to have the Justice Department increase the number of federal marshals in the Deep South.

Kendall was walking out of the office of Illinois Senator Paul Douglas when he heard the radio bulletin that Goodman and his two companions, James Chaney and Michael Schwerner, had disappeared. It would turn out that they had been captured by a band of racist thugs—aided by the county sheriff and his deputies—and shot to death after being beaten. "I was sure then that he was dead," Kendall recalled, "though they didn't find the bodies until August."

When David finally arrived to do fieldwork in Mississippi, he was a different person. Kendall was lucky not to be physically harmed during his tenure in the Deep South, but psychologically he would never view life in the same way. Goodman, Schwerner, and Chaney's murders became one of the most tragic and galvanizing episodes of the civil rights era in Mississippi, and for no individual any more so than for David. On eight separate occasions he was roughly arrested by various county sheriffs and thrown into jail for his "agitating" civil rights activities. Some of Kendall's arrests were the result of his own sloppiness, like the time he was jailed for driving his Volkswagen with Mississippi plates but without a Mississippi inspection sticker. On another occasion, Kendall was jailed for no particular cause other than "investigation." After three days in jail he was brought before a county magistrate, who gave him the arrest warrant to read, which contained references to a fictional defendant. Kendall read it, then blurted out, "There's something wrong here. This warrant says take the body of John Doe—I'm not John Doe!" As the magistrate glowered and sheriff's deputies grabbed their nightsticks, Kendall's lawyer, Faith Seidenberg, whispered in his ear what would become classic Williams & Connolly dogma, "I'm your lawyer. When I want you to talk, you'll talk. Unless I tell you to talk, keep your mouth shut."

Kendall was reduced to smuggling letters out of jail on toilet paper. One read, "This isn't a bad jail...I'm alone, which is very good. One of the chief dangers of being arrested is getting beaten up by white prisoners (sometimes with the Sheriff's encouragement) who find out you're a Civil Rights worker (they always call us 'Freedom Riders'). The ironic thing is that twenty-four hours ago I was in jail at Hernando, Miss. for 'investigation.' I was released after eight hours though."

Frequently, Kendall's bail was posted by lawyers from the NAACP Legal Defense and Educational Fund. Kendall made a mental note to pay them back someday. He proudly described himself as an "agitator," the very term that Ku Klux Klan members used to derogate the students who came south to push for civil rights

"We were in fact agitators, I hope and believe," Kendall said at a memorial service for Goodman and the others, forty years later, "but we weren't really outsiders even though we didn't live here permanently and even though at the end of the summer, we would, except for Andy Goodman, return to a comfortable college life. We weren't outsiders here because the civil rights struggle we were engaged in, and which others had been engaged in for a long time before and after the summer of 1964, wasn't just about Mississippi or the people who live here, it was about the entire United States, and we, the summer volunteers weren't outsiders there. . . . James Chaney and Andy Goodman and Mickey Schwerner died for their country—our country—just as much as the U.S. GIs who died on Omaha Beach in Normandy almost exactly twenty years earlier. Their struggle and their deaths, and the struggle and deaths of so many others in the movement, have established that this is not the country of the racists and the haters—that they are the outsiders here."

As the days passed in the humid and impossibly depressing hills of rural Mississippi, Kendall began to ponder the power and utility of the law. A doctor could save lives one at a time. A lawyer, he was discovering, had the power to change the world.

Said Kendall, "I felt deeply committed to the goals of racial equality and non-discriminatory voter registration but increasingly uncomfortable with the heated rhetoric and seemingly endless staff meetings of movement life that summer in [Mississippi]. But at the same time I became attracted to the civil rights lawyers who got us off when we got arrested or jailed for specious alleged infractions."

Kendall came to believe that "lawyers had a powerful weapon in their hands, and I began to regard the law in a new way. Our lawyers didn't speechify, they marshaled facts, filed affidavits and pleadings, appeared in court, and argued skillfully—they got themselves listened to and even occasionally feared by the white power structure that seemed to be so successfully harassing us would-be voting registers."

Kendall came to realize that the best lawyers "knew the rules of a mysterious and tricky game, one that they played skillfully against ill-intentioned opponents who often seemed less knowledgeable about the law."

Kendall's travels across Mississippi shaped his social consciousness and even made him question the pacifism of his Quaker parents. He rebelled against the simplicity of the description. "I am a member of the Religious Society of Friends, or my ancestors were, but that tag gets hung around me a lot in ways that I really don't understand and don't much like," he would say in an interview with a Wabash College magazine. "I don't know what it signifies. I served in the army. I have a very complicated relationship with my religious heritage, I guess."

He returned to Wabash in 1966, winning a Rhodes Scholarship to study in England. He was not impressed, however. Writing an essay later for the quarterly *Wabash Bulletin*, Kendall declared his surprise at the extremely low quality of lecturing at Oxford. "Lecturers such as Isaiah Berlin and J. R. R. Tolkien are excellent and draw large crowds, but the average lecture is likely to be on a trivial topic, badly delivered, dull, and ill attended," he observed. Kendall's own lectures weren't bad, however; he had won first place in the college's nationally known and prestigious oratory contest.

Chosen to give the valedictory address at Wabash in 1966, Kendall electrified some in the student body with his passionate speech. "We need cynicism in order to be honest, to avoid a blind optimism, to realize the human origin of our values ... We need commitment because beliefs should not be separated from knowledge, and values are not separated from actions. We must be committed to the humanistic ideals of tolerance and rationality because there will always be Grand Inquisitors ready to build concentration camps to sacrifice human dignity to the purity of an ideal," he said.

David's parents still hoped that he would go to medical school, and he was accepted at several of the top ones in the country. Becoming a lawyer was considered by his neighbors almost as disreputable as becoming an actor or a writer. "In the small Indiana farming community where I grew up," Kendall said, "doctors were revered, lawyers were not."

His experiences in Mississippi were indelibly imprinted into him, though, so instead of medical school Kendall enrolled at Yale University Law School, graduating in the class of 1971. He then got the job as a clerk for Justice Byron "Whizzer" White, a year before Barnett got the same clerkship. Frequently Supreme Court clerks are chosen from the ranks of clerks for federal judges, referred by judge to judge, but Kendall and a close friend of his, Richard Danzig, both applied directly to White. Even though they assumed only one of them would get the clerkship, Kendall, who was interviewed first, came back and revealed all the questions to Danzig. "It was an amazingly selfless act," Danzig would say later. It was also one of those rare times when decency was rewarded. White hired both law graduates, who would be lifelong friends, as his two clerks.

Kendall and Barnett overlapped briefly, both working on White's opinion in *Roe v. Wade*, where the JFK-appointee surprised liberals by opposing the 7–2 decision of the Court, handed down on January 22, 1973. While both were publicly loyal to their judge, Barnett would always consider Judge Wisdom his idol. Kendall would always be puzzled by White's approach to law. One of the most liberal students at Yale had wound up with one of the most conservative justices on the Court. "His philosophy wasn't mine," Kendall says, "but no one ever appointed me to the Supreme Court."

Kendall, who was nothing if not committed, would say, "With each case he spreads a deck of cards with every conceivable factual variation. . . . He wasn't invested in an argument; you could hit him with a chair, intellectually speaking, and he could be convinced." Kendall added, "He was a good boss, a tough basketball player at the court over the courtroom, and a lifelong friend who was not above giving me the occasional needle."

When Kendall emerged from his clerkship, he had the credentials to get an associate's position at any top law firm in the country. Instead, he fulfilled his vow to change the world and joined the NAACP's Legal Defense and Educational Fund, the preeminent organization in the United States working on public interest suits for voting rights and fair housing and against capital punishment. It was in the area of the death penalty that Kendall would become best known.

It was while Kendall was clerking for Justice White that the Supreme Court had temporarily suspended the death penalty in America, in a 1972 case called *Furman v. Georgia*. The way capital punishment was applied in the United States was judged too inconsistent and haphazard. The penalty was not uniformly applied for the same crimes, nor was it dispensed equally with regard to race or gender or region of the country. Although White voted in the majority to put a moratorium on the death penalty, he would not go so far as to say that the electric chair was unconstitutional under the "cruel and unusual punishment" provision of the Constitution.

In the four subsequent years, states hustled to pass new death penalty statutes that would comply with the problems that the five concurring judges, albeit with different rationales, had identified in their landmark decision. Florida was among the first states to repass a death penalty statute. Although both Kendall and Barnett had left Justice White's chambers, it was their former boss who wrote a key opinion on July 2, 1976, in a group of cases generally referred to by the date they were handed down— the *July 2 Cases*—that brought the death penalty back. In that group of decisions, the court upheld the rights of states to execute prisoners and concluded that capital punishment was not constitutionally barred by the "cruel and unusual" provision. White proved considerably more tolerant of capital punishment than his erstwhile former clerk would turn out to be. At the Legal Defense Fund, every one of Kendall's clients was a death row inmate. Having learned that the preferred game on all death rows in America was chess, Kendall challenged each of his clients to a game by mail, and he filled his office with a dozen plastic chessboards, each one representing a different prisoner.

Having gotten their new pro-death-penalty statute through the legislature, Florida worked hard to execute its first death row inmate since the *Furman* decision. That first case involved a ne'er-do-well Iowa drifter named John Spenkelink—one of numerous clients represented by the checkered squares on Kendall's office tables.

Kendall could identify with the midwestern life that had produced Spenkelink. The cerebral, decent Kendall was a poster child for the rock-solid Middle America that politicians make speeches about, but Spenkelink represented a more desperate, hardscrabble heartland not often mentioned in slogans or lauded on the political stump. Growing up with no mother, he had learned early in life how to drive a truck, and by the time John was nine, his main chore was keeping his father alive after drunken benders.

On May 3, 1961, he hadn't arrived home early enough to save his father. Instead he found his father's dead body on the front seat of a rusting 1953

Chevy panel truck, asphyxiated from carbon monoxide poisoning. John was eleven then. By the time he was twenty, Spenkelink was serving a possible life sentence for a series of armed robberies. When he got word that because of a bad prison record he would not be paroled, Spenkelink walked off the grounds of Slack Canyon Conservation Camp in California and headed north, then eventually began working his way toward Florida. Along the way, in Nebraska, he picked up a hitchhiker in his stolen car. The rider was Joe Szymankiewicz, who had just gotten out of prison after doing sixteen years for forgery, burglary, and theft. By early February, they had found their way to Florida, checking into room 4 at the Ponce de Leon Motel in Tallahassee.

On February 4, 1973, a maid discovered Joe's 230-pound dead body in the motel bed, bludgeoned and shot twice.

Spenkelink was arrested fairly quickly and accused of murder. At his trial, he would claim that Szymankiewicz had stolen $8,000 from him, demanded that he perform fellatio, and made him play Russian roulette with their guns. Spenkelink's claim that he had acted in self-defense was undermined by forensic evidence that the wounds were all inflicted from behind. Spenkelink was convicted of murder and sentenced on December 20, 1973, to die in Florida's electric chair. His life had initially been spared by the *Furman* decision, but the *July 2 Cases* had put Spenkelink's life back in jeopardy.

If Spenkelink's original lawyer had accepted a plea bargain arrangement, Spenkelink would likely have been a candidate for parole on May 18, 1979. Instead, that was the day Florida governor Bob Graham signed his death warrant. Graham's half brother was Philip Graham. On the day in 1963 that Phil Graham killed himself, Bob was a twenty-seven-year-old playing golf at Miami Lakes Country Club. Just elected governor a few months before the signing of the warrant, Graham, a former state senator who seemed to be far too liberal and cerebral for even a Democrat in Florida, was perceived as being rich and spineless. His election was a shock to the establishment in Florida, but Graham had caught on through a campaign of workdays, spending time doing different jobs every day. Elderly Floridians and especially teachers made Bob their favorite politician. He was able to overcome his privileged image and become a powerful force in Florida politics for the next three decades.

Prisoners on death row were among those optimistic that this left-wing

Harvard boy would never sign a death warrant. The view was shared by the state's powerful daily newspaper editorial writers. Graham, however, was anxious to prove to the Florida voters that he was tough. Spenkelink was viewed as the perfect inmate for execution—largely because he was not black, so the issue of the double standard for black defendants would not arise.

For nearly five years, from 1973 until 1978, Kendall had intensely battled capital punishment. When, in 1978, he was hired to join law school buddies Lucchino and Craig at Williams & Connolly, Kendall insisted on bringing the death row defense of John Spenkelink with him. The firm debated vigorously whether Kendall should even be hired since he had come from what in effect was a public interest law firm. It seemed to violate the rule against hiring laterals, those who had worked at other law firms. In the end, he was narrowly voted in on what would always thereafter be called "the Kendall exception," almost a lateral but not quite.

After his hiring, Williams took Kendall aside for one of his favorite lines. "Washington burns a witch every three months," he said. "It's important not to be that witch." Witch burnings, especially around a governor's reelection campaign, were something Kendall understood better than most.

His role in the Spenkelink execution would eventually be the subject of a dramatic death row narrative by *Washington Post* staff writer David Von Drehle titled *Among the Lowest of the Dead*, on which the following account is based.

On May 19, 1979, Kendall received a call from Spenkelink, who said his death warrant had been signed. "Read it to me," Kendall said.

Spenkelink stopped when he got to the date of the execution, May 23, in just four days. "What are we going to do?" Spenkelink asked.

Kendall assured Spenkelink that he had some new areas of appeal and was confident he could win yet another delay. He ended the conversation promising to call the prisoner's mother and give her the news. No prisoner had been executed in the United States for some twelve years. Now, Kendall stood on the verge of being the first lawyer in the United States to lose a client.

Florida prison officials allowed Kendall an hour to meet with Spenkelink on May 20 at the Florida State Prison. Kendall had planned to discuss possible avenues of appeal, but Spenkelink was in a mood to ramble and spent most of the time talking about his father. At one point, Spen-kelink pointed to the microphone between them.

"Do you think this thing is bugged?" he asked.

"I imagine so," Kendall replied.

"Well then, fuck you, whoever is listening," Spenkelink said.

The session ended with Kendall pondering whether Spenkelink fully comprehended the immediacy of his predicament. He noticed that several of the books Spenkelink had taken from the prison library were about re-incarnation.

Kendall returned to a Best Western motel on Highway 301 in Starke to take some notes. At 1:00 P.M., he met with the prison warden to discuss visits. Warden David Brierton told Kendall that Spenkelink could have no "contact visits" because of security concerns.

"I think you've got things mixed up," Kendall countered. "I can assure you, no one intends to help John kill himself. John doesn't want to die. It's the state that wants him dead."

Brierton relented, but only slightly. "We'll see what we can do for his mother," he said. He would not, however, consent to letting Spenkelink give his girlfriend a farewell kiss.

"You're telling me that John's going to be executed without a chance to kiss his girlfriend good-bye?" Kendall asked.

Brierton replied, "I'm telling you that we're not going to have a circus."

Kendall left the warden and went back to report on the meeting to Spenkelink. "I've been thinking," Spenkelink said. "Maybe I should give a press conference. Let 'em hear my side of the story."

"I don't think they would allow that," Kendall said. "Why don't you write out a statement. That way you can be sure it says what you want."

Spenkelink said nothing for more than a minute, curling smoke rings up into the air. "You better check the phone line to the governor's office," he said. "If I know those clowns, they'll probably leave it off the hook. Or short the damn thing out."

Kendall told Spenkelink that he planned to file an appeal on the follow-ing morning, Monday, to ask for a new trial. His grounds would be that the state had never proved premeditation or that the killing had been un-provoked.

"Man, that's what I need," Spenkelink said, "and you would be my law-yer? What would you do different?"

"Well, for one thing I would work with you for days getting your testimony straight. We wouldn't just set you up there and see what comes out of your mouth," Kendall said.

"I guess I couldn't do any worse with you," Spenkelink said.

Kendall was a little hurt. "That's not exactly a ringing vote of confidence," he said.

"Oh, you know what I mean," the inmate replied.

As they left, Spenkelink tried to slip Kendall a packet of letters for his relatives and some friends, but the exchange was not allowed. Spenkelink held one up to the thick glass that separated them.

"I've changed the way I end my letters," he said. "You know how I used to say 'Yours Truly'? Well, now I write 'Capital Punishment—Them without the capital get the punishment.'"

The next morning, Kendall drove to Tallahassee, practicing his oral argument over the music from the car radio. He barely noticed the police car that pulled up behind him and gave him a ticket for speeding. He registered in the Driftwood Motel and waited for a call from the Florida Supreme Court telling him a hearing would be scheduled. Finally at 5:15 P.M., he got a call asking him to stop by the courthouse. There he found that the court had voted not to give Spenkelink any additional hearing time. Kendall's magnificent oratory on Florida's I-10 had been wasted. He got back in the rental car and drove back to the Best Western in Starke.

The following hours would be filled with desperate last-minute appeals and falsely encouraging brief stays of execution. Ultimately, on May 25, at 10:18 A.M., capital punishment returned to America not as a political argument but as reality. It occurred on the watch of the most passionate opponent of the measure that the community of young committed lawyers could summon.

After the execution, Kendall would return to deliver an address at Wabash, predicting that by the end of the twentieth century, the death penalty would be abolished on moral grounds. It was a prediction that would prove to be wildly optimistic. "I was rash to have said twenty years," Kendall admits, "but I think society is trending in that direction. It will eventually wither away because it is a counterproductive and inefficient way to deal with violent crime. Ah, youthful optimism!"

Kendall was coming to Washington to live for the first time. His wife, Anne, whom he had met on a trip to the Soviet Union and then married after receiving his Rhodes Scholarship in 1968, had an influential family there, prominent in American journalism. She was the daughter of powerful Time-Life magazine executive Larry Laybourne, who started as a reporter with the *St. Louis Post-Dispatch*, then came to *Time* magazine in 1944, rising by 1950 to be the *Life* magazine bureau chief in New York City. Later he became the chief of all Time-Life correspondents, one of the most prized jobs in journalism, when being a correspondent for *Time*, much less the chief of correspondents, was one of the most prestigious jobs at what was then the most powerful newsmagazine around.

By the early 1970s, Laybourne had been moved to a corporate position, *Time*'s highest-ranking vice president in Washington, in the very Sixteenth Street office where I would work for the magazine. Laybourne's area was in a separate part of our floor, completely separate from the editorial operations, and never did I see him having a role in the editorial process. Laybourne's job was to lobby on *Time*'s behalf, mostly with the federal Postal Regulatory Commission, to keep mailing costs for newsmagazines as low as possible. In those days, Time-Life, in addition to publishing its flagship magazine, was well known for its very classy Time-Life Books division, which published well-done books on everything from gardening to cooking. It was Laybourne's practice to send copies of these books to key members of Congress who oversaw the commission. Most of the time the boxing and mailing of the books was done by Laybourne's secretary, but if she was busy on something else, I would get the assignment to put them in the mail. It was the time of Watergate, and maybe a day when I had something else to do also, but somehow, some words found their way out of my mouth and into her ears to the effect that Laybourne shouldn't be bribing congressmen with free books, or something equally as tactful.

Probably not two minutes had passed after his secretary disappeared back to his area. Then I saw Laybourne, his face redder than the famous border of the weekly newsmagazine, come storming down the hall. I am sure if it had been legal, he would have strangled me. If I hadn't worked for editorial, and he for corporate, I would have been a goner. Fortunately the mythical wall between the business people and the editorial people wasn't totally a fantasy. It was a horrible experience, because he was a wonderful gentleman, who had always been gracious and friendly to me up until then. After that I could only be grateful that I didn't have to pass his open door too many times. I mouthed some apologies and weathered the storm. I never knew that he had two daughters who would go on to be so distinguished. His older daughter, Geraldine, would become a powerful media executive. Both at Nickelodeon and later Oxygen Media, a publishing house and cable television channel aimed at women. Anne would become one of the top private psychologists in Washington. At the time of my contretemps with her father, she had been married to David for just five years. I could have used him to plead my case.

12.

THE COURTESY MAN

———— ■ ————

While Kendall explored Mississippi's dark shadows, trying to change the world, Barnett's year-long clerkship with Justice White ended with him deciding that he wanted to try something political—though not perhaps so idealistic. While Kendall had been deeply affected by Mississipppi, Barnett never really noticed that it existed.

He went on interviews, he recalls, at the offices of twelve different U.S. senators. With his Supreme Court clerkship as a credential, he got a handful of offers. Barnett sifted through them, methodically weighing the pros and the cons of each one with a sharp No. 2 pencil, just as years earlier he had done with New Orleans restaurants. He ultimately settled on an offer from Walter Mondale of Minnesota.

Mondale quickly assigned Barnett to work on a floor debate on a measure that was intended to curb filibusters, especially those of conservative Alabama senator James Allen. In about two weeks, with his unusual focus, Barnett knew more about Senate rules and procedures than Mondale did.

Later, as a lawyer in Minneapolis, Mondale would say he was struck most by Barnett's ability for power naps. "We would be in a car going somewhere and he was out like a light, then when we got there, totally alert," Mondale recalls. "He was a famous sleeper."

Barnett has no recollection of sleeping when his boss was around at all. "He must have me mixed up with somebody else," Barnett told me. He didn't seem appreciative of that particular memory.

In 1976, Mondale was selected by Jimmy Carter to be the vice-presidential candidate on the Democratic ticket. As he was going to be leaving his Senate seat, Mondale recommended Barnett to Califano as a very smart up-and-comer that he would want to hire. Califano looked very favorably on job candidates that had experience both at the Supreme Court and on Capitol Hill. He quickly snapped Barnett up, outbidding several rival firms in the process. Unlike Lucchino and Sullivan, who constituted Williams's "War Department," Barnett was brought in as a member of Califano's "State Department," someone more familiar with politics and diplomacy than with litigation and intimidation.

In the 1976 presidential election, Barnett served as a key but junior member of the Mondale campaign team. When Carter-Mondale won the election, most of the outside campaign aides took jobs in the administration. Califano, of course, was the short-lived secretary of health, education, and welfare. His mentor, Cyrus Vance, was chosen to be Carter's secretary of state. Barnett, however, decided to return to Williams & Connolly. He had not yet really worked there, and friends impressed upon him that it would be useful to have a "Mr. Outside" to complement and advise all the Mondale people who were going into the government.

While Craig was grabbing all the headlines—or, more apt for Williams & Connolly, dodging big headlines—Barnett had quietly grabbed the profitable representation of the nation's largest automobile importer, Southeast Toyota. The company was owned by Jim Moran, the flamboyant son of a Chicago cigar store clerk. Moran started in the business by buying a 1936 Ford for $75 and selling it later for $235. He was off to the races. By the early 1950s, he advertised himself as "Jim Moran the Courtesy Man." He built his own television studio and produced his own program on which to sell his Fords. Moran also sponsored and hosted *Wrestling from Rainbow*, *Barn Dance*, and *Sunday Night Movies*. During wrestling matches that featured Gorgeous George and Dick the Bruiser, Moran would drive used cars in front of the camera.

Courtesy Motors became the world's largest Ford dealership, and, once, Moran beat out Ed Sullivan and Steve Allen in the category of best television host, according to a 1989 article in *Forbes*. That show, which featured a crazy running character known as Professor Irwin Corey, was called *The Jim Moran Courtesy Hour*. In 1961, Moran made the cover of *Time* magazine. By 1966, he was a multimillionaire and living in a mansion with his wife, three kids, and a giant outdoor swimming pool. He had everything he wanted, but he didn't need the pesky doctors who diagnosed him with cancer and gave him a year to live. Moran refused to accept the diagnosis, moved to Florida, and did not die. When he purchased a Pontiac dealership in Homestead, General Motors executives made him sign a pledge that he would not appear in front of a television camera. People wonder why GM went bankrupt.

Barnett had been referred to Moran through friends back in Chicago, and the two immediately formed a close bond. By the time they became involved, the entrepreneur had 2,300 employees and more than $2.4 billion in car sales. He controlled twenty-five separate subsidiaries, the largest of which was Southeast Toyota Distributors, which supplied cars, trucks, and vans to more than 165 dealers in the southeastern United States. He owned a seventy-acre lot at the port of Jacksonville, where most Toyotas arrived from Japan.

The umbrella corporation for his ventures was JM Family Enterprises, generally listed by business publications as one of the twenty largest privately held companies in the United States. Moran was a lawyer's dream. His company was litigious, constantly suing or being sued by the dealers with which it signed contracts. On a personal level, Moran was always in trouble with the IRS and other federal agencies. To stay in the good graces of the Japanese businessmen with whom he dealt, according to federal agents and a later plea agreement, Moran paid what Americans consider bribes. The Japanese had a different, more tolerant, view of such transactions, but Moran was not from Japan. In 1978, he was indicted for criminal tax fraud in a massive undercover investigation termed Project Haven by the FBI. The allegations spanned continents and were so complicated that one of the charges had to do with the establishment of an entire bank, Castle Bank, which was operated by suspected organized crime figures and was used to launder bribes and kickbacks.

Barnett became his loyal and trusted private attorney and for six years spent most of his lawyer billing time trying to ensure that Moran hadn't beaten cancer only to lose out to federal prison—a less implacable foe, one would think. In 1984, the pressure of the federal case caused Moran to suffer a stroke. To speed things up, Barnett successfully reached a deal with prosecutors to end the long-running legal drama. Moran agreed to a two-year suspended sentence, a fine, and community service that consisted of his companies teaching underprivileged children to learn to be auto mechanics.

Still, in a firm where the stars were Brendan Sullivan, Gregory Craig, and Larry Lucchino, Barnett was restless playing fourth fiddle. Not only had his partners vaulted into the headlines before him, so had his wife, who was now one of the leading reporters on the top-ranked network news program.

13.

THE HIGH WATERMARK

———————■———————

It was Sullivan who continued to get the well-publicized cases that were the fodder for the front pages of the *Washington Post* and *Baltimore Sun*.

In 1976, as Howard Baker was lobbying heavily to get named as vice president on President Gerald Ford's ticket, his wife, Joy, was stopped for what newspaper columnists, the predecessors to what are today called bloggers, were saying was drunk driving. It fell on A. B. Culvahouse to figure out who the best attorney was in town, and he was directed to Sullivan. Sullivan took to the task with his usual intensity, quickly pressuring local authorities not to press charges and forcing them, with the threat of an expensive suit, to make a statement that the senator's wife had not been drinking. His work impressed A. B., but it was too late to save Baker's vice-presidential selection; the slot went to Kansas Senator Bob Dole.

Sullivan then took on the representation of a Yugoslavian-born Catholic priest, Guido John Carcich, alleged by prosecutors to have embezzled $16 million from his Maryland parishioners. Carcich was a despised figure even in his own church. Reporters from the *Baltimore Sun* found employees who complained that Carcich wouldn't allow them to wear a coat at their desk when it was cold. Carcich, the *Sun* uncovered, owned a posh apartment in Florida and spent a considerable amount of time spending the alledgedly embezzled cash at Caesars Palace in Las Vegas.

From the moment Sullivan entered the case, it was the prosecutors who were on trial, not Carcich. Sullivan began by accusing an assistant Maryland attorney general of intimidating witnesses. In a document filed in court, Sullivan said the prosecution had "fashioned the grand jury into its own private vehicle for investigation by terrorism."

Sullivan's hyperbolic arguments were considered outlandish by his courtroom opponents. However, Sullivan seemed much less preposterous when a witness, an accountant familiar with the priest's financial machinations, killed himself on December 9, 1977. Sullivan claimed that the death was not suicide but a brand of "state-incited manslaughter," and that the accountant took the desperate step of taking his own life only after the prosecutors threatened to indict him if he did not testify the way they wished. Backed into a corner by a relentless opponent, the prosecutors began worrying about their own careers and became increasingly anxious to unload the case rather than defend accusations of prosecutorial misconduct, with which Sullivan continued to threaten them.

On May 9, 1978, Sullivan cut a deal allowing Carcich to serve only one year of house arrest at his parish. This time Sullivan made sure he had all bases covered, and the agreement stuck. The Father Carcich case began to create the "legend" around the young attorney that when he was involved in a case, it was more likely that the prosecutor would end up in jail—or some other earthly purgatory—than his client.

Carcich never spent a day in prison. The clamor from the case, basically allowing the unpopular priest to walk free, forced Maryland's Republican attorney general, Francis Burch, to drop his campaign for governor and abruptly ended what had been a promising political career. Carcich died in 2002, the respected pastor emeritus of Sacred Heart Catholic Church in Southport, North Carolina, and he was honorably buried in the priests' section of the parish cemetery. Not even in his obituaries was there the mention of his past sins.

In May 1984, officials in the Criminal Tax Fraud Division of the Justice Department convened a well-attended press conference to announce the indictment of a well-known company that specialized in leasing private jets to the rich and famous, including Frank Sinatra. Omni International was accused in both the press conference and in an indictment of sneakily siphoning off millions of dollars in income to a foreign subsidiary to avoid having to pay U.S. taxes on the money. Inside the federal law enforcement agency, there were high fives before the case even got under way. It was the type of splashy tax case that figured to get a lot of publicity, thanks to the Sinatra angle, and make the reputation and careers of the Justice Department and IRS agents who had cracked the case.

Omni found that the Feds already had three years of documents and investigation to prove their case. Seven IRS agents had worked on nothing but the Omni case, and millions had been spent on the prosecution even before the announcement of the indictment.

Most attorneys would have just read the documents that the government provided to Omni's attorneys, Brendan Sullivan and his most clever but also more volatile (if that was possible) associate, Barry Simon. Sullivan and Simon, though, took their research to a second level. Instead of merely reading what was on the papers, they began looking at the papers themselves. Sullivan began studying not just the tax laws about sheltering income but the process by which paper is made. Thus it was that Sullivan was able to conclude that the watermark on a Justice Department document couldn't possibly have been in existence at the time prosecutors claimed it was. The watermark proved that the document was printed on paper that wasn't manufactured until 1984, but the government claimed it had been written upon in 1983. Later Sullivan claimed that he became suspicious of the documents' authenticity because "something was fishy—they looked too good."

Armed with that bit of information, Sullivan began interrogating the prosecutors, eventually learning that one lawyer in the department had warned superiors that their case was not as strong as they thought and would be difficult to prove, as they were missing some key documents. Rather than give up their quest, the Justice Department decided to re-create the missing papers and letters.

Sullivan insisted that the federal prosecutors themselves, including a popular assistant U.S. attorney, Elizabeth Trimble, testify about the documents. On the stand Sullivan accused her of perjury and obstruction of justice and, in the eyes of her sympathetic colleagues, viciously reduced her to tears. In doing so, Sullivan earned the cold hatred of many lawyers in Maryland. "It was hard for us to go into Maryland for many years after that," Sullivan admitted.

Those whom Sullivan offended did not include the federal judge in the case. In May 1986, U.S. District Judge Walter Black dismissed Omni's tax fraud indictment on the grounds that prosecutors can't re-create a document just because they can't find the original. Black observed, "The government's conduct was patently egregious and cannot be tolerated or condoned. Its manner of proceeding shocks the court's conscience."

Prosecutors denounced Sullivan's tactics as "Kafkaesque."

"It was one of the most difficult cases in which we have ever been involved," Sullivan confided to me once. "We didn't just accuse the government of prosecutorial misconduct, we were accusing them, and the IRS agents, of committing criminal conduct. After that we were ostracized by the Maryland bar—people there felt we were making reckless allegations— but the judge agreed with us."

Trying to explain Sullivan and his cohort Simon, a former associate said, "First they go over the ground with a fine-tooth comb. Then they scorch it." A CNN commentator observed of them, "There are no schoolyard fights with them. Every battle is nuclear warfare. Everything is prosecutorial misconduct."

No action was ever taken against Trimble and she eventually landed a job as principal counsel for the Maryland Office of Cemetery Oversight.

In the mid-1980s, Sullivan offered to come to the rescue of Ted Olson, who in 1981 had become the attorney for newly appointed attorney general William French Smith. In that position, for what were essentially political acts, Congress had named a special prosecutor to investigate him.

Gibson, Dunn & Crutcher was the favored Los Angeles firm of President Ronald Reagan. Reagan's pick for attorney general was the leader of that firm, William French Smith. Olson was a Smith protégé. Olson had his own protégé, Kenneth Starr, whom he had hired on a recommendation from Chief Justice Warren Burger, for whom Starr clerked. The three of them, Smith, Olson, and Starr, all came to Washington together after Reagan's election. Olson was named to head the Justice Department's Office of Legal Counsel; essentially he would function as the lawyer and adviser to the attorney general. Unfortunately, things did not go that well for Olson in government.

His woes began when officials at the Environmental Protection Agency refused to provide documents about their environmental cleanup work to a congressional committee. This was at a time when chemical waste dumps were plaguing cities and towns, literally making ghost towns out of several communities. The suspicion of Democrats was that the administration was expending funds for cleanup in a way that would favor certain congressional candidates.

Olson drew the short straw of defending administration policy by testifying at the committee, but he refused to turn over the documents that the committee members wanted. An outraged Democratic committee chairman referred the matter to the attorney general, asking that he consider appointing a special prosecutor to possibly indict and imprison Olson for what was essentially a political act. Sullivan was so outraged, he called Olson and offered to represent him for nothing. Olson already had a top-drawer lawyer, so he declined. After a legal duel that lasted almost five years and was fought all the way to the Supreme Court itself, Olson was finally exonerated and freed of what is considered in Washington legal history a runaway special counsel investigation. Something good came of it: Olson and Sullivan became lifelong friends.

If no stone was left unturned by Sullivan and his court battles, Barnett and Craig would use the same approach in their political fights.

14.

CIGARS WITH CASTRO, FLOWERS FOR FERRARO

———————■———————

In 1984, Greg Craig took a leave of absence from Williams & Connolly to take a job as national security aide for Massachusetts senator Edward Kennedy. Craig was a rare bird as far as Williams & Connolly was concerned, who flitted back and forth between the firm and political work. "We're like a bus to him, and he keeps getting on and off," complained one of his partners. Craig's specialty for Kennedy was his work with Latin America, and one of his first assignments was to extract from a Cuban prison the last man being held from the 1961 Bay of Pigs invasion, which many people felt had been botched by Senator Kennedy's brother the president. After intense negotiations with Cuban emissaries at the Swiss Embassy in Washington, Craig received word that Colonel Ricardo Miguel Montero-Duque would be released, but only to a representative of Senator Kennedy's. Cuban president Fidel Castro, always concerned about appearances, wanted it clear that the release was a special favor to the senator, not a sign of capitulation to the United States.

On June 4, 1986, Craig boarded the once-a-week flight from Miami and was driven to the Combinido del Este prison outside of Havana. When he was introduced to the prisoner, Montero-Duque surprised him by saying that he was not, in fact, the last Bay of Pigs prisoner in Cuba, and thus he could not accept the offer to leave the country. "I'm an officer. I cannot leave my soldier here," he said.

This brought the mission to a standstill, as Cuban authorities said it would take the permission of Castro personally to be able to release the other prisoner, Ramon Conte Hernandez. Craig was eventually brought to Castro's presidential palace, where he spent two hours smoking cigars and drinking liquor while he tried to convince the Cuban president to let him take both men back to the United States. Castro was noncommittal, but Montero-Duque felt they had made enough progress so that he would, after all, go home first. Craig assured him that Conte Hernandez would soon be freed, and four months later he was. Craig flew back to Havana a second time, with the last prisoner's mother. As they reboarded the charter flight to come back to free soil, Conte Hernandez told reporters, "I'd love to do it again sometime."

Conte Hernandez would not get the chance, but Greg Craig would later use his Castro connections to his advantage in one of the great international incidents of the era—the Elián González case.

Craig put in five years with Kennedy, staying on Capitol Hill until 1988. Meanwhile, Barnett's Senate mentor, Walter Mondale, reemerged in the American political landscape to run away with the Democratic nomination for president of the United States. This time the stakes were higher for Bob.

Mondale's vice-presidential selection was a forty-nine-year-old former schoolteacher from Queens, New York, three-term congresswoman Geraldine Ferraro. She was vetted by a former Mondale aide, Michael Berman, who happened to be Barnett's best friend and next-door neighbor at an up-scale Washington condo known as the Colonnade. Around Washington, the Colonnade was known as the "Democrats' Watergate"—referring to the apartments, where more Republicans seemed to live, not the scandal. When Berman asked Ferraro's husband, John Zaccaro, about his tax returns, he said there would be no problem releasing them, but he had no intention of letting them out, or of truthfully telling what was in them.

With that bombshell waiting to go off, on July 19, 1984, Ferraro became the first woman in American history to accept a nomination for one of the two highest political offices in the land. Within a month, stories began to emerge in the press that Zaccaro had lied about fund-raising activities for Ferraro's 1978 congressional campaign. When Ferraro was asked whether Zaccaro would release his tax returns, she said she was powerless to force him and replied with a weak joke, "You people who are married to Italian men, you know what it's like."

Ferraro's troubles multiplied in the ensuing days as the adviser to her 1978 congressional campaign, David Stein, contradicted her account of how illegal family loans got into her campaign coffers. He was saying he told Ferraro *not* to put family money into the campaign; she was now saying that he had said it was OK. Zaccaro was dragged into an interrogation by the U.S. attorney for the Southern District of New York, the former Reagan Justice Department aide who didn't negotiate with assassins, Rudolph Giuliani. By August 20, various newsmagazines were linking Zaccaro to alleged organized crime figures. The stories were based, in part, on a report by a New York police sergeant who had observed Zaccaro speaking to a lieutenant in the Gambino crime family. Obviously the observation meant nothing—it was just a conversation—but it gave the New York City tabloids plenty of fodder with which to speculate. Ferraro admitted being "sickened" by the allegations, but she was even more devastated by revelations that turned out to be true, wheeling and dealing by her husband to which she was indeed not privy. Ferraro's travails made anything that the next female candidate for vice president, Sarah Palin, would have to go through look trivial by comparison. It made Palin's oft-stated claim, that if she had just been a Democrat her treatment by the press would have been different, seem rather uninformed.

Ferraro felt compelled to call a two-hour news conference to answer all the questions about her tax returns, which she accomplished masterfully, saving both her candidacy and her reputation. Republican columnist George Will obsequiously sent Ferraro a dozen roses after the show with a note that read, "Has anyone told you, you are cute when you are mad?"

To avoid any further disasters, as Ferraro prepared for her October 11 debate in Philadelphia with Vice President George H. W. Bush, Mondale decided not to take any chances. He dispatched Barnett to prepare her for the confrontation. The aide arrived in Philadelphia with an eight-pound three-ring binder that included a full rundown of Bush's stated position on more than one hundred issues, an analysis of Ferrraro's congressional voting record, a compendium of major speeches, and the complete set of Q&A on her husband's tax flaps. The Bush material was voluminous: a section on "General Issues," another on "George Bush Materials," plus another exhaustive compilation on "Inconsistencies and Errors."

For two weeks, Ferraro lugged around the briefing book, studying it intermittently, the way, she imagined, one might "pick away at a three-pound T-bone steak." When the staff asked her to watch a rented copy of Frank Capra's *Mr. Smith Goes to Washington*, Ferraro fell asleep halfway through the movie.

While Ferraro studied Barnett's book, the longtime musical comedy buff from Waukegan began learning to play the speaking part of George

Bush. He was not starting from scratch; Barnett had kept a similar brief-ing book when he helped Mondale debate Republican Robert Dole in the 1976 vice-presidential debate. Four days before the debate in 1980, the prep team moved into a suite at a hotel in midtown Manhattan.

Barnett, though he didn't know it, was preparing for the role of a life-time. Playing one Bush or another would be pretty good business for the next three decades. What all of Edward Bennett Williams's protégés had learned from their mentor was that you go into every battle knowing more about a witness or an adversary than he even knows about himself. Thus Barnett, in this darkened New York City hotel suite, began thinking and dressing like George Bush. He had obtained information that Bush liked to constantly change his watchband, so he started collecting watchbands and wearing a different one every day, or hour. Barnett was in the process of not just playing Bush but becoming Bush.

Always easily irritated, Ferraro found the whole process "artificial" and insulting, as she found many things. The idea that she had to practice sound-ing spontaneous grated her the most. It was an embarrassing waste of time, she felt, "giving thoughtful answers in such an artificial circumstance."

A real debate, she naively argued, was all about spontaneity and intellec-tual jousting. It was supposed to be about how quickly people could think on their feet, not a memorization-of-the-answers contest. Oh, how wrong she was. Politics, she discovered, was completely contrived, "more like theater than an intellectual contest." Barnett, the onetime Stage Manager in *Our Town* was well equipped for the intersection of politics and theater.

The analysis from inside the Mondale camp was beginning to slide into conformity with the assessment of her opponent's wife, Barbara Bush. On Air Force Two, the future first lady described Ferraro as having a personal-ity that "rhymes with rich." Mrs. Bush later apologized for the indiscre-tion, but not for her accuracy.

Ferraro says she had never encountered any aide as detail-oriented as Barnett. He ordered a total re-creation of the debate set to be installed at a rented television studio on East Forty-seventh Street. The height of the podiums, the distance between them, the positioning of the cameras and the moderator, even the different-colored lights on the podiums that would remind the participants of how much time they had remaining—everything was just as it would be on the night.

Bush was Barnett, Barnett was Bush. Ferraro would later observe, "He had studied Bush's habits and his speeches and clips so much that he was actually a much more impressive Bush than Bush himself would be."

Barnett insisted that Ferraro be prepared for three separate Bush lines of attack: that he would attack Mondale, that he would attack Ferraro herself, or that he would not attack anybody. In order to get ready, Barnett declared, they had to go through all three scenarios. Barnett also wanted Ferraro to do something to rattle her opponent, the way Mondale had put Reagan off stride by confronting him directly with his "Where's the beef?" remark.

"Say "Good luck, Poppy,'" Barnett told Ferraro. "He hates that. He'll get furious."

Ferraro responded, "What I am going to do is go up onstage, grab him, and give him a kiss straight on the lips."

For once Barnett was speechless. "Just kidding," Ferraro said—although she was such an enigma, nobody was quite sure.

The two answered questions from an expert panel during four separate and intense ninety-minute sessions. She was as ready as she could be, although not as ready as he would have been.

When the debate time arrived, Barnett's role was to win the predebate coin toss and elect for Ferraro to speak last. The ninety minutes in the ring with the real Bush turned into a piece of cake for the overly prepared Geraldine. After the debate ended, she rushed into Barnett's arms. "You were ten times tougher than George Bush," she said.

Unfortunately for Ferraro, however, Mondale was running against Ronald Reagan, not George Bush, and destiny did not have a place for the stubborn, often petulant congresswoman from Queens. Mondale carried only one state and the District of Columbia.

Bob was already thinking ahead. He was, after all, the man who routinely thought of everything. "You must record your emotions on the day of the election," he advised. "Think of history." It was the same word Haldeman had once uttered to Nixon in urging him to tape his conversations, but this time the sentiment had a better result.

Ferraro was more than willing to oblige, and while she thought of history, per Barnett's suggestion, the lawyer was thinking about how books were sold and published. Ferraro was from Queens, not Manhattan. As a teenager, Ferraro recalled, she had a natural inclination toward writing and English. After her mother told her there was no money in writing, she lost interest fast. Now Barnett seemed sure that there could be money in it after all. She confided to Barnett that while she was very happy to write a book about her experience as the first female in American history to run for one of the two highest offices, she had no idea how to go about it. Barnett had never sold a book for one of his clients, but he couldn't imagine it was that difficult.

On his first pass in the book business, Barnett helped Ferraro navigate the traditional way that prospective authors sell books. He located a well-known New York City–based agent, Esther Newberg. She then negotiated the sale by auction of Ferraro's memoirs to Bantam Books for what was, at the time, an eye-popping sum of $1 million. Bantam executives later revealed that they bought the book not because of the written proposal but because of their interview with Ferraro and the pitch that Barnett made alongside her. Said one of the executives in the room, "Books are not always sold with outlines and proposals. We went with it based on our discussions with her and her lawyers."

The lawyer in him was particularly intrigued with the part of the transaction in which Newberg took 15 percent of Ferraro's guaranteed advance. In the case of a $1 million book, Newberg had pocketed a quick $150,000. His attorney's rate of $350 an hour was equivalent to Newberg's spending some 428 hours on the project, roughly the equivalent of forty-two full-time lawyer days. Barnett could barely believe the figures as he began making meticulous notes on the process. While it was too late to do anything about Ferraro's book, he told her to spread the word that someone who needed a book sold should see him first. He was sure that he could do the job in fewer than 428 billing hours. The first test of his theory would come the following year, in 1985.

Ferraro had been friendly with her former colleague from the House David Stockman, who had left Congress in 1984 to become Reagan's director of the Office of Management and Budget. He quickly became frustrated in the Reagan administration and clashed repeatedly with Treasury Secretary Donald Regan. In 1981, barely a year into the Reagan presidency, Stockman took the almost radical step of giving an interview to *Atlantic Monthly* magazine's Bill Greider, which questioned the central "trickle-down" principal of the Reagan economic team. At one point he was quoted as saying, "None of us really understand what's going on with all these numbers."

During the 1984 campaign, Stockman had been Reagan's debate coach. After Reagan appeared disoriented and confused in his first round with

Mondale, the president privately blamed Stockman, who Reagan's campaign manager claimed had "brutalized" him as a debate preparer. Soon thereafter, Stockman began preparing to leave the administration.

Stockman was widely praised and admired for being the one person in the Reagan administration who would dare speak the truth in public. After leaving government, Stockman ended up as the CEO of Collins & Aikman, a Detroit auto parts manufacturer. The company went bankrupt in 2005, and Stockman was subsequently indicted for manipulating financial statements, though never convicted. The charges were dropped.

Meanwhile, back in 1985, aware that Stockman was contemplating what had the potential to be an explosive inside-the-administration tell-all, Barnett made a pitch for his business. Being an economist, and a fiscally conservative penny-pinching one, Stockman was intrigued by the proposal, so he decided to let Barnett give it a try. Barnett notified publishers that he would be holding an auction for Stockman's memoir. He sold the book, *The Triumph of Politics*, for $2.4 million, the largest sum that Harper & Row had ever paid for a political memoir. *Time* calculated that Stockman's advance computed out to more than twenty-six years' worth of salary at his $75,000-a-year White House job. Book industry sources say Harper & Row ended up losing at least $300,000 on the publication of the book, justifying the view of one that "political figures don't create big books. Elvis creates big books." By the time Harper & Row's accounting was completed, though, Barnett was off to his next project, and Stockman was laughing all the way to the bank.

Stockman was pleased with his agent. "Barnett's fee for representing me on the book was $15,000, or 0.6% of the $2.4 million advance compared to 15% or $360,000, which would have pertained under a standard book agent arrangement. This was back in the days when lawyers got paid what they were worth," he told me.

Barnett's foray into publishing was an intriguing sideline, but his fellow partners, including Edward Bennett Williams, wondered what it all had to do with hard-boiled litigation as they had traditionally practiced it at Williams & Connolly.

In fact, if Williams had a personal favorite member of his team, it was neither Brendan Sullivan nor Bob Barnett. It was still Larry Lucchino.

15.

NON-HODGKIN'S STRIKES OUT

————■————

In the last years of his life, his body ravaged by cancer, Williams spent more time having lunch with the two men who were closest to him at the legendary, now-defunct, old Duke Zeibert's Restaurant on Connecticut and L streets in downtown Washington. Williams loved to talk to Lucchino about sports. Only when he was done did he turn and talk about cases with the lawyer he habitually called "Solomon."

One of Lucchino's favorite topics at Duke's was the idea he had for the new downtown baseball park that would change both baseball and the direction of his life forever.

For many years, the Orioles and the Baltimore Colts had shared the use of Baltimore's Memorial Stadium. When the Colts were stolen away to Indianapolis in the middle of the night on March 29, 1984, Lucchino immediately began considering the possibilities.

Lucchino was the first person to suggest a baseball-only park to Ed Williams. Lucchino had looked at baseball's most storied franchises: the Dodgers, the Red Sox, the Yankees, and the Cubs. What did they all have in common? They all had single-team baseball stadiums. In truth, he had never quite gotten over the demolition of his hometown ballpark in Pittsburgh, Forbes Field. "They replaced it with the University of Pittsburgh Law School," Lucchino would complain throughout his life. "It was the worst trade in history."

In the 1970s, in Pittsburgh, in Cincinnati, and in Washington, the trend had been to build monotonous multiuse circular stadiums that would accommodate football, baseball, and even monster truck races but in reality were not hospitable for any one particular sport.

Lucchino's dream quickly took shape both in his mind and in early architectural drawings. He wanted to build a park with modern amenities but one that would evoke the old historic ballparks like Ebbets Field, the Polo Grounds, and especially Forbes Field. Just as his idea began taking shape, however, the reality of human life intervened and put the discussions about where to play games into a different perspective.

In the summer of 1985, Lucchino arranged to rent a Yamaha and take a world-class motorcycle trip, visiting wineries and nude beaches across southern France with friend and client Jay Emmett, an executive at Warner Brothers. For years, Emmett, with his show business experience, had advised Williams and Lucchino about how to promote the Orioles to fans in Maryland and central Pennsylvania. They had become extremely close friends, with Emmett playing the wizened mentor to a younger man discovering a world as far from Pittsburgh as could be. "He was a moron when it came to gambling," Emmett complained. "I was an expert in blackjack and kept losing. This annoyed me quite a bit because even though he didn't know what he was doing, he kept winning and I kept losing."

Emmett was amused at Lucchino's naïveté when it came to the ways of the world. One day Lucchino, who spoke excellent French, got into a discussion with a Provence shopkeeper over a poster he wanted. He tried to persuade the owner to give him the poster, but he was rebuffed because the event it was advertising had not yet taken place. Emmett looked on with fatherly amusement. After Lucchino emerged, posterless, Emmett went into the store and came out with it. "I guess my French works better than your French," he said, pointing to his wallet.

In France, Lucchino noticed an annoying and persistent cough and an occasional shortness of breath. "He had this cough," Emmett remembered. "I'd say to him, 'What's what with all this coughing?' We figured he had a cold."

Until the beginning of September, as his fortieth birthday approached, Lucchino tried to "play through" his perplexing symptoms. He finally agreed to see a doctor and try to find out what was going on.

On Friday, the thirteenth of September, came the worst possible news imaginable. At Georgetown University Medical Center, Lucchino was diagnosed with non-Hodgkin's lymphoma, a virulent disease of the lymph node glands. Coincidentally, Georgetown had been one of Lucchino's most regular clients in the firm's malpractice defense work, although no case had ever involved this particular cancer. With his brother, Frank, arriving to help him through the medical thicket, Lucchino pondered who he should see and what he should do. "I had heard of Hodgkin's disease," he would say later, "but not non-Hodgkin's lymphoma. I didn't even know if I could spell it—but I had it.

"I knew that the cutting edge of cancer research was in Boston at the Dana-Farber Cancer Institute," Lucchino said. In October, Williams directed him to see one of the nation's leading cancer specialists, Dr. Lee Nadler, a Bronx native who had literally been born in the shadow of Yankee Stadium.

Lucchino instantly felt at home in Nadler's office at Harvard University Medical School. Instead of labeling it a doctor's office, Nadler's sign informed Lucchino that he was entering a "war room." Lucchino had to almost laugh through his tears. Brendan Sullivan had always joked that Williams & Connolly was not a law office but a military barracks. Inside Nadler's sanctum was a bust of Winston Churchill, with the motto "We will never surrender." "I don't believe that any other single institution can break the back of a human illness," Nadler would say, "but *Harvard* can." Impressed by Nadler's self-confidence and his penchant—like that of television doctor Gregory House—for ignoring bureaucratic red tape, Lucchino began calling him simply "the bulldozer." Then he was stunned to read, on December 14, 1985, that non-Hodgkin's had killed former Yankee home run king Roger Maris. "Cancer is a miserable disease," Lucchino said. "It strikes without regard to who you are, what you are, or where you've been, what you've done. I didn't fool myself into thinking that being a former athlete myself was going to make any difference whatsoever."

Nadler informed Lucchino that after undergoing radiation, chemotherapy, and surgery, his last and only hope was an autologous bone marrow transplant. At best, Nadler said, Lucchino had about a 40 percent chance of survival beyond six months. They would use Lucchino's own bone marrow for the operation, bone marrow that itself had tumor cells that had to be cleansed with experimental monoclonal antibodies, accelerating the risk. Larry would only be the thirty-third person in recorded medical history to have such an operation, which took place in May 1986 and lasted for nearly eight hours.

Following the surgery, Larry teetered on the brink of death for thirty-seven days. He doubted that he would survive sometimes. A fellow patient warned him against such thoughts, which came mostly while he was alone. Yet while he wanted always to have a friend nearby, he couldn't. Larry's immune system was so fragile he had to be kept in total isolation for more than a month. It was more difficult than he could imagine, he recalled. One day he announced to Nadler that he was leaving the hospital. "No you're not," Nadler replied. "Leave the room and you die." Larry decided to stay.

Emmett and Williams paid for a special satellite dish so Larry could at least watch the Orioles from his bed. Just as much, he loved watching the Red Sox play in Fenway Park, with its odd right field angles and the short left field wall, the "green monster." In a way it was the company of those games that saved him from being overwhelmed by the bad thoughts. More than that, he thought; they had saved him, period.

Emmett, Frank, and his partners filed by regularly to look forlornly into his room, but they could not speak to him. For more than a month, the partner whose hedonist credo was framed on his wall wondered whether he would live or die. Some days he could see Edward Bennett Williams, who came to Dana-Farber for his own cancer checks, staring through a window, giving him the thumbs-up. On the thirty-eighth day, the worst of the cancer seemed to have abated.

On that day Nadler announced that Lucchino's bubble-boy existence was over and he could go outside for the first time in six weeks, Lucchino thought of the one place and thing he had missed during his ordeal. He asked to go to a baseball game at Fenway. Nadler said it was okay, as long as he took a box a reasonable distance away from other people at the park and no one in the hospital administration knew. It turned out that the Red Sox were out of town that week. John Harrington, a Red Sox executive, told Larry he could come over and walk around the field. So Emmett took Lucchino over to the historic park, where they walked around the bases and stood on the pitching mound pretending to throw strikes off the pitching rubber. Larry told Emmett he could only imagine what it must be like to own a historic franchise like the Red Sox.

"When I was allowed out into civilized society, it was a Saturday, and I wanted to come to Fenway. It struck me as the best place to reemerge from the hospital," he said. "The Red Sox had a list of official charities, and one of the most publicized and prized was their sponsorship of Dana-Farber's Jimmy Fund, to raise money to fight childhood diseases."

Finally, in the late fall of 1986, Lucchino returned home to Washington and immersed himself once again in running the Orioles.

In the end, Larry lived, embracing, more than any other partner, even Sullivan, what he perceived to be Williams's philosophy of life, roughly defined as "contest living," where every encounter and every struggle was a battle to the death. They traveled together, drank together, and most mornings went to mass at the great downtown St. Matthew's Cathedral. After Larry's cancer was in remission, they became closer than before, if such a thing was possible. When Lucchino was depressed from his cancer treatments, Williams would take him out for a drink, saying, "Let's have some real chemotherapy."

A former Williams & Connolly summer associate remembered that, once, Lucchino came to address the group of summer employees, some of whom would later be offered full-time jobs. Lucchino entered the meeting room, and there was Williams right behind him. "Williams hated meeting with the summer associates," this lawyer told me, "but he loved being with Larry."

Lucchino was an exemplar as well of the philosophy of work hard, play hard. His sometimes militaristic attitudes toward his cases often scared the young associates with whom he interacted. To Williams, Lucchino was the living example of all that he believed. Life was a constant battle, a war. He and Lucchino were going through the ultimate combat, the struggle for life itself.

Even as the Orioles played a large role in providing Lucchino with hope that he would live and have something to return to, Ed Williams wasn't joking when he said that the team was pushing him closer to the grave.

During the 1987 season, the last full baseball year that Williams would live through, the Orioles collapsed on the field, perhaps the result of the necessary absence of Lucchino from the decision-making process. On October 5, after the last game of a horrible season, Lucchino fired Orioles general manager Hank Peters and took over the operational control of the team, which included negotiating contracts with star players like Cal Ripken Jr.

Before Peters was fired, the players and their agents had frequently complained that the Orioles had too many layers of authority. When Lucchino was handed the new role of running the baseball aspects of the club, Williams wanted no confusion. He called the team together. "When Larry speaks," Williams said, "you are listening to me." After that there was no confusion about roles. It was the last year of Williams's life, and there was no doubt in his mind that he had found the person to inherit his mantle.

Cal Ripken's agent, Ron Shapiro, said of Lucchino, "He prepared for a negotiation the way he prepared for litigation. He had the facts marshaled and analyzed, and when he came to the table he presented a formidable position."

Lucchino blanched at the idea that he was a baseball executive, or even a sports lawyer. Likewise, his partner Bob Barnett would later always insist he was not a literary agent, despite that avocation consuming his more traditional law practice. Both men would claim to be a lawyer first, a businessman, sportsman, or agent later.

Lucchino's personal storm had passed. On the other side was not death but a life that would be spent in baseball, or, as Lucchino often referred to his place on earth, "the toy store of life." Like Kevin Costner in the soon-to-be-released *Field of Dreams*, Lucchino was very much alive, and he still had his own park to build and a game to save.

16.

THE POTTED PLANT

———■———

By 1987, the law firm was approaching a crossroads. Barnett, Craig, Lucchino, Kendall, and Sullivan were moving in different directions, but somehow their gears all interlocked in one way or another. Each had made giant strides in building his own personal practice, but none yet seemed ready to take over from a leader whose health was rapidly deteriorating. It seemed almost inevitable that Williams & Connolly could not survive the death of its bigger-than-life founding partner, and in Lucchino's case, life itself still hung in the balance. Larry awoke every morning checking all his body parts, full of nervous anticipation and hope that he would live another day.

Then a case arose that would shake America's faith in its president but at the same time cement the future of Williams & Connolly for the next thirty years. There are in American business such things as the "bet the company case." For Williams & Connolly, Iran-Contra would become the "bet the firm case."

The game-changing saga began on November 3, 1986, when a Lebanese newspaper, *Al Shiraa*, broke a story that U.S. government officials were selling ammunition and spare parts to the newly anti-American government of Iran, in exchange for Iran's helping facilitate the release of seven hostages being held by radical groups in Beirut. Responding to questions at a press conference, the White House initially assured the American people that there was "no foundation" to the reports.

Within days, American newspapers, including the *Washington Post*, were reporting that the arms-for-hostages deal was being run by a small group of National Security Council staffers, directed by Marine Lt. Col. Oliver North, a White House aide working for the presidential adviser on national security.

At first, President Reagan denied any knowledge of trading arms for hostages, which would have violated both United States policy and law. On November 8, just five days after the disclosure, Robert McFarlane, the president's former national security adviser, who had played a critical role in the arms sales, sent a memo to North. "I hope to daylights that somebody has been purging the National Security Agency's files on this episode," he wrote. The zealous North was one step ahead of McFarlane and had already ordered what he would later describe as "a shredding party" to get rid of incriminating documents.

On November 13, President Reagan went on national television to partially debunk the Lebanese account, saying that the charge that the United States was "trafficking with terrorists" was completely false. Nevertheless, widespread skepticism over whether Reagan was telling the truth prompted calls for Congress to conduct an investigation.

On November 21, Attorney General Ed Meese, who had succeeded William French Smith, was ordered to conduct an investigation and report back to the president. Reagan acknowledged to his aides that he knew he had approved the sale of Hawk missiles to Iran but didn't consider that trading "arms for hostages." His view was that he was simply trying to show goodwill toward the hostage takers, so that they would release the hostages. It was a subtle distinction lost on many.

To "protect" the president's story, North and his secretary, Fawn Hall, stepped up the pace of the "shredding party." Admiral John Poindexter, who had succeeded McFarlane as national security adviser, joined in what North termed "the festivities." Poindexter personally tore up and dispatched one of the most incriminating pieces of evidence, a presidential finding, signed by a forgetful President Reagan, approving the sale of Hawk missiles to Iran.

In the course of his investigation, Meese then discovered a note, written by North, that outlined a plan to divert $12 million from the sale of weapons to Iran to fund a group of antigovernment rebels in Nicaragua, known as the Contras. This marked an escalation of the story both from a journalistic and geographical perspective. Congress had specifically passed amendments to the Defense Appropriations Bill that made it unlawful to provide U.S. government assistance to the Contras. So now the Reagan administration wasn't just breaking one law in violating the arms embargo to Tehran, it was abusing two laws.

Meese questioned North for four hours about the whereabouts of the $12 million, suspecting many in the press might presume that money from the sale of stockpiled U.S. missiles would go to the U.S. Treasury, not to a private secret bank account. Meese discovered that the funds had indeed found their way into slippery Swiss bank accounts that North and others in his "enterprise" controlled.

On November 24, a stormy meeting was held in the White House situation room, where Reagan, whose memory had not been good for years, asked Meese if, in fact, he as president had approved the sale of missiles to Iran in 1985. Although Reagan had actually signed the approval for the transfer, the document no longer existed. As it would later be revealed, Reagan's memory lapses were real. He was in the very early stages of the Alzheimer's disease that would ultimately take his life. He and Nancy had talked often about his memory loss—one of the reasons that for years he had carefully kept a diary of every day's activities—but it was not a weakness that a president of the United States could acknowledge, either to the country or to other world leaders.

Meese said that McFarlane had handled the operation and that, while he had mentioned it to Secretary of State George Shultz, no one had informed the president that this had actually taken place. A White House memo stated the president's strategy: "blame must be put at NSC's door—a rogue operation, going on without President's knowledge or sanction."

The next day Poindexter was fired, and North was reassigned from the White House to Marine Corps barracks in southeast Washington. The president and Meese held a press conference announcing that the bad guys had been found out and summarily dismissed. Meese revealed his discovery that North had been aware of the secret Swiss bank account that was redirecting the money from Iran to the Contras in Nicaragua. So-called White House sources leaked information to the major newspapers that the whole idea of the diversion was North's. This was not a total shock to North. He was well aware that as part of the plan, he might well have to be the fall guy for what CBS anchor Dan Rather was calling the "weapons for Iran, aid to the Contras" operation. North was willing to fall on his sword for the president and to insist, for as long as Reagan was president, that the leader he idolized was unaware of the enterprise. That's what a soldier did.

However, North had envisioned his sacrifice in political or career terms, which he figured his friends would repay at some point. The notion that he might have to go to prison and face criminal charges was not something he felt he had signed on to.

After Meese had secured Oliver North's office, Fawn Hall called North to say that the shredding had been stopped and asked what to do. North suggested she stuff whatever she could under her clothes and meet both him and a veteran Washington lawyer named Tom Green in an anteroom outside North's White House office. A decorated army captain from Minnesota, Green had served serious combat duty in the Vietnam War and was the first high-powered defense lawyer of choice for many Vietnam veterans and other military types, including North's collaborator in Iran-Contra, a retired general named Richard Secord.

Green had represented Secord in past legal matters, and it was as a favor to Secord that he promised initially to advise both him and North. After Hall and North exited the White House, they walked to Green's car, where he noticed papers spilling out of Hall's bra and skirt band.

"Whoa," said Green. He took them back to his office to confer with one of his law partners, and they informed North that they could not now represent him, as Green had instantly become a witness in the case. "So we called and got him Brendan Sullivan," Green said.

At Sullivan's suggestion, Hall then hired Plato Cacheris as her attorney. As often would happen with his clients, she turned into a witness for the government in exchange for a promise that she would not be prosecuted. Reagan would come to be personally represented by Ted Olson, who had finally been cleared of allegations against him by his own runaway special counsel in the EPA documents case. Reagan's official government lawyer was A. B. Culvahouse. As Bob Woodward would later write, "He would not have been on anyone's list of the top 100 people to be White House counsel. Probably he wouldn't have been on the list of the top 1,000."

A. B. was Baker's boy, though, and the most important consideration was trust. Baker, who had been hired to be the new White House chief of staff, didn't have time to learn to trust anyone he didn't already know.

Green continued to represent Secord, a retired Air Force major general who had been an operational officer in establishing an illegal private supply network for the Contras, the pro-American opposition to leftist Sandinista president Daniel Ortega. Secord had told authorities that his activities in Central America all had the approval of high-ups in the administration. His role had come to light, and begun to unravel, when on

October 5, 1986, one of the supply planes he was operating was shot down by Nicaraguan soldiers. Administration officials quickly denied that the plane had any connection to the U.S. government, which was not true. The government official who made those assurances and ultimately pleaded guilty to two misdemeanor counts of withholding information from Congress, Elliot Abrams, would later be hired for a prominent foreign policy position in the administration of George W. Bush. Apparently there are never enough individuals in America who have not committed crimes to fill the available government slots.

Secord's defense strategy would ultimately be to put everything on North and Poindexter. They were to say that they were doing what the president wanted, though not necessarily what he specifically ordered. So to make sure North still got the best possible shake, Green arranged for North to meet and eventually hire Brendan Sullivan.

No one in Washington thought it even remotely odd that Secord's attorney—who would be advancing that argument—would basically find lawyers for the other players in the case. That was the way things worked in Washington, and still is. For the last thirty years, a small coterie of Washington D.C., defense attorneys have divided up the work among themselves when there is a scandal. Green is often one of the first aboard, as he is one of the most ferocious courtroom battlers in the entire United States. For Major General Secord, he eventually secured a sentence of probation for making a false statement to investigators. The lie that Secord admitted telling was that he didn't know that some of the money he had received to aid the Contras had actually gone to finance a $13,800 security system at Colonel North's Virginia home.

All this prompted an immediate investigation by Congress, and the clamor to have North testify in public was intense. Only he was supposed to know whether President Reagan was the real mastermind of all this or not.

If Oliver North was coming across as the gung-ho marine, Sullivan, then forty-five years old, would be the can-do warrior attorney. Sullivan's career had been launched while he was in the U.S Army, representing disaffected servicemen. Here was yet another example, Sullivan believed, of a soldier being made the scapegoat for politicians. There was no attorney in the United States more prepared or motivated to take up the defense of North than Brendan Sullivan. In a sense it was the case that became the perfect paradigm for the firm, since Sullivan always compared his partners to an elite military unit. Now he was defending a client who was in turn very much the real-life personification of Williams & Connolly.

At first, North was concerned with the results of his initial inquiry into Sullivan's bio. On the surface, Sullivan tended to be sympathetic to liberals and Democrats. Sullivan's Presidio clients had been soldiers who didn't want to go to Vietnam. To the extent North had done some research on the man who became his counsel, he was slightly concerned about Sullivan's actions during Vietnam, or lack of action. In asking around, though, any fears were allayed when he was assured that Sullivan took no guff from anyone. Sullivan explained to North that he had avoided going to Vietnam, but only because the army tried to send him for all the wrong reasons and because Walter Cronkite had taken up his cause. North accepted the explanation.

If he had been in Vietnam, Sullivan would no doubt have been every bit the officer and leader that North was. Both men were cut from steel, and while politically they may not have been on the same side of the fence— Sullivan was basically an anti-big-government Democrat—they hit it off immediately, each no doubt seeing a little of the warrior in the other. In pursuing his orders as national security liaison, Oliver North had proven to be, without really knowing it, a disciple in his own way of Williams's "scorched earth" philosophy. North's job was to get money and aid to the freedom fighters in Nicaragua. Brendan Sullivan had once said that his job was to acquit his client, and if the world fell apart in the process, that wasn't his problem. North was willing to do whatever was necessary to successfully complete his mission for President Reagan. Had North become an attorney, instead of a career marine officer, there is no doubt that Williams & Connolly would have been the place for him. Sullivan and North were, in some ways, interchangeable.

There were also significant differences between them. Sullivan was a deadly serious man. North was a cut-up with the propensity to be an annoying smart-ass. Sullivan seemed to be much the older of the two men; in fact, there was only a one-year age gap between them, but he was clearly the more mature. Even so, North was eminently likable and considered a great client by all directly involved in the case—all but one person.

In the months leading up to the congressional public hearings that would begin in May 1987, North and Sullivan, both strong personalities, had clashed many times. A stream of men claiming to be go-betweens between North and President Reagan appeared at various times at Williams & Connolly, begging North to forgo his constitutional rights and tell the country that he was in fact operating the rogue operation that the president claimed. According to North, one of the visitors was businessman Ross Perot.

"Why doesn't Ollie just end this and explain to the FBI that the president didn't know?" Perot asked. "If he goes to jail I will take care of his family, and I'll be happy to give him a job when he gets out." North flushed at the word "jail." Neither Sullivan nor North wanted anything to do with jail. Sullivan's guiding principle was that Williams & Connolly clients don't go to jail. Nor did the concept do much for North, who couldn't figure out why Reagan wasn't sending a more positive signal, like a promise of a pardon or some other indication that he would never go to jail. The fact was that Ollie wasn't going to be explaining anything, if Sullivan had his way. His clients almost always remained stonily silent behind the protections of the Fifth Amendment. One of the central tenets of a Sullivan defense was that it was up to the prosecutors to prove their case, and they shouldn't expect any help from his client.

Perot later disputed North's implication that he was suggesting North lie, and Perot released a tape recording that he said proved that North's implication of hush money was false. In a 1991 interview, Perot acknowledged, "I did not want Colonel North to take the Fifth Amendment," but said the reason was "I wanted the truth to come out." On the tape, Perot is heard telling North, in Sullivan's presence, "The smart thing for you to do is dump it all out there and dump it fast." The promise to take care of his family was not on Perot's tape.

Although North gagged over the idea of taking the Fifth Amendment, if he spoke out publicly it was not going to be to say that he was acting without the implicit wishes of the president. He was a soldier, first and foremost. In a nutshell, North believed that Reagan approved of everything that he had done, but he would never have a shred of evidence to prove that the president knew. What Reagan was told, and by whom, would forever be shrouded in debate and doubt, a situation not made any clearer by Reagan's early stage Alzheimer's.

In the wake of the Iran-Contra revelations, Attorney General Meese, under intense political pressure, appointed a special prosecutor, Lawrence

E. Walsh, to investigate the burgeoning controversy. In addition, both the House of Representatives and the Senate set up investigating committees to hold joint hearings on North's "enterprise." Sullivan was more than ready to make the most of the rivalries and confusion that such competing investigations would engender. Confusion is always the best friend of the defense attorney.

He ordered his loquacious client to remain silent at all costs, no matter how provocative the questions. Sullivan's co-counsels, Barry Simon and their striking young associate Nicole Seligman, maintained their own strict code of silence. North felt Simon was the smartest man he had ever met. It was an opinion shared by Simon's partners as well, though Simon was not always tolerant of those who didn't match up to his brainpower, which could be everybody but Sullivan, in his view. If you needed someone to ingratiate himself with a judge, Simon was not the man. Then again, Williams & Connolly did not operate under the good-old-boy, suck-up-to-the-judge theory of trial work.

Seligman was a Harvard Law grad, no slouch in the intellect department, but she also had a sensitive female side. During the congressional hearings, she would be the somewhat mysterious 1940's-like movie-star figure sitting directly behind Sullivan and North but not participating directly in the verbal exchanges. Television commentators had no idea who she was, and at Williams & Connolly, there was hardly anyone to ask. If Williams & Connolly was sort of a white guys' club, Seligman showed just how talented a woman had to be to break into it. She was a product of Manhattan's Central Park. Her father, her uncle, and her sister, Stephanie Seligman, were all lawyers. She and her sister had both attended the elite Fieldston School, where in ninth grade she decided to master Japanese as her foreign language. At Harvard, Seligman became best friends with Caroline Kennedy, and at Harvard Law, she was editor of the *Harvard Law Review*. Before enrolling in law school Nicole had used her language skills as a reporter with the Asian edition of the *Wall Street Journal*. Stephanie would ultimately become a wealthy attorney at a New York City mergers and acquisitions firm, Wachtell, Lipton, Rosen & Katz.

After a clerkship with Supreme Court Justice Thurgood Marshall, Nicole was offered a job by Williams & Connolly, which was under self-imposed internal pressure to hire more women. In one of her first cases, she was assigned to the defense of James Beggs, a General Dynamics executive accused by government prosecutors of committing fraud in the acquistion of certain government contracts. Seligman got a quick object lesson in the Williams & Connolly method. Not only did she help get the charges dropped, her defense team won an apology from the judge and the prosecutors for what they had done to Beggs's reputation and career. In one case, Seligman had made it clear to her mostly white male partners that she had the right stuff. "She was a superstar from the moment she walked in the door," Bob Barnett observed. In the firm dining room, Seligman skipped past all the lawyers her own age and regularly sidled up to the most senior, and to some of her peers the most intimidating, of her bosses. Her connections weren't bad, either. When Caroline Kennedy married Edwin Schlossberg on Cape Cod on July 19, 1986, Nicole was a bridesmaid.

Like most of the other lawyers on the North case, she was personally sympathetic to North and often commented that he would make a better U.S. senator than most of those on the committee investigating him. Her liberal friends were amazed to hear her express her support for North so enthusiastically, but politics had nothing to do with a lawyer's loyalty to a client. At Williams & Connolly loyalty to a client was absolute.

North loved her. After allegations swirled that he had bought gifts, even a car, with his Iran-Contra money for Fawn Hall, Seligman sat down with his wife, Betsy, and assured her that none of it was true. North later told Ruth Marcus of the *Washington Post*, "Nicole was absolutely crucial in getting to the bottom of that and reassuring my best friend and the mother of my four children that there was nothing to that. She knew how terribly hurtful and painful that was to me and she went out of her way to make sure that Betsy knew there was nothing to it. A man wouldn't have done that."

The other attorneys in the case might have made a show of not talking to reporters, but they loved to leak information favorable to their clients behind the scenes. Sullivan kept all his press messages in a folder but returned virtually none of them. Reporters camped at the entrances to Williams & Connolly shouting questions at him, but he ignored them. Seligman also declined any conversations that might shed light on who she was or what she was doing. "It's not appropriate for me to talk about any of my clients, and I don't like talking about me," she told potential interviewers.

While Congress and the special prosecutor feuded over who would get to interrogate or question North first, Sullivan sat back. Keeping North quiet was a full-time job. He kept insisting that one way or the other, he was going to tell his story to the public.

"I know that's what you want," Sullivan told him, "but that's not what you are going to do."

North protested that it was his life, and he demanded a chance to explain his role to the public.

Sullivan leaned forward across his desk. "Let me explain it to you this way," he said. "If you and I were on a plane that crashed in the jungle behind enemy lines and we were fortunate enough to survive, I'd rely on you to get us out of there alive. Well, today you are in a different jungle, and you've got to rely on me to get you out. You may not like everything you have to do, but as long as I am your lawyer, that's the way it is going to be."

The joint congressional committee investigating the sale of weapons to Iran set the date of May 5, 1987, to begin its hearings. The members were worried that because of the threat of prosecution from Walsh, North and his superior, Admiral Poindexter, would take the Fifth Amendment and refuse to answer questions. Senator Warren Rudman, the New Hampshire Republican who cochaired the Senate side of the committee with Hawaii Democrat Daniel Inouye, asked Walsh to speed up the prosecution of North on charges of illegally shredding documents. When Walsh refused, preferring to work at his own pace, that left the investigating committee with two options: either suspend its investigation or grant North what is called "use immunity." This meant that North would be free to speak without fear that his words would later be used against him in a court of law or by Walsh's team of prosecutors. Democrats on the committee were anxious to hear from North, hoping that his testimony would embarrass the president. Republicans on the committee, led by Wyoming congressman Richard Cheney, wanted the committee to just not call North at all.

House Chairman Lee Hamilton had expended all the political capital he could muster to persuade the committee that the national interest required a complete accounting of the episode, just as much as the justice system required indictments and convictions. Use immunity, Hamilton believed, could get the country both.

Realizing that Hamilton was backed into a corner, Sullivan pounced, eager to take full advantage of the constitutional guarantee that his client would not be compelled to incriminate himself. Sullivan accepted the offer of use immunity, which would mean that North's congressional testimony could not be used against him in a courtroom. Sullivan also elicited from the committee a couple of other special conditions. Unlike other witnesses, North would not agree to give committee lawyers a deposition before his public testimony. This would require that committee members and their lawyers be able to think on their feet. This was not, as Geraldine Ferraro had observed over the years, Washington's strong point. In addition, they would get just one shot at North. When his testimony ended, that would be it. There would be no calling him back for further testimony or rebuttal.

Rather than lose North, Hamilton agreed to every one of Sullivan's demands. Later, in his committee's final report, Hamilton revealed that Sullivan had informed the committee that if it did not agree to his demands, he would defend North against criminal contempt citations, an action that might take years to litigate, based on Sullivan's past track record. Unlike the court system, a congressional committee doesn't usually have forever. Was it a one-sided arrangement? Commentator and author Richard Reeves, who covered the hearings, summed it up this way: "North could interrupt questions and statements by committee members and attorneys. More importantly, *he* could not be interrupted."

By this time, the country was salivating to hear whether North would implicate President Reagan or not. Rather than have Sullivan change his mind about allowing North to testify even under those conditions, Hamilton agreed, writing, "Although the committee believed North's legal arguments were without merit, it was not clear that a jury would agree."

Every night after work at the marine barracks in southeast Washington, North showed up at Williams & Connolly to prepare for his congressional testimony. One of the more interesting decisions that Sullivan made was to have North wear his Marine Corps uniform while he spoke. North was worried that if things went poorly, he could damage the reputation of the Corps as an institution.

"You are still a marine," Sullivan instructed him. "You spend every day at marine headquarters. You need to wear the uniform." Besides that, Sullivan said, North wasn't about to damage the Marine Corps. "We have a policy here at Williams & Connolly," Sullivan explained. "Our clients don't end up in jail."

When North continued to object, he told him to call the marine commandant, Paul X. Kelley, for his opinion. "All marines wear the uniform when they testify," he said. In January 1989, Kelley gave up his own uniform to become a lobbyist for Washington's most prominent lobby shop, Cassidy & Associates. His advice to North proved to be wise.

The day that would raise the public profile of both Brendan Sullivan and Williams & Connolly began at 9:00 A.M. on July 8, 1987. I was living on Capitol Hill at the time as the correspondent at the hearings for *Legal Times*, a once influential but now mostly defunct publication that was sold and marketed directly to lawyers. Although Sullivan was not obscure, most people didn't know that much about him. Williams & Connolly was connected to the name and reputation of one giant figure who, even though nearing the end of his life, was still the 800-pound gorilla of Washington law.

The two most formidable men across the table from North and Sullivan were Arthur Liman and John Nields. Like Sullivan, both were big-firm corporate lawyer types. Liman had been hired by the committee out of the New York law firm of Paul, Weiss, Rifkind, Wharton & Garrison. His top deputy was Mark Belnick, a protégé from the same firm. Historically lawyers from New York hadn't fared that well in Washington. Attorney General John Mitchell had come there from New York's Mudge Rose and ended up in prison. Wall Streeters who tried to operate a New York–style practice didn't last long in Washington. Nevertheless, Co-chairman Rudman was anxious that Liman, who had a giant reputation and ego, be hired. Among Liman's many credentials had been his representation of Geraldine Ferraro's husband, John Zaccaro, on tax charges. Liman had also worked on the defense of indicted Wall Street titan Michael Milken, alongside Edward Bennett Williams. Later, after Rudman left the Senate, the senator went to work as a million-dollar-a-year attorney as Liman's partner.

The House of Representatives picked Nields, a Washington defense attorney who looked young enough, with his longish brown locks, to be the fast-graying Sullivan's son. In fact, Nields and Sullivan were both the same age. Like Sullivan's partners Barnett and Kendall, Nields was a former clerk for Justice White. After that he became a partner at a rather dull but self-important Washington law firm then called Howrey & Simon. He had been hired by the House of Representatives in 1977 to conduct an investigation into Korean influence on the U.S government. Now, ten years later, the House of Representatives had summoned him again for this joint House-Senate inquiry into the Iran-Contra scandal.

Nields and Liman had divided up the witnesses, and it fell on Nields to begin the questioning of North, which meant he would have to deal with a string of scene-setting objections from Sullivan.

Nields, however, was not the only person in the historic hearing room to feel Sullivan's stinging presence as the questions commenced. Over and over again at their rehearsals, Sullivan had admonished North not to be sarcastic. "Just explain things to them, the way you do to us," Sullivan said. *"Minus the wisecracks!"* He also reminded his client, "No one is going to jail for what they did in the White House, but they might go to jail for what they do now. People could be indicted for perjury, for example."

The table at which Sullivan and North were seated was covered with a full tablecloth. No one could see their feet. Despite Sullivan's strenuous admonitions, North simply could not repress himself. He didn't like Nields one bit and found him arrogant and funny-looking, both long-haired and balding at the same time. The sarcastic wisecracks started almost immediately, and every time North uttered one, Sullivan would kick him under the table. As the pattern continued, the kicks got harder. By the time they broke for lunch, North says, he could barely limp out of the room.

Occasionally, Sullivan would lean over to consult with North about a question from the committee. In fact, often those conversations were more reminiscent of a pitcher's mound conference in another popular Kevin Costner movie, *Bull Durham*, where the manager-pitcher dialogue didn't necessarily have much to do with baseball.

On the occasions when Sullivan needed to confer with North, he took the precaution of covering his mouth so that lip readers watching on television couldn't see what he was saying. If they had been able to, they might have seen Sullivan say on one occasion, "Hi, it's been a while since you and I had a chat, so I thought I would say hello. Look serious, and if you smile now I'll kick you so hard your ankle will bleed."

Another time, Sullivan was informed that Betsy North had fallen asleep during her husband's testimony. During a recess, she was mortified and offered to go home, rather than be seen on the television cameras snoozing through Ollie's best lines. Sullivan told her to go back into the hearing room and fall asleep again. "It will show that you are totally relaxed and believing everything your husband says," Sullivan assured her.

Ordinarily at congressional hearings, attorneys tend to stay in the background. Occasionally they will be seen holding up a hand and whispering into the ear of their client. There have been some notable exceptions. During the Army-McCarthy hearings, attorney Joseph Welch challenged Senator Joseph McCarthy after McCarthy insinuated that Welch had an attorney working in his own office who was associated with a Communist front organization. Taken aback, Welch cried, "Until this moment, Senator, I think I never really gauged your cruelty, or your recklessness." When McCarthy resumed his attack, Welch cut him short. "Let us not assassinate this lad further, Senator . . . You've done enough. Have you no sense of decency, sir, at long last? Have you left no sense of decency?" McCarthy's attorney and closest adviser during that period had been Sullivan's mentor, Ed Williams.

Sullivan's frustration stemmed from the total lack of control he felt in the public portion of this process. He could neither ask the questions, as during a normal cross-examination, nor make North's argument for him, in the manner of addressing a jury.

It was forty-five minutes into the inquiry when North felt that Nields had cut him off from answering a question about a shipment of missiles to Iran from Israel. It sounds odd in the politics of today, but Israel was sending weapons to Iran, and getting the United States to replace them, since the United States had an embargo on arms shipments to the country that had seized our embassy and taken its workers hostage. Israel, whose leaders now wish they could bomb Iran, then had no qualms about scrubbing off the blue and white Jewish stars from their missiles and handing them over to radical ayatollahs. North had gone on for quite a while about his relationships with Israeli intermediaries, and Nields was chomping at the bit for North to wind up so he could ask another question and move on. North's loquacious replies were beginning to get tiring. After all, congressional interrogators like it better when the witnesses refuse to answer questions and the questioner gets to do all the talking. Members of Congress aren't usually interested in hearing anyone else talk.

North, a future success on radio and cable television, was nothing if not chatty. His former boss Robert MacFarlane even used the word "sophomoric," to describe him. One would think that somebody entrusted with so many national security secrets would have been more circumspect, like Sullivan or Seligman, but that was not Ollie North. When Nields

MASTERS OF THE GAME

interrupted him, North protested that even after about four minutes of answers, he was just getting started. Nields continued to interrupt and tried to move on, and that was when Sullivan dove in for the first time that morning. "Counsel, it might be obvious that the colonel is trying to answer your question, and I think it's up to counsel, Mr. Chairman, to permit the witness to answer the question fully."

"I have not put a question to him," Nields sputtered. "I am about to put—"

"You're interrupting," Sullivan said. "You're interrupting his answer."

Sullivan had an authoritative manner of making a statement that made it very difficult to challenge him. Even so Cochairman Inouye chastised Sullivan for directing his objections to the staff counsel, Nields. He reminded Sullivan that the rules called for objections to be directed to the committee chairman, not to the lawyer for the committee.

"I thought I did, Mr. Chairman . . . Of course, I didn't get any favorable rulings yesterday, so I thought I would take a straight shot at counsel," he replied.

"My point is," Sullivan went on, "it's absolutely clear, the counsel interrupted the witness. That's why I am compelled to bring it to your attention and I think the witness feels he has been interrupted because for several moments he tried to say, 'No, I want to say something else.' So please, Mr. Chairman, direct your counsel to permit Colonel North to answer the question the way he sees fit."

North continued to ramble on over Nield's protestations for another half hour or so. After one particularly lengthy answer about the cost of TOW antitank missiles, Sullivan again interceded, accusing Nields of stalling with his continuing interruptions. "Colonel North is attempting to do the very best he can," Sullivan explained. "I want to state to the chairman, and I should put it on the record right now, that we're being subjected to a stall job."

"Who is responsible for the stall?" Chairman Inouye responded.

It only took one little comment to set Sullivan off on another indignant rant. Only one ex-military man was going to control these proceedings, and it wasn't going to be the senator from Hawaii who had lost his arm fighting the Germans in Italy. Inouye, after being wounded in the stomach by machine-gun fire near San Terenzo, single-handedly charged and destroyed three separate machine-gun nests. He had drawn back his right arm to throw a grenade at the third one when his right elbow was struck by a rifle grenade, which almost tore off his arm. Reaching down with his good left hand, Inouye removed the hand grenade from his lifeless, clenched fingers and threw it, destroying the remaining machine gun. Then, despite a right arm flapping uselessly—it was later amputated—and a new bullet wound in the leg, he ordered his men out of danger and continued firing a tommy gun with his left hand, eventually killing twenty-five enemy troops and capturing eight others. Inouye's Medal of Honor recommendation was turned down by the Truman White House because of his Japanese heritage. Instead, he was awarded a Distinguished Service Cross. In 2000, before President Clinton left office, he finally received his Medal of Honor. Inouye was a worthy opponent for Sullivan's gladiatorial legal style.

"As a trial lawyer, I know a stall when I see one," Sullivan continued. He accused the committee of "meandering through questions in a disjointed fashion," so that North's testimony would ultimately spill over the weekend and give Nields and his investigators time to impugn North's veracity. When Sullivan was finally finished addressing the committee, Inouye said bemusedly, "May the records show that it took four and a half minutes to explain the stall." No one could have predicted at that moment that twenty-two years later, with Inouye still a senator and Sullivan still a lawyer, they would meet again.

By 2:00 P.M. televisions all over America were being turned on to see the extraordinary drama that was now taking place between North, Sullivan, and the committee. The public was accustomed to witnesses at congressional committees prostrating themselves before senators and representatives. Most had seen what happened to Robert Bork when he wouldn't play the game. This was quite different, though: a marine and his like-minded attorney blasting back at the clueless members of Congress. The David v. Goliath show made for great television and turned both lawyer and client into national celebrities. Networks covering the hearings live noticed that viewership was picking up exponentially as news traveled by word of mouth and telephone about what was happening. Then it became the task of the Senate counsel, Arthur Liman, to see what he could do with this plucky adversary.

"Colonel, is it fair to say that November 25, 1986, was one of the worst days of your life?"

North turned to whisper in Sullivan's ear.

"I wasn't asking whether it was one of the worst days in Mr. Sullivan's life," Liman said.

"I didn't meet him until the next day," North quipped. Sullivan gave his ankle a particularly painful pop, but North was practiced in not showing pain.

A few moments later, when North hesitated in giving an answer to a question referring to a conversation with Admiral Poindexter, Liman attempted to pounce. "You seem to be hesitating. Is there any doubt in your mind?" Liman asked.

"You're just looking for tricks, Mr. Liman," Sullivan said, seething. "Excuse me, Mr. Chairman, I just thought we'd be on to some new important subject by now."

The sarcasm dripped off Sullivan's tongue, and he seemed to become increasingly annoyed. His anger exploded when Liman instructed North to "look at whatever is in front of you" to refresh his memory.

"Mr. Liman, when he wants to look at something, he will look at it. Don't you suggest what he looks at," Sullivan almost shrieked.

"Our public address system is working very well," Inouye said. "You need not shout, sir."

Liman repeated his permission for North to refresh his memory.

Sullivan exploded. "If the witness wants to look at his notes, his whole book that he has here, he'll do so for the answer. If he doesn't he won't do so. He will look at the book when he wants to look at his book, and it's improper for any questioner to say, 'Look at your book and see if you can find an answer.'"

"I think the question was proper," Inouye concluded. "Please proceed."

"Are you directing him to look at the book, Mr. Chairman? Would you like him to start at page one?"

"He may look at it or he need not look at it. It's up to him."

Sullivan quickly claimed victory. "That's the ruling I was looking for," he told Inouye.

Sullivan was only satisfied for a moment, though. As the day wore on and Liman's repetitive questioning sauntered into the realm of shredding classified documents, Sullivan's periods of calm cycled in and out.

"Would you have shredded less documents, if you had been told that the attorney general was acting at the specific request of the president, your commander in chief?" Liman asked.

"Pure speculation, dreamland," Sullivan interjected. "It has two ifs in it. And Mr. Liman knows better than most . . . that those kinds of questions are wholly inappropriate, not just because of the rules of evidence, not because you couldn't say it in a court, but because it's just dreamland. It's speculation. He says, 'If you'd done this, and if you had done that, what about this.' Come on. Let's have, Mr. Chairman, plain fairness, plain fairness. That's all we are asking."

"I'm certain counsel realizes this is not a court of law," Inouye said.

"Believe me, I know that," Sullivan said.

"And I am certain you realize that the rules of evidence do not apply to this inquiry," Inouye continued.

"That I know as well," Sullivan said. "I'm just asking for fairness— fairness. I know the rules don't apply. I know that Congress doesn't recognize attorney-client privilege, a husband-and-wife privilege, a priest-penitent privilege. I know those things are out the window."

Then Inouye said, "Let the witness object, if he wishes to."

Sullivan nearly leaped off his chair in exasperation. "Well, sir, I'm not a potted plant. I'm here as the lawyer. That's my job."

With that line, Sullivan vaulted from the case files in the law library into the reference pages of Bartlett's Quotations. Nobody else in Washington would dare make such a remark to a sacred United States senator. He had hit a good chord with the segment of the American people fed up with senatorial pomposity. The next morning, Sullivan was deluged with potted plants from both friends and enthusiastic television watchers. One of the plants that he received went on to live in the firm's offices for the next fifteen years.

Sullivan immediately and unexpectedly became one of the most recognizable attorney names in the world. Among those who was not amused at the sudden rush of fame and recognition, however, was his mentor, Edward Bennett Williams. One of Williams's best friends in the legal profession was Liman, whom Sullivan had exposed during the hearings as not the oh-so-smart New York lawyer people had thought that he was.

Williams was initially pleased that Sullivan's high-profile aggressive defense had sparked a huge increase in giving to the Oliver North Legal Defense Fund. "Thank God, that's the end of this pro bono shit," Williams told a priest, who relayed the conversation to Evan Thomas. On the other hand, Williams didn't care for how close North and Sullivan had gotten. "All that guy [North] does is hang around," Williams bitched. He was also displeased by the some hundred thousand pieces of mail that came into the firm about the case. Even though the vast majority of the letters were supportive of North, each one had to be sniffed for powder by a trained German shepherd before it could be opened. The volume of the mail necessitated hiring three additional dogs, lest work in the mailroom come to a complete halt, which it did anyway when a full-scale noisy dog-fight broke out between the sniffers. Just like their humans, FBI-trained dogs and local police dogs simply can't share authority. The only thing that made Williams feel any better about this was that many of the letters contained checks for North's Legal Defense Fund. North's popularity also occasionally miffed Williams's other high-profile clients. One day both North and indicted corporate bond swindler Michael Milken were in the Williams & Connolly offices, and Milken noticed the swarm of cameramen and paparazzi outside the firm's building. Milken was annoyed that the media had gotten wind of his presence in Washington and curious about how. Williams had to straddle the divide in Milken's psyche, between wanting to be famous and not wanting to be hunted, to explain to him that the crowd of reporters had gathered to see Ollie North and not him. The New York–based corporate raider wasn't so sure. He asked Williams if there wasn't a side or a back entrance that they could use to get out. Williams called down to the limousine and asked that it come around to the back. As it did, the swarm followed it into the alley, where Williams and Milken emerged from a back door and climbed into the black Lincoln Continental. The photographers had no idea who Milken was and didn't snap a single picture. They just knew it wasn't Ollie. Still, Milken for years continued to insist to Williams that he had been right, and that the photographers had been there for him and not North. The whole incident distressed Williams, who chalked it up as another example of North embarrassing either the firm or one of its clients.

The performances, both North's and Sullivan's, had made the committee and Liman look foolish. Leaning over a rail during a break, ABC News correspondent Brit Hume made what seemed at the time like a bold prediction, "Sullivan just made Ollie the next U.S. senator from Virginia."

Hume's prophecy was not far off. North would later run for the Senate from Virginia and come remarkably close to joining his inquisitors on the other side of the paneled desk. In most investigations or court hearings, a witness like Oliver North would feel his career shrinking, but Sullivan had more in mind than simply exonerating an embattled marine officer. He wouldn't just restore North's honor and reputation, to say nothing of his freedom. Sullivan had made North into a national hero. North didn't quite win his Senate seat, though he came close. He did, however, go on to become an important voice on radio and cable television news, a popular author of nearly twenty books, and a well-compensated dinner speaker. When the case started, North couldn't even begin to pay the millions of dollars in fees generated by the hourly rates of Sullivan, Seligman, and others on his legal team. Sullivan had made sure that North not only didn't have to spend a day in jail but could pay the bills and much more for the rest of his life.

Liman returned to his law firm, chastened about the ability of a know-it-all New Yorker to understand the particular ways of Washington. Jay Leno made jokes about his sparse stringy hair. When he went to the Mayflower Hotel one day to accept an award from a Jewish organization, the hotel served a Spanish omelet of ham and eggs, which Liman could not eat, nor could any of the guests. His top assistant, Mark Belnick, would later be arrested, handcuffed, jailed, and prosecuted for allegedly participating in a scheme to falsify the business records of a client. Eventually Belnick was acquitted. Liman died in 1997, looking much older than his age of sixty-four. His obituary reflected the shortcomings that Iran-Contra had exposed, as much as his successes. However, he did live long enough to hire Iran-Contra's Republican cochairman, Warren Rudman, as a million-dollar-a-year Paul, Weiss partner in 1993. John Nields returned to Howrey & Simon. His name, however, would become better known in the 1990s in the form of a popular and successful singing group named the Nields, which consisted of two of his daughters, Katryna and Nerissa.

By contrast to the gloom that enveloped his opponents, Sullivan could have happily gone into the floral business. His performance had done more than help make Ollie North into an overnight folk hero. He had also saved the law firm, in a way that would not be clear until years later.

Indeed, while Sullivan's antics in Iran-Contra woke up the country, he and Barry Simon were simultaneously working on another case that would make them attractive to any American businessman under indictment.

17.

NO APPLE FOR THE TEACHER

———— ■ ————

Niels Hoyvald was the chief executive officer of Beech-Nut Nutrition, then the second-largest seller of baby food—after Gerber—in the world.

Founded in 1891, Beech-Nut by the 1960s had become known for its Life Savers, Tetley tea, Martinson's coffee, and the chewing gum and baby food that it sold under its own name. In 1969, Beech-Nut was bought out by the large drug company Squibb. Four years later, Squibb sold off the baby food business to a private equity group. The new Beech-Nut company sold only baby food. Its biggest and most profitable product was apple juice, targeted at, yes, babies. Although apple juice is not particularly nutritious, many new mothers don't know that. Their babies like it, it is easily digested, and many parents consider it as natural as breast milk. The apple industry has spent millions over the years polishing its brand. Just the word "apple" in a product, especially in juice for toddlers, is worth millions in sales.

At least that was what the company hoped and claimed, as during the 1970s its ad agencies heavily promoted Beech-Nut apple juice as the "natural" baby food. The campaign was only a partial success, and in the Jimmy Carter recession/malaise of the late 1970s, Beech-Nut began to bleed red ink. In 1977, a Bronx juice supplier, Universal Juice, offered Beech-Nut executives a less expensive concentrate that it said would save the company some $250,000 a year, actually a drop in the apple juice pail for a company that was still doing $50 million in annual sales. The research director of one of Beech-Nut's plants, Jerome LiCari, was curious about the quality of the new juice and sent two employees to Universal's plant in New Jersey. When the company's investigators got there, all they reported finding was a few fifty-five-gallon drums, supposedly filled with the concentrate from apples imported from Israel. The honest guy then sent samples of the concentrate to an outside laboratory for testing. The results came back that the concentrate had little in common with apples and was mostly corn syrup. Sensing that there might be potential for trouble, Beech-Nut demanded that the owner of Universal, Zeev Kaplansky, sign a document holding Beech-Nut harmless against any damages that might stem from complaints or lawsuits.

Two years later, in 1979, the company was sold to the Swiss food giant Nestlé. To run the division, Nestlé hired Niels Hoyvald, a Danish businessman with an MBA degree from the University of Wisconsin. Certifiably ambitious, Hoyvald took a position as head of marketing with the promise that he would become CEO within a year. He had turned around another food company, Plumrose, and was extremely confident that he could do the same for Beech-Nut. The plant manager who had ordered the inquiry was still not happy, and in mid-1979 he sent more samples to a second laboratory. Those tests revealed that Universal had switched from corn syrup to beet sugar—closer, but still not apples. He circulated a memorandum to that effect and urged the company's executives to end the contract. As he would later testify, he was told that he was not being a team player and that he would be fired if his pestering didn't stop.

Four months after Hoyvald's promotion to president of the company, in late 1979, LiCari appeared in the Dane's office to make one last plea to stop selling products with the obviously apple-less juice. Hoyvald, according to testimony, appeared "shocked and surprised" and indicated that something would be done. Nothing was, and after confronting Hoyvald at a company retreat in Vermont, the whistle-blowing employee resigned. He then alerted state and federal authorities about his suspicions.

In 1982, sensing that the FDA was about to seize the juice, Hoyvald arranged for nine tractor-trailers to haul the company's entire inventory to a warehouse in Secaucus, New Jersey. He then had that juice transferred by ship to a company distributor in the Caribbean. Company lawyers by this time were urging Hoyvald to recall the adulterated juice, but Hoyvald rejected that advice and decided to try to get rid of the evidence by ordering a "foreign promotion" that would sell the juice overseas at reduced prices. Within days, twenty-three thousand cases were shipped from a warehouse in San Jose, California, to the Dominican Republic for a half-price sale.

Hoyvald later revealed that he took this action after being advised by company lawyers that U.S. law does not prohibit the overseas sale of items banned in the United States. Cigarettes, for example, that don't meet U.S. regulations can still be made in the United States, as long as they are sold overseas and are in compliance with the laws of the country in which they are being sold.

Hoyvald reported to his bosses at Nestlé, "The recall has now been completed, and . . . we were only faced with having to destroy approximately 20,000 cases." He boasted that they had received adverse publicity in "only one magazine."

However, Hoyvald underestimated the tenacity of federal prosecutors. New York state sued Beech-Nut and imposed a $250,000 fine on the company. Then, in 1986, the federal government indicted Hoyvald and the other executives involved in the matter for fraud. The Food and Drug Administration persuaded the corporation to pay a $2 million fine, at the time the largest ever collected.

The case was considered as open and shut as any prosecution could possibly be. Not since Robert Kennedy had been sure enough to bet everything that he would put Jimmy Hoffa away had opponents of Williams & Connolly been more confident. Sullivan confided, "Listening to the prosecutors' presentation was a little bit like being a soldier in a foxhole with your rifle empty and the bombs coming in. It's like being at the bottom of the Grand Canyon and somebody gives you matchsticks. It's the time when you start to think about medical school."

The federal government had everything in place. It just hadn't counted on Sullivan and Simon.

Hot off his nationally televised Oliver North defense, Sullivan had become one of the most recognized attorneys in the world, almost overnight. *American Lawyer* magazine put a full-time reporter on the trial, largely to determine if Sullivan's new national profile was justified or just hype. Since the magazine was largely founded on the concept of bursting bubbles and defying conventional wisdom, one could guess in advance what the conclusion would likely be.

The Beech-Nut case had actually begun before the North case, but the slow pace of litigation had made it lag behind. On November 16, 1987, while his North representation was still his most obvious claim to notoriety, Sullivan walked with Hoyvald into a federal courtroom in Brooklyn. Immediately, according to the *American Lawyer* reports, there was a twitter.

"That's Oliver North's lawyer," juror Frank Livorsi exclaimed. "Big time," said another. There was a smattering of "oh my goodness" from several of the others.

Simon was seven years younger than Sullivan, just thirty-eight, but he had already gained a ferocious reputation among his peers. If Sullivan and Simon were participants in acts of torture, Sullivan for all his notoriety was the good cop. Simon, a onetime clerk to liberal Supreme Court Justice William J. Brennan Jr., was the bad cop. Lawyers would say that Simon was so difficult to deal with that when Sullivan walked in the door, it was a breath of fresh air. Brendan, as he had shown with the Iran-Contra committee, could get almost anything he wanted, often so prosecutors wouldn't have to deal with Simon, who treated his opponents with total disdain, usually even refusing to shake hands with them when they entered the courtroom in the morning. Another unusual Simon antic was his routinely refusing to sign a building register if he had to go to a lawyer's office for a meeting. Simon claimed that he didn't want his courtroom opponents having his handwriting analyzed to detect his mood. He didn't want to take the chance that by signing his name he might inadvertently help the opposition's investigations.

American Lawyer, the legal profession's often critical antimagazine, was eager to debunk the myth of Brendan Sullivan. It quoted jurors, who initially had been excited about being in the same courtroom with North's attorney, as saying that Sullivan "used every trick in the book" and that "from the opening moment, his thing was, how can I deceive the jury."

Sullivan later acknowledged in an interview that his argument that the experienced Hoyvald was relying on bad legal advice wasn't the best argument in the world. "I just wanted the jury to think that I had one," he said in a rare moment of levity.

After the jury voted to convict Hoyvald, *American Lawyer*'s Tim O'Brien slyly observed, "Perhaps a potted plant would have been better." The writer noted that Hoyvald would soon be the first Sullivan client since Allen Green in 1973 to go to prison. The headline of the *American Lawyer* story was "Brendan Sullivan Bombs in Brooklyn." Sullivan, however, was not about to let his fifteen-year-old winning streak end. In a presentencing memorandum to the judge, Sullivan made what was considered one of the most audacious legal arguments ever offered in a criminal prosecution.

His client had just been convicted of 351 felony counts. He had been integral to a conspiracy to cheat little teeny babies out of the genuine apple part of their juice. Each of the individual counts carried a potential jail sentence of three years in prison. Nevertheless, on June 6, 1988, Sullivan stood before U.S. District Judge Thomas C. Platt and asked that Hoyvald be sentenced to lecturing business students. He asked that Hoyvald pay his penance by being forced to teach an accredited class in business ethics. "Business students undoubtedly hear this principle regularly in their ethics classes," Sullivan said, "but the impact of this message would be far clearer coming from Niels Hoyvald, whose career has been shattered because he did not heed it, than it could ever be coming from a textbook or a professor."

To say that Hoyvald was petrified at the thought of going to prison was a tremendous understatement. When sentencing day arrived, a week after Sullivan's remarkable request, Hoyvald tearfully begged the judge, "Please don't send me to jail." Talking about his eighty-three-year-old mother and his wife of twenty-eight years, Hoyvald said, "I can see in their eyes disappointment, hurt, disgust, and fear of their future. I ask for them and myself, please don't send me to jail."

Judge Platt was not *that* cooperative, though many thought he was lenient to the extreme. Saying that he believed some period of incarceration was necessary, Platt sentenced Hoyvald to a mere one year and one day in prison. One might have thought that Hoyvald would be relieved and that Sullivan, all things considered, would be satisfied. The prosecutor, though he had hoped for a longer sentence, was relieved that he had won. "We're not talking about the Mafia here, or a bunch of bank robbers," U.S. Attorney Andrew J. Maloney said. "A message has been sent out to corporate America that these cases will get the highest priority."

Sullivan announced his intention to appeal, and Hoyvald was released on a million-dollar bond. In March 1989, Hoyvald's conviction was overturned by a federal appeals court, which ruled that the government had tried the case in the wrong venue. Losing lawyers claim this is a technicality. The winning side will always object to the characterization and point out that the law is not a technicality. Still, most people would consider it one.

A second trial ensued. Sullivan and Simon argued that Hoyvald had been consulting with attorneys and acted not maliciously but in concert with their advice. This time the jury deadlocked and a mistrial was declared.

Rather than try Hoyvald for yet a third time, the government decided to negotiate a plea bargain with Sullivan. The result of the negotiations was that Hoyvald agreed to perform approximately a thousand hours of community service, some of it to be spent teaching a business class on ethics.

If there was one thing to recognize about Sullivan's tenacity, it was that a case was never over until it was over. The prosecutor in this case had spent over four years of the public's resources on the prosecution, but in the end had only made the contribution of adding one more teacher to the education system. Prosecutor Thomas Roche was later quoted by the Associated Press as saying it was all worth it, because he had, in the end, gotten Hoyvald to admit that he was guilty. "We're gratified that this defendant has finally admitted his involvement," Roche said, as his legal prey walked out of the courthouse a free man.

18.

ST. GABRIEL'S CEMETERY

———■———

Sullivan's national notoriety caught Williams more than a little off guard. For years, it had been Edward Bennett Williams and the other nameless guys. If there was a model, it was the Washington Redskins that he once owned. There it was Sonny Jurgensen and a nameless corps of receivers simply designated as the Smurfs. The offensive line was the Hogs. Until Sullivan came along, that was an apt description of Williams & Connolly. It was the superstar quarterback and the other guys, the Smurfs.

For the first time in his law firm life, Williams was jealous, and his petulance was obvious to all. When Williams had returned to the office after Sullivan's dramatic confrontation with Liman, he said little.

Although testimony at the congressional hearings had ended, Sullivan now had to run the gauntlet of Walsh's special prosecutor task force.

The Iran-Contra hearings had not ended North's case, only the public phase of it. He was still a ubiquitous presence around the firm. North once walked into Barry Simon's office wearing an old gray wig that had belonged to his wife Betsy's mom. Simon, the toughest guy at Williams & Connolly, nearly jumped out of his seat. "How the hell did you get in here?" he yelled. Then North pulled off the wig. Simon didn't laugh. Williams complained loudly about North on one occasion, "Fucking guy, all he does is hang around here getting you coffee."

North, however, loved the access to Washington's true power players. He was already thinking along the same political lines as Brit Hume—that is, turning his national fame and approval into a political career. He tried to get Williams to encourage him, but the famous lawyer would have none of it. "The day you run for office will be the end of you," Williams said.

In fact, it was closer to the end of Williams.

Although he had never held public office, Williams had held the lives of many in his hands. Presidents, cabinet members, even Supreme Court justices fought for his approval and respect. At various times, as owner of both the Washington Redskins and the Baltimore Orioles, he controlled the most revered sports obsessions of the population in which he lived. In Washington, the Redskins in particular were as much a unifying religion as they were a football team. As treasurer of the Democratic National Committee, Williams exercised a disproportionate influence over politics, not just for Democrats but for Republicans as well. As best friend of *Washington Post* management, and personal attorney for owner Katharine Graham, he could, as John Connally had believed, kill stories embarrassing to his clients. One example cited by Evan Thomas involved his representation of Jack Kent Cooke's then-girlfriend Suzanne Martin, who later married Cooke. She originally hired Williams to sue the owner of the Washington Redskins, who had once been Edward Bennett Williams's partner in the ownership of that very team. Martin alleged that Cooke had forced her to have two abortions against her will. Then, in an abrupt about-face, Martin married the billionaire team owner. Cooke's attorney, Milton Gould, accused Williams of extortion and conflict of interest for representing Suzanne against the man who had been his own business partner. It was exactly the kind of juicy internecine warfare that newspapers live on, but the paper that broke Watergate and published the Pentagon Papers never wrote a word about it. One call from Williams to his buddy *Post* executive editor Ben Bradlee killed the story. Bradlee explained to Evan Thomas, "It was a nothing story." No one at the *Washington Post* would concede that they ever would do any such thing; they are too filled with high-minded journalistic principles to ever do anything like that. They did it, though.

The *Post* didn't mention the case until after Cooke's death. Oddly enough, when a county judge in Virginia's Hunt Country finally ruled on the suit, and the *Post* could keep it quiet no longer, the reporter for the paper termed it "a domestic soap opera that has rivaled 'Dynasty' in its big-bucks nastiness and use of choice words." So much for the Cooke controversy having been a "nothing case."

Not many lawyers have ever had that ability to control press coverage in their hometown paper, much less in the revered and ethically pristine *Washington Post*.

On December 7, 1987, some five months after North's testimony had ended, and while Sullivan was immersed in the Hoyvald case, Williams's cancer worsened. A tumor in his liver was growing. It was the beginning of the final painful end for one of Washington's most enduring landmarks. In January, Williams rallied to escort his daughter down the aisle of Holy Trinity Church. For those in the pews, it was a shocking and uncomfortable sight. Jack Valenti, who had once been so annoyed that he wouldn't be questioned by Williams at the Connally trial, couldn't hold back the tears. Williams made it to the altar without collapsing, and his voice was still strong as he read a passage from Isaiah. Evan Thomas reported that at the wedding reception, Williams told David Brinkley, "I'm going to get through this and then go home and croak."

That night, Williams checked into Georgetown University Hospital and received last rites. As usual, though, he refused to die. On May 31, 1988, he celebrated his sixty-eighth birthday. For his son Kevin's graduation, he was well enough to deliver the commencement address at Spring Hill College in Alabama, the last speech he would ever give. At the end of July, Williams went to visit Msgr. W. Louis Quinn. "I don't think I can beat it this time," he said.

In early August, Williams was reading a copy of *Regardie's* magazine, a Washington business publication, about the most powerful people in the city. Even as death enveloped him, he had made the list for one last time. "They don't realize what power really is," Williams told his son. "I'm about to see true power. Fighting death is selfish. It's time to go and see what real power is."

On a Sunday night, in 1988, Williams fell and was taken by ambulance to Georgetown. Although he claimed to be ready to die, he simply would not. By the following Friday, he began planning his funeral, listing who should give the eulogies and what priests should be at the altar. On August 13, heavily sedated with morphine, his cancer-ravaged body finally gave up.

Among the most recognizeable pallbearers for Edward Bennett Williams were his best friends and drinking buddies Ben Bradlee and Art Buchwald. Also dressed in dark suits were the two less-recognized protégés closest to him, Sullivan and Lucchino. Lucchino, who had been diagnosed with cancer on Friday, September 13, 1985, seemed more devastated than most. Williams had succumbed on Friday the thirteenth. Lucchino had trouble shaking the significance of the date and for the rest of his life would dread Friday the thirteenth, like no other day on the calendar.

Williams was buried under the spreading branches of a large maple tree in St. Gabriel's Cemetery in Potomac, Maryland. The obituary in the *Washington Post* noted that "a sultry wind rustled in the trees and birds chirped softly."

How could there be a Williams & Connolly after Williams? It was as unimaginable as that there could be a Disney after the death of Walt or a Ford Motor Company after Henry. The former Captain Sullivan, however, was prepared to lead.

If Williams had died ten years earlier, when he had his first serious face-to-face with death, there would have been no Williams & Connolly. The loss of both Williams and Paul Connolly, who died of a heart attack in 1978, would have been too much to overcome. Sullivan would have been too young to carry it off. It was the juxtaposition of the fame from the Oliver North case and Williams's demise that saved Williams & Connolly. The Iran-Contra case had gotten the firm millions of dollars' worth of free publicity. Suddenly everyone wanted to hire the smart aleck who had told the U.S. senators where to go.

"A decade before, we would have been toast," Sullivan recalled, "but in 1988 there was no question but that we would survive."

When Edward Bennett Williams died, it was Sullivan to whom the other partners awarded a mammoth eighth-floor office, near a building whose street-level retail outlet was a store for the firm-run Baltimore Orioles baseball team. The pictures of Williams with presidents, politicians, and, yes, crooked labor leaders had been replaced with a TV-sized portrait of Sullivan's new yacht, the *Confrontation*, its spectacular red, white, and blue spinnaker filled with wind. Members of his family, including young Brendan Sullivan III, "Sully," were displayed prominently. Sully, who had gone to Stanford like his idol, Yankee pitching star Mike Mussina (a former Oriole), would become a strong-armed relief pitcher in the San Diego Padres minor league system.

The most prominent picture in Sullivan's office today is a wide-angle shot of Oliver North being sworn in for testimony before the joint congressional committee. Just behind Sullivan in the picture, sitting at a press table a little to the right, there I am, glasses and all—my picture on Sullivan's wall, among a hundred or so, of course.

In the criminal phase of the case, Sullivan had gone on to defeat Walsh on virtually every important point of North's indictment. In a tour de force of lawyering on April 20, 1989, Sullivan told a Washington criminal jury that Oliver North was a hostage. "I ask you on the evidence to set him free," Sullivan said. "Greater love has no man than he be willing to lay down his life for another. That's Ollie North. That's the kind of man Ollie North is."

He portrayed North to the jury as a man who was willing to do anything for his country—but now, Sullivan said, North "doesn't want to be a hero, he wants to go home."

On May 4, North was convicted of destroying documents, obstructing the investigation, and accepting the gift of the $13,800 home security system. On the nine most serious charges against him, he was found not guilty. The convictions would eventually be thrown out by a federal judge, and as Sullivan had promised, North never spent a day in prison. After spending $30 million and hiring teams and teams of lawyers, Walsh and his investigation had been solidly beaten by Sullivan. His cardinal rule—our clients don't go to jail—had been preserved.

The first time I met Sullivan in his office, it was the first press interview he had given in over three years. I worried he was going to be mean, but he wasn't at all. He was apologetic about the size of his office. "It was even larger when Ed had it," he told me. "He had the whole side of this building. I had a wall put in. I didn't want people saying I was the next Edward Bennett Williams.

"I am not the next Edward Bennett Williams," he said. "He was my friend, he was my teacher, and he was my law partner. But I am not Edward Bennett Williams."

Sullivan is, though, the living embodiment of the central philosophy and principal tenet of the firm that his mentor left behind. At Williams & Connolly, they have a simple proud name for what every partner believes and must live by. They call it "scorched earth." Opponents of Williams & Connolly had a different term for their tactics, calling their methods "the scorpion defense." A prospective adversary knows that if you attack them, you are the one who is going to get stung.

At the very mention of the phrase "scorched earth," Sullivan sat taller. "Somebody wrote during the Iran-Contra hearings that the lawyers for North wouldn't care if all America came tumbling down, because some secret document or classified revelation might come out," he said. "Well, that's right. I don't care if the whole world comes down. My duty is to defend my client. If the world comes apart as a result, so be it."

It was hard to get one's hands around the fact that this scrappy pillar of the Washington establishment, this supporter of the arts, this millionaire establishment attorney for Colonel North and all that he did, could be some sort of unlikely closet radical, willing to drop his own bomb on a Republican president, if that freed his ideologically conservative client from prosecutorial inquisition. As he had with Niels Hoyvald, and with every other one of his clients up to that time since the unfortunate Agnew briber Allen Green, Sullivan had ultimately saved North from spending even a single day in prison.

As a client newly freed from indictment, conviction, and congressional scrutiny, North was turned over to Robert Barnett, whose job it would be to sell Ollie's memoirs, get him a new job, and put him back on the path to public redemption. In some law firms, the plaint of labor secretary Raymond Donovan was just theoretical: Where do you go to get your reputation back? When Donovan said it, it was a rhetorical question. At Williams & Connolly, there was nothing rhetorical about it. If you wanted your reputation back, you merely walked down the hall to Bob Barnett's office. Reputation restored. That was his department.

On September 24, 1988, Barnett was walking into the presidential suite of the Lafayette Hotel across the street from Governor Michael Dukakis's presidential campaign headquarters in Boston. Barnett was adorned in a pin-striped suit with a Spiro Agnew watch and a red, white, and blue watchband. Aides—including former Princeton basketball star Bill Bradley, by now the U.S. senator from New Jersey—helped push cream-colored contemporary furniture out of the way. Lucchino's old hardcourt pal had some advice for Dukakis as well. "Take open shots and play tough defense," he said.

In a practice debate, Dukakis played himself; Barnett played Bush. Barnett clearly won the debate, as Bush would later in the real-life version.

Dukakis didn't fare much better in the presidential election than the 1988 Williams & Connolly Orioles, who ended the season after Williams's death with a record of 54 wins and 107 losses. Barnett, though, could always sense opportunity in political defeat, as he had with Ferraro. Within months, he had put a contract worth $175,000 into the pocket of spurned first lady Kitty Dukakis, although, as it was noted at the time, she had failed to take a single note or keep a diary. No matter, Barnett then found her a ghostwriter and arranged a speaking tour for her at $15,000 a pop. If you can't make a buck in Washington confessing to drug addiction and alcoholism, you just aren't trying hard enough.

Despite the fact that Kitty Dukakis was a public figure, she quickly adopted the Williams & Connolly style of dealing with the press. So that the information in her book would remain fresh, Barnett had inserted a clause in her speaking agreements that her appearances would be closed to the press. Dukakis therefore refused to say whom she was speaking to, much less where or when. "It's a private matter," Barnett explained. "We tend to forget that people do have privacy. You shouldn't be shocked or amazed."

19.

SPYING ON THE BIRDS

———■———

With the death of his father figure and mentor, Larry Lucchino suddenly had more power over a baseball team than any forty-three-year-old Yale law grad could possibly have hoped for.

On December 7, 1988, the actual majority ownership in the team passed to Eli Jacobs, a friend and client of Williams who was head of Memorex. *Business Week* described Jacobs as "a shadowy figure who refused even to disclose so much as the names of the various operating companies he controls."

Raised in Newton, Massachusetts, Jacobs was the son of a successful real estate developer. He attended Phillips Academy in Andover and then enrolled at Yale, where he received both an undergraduate degree and his law degree. His best friend from college was David L. Boren, who would become the governor of Oklahoma and later a U.S. senator from that state, serving as chairman of the Senate Intelligence Committee and a prominent member of the Iran-Contra committee. When asked about Jacobs by the *Wall Street Journal*, though, Boren claimed to know nothing, writing, "Few, if any, of his friends know anything about Mr. Jacobs's business interests, much less take advantage of them."

Another pal was conservative New York state politician Lewis Lehrman, with whom Jacobs founded an investment bank in 1970. They invested in some oil wells in Texas and, according to Jacobs, "hit a couple of gushers." Exactly how much money their other business ventures made—or lost— was open to debate, but by 1983 the partnership was sour and Jacobs and Lehrman had split up. An acquaintance of both men later said it was difficult to decode who was screwing who. A new partnership with investor Peter Peterson failed to turn out much better.

Jacobs's best-known investment had been in Memorex, which made cassette tapes. It became best known for a brilliant and classic television advertising campaign in which Ella Fitzgerald would shatter a glass with her singing and then ask, "Is it live or is it Memorex?"

Jacobs used his Memorex investment, with the help of junk bond king Milken, to buy Telex, as well as some other businesses. According to *Business Week*, Jacobs managed to complete a trio of deals worth over $1.5 billion by putting in no more than $8 million of his own money.

Business Week reported that of the twenty-nine companies he owned, nearly half had been liquidated at a loss or were operating with sharply negative shareholder's equity. "The overriding question that emerges from an analysis of Jacobs' documented history as a corporate owner is: Where did he get the $35 million he put down in buying the Orioles for $70 million?" *Business Week* asked. The writers couldn't exactly figure that out, but after a four-month investigation, the magazine concluded, "Jacobs' acquisition of the Orioles was not only the best deal of his life, but a fluke."

Jacobs never did bother to explain where the money came from, and Major League Baseball didn't seem to care. He did provide *Business Week* with a list of character witnesses that included Boren, Senator Joseph Lieberman, and Howard Baker, always the best person to have on any Washington reference list.

If Jacobs's purchase was all right with Lucchino, baseball commissioner Bud Selig would not stand in the way. Oddly, Lucchino had little use for or patience with Jacobs, but Jacobs's willingness to stand aside from baseball-related decisions was all Lucchino really wanted from him. Just stay out of the way and do as little damage as possible.

Although Jacobs had little interest in baseball that anyone could discern, he was attracted to the idea that the owner's suite at what was then Memorial Stadium would be an attractive site in which to meet and greet. If he had one compelling interest outside of business, it was the CIA. Boren, his best friend since college days, was the longest-standing chairman of the Senate Intelligence Committee up to that point. Boren was a Skull and Bonesman at Yale, the traditional route by which well-bred, well-educated young men were directed into the national intelligence services.

Using Boren's influence as a senator, Jacobs was appointed to the federal Defense Policy Board, the General Advisory Committee on Arms Control and Disarmament, the Chief of Naval Operations Executive Panel, and the National Reconnaissance Program Task Force. After the fiasco of

Iran-Contra, Boren had Jacobs appointed to chair what became known as the Jacobs Panel, to recommend structural changes in counterintelligence at the CIA. On at least one occasion Jacobs took Lucchino along to Langley to introduce him around CIA headquarters. Jacobs's taste in reading was tilted toward long and sometimes bizarre tomes of military history.

When he and Lucchino went to lunch or dinner, Jacobs would never allow them to be seated near a lone diner, fearing that anyone eating alone was probably either overhearing or recording their conversation. For the most part, Jacobs claimed to be so worried about being spied upon, that he preferred not to go out at all, once advising Lucchino, "Dine in your office. You have more privacy."

Lucchino suspected that Jacobs was a major "bullshit artist," but he didn't know what to make of Jacobs and his high-flying spy friends any more than *Business Week* did. According to an Orioles financial official, Jacobs actually borrowed nearly his entire stake from friends at Citicorp. "Jacobs," he said, "didn't have to put up a penny."

Lucchino observed in a published oral history of the Orioles, "These were the go-go '80s, and Eli was a classic of the times. He was LBO (leveraged buyout) all the way—borrow the money and pump the revenues up to pay the debt."

For his $70 million investment, Jacobs took 87 percent of the Orioles, and he quickly began reciprocating his friends' favors. Boren's wife was put on the Orioles board of directors. Boren's top legislative aide during the Iran-Contra hearings, Sven Erik Holmes, was rehired at Williams & Connolly and quickly named to be the team's club counsel and vice president. Jacobs endlessly lobbied for Boren's Intelligence Committee protégé, George Tenet, to be moved over to the CIA, an appointment Tenet received when he was named deputy director of central intelligence in July 1995. He became acting director in December 1996; confirmed as director in July 1997, he would have one of the longest tenures in that post in history, thanks in part to Jacobs's high-level lobbying on his behalf. Although Tenet originally was named to the CIA post in the Clinton administration, Jacobs intervened on his behalf with President George W. Bush, who kept him on. Jacobs's ownership of the Orioles had gotten him well acquainted with Bush, who had been an executive with another American League baseball team, the Texas Rangers. An article in the *Wall Street Journal* at the time described how he chose former Vice President Dan

Quayle to throw out the first ball for the 1991 season and cited Jacobs's "endless courting" of former defense secretary Dick Cheney.

Jacobs also availed himself of the social company of the best-looking and smartest female lawyer at the firm, Nicole Seligman. Although he was twenty years her senior, they openly became a couple and were the occasional subject of gossip columns, though not usually in the *Washington Post*, whose chief gossip writer, Lois Romano, had married Sven Holmes. The romance was inexplicable to the male partners, many of whom drooled over Seligman and despised Jacobs. "When you ever figure that one out, you tell me," one partner growled, a sentiment echoed by others with similar words.

In dire financial trouble almost from the moment he arrived in Baltimore, Jacobs began to try to resell the team nearly as quickly as he had bought it. Within two years of his original purchase, the supposed billionaire Jacobs would default on the mortgage payments on his $2.25 million Baltimore-area home, which sold at auction for $ 1.4 million.

The other principal partners in the Orioles purchase were Sargent Shriver, a prominent partner in the firm of Fried, Frank, Harris, Shriver & Jacobson and the Democratic Party's vice-presidential nominee in 1972, and Shriver's son Bobby. Bobby's mother was Eunice Shriver, President Kennedy's sister. His sister was Maria Shriver, whom Lucchino dated. Eunice Shriver was said to pray every night that Larry and Maria would get married, but his attentions only made Arnold Schwarzenegger more determined to have Maria for himself. Arnold won the scrum, and he and Larry have avoided each other ever after.

Lucchino was in effect both the team's active owner and its general manager and negotiator-in-chief. His mediation skills would be tested by umpiring disputes between Jacobs and the two Shrivers, who didn't get along. Lucchino would claim that "I didn't know Jacobs from the man in the moon before he bought the Orioles. It looked like Sarge was going to be active and Eli was going to be the passive investor. That didn't prove to be the case. I was the president and the CEO, but the budgets had to be determined with Eli and Sarge. Then they had a falling-out and essentially only communicated through me. It was a hard and anxious time for all of us."

The friction between the two principal owners worked to Lucchino's strategic advantage. Both were rather caught up in the prestige that came with owning a Major League Baseball club, and both were happy to leave the actual operation of the team to Larry, who wanted to continue to run a baseball club more than anything. He was living out a dream. In fact, more than a dream. In the last six years that he was associated with the team, the Orioles appreciated in value by five times, and Williams's estate had awarded him a little less than 10 percent of the team to compensate him for the "sweat equity" he had put into it. The Orioles, after all, had been technically owned by Williams, not by the law firm. The pint-sized point guard from Squirrel Hill in Pittsburgh, who had roamed the world as a "generalist," was suddenly a multimillionaire, his equity stake in the team now worth over $7 million. "It was ironic," observed one of his best friends. "If Ed had lived, Larry would not have been a rich man."

Lucchino's good fortune was not lost on the partners. Sullivan complained to friends, "Maybe I should have been talking about sports at our lunches. Then I wouldn't be the one tethered to the billable hour."

On April 6, 1992, Lucchino finally opened Oriole Park at Camden Yards, a spanking new ballpark that accomplished every goal Lucchino had mapped out for it. It was a true baseball marvel, incorporating an old warehouse as a backdrop in right field. Professional architects had recommended the old structure be torn down; Lucchino was the one with the vision to see how it could be incorporated into the classic old-time design. Between the outfield and the building was Eutaw Street, which became the home of Oriole slugger Boog Powell's iconic barbecue pit and other bustling eateries. Babe Ruth's actual birthplace was just around the corner. Over the years as home runs sailed over the right field fence and onto the pavement, the exact location of each gargantuan hit was marked with a little baseball insignia on the pavement, showing where it landed and who hit it. One of the Oriole summer interns who kept track of the home run landings in that first season at the new park was an enthusiastic Yale freshman, Theo Epstein.

Camden Yards would become the most important single factor in the resurrection of a game that had almost been destroyed by the bad architecture of multiuse parks built in the 1970s and 1980s. Attendance was down, interest in the game was lessening, and labor troubles had alienated fans. Baseball wasn't fun anymore, and there was even talk of contracting to fewer teams. Then Camden Yards reversed the downtrend. Before long copycat parks would appear in San Francisco, Houston, and Chicago, among a total of sixteen teams that would commission "Lucchino"-type ballparks. Just seven years after Dr. Nadler had saved Larry, Larry, in a very tangible way, had arguably saved baseball.

Williams & Connolly now had yet another distinctive cachet. It was customary during the summers for big law firms to bestow sports and theater tickets on their summer associates. Industry publications even ranked which firms offered the best and most extravagant perks to their would-be hires. With 250 lawyers on its staff by 1992, Williams & Connolly could do more than just buy tickets; the eighty-some partners virtually had their own team. No industry competitor for top law school talent could top that claim.

As things turned out, the opening of Camden Yards in the spring of 1992 was only the first gleam of the notoriety that was about to shine on the partners who had so long lived in Williams's shadow.

20.

THE *ENQUIRER* MEETS THE RENAISSANCE

———■———

In the elections of 1980, 1984, and 1988, Robert Barnett had a mixed record. Impersonating George H. W. Bush, he had a great winning percentage. Unfortunately, what he was really trying to do was beat George Bush, and Barnett's favored candidates had not yet tasted electoral victory. However, 1992 promised to be different. If Brendan Sullivan was replicating the persona of Edward Bennett Williams as a lawyer, and if Lucchino had become Williams the sports figure, Barnett was on his way to filling in the political side of Williams, the kingmaker who had once been the treasurer and attorney of the Democratic National Committee.

In the early 1980s, Philip Lader, a Charleston, South Carolina, lawyer, and his wife, Linda, a Yale Divinity School graduate, created an event called Renaissance Weekend. Held in Hilton Head, South Carolina, after Christmas, it was billed as a time to reflect on the issues of the day. The Laders were politically connected in the South, and among their friends who participated in Renaissance Weekends was Richard Riley, the progressive governor of South Carolina. In 1984, Riley suggested that the Laders invite the new governor of Arkansas and his dynamic lawyer wife. They came, and became fixtures at the event. The arrival of the Clintons in turn sparked interest in the event from journalists, who already had their eye on Bill Clinton as a forty-one-year-old up-and-comer in the Democratic Party.

For Bob Barnett and his increasingly prominent CBS correspondent wife, Rita Braver, Renaissance Weekend became an important part of their year. It gave Braver an opportunity to hobnob with sources for her CBS News shows, while Barnett could size up future authors and clients.

From the various connections and friendships that existed with his partners, Barnett and Hillary Clinton were already well acquainted. They found additional common ground in their backgrounds as natives of Illinois. As Bill Clinton planned to run for the presidency against incumbent George H. W. Bush in 1992, he, too, was well aware of Barnett's remarkable talent for impersonation.

As the 1992 election rolled around, Barnett was once more called on to participate in the debate preparation. That year, however, there was a twist on the quadrennial plot line: Clinton won the election. It was the first time since Barnett had started "being" a Bush that the real Bush had actually lost.

Philip Lader was named administrator of the Small Business Administration and given a seat in the administration's cabinet meetings. Other participants in Renaissance Weekends got juicy federal jobs, too. Richard Riley became the secretary of education and would be considered years later one of the best, if not the best, leader that relatively new cabinet department has ever had.

Barnett was certainly in line for some role in the Clinton government, but he had no interest in either a cabinet post or an ambassadorship. He was too important where he was. Instead, Hillary selected him to be the Clinton family's personal attorney as they entered the White House.

The year that Bill Clinton was elected president was a heady time for the law firm. David Kendall and partner Paul Wolff were busy defending the *National Enquirer* in a suit brought by entertainer Carol Burnett. Before Williams & Connolly got involved, Burnett had won $1.6 million from the *National Enquirer* for printing a story about her getting drunk at Rive Gauche, an upscale French restaurant in Washington. Up to that point it was the biggest libel judgment that the *Enquirer* had ever lost, and it soured the paper's owner, Generoso Pope, on Rogers & Wells, the attorneys he blamed for blowing the case. Pope, who for a while worked at the CIA, was the godson of mobster Frank Costello, whom Williams had once saved from a federal deportation proceeding. Costello recommended Williams to Pope. Pope was pleased to learn that Williams could handle an appeal as well as jury trial work and asked him to get involved in the case. By the time Williams & Connolly was finished Carol Burnett was happy to accept $200,000 and walk away. She quickly realized that being opposed by staid Rogers & Wells was light-years different from taking on a band of gladiators who seemed to miss nothing and were not afraid to use anything to make her stand down. Pope was thrilled with the result, and for the next twenty years Williams & Connolly would be the principal attorneys behind the tabloid, approving what it wrote prepublication and defending it postpublication.

The *Enquirer's* principal litigator at the firm, Wolff, had long been one of Williams & Connolly's most iconoclastic attorneys. Like many of his partners, the elfin Kansas City native had a personality that probably wouldn't have been appreciated at stodgy rivals like Covington & Burling. His desk was made from a ninety-year-old industrial ironing board that was bolted to the floor. The base of the board was emblazoned with the words TROY LAUNDRY MACHINE CO. Elsewhere in the office sat a toy wooden train and a gumball machine filled with salted peanuts.

Wolff assigned David Kendall to be in charge of prepublication "content review." Almost every week, Kendall would fly to Lantana, Florida, to go over the following week's issues of the *Enquirer,* the *Examiner,* the *Globe,* and even the *Weekly World News,* all part of Pope's tabloid empire.

Kendall enjoyed the same job for the *Washington Post,* and he also vetted several magazines that were owned by a German publishing company client. In addition to merely representing the *Post,* Williams & Connolly had hired Bill Graham, Katharine's son, as an associate. Later the firm would also hire Mrs. Graham's granddaughter, Katharine Weymouth.

Weymouth, a Stanford Law grad, was hired by Barnett as an associate in 1993. Three years later the *Washington Post* called the head of the department that represented the *Post* and asked if anybody wanted to come across the street for a temporary assignment in the client's offices. Weymouth volunteered, later telling a Washington writer, "I thought this might be the perfect way to dip my toe in and not make a commitment." She never went back to Williams & Connolly.

The reading of the various papers before publication often took the time of as many as seven Williams & Connolly lawyers, including David Kendall and Jeffrey Kindler, but they didn't always catch everything. Even Wolff had trouble justifying a story in the *Enquirer* that claimed Elizabeth Taylor's face was ravaged by lupus and that she had been drinking in the hospital while recovering from pneumonia. Taylor sued, asking for $20 million in damages. Wolff had to give up the fight on that one, and Liz ended up settling for a large sum. Years later he would still refer to it as the *Enquirer's* "biggest blunder."

Wolff ended up getting the last word, though. Liz's husband, Larry

Fortensky, thought they had the paper on the run, and he sued the *Enquirer* for a second time over a story claiming that he had beaten up a neighbor. Wolff took the position that the *Enquirer* account was correct. Wolff and Kendall countersued and won several hundred thousand dollars in damages against them. It was the first time a court had ever awarded money *to* the *Enquirer* in a libel case.

He also settled a suit for Roseanne Barr and Tom Arnold, after it turned out a love letter published in the tabloid hadn't been discarded and found, as the *Enquirer* claimed, but rather stolen from Tom's briefcase. Editor Iain Calder issued a rare apology, "We do sympathize with the distress felt by Roseanne and Tom at the loss of the letter and are sorry they were upset by this incident."

In the middle of these battles on behalf of the *Enquirer* was Kendall, the eggheaded but mischievous leader of the firm, a guy who liked to read *Wuthering Heights* for the fun of it. Yet his utter lack of pretension was obvious when he talked about the *Enquirer*. "The *Enquirer* is a very interesting story," he would say. "It's not what people imagine it to be. The people who talk about it haven't read it very much. It has done a lot of incredibly good journalistic work." In his office, Kendall maintained bound volumes not just of the *Enquirer* but of Pope's wackier sister paper, the *Weekly World News*, and when it came to the hard calls on stories, it was Kendall to whom chief editor Iain Calder would look. When the publication itself had doubts about running a story on whether Liberace had AIDS, it was Kendall who made the final decision to go with the story. When Eddie Murphy threatened to sue over an *Enquirer* claim that he had been arrested on May 2, 1997, for meeting a transvestite prostitute lover early in the morning, Wolff and Kendall were dubious about Murphy's claim that he had just gone out to get a newspaper—not a prostitute—that morning. The Williams & Connolly team flew to Los Angeles, drove to Murphy's house, and proceeded to count each and every *Los Angeles Times* newspaper box between his home and the place where he had been seen by the *Enquirer* spy. The research made it highly dubious that Murphy would have gone there to buy a newspaper, and the $5 million suit not only disappeared, Murphy ended up reimbursing the *Enquirer* for its fees.

New attorneys at the firm delighted in the *Enquirer* work, as it gave them surprising freedom to make decisions, as well as the opportunity to meet famous people.

Jeffrey Kindler was the son of a Montclair, New Jersey, doctor, more interested in journalism than in medicine. As an undergraduate, he became the editor of the *Tufts Observer*. Kindler then attended Harvard Law School and first came to Washington as a law clerk for Circuit Court of Appeals Judge David Bazelon, one of the most highly sought-after clerkships in the country. After a clerkship with Justice Brennan on the Supreme Court, Kindler followed a fellow Bazelon clerk, Gerson Zweifach, to Williams & Connolly. Kindler was hired and in his first few weeks on the job was instructed to fly to the home office of the *National Enquirer* and do copy review for the newspaper.

Just as Lucchino's basketball past had singled him out to be the chief negotiator for the Washington Redskins and the Orioles, Kindler's college newspaper editorship had marked him as an instant expert in libel law. Kindler, however, was not so confident that he really knew anything about the fine points of libel, so on the way to the airport he purchased a "hornbook," a lawyer's basic primer on a subject, then flew to Florida.

The offices of the *Enquirer* were long and open, and the whole place gave off the atmosphere of the old movie about Chicago newspapering, *The Front Page*. Kindler strolled the length of the building to a glass-enclosed booth, where a Post-it note simply read LAWYER. Kindler took the hot seat, and a parade of writers and editors marched up to have him read their stories and green-light them for publication. Kindler still had no idea what he was doing when an editor came up in a hurry and breathlessly explained to him that they had a stringer in Los Angeles who had just spotted Elizabeth Taylor in a spa. He wanted to know if it was OK for her to take a picture of the star.

Kindler begged for a few moments to ponder this dilemma but was heatedly informed that the photographer was standing there waiting to hear from him and that they needed an answer. Kindler again asked for and this time received a couple of minutes to make a decision. He thumbed through the thin book on libel law that he had purchased in the airport and spotted a reference to invasion of privacy. Still not sure, he called his wife, Sharon Sullivan, who was an associate editor at *U.S. News & World Report*. She replied that if she were in a spa and somebody tried to take her picture, she would definitely consider that an invasion of privacy. While Kindler pondered in the glass-enclosed "office," the *National Enquirer* editors gathered in a circle outside. "They were all watching me," said Kindler.

Finally, on the authority of his wife, Kindler emerged and proclaimed that invasion of privacy was his decision and that if they ran the picture they would be liable for a suit. The photo, if ever taken, never ran in the paper. Later, Kindler was sent to Palm Springs to defend a suit filed by Frank Sinatra. The crooner objected to an article that claimed he was obsessed about growing old and had gone to a spa to have "youthful regeneration" cells implanted in his buttocks that would make him younger. The head-line of the story, which Kendall personally approved, was "Sinatra Injected with Youth Serum—He's Secretly Treated with Sheep Cells at Swiss Clinic."

Kindler took Sinatra's deposition. "Let's put it this way," Kindler said. "He wasn't singing 'My Way.'"

Sinatra's suit against the *Enquirer* was eventually dropped, though he did win $450,000 from the clinic for violating his privacy by talking to the *Enquirer*. Sinatra's case, though, was not the end of Kindler's seeming des-tiny to connect to fatty cells. After leaving Williams & Connolly, he would become the general counsel of McDonald's. Then, in 2002, he became the general counsel of Pfizer, the manufacturer of the anticholesterol medica-tion Lipitor. In 2006 he was elevated to chairman and CEO. Kindler's seemingly chaotic journey from fat cells to fatty fast-food hamburgers to Lipitor proves that there is some order in the worlds of law and business after all.

Two other partners, Gerald Feffer and James Bruton, were hired by Leona Helmsley to defend her against tax charges brought by the IRS. The IRS maintained she owed over a million dollars after claiming $4 million in home improvements as a business expense. Bruton, with typical Williams & Conolly chutzpah, countered that she was owed a $681,000 refund. In the most memorable line from the trial, Feffer absorbed days of testimony about what a horrible person Mrs. Helmsley was. "I do not be-lieve Mrs. Helmsley is charged in this indictment with being a bitch," her lawyer countered.

Unfortunately Mrs. Helmsley was convicted of thirty-three tax evasion and fraud counts on August 30, 1989, and ended up going to prison in 1992 for seventeen months, being released in October 1993. After she passed away at the age of eighty-seven, she left a large part of her fortune to Trouble, her white Maltese bitch.

Greg Craig had returned to the firm from his five-year stint with Senator Kennedy in 1988. His work for Kennedy had largely been centered on international affairs and foreign policy, especially with regard to issues in Latin America. Now back in private practice, he became a board member and influential player for the Carnegie Endowment for International Peace, as well as the Human Rights Law Group. After the arrest of Manuel Noriega, Craig became the lead attorney in a $6 billion lawsuit seeking damages for Panamanians allegedly oppressed by the drug-selling dictator. Between Nicole Seligman, who had the JFK side of the family wired, and Craig, who by now had the total trust of Ted Kennedy, Williams & Connolly had the powerful Kennedy clan covered. Just as Barnett had become Mondale's guy in Washington over the years, Craig had the distinction of having become Ted's main Washington man. In his work for Senator Kennedy he often spearheaded Kennedy's human-rights-oriented foreign policy stances. The Kennedys provided more than the prestige and influence that came from the connection; they also generated a lot of fees from the nonstop hijinks of their family members, from the senator on down to the arrest-prone cousins. The best illustration of the point came in 1991 when Senator Kennedy called Craig to help in the trial of his nephew William Kennedy Smith, the son of his sister Jean Kennedy Smith.

"Willie" Smith had been accused of an inebriated rape on a beach outside the Kennedy house in Palm Beach, Florida. Smith had hired the noted Miami criminal defense attorney Roy Black to defend him, but Senator Kennedy was going to be called as a witness, and he asked Craig to help prepare him for his testimony. Craig provided Kennedy with a tear-jerking soliloquy about Smith's father, Steven Smith, who had died shortly before the case was brought. "We lost a brother in the war, and when Jean married Steven, we had another brother," Kennedy said. "When he died something left all of us." There wasn't a dry eye in the courtroom.

Craig left the courtroom performance to Black, the forty-six-year-old maestro of Miami trial work and a familiar courtroom presence from his extensive television work during the O. J. Simpson case. Still, Craig's behind-the-scenes touches were unmistakable to his colleagues watching the case on television back home. When Kennedy was asked about the times of certain events—when he and his nephew left the bar, for example—he had a good response ready. "When I am in the Senate, I have to watch time very carefully," he said. "When I am on vacation, I don't."

An especially poignant moment came when Black asked Senator

Kennedy to identify Bill Barry, who had been head of security when his brother Robert Kennedy was slain in 1968 and who had been in Palm Beach at the time of the alleged rape. The illustrious bodyguard had been accused by the prosecution of misleading investigators in the early stages of the rape inquest. Kennedy, well prepared for the question, responded with a dramatic retelling of how his brother had been assassinated in 1968, and how it was Barry who had wrested the murder weapon away from assassin Sirhan Sirhan. By the time Senator Kennedy's testimony was over, both he and the jury were once again sharing tears.

Kennedy was judged to have done a good job, and though he was called as a prosecution witness against his nephew, he ended up helping the defense enormously. The most damaging revelation, however, was when one of the other prosecution witnesses, Anne Mercer, revealed on the witness stand that she had been paid $40,000 for an interview on a tabloid television show, *A Current Affair*. Mercer had driven the alleged rape victim home from the Kennedy mansion that night. However, her credibility in claiming that the victim told her of the rape was destroyed after she was exposed by Black and Craig as someone who was willing to sell her—and her friend's—story for money.

When the not-guilty verdict was announced after seventy-two stressful hours of deliberation, Black effusively thanked the show's producer, Steve Dunleavy. Of course, there was no other firm in the country that understood the press as well as Williams & Connolly. Could they possibly have used their tabloid connections to sabotage the prosecution case? There was never any suggestion or evidence that they did, but the reputation of Williams & Connolly was such that no one would have put it past them.

Three years later, William Kennedy Smith decked a bar bouncer in Clarendon, Virginia. Craig negotiated a deal that got Smith unsupervised probation and a hundred hours of community service. He then settled a $500,000 civil lawsuit brought against Smith by the bouncer. The Kennedys were the gift that kept on giving. As Craig himself observed about his legal work on a different occasion, "Once you start working for Ted Kennedy, you do it for life."

A little more than two years after Williams's death, the firm announced it would jump the pay of starting associates to more than $70,000 a year, then the highest pay in the city for incoming new lawyers—but the executive committee also reiterated its policy that it would only grow its own attorneys. All around them firms were leaping at lateral partners and raid-ing competitors for obscene sums. The new guard of Sullivan, Kendall, and Barnett pledged not to play that game. They had been brought up through a farm system. Like the Oriole stars in the team's heyday, Cal Ripken Jr., Brooks Robinson, and Jim Palmer, the all-stars of Williams & Connolly did not play for other teams. Legal stars came up through the organization, and anyone who had played for another firm, and especially for the government, was very suspect.

The transition from the Republican administration to the Democratic Clinton one provided Barnett with almost unparalleled opportunities. Through Rita's professional friends and colleagues, he already built a small cottage practice negotiating contracts for local and national television cor-respondents and anchors. He had been an enormous help to the ambitious wife of one of his own partners, Jay Monahan, who wanted to leap from local news to a national stage. Her name was Katie Couric. She had met Monahan at a Williams & Connolly party, and he was listening when she loudly asked several young men what they did for a living. After they re-plied, "We're lawyers," Katie, dressed in a tight black miniskirt, responded by sticking her finger down her throat in a mock gag. She then turned to the twenty-four-year-old Washington & Lee University grad. "What do you do?" she asked. "I'm a painter," Monahan replied. She thought that was cute, and Jay and Katie were engaged ten months later in 1989.

Barnett also had Andrea Mitchell, George Will, and Sam Donaldson in the fold. Barnett's role in their careers was not that of the typical "agent" who simply negotiated money issues and then disappeared until the con-tract had expired. Barnett liked to think on a more expansive scale. In Andrea Mitchell's case, she has revealed, Barnett instructed NBC how to define and protect her foreign affairs beat when she moved from the White House to the State Department. He was so successful on Mitch-ell's behalf that she has almost become a one-person band in the ever-dwindling news-correspondent role, part anchor, frequent guest on *Meet the Press* and *Morning Joe*, and dean of the traveling press corps when the president goes on foreign trips. Neither Mitchell nor most of Barnett's other clients have to worry very much about expenses. Television news ex-ecutives, keenly aware of whom Barnett represents and whom he doesn't, admit they don't dare nickel-and-dime his clients. As one admits, "If he says his anchor needs Perrier on a cross-country flight, who are we to argue?"

The media practice of the firm had handled libel defense work for ABC. Another client, in a massive price-fixing case, was the agricultural and chemical giant Archer Daniels Midland. On virtually any Sunday morning, Barnett would awake at a fairly civilized hour, collect his newspapers, and begin reading while working out on his exercise bicycle. An accomplished multitasker, Barnett would glance up at Washington's ABC affiliate where an entire panel of his clients on the David Brinkley Sunday news show were appearing on a network represented corporately by his firm and on a program that was sponsored each and every week by client ADM, "the Supermarket to the World," as its ads used to say. Barnett rarely headed to the real supermarket. With Braver spending nearly half her professional career on the road, he had sketched out a particular order for his meals: Sushi Ko on Monday, Chicken Out on Tuesday, Cafe Divan on Wednesday, and the Chinese restaurant City Lights on Thursday. "Hopefully, Rita is back by Friday," he would say.

Barnett claimed to look on this part of his law practice as mostly "favors to friends." Denying that this work generated all that much income, he says that the contracts he negotiated for his clients usually lasted three or four years, so it wasn't like those clients provided constant work. Barnett would joke that he wasn't quitting his day job, which was often handling the extensive litigation portfolio of JM Family Enterprises. The company was the largest distributor of Toyotas in the entire country and, better yet, had a contentious, litigious relationship with the dozens of automobile dealerships that it supplied. Barnett also did a lot of work for McDonald's and some other business clients he had gathered from his connections to Chicago and the Midwest. As with his colleagues, it was hard to figure out exactly what true litigation work Barnett was doing, since he didn't publicize his cases or clients. In his case, though, even his partners had trouble figuring him out. One pointed out that Barnett through his prominent media connections was excellent at bringing in business but, once he did, usually had to find another lawyer in the firm to handle courtroom chores. Barnett defined the term "rainmaker," an appellation in the legal world for lawyers who are expert at attracting business rather than writing briefs or making legal arguments.

He definitely knew more about President Bush than Bush. Barnett's flawless performance was attributed by many as making the difference in the 1992 election. The *Chicago Tribune* once noted, "Barbara Bush may think she knows her husband well, but Bob Barnett, a Waukegan-born attorney, might know his mind even better."

What prompted the comments was an interview several weeks before the election between Bush and Katie Couric. Barnett watched the interview in his Washington kitchen and claimed to the *Chicago Tribune* that he answered 99 percent of Couric's questions exactly as Bush did, but much more quickly, *Jeopardy*–style quick.

January 1992 was the beginning of a watershed year in his career. Democrat Barnett suddenly became the favorite lawyer not just of Democrats but of Republicans. After negotiating a $1 million advance for the memoirs of Vice President Dan Quayle, he arranged the sale of a 284-page novel by Marilyn Quayle. Quayle was a golfing partner and friend of one of Barnett's partners, Jack Vardaman. Vardaman had been captain of the Washington and Lee University golf team before going to Harvard Law and becoming a law clerk to Justice Hugo Black, a fellow Alabamian. At one time he had seriously considered a career in professional golf. Then, while still a seventeen-year-old student, in 1957 he went to Ohio to play in the national Jaycees tournament. There was one teenaged player that caught his eye, a chubby kid from Columbus named Jack Nicklaus. Vardaman says watching Nicklaus play convinced him that he could never compete with that and would have a better chance in law school than on the PGA Tour.

He was one of several prominent Williams & Connolly partners with convenient ties to Republicans. One of the others was Terrence O'Donnell, a close friend and attorney for Dick Cheney, who was almost as powerful in Republican Party circles as Barnett was with the Democratic Party and had worked in the Nixon and then Ford White House as a young aide during Watergate.

Barnett also handled the exit from government or the publication of memoirs from former secretary of state James Baker, press secretary Marlin Fitzwater, and Lynne Cheney, the novel-writing wife of G. H. W. Bush defense secretary Dick Cheney.

After the Clinton inauguration in January 1993, Barnett was approached by the bipartisan romantic couple of Mary Matalin and James Carville. During the political campaign, Matalin had been a vociferous Bush supporter. Carville, a Louisianian, had been the "war room" mastermind of Clinton's upset of incumbent President Bush. Their bickering appearances on national morning news shows was intriguing, to say the least. How were they able to set aside their political disputes and still have a happy marriage? Surely the country would want to know.

On February 4, 1993, Barnett held an auction in his office for the proposed Carville-Matalin book, *All's Fair: Love, War, and Running for President*. No one publisher wanted to accept all the risk for this project, so Random House and Simon & Schuster agreed to split the $900,000 advance and publish the book jointly, the first time that had ever happened. Said Carville, "By the time this is over, I'll either have married her or killed her."

Having two publishers split the cost of a book of two feuding political commentators and consultants struck Barnett's fancy. "We were the Hatfields and the McCoys, published by the Capulets and the Montagues," Barnett said, laughing. Carville's prediction came true. After publication of the book, he and Matalin were married on November 25, 1993, at a hotel in New Orleans. The marriage license made their subsequent cable television and cruise ship act all the more believable.

21.

SWANK HILLARY

———■———

Contrary to the nostalgia that wrapped around the Clinton administration after eight years of George W. Bush, in reality, his presidency had begun to unravel before it even got started. Almost immediately after taking over the White House, the Clintons were in political and personal trouble. There was the needless firing of good old boy Billy Dale, who had run the White House Travel Office for years and was beloved by the members of the traveling press. Hillary Clinton claimed Dale was incompetent and disorganized. To fill his place, the Clintons found a more disorganized distant relative from Arkansas with no experience for the job. Finding someone to serve as attorney general seemed an impossibility as the Clintons blazed through a series of flawed candidates. Eventually Hillary settled on Janet Reno, a lanky alligator-wrestling former state's attorney from Miami. She took over from the acting deputy attorney general, Webb Hubbell; another inept Arkansas crony of the Clintons, he had been a law partner of Hillary's in the Rose Law Firm in Little Rock. Then came the news on July 20, 1993, that another Arkansas member of the administration, Vincent Foster, had killed himself at a scenic Virginia overlook by the Potomac River. No one would ever know why Foster committed suicide, but in her memoirs, Mrs. Clinton would claim it was because he was stung by criticism of his abilities and job performance in the *Wall Street Journal*. If that was the criterion for a decision about whether to end your life, it's amazing Washington has any population whatsoever, but no one has ever come up with a better explanation.

Two days after Foster's suicide, White House counsel Bernard Nussbaum went into Foster's office to search for a suicide note. The note was not immediately found, but Nussbaum did collect Foster's files on the Clintons' personal businesses and investments, and within a week they were designated to be given to Bob Barnett. Now that Foster was dead,

Barnett seemed to be number one in the hierarchy of first-lady lawyers. Nussbaum had been a partner at Wachtell Lipton, the same firm where Nicole Seligman's sister, Stephanie, worked. His top assistant at the White House was a lawyer named Joel Klein, who was in the same Washington book club as Kendall.

After less than eighteen months in office, the Clintons were being ravaged by events that they seemed unable to control. Their initiation into what became the blood sport of Washington was undoubtedly the most brutal in American presidential history, if one excepts the presidency of William Henry Harrison, who spent his thirty-two days in office bedridden with pneumonia, and then died. As Mrs. Clinton summed it up in her memoir, "My father and close friend dead; Vince's wife, children, family, and friends devastated; my mother-in-law dying; the faltering missteps of a new administration being literally turned into federal cases."

The job of reporting on all this for the then still influential *CBS Evening News with Dan Rather* fell on the network's newly appointed White House correspondent, Rita Braver. Although she was competent and likable, the manner in which Braver got her plum assignment had ruffled feathers in the world of Washington news. The job had belonged originally to the equally personable Susan Spencer, and there was a feeling that CBS brass had promoted Braver, and ditched Spencer, because of Braver's friendship with the Clintons. Braver had become a Renaissance Weekend regular, and it was no secret that her husband was the Clintons' outside lawyer.

On the night of Foster's death, Nussbaum searched his associate's office, apparently looking for a suicide note, or some other document that might reveal a motive for his desperate final act. As Hillary Clinton explained the sequence of events, Nussbaum discovered that Vince had stored personal files in his office, some of them related to personal work he had done for Bill and Hillary when they were in Arkansas. Among those papers were documents that related to the Clintons' purchase of land at the Whitewater development.

She wrote, "Bernie gave these files to Maggie Williams [the first lady's chief of staff], who delivered them to the residence, and soon they were transferred to the office of Bob Barnett, our private attorney in Washington."

Hillary's published account was not entirely accurate. In reality, Barnett had come to the White House on July 27. He had opened the box of Foster's files. He had gone through the box, labeled everything, and taped the box back up. Barnett then had a firm van carry the taped box of personal Clinton files back to his office, only three blocks from the White House.

Despite the suggestion that it was the paper's own editorials that had killed Vincent Foster, the *Wall Street Journal* began homing in on the Barnett-Braver relationship. All sorts of rumors were swirling through Washington at the time. Conservative radio talk show hosts were making sexual insinuations about Hillary and Foster. One of the most popular was a rumor that they were lovers and that she had killed Foster after a Washington apartment tryst before having Secret Service agents drive his body out to be dumped by a Virginia parkway. On August 6, 1993, the *Wall Street Journal* raised new questions about the ethics of Barnett representing the first lady and the president while Braver served as the CBS White House correspondent.

"The fact that Mr. Barnett is working for the President at the same time that his journalist clients are covering the President may raise questions about potential conflicts of interest," wrote the *Journal*. How thorny was Barnett's web of conflicting interests? At the very paper that was questioning his influence, some top-level journalists were also his clients.

Two weeks later, a respected television columnist, Marvin Kitman, wrote a widely syndicated article in the Long Island newspaper *Newsday* that raised the Barnett-Braver issue again. "Every once in a while," he wrote, "there is a seeming breach in TV journalism that is so appalling it takes one's breath away. The case of CBS News correspondent Rita Braver and her husband Robert Barnett called for a giant family-sized cylinder of oxygen.

"She was appointed to be the new White House correspondent on Aug. 4, replacing Susan Spencer, who people felt was getting a raw deal," Kitman noted, adding the irony that Spencer, like CNN's Wolf Blitzer, Fox's Brit Hume, and NBC's Andrea Mitchell, was a client of Barnett's burgeoning media practice. "I don't think anyone covering the White House should be accepting invitations to dine at the White House," Kitman wrote, rather quaintly by today's standards.

It became obvious to Rita and Bob that one of them would have to yield. Journalistically speaking, Kitman had a fairly valid point. Practically, the Barnetts felt the criticisms were ridiculous, since Bob, like the rest of the crew at Williams & Connolly, hardly ever mentioned work outside of the office. Barnett liked to joke that because of their conflicting travel schedules, the chances of them actually engaging in "pillow talk" were slim.

Still, when Rita did inevitably end up getting some incredible scoop, nobody in cynical Washington would believe that her husband didn't have something to do with it. They would both be in an uncomfortable spot. Although he had only cemented a business relationship with Hillary in 1992, according to her memoir, he already had maneuvered into a situation where he would have to step aside from that plum representation. Bob was willing to yield to what for Rita was the most prestigious assignment she had ever gotten at CBS News. Barnett felt the whole thing was silly. "There would have been no conflict," he said stubbornly. "I do not discuss client matters with her, and she doesn't check her stories with me. But we did not want any appearance, and therefore we thought it best that although my law firm would continue the representation, I would not personally do so."

In that spirit, Barnett asked Hillary if she would accept the representation of David Kendall, which was more than fine with her. The shift was made with hardly any notice by the White House press. They were all either clients of Barnett's already or people who hoped they might be. Nobody had any interest in pissing off someone who stood to be so helpful later. Before he "departed," Barnett lobbied President Clinton to award his most beloved role model, John Minor Wisdom, the Presidential Medal of Freedom, a request to which Clinton quickly acceded. Acknowledging that he "recommended the judge for the job," Barnett claims it didn't really take that much convincing. "The president had been a big admirer of Wisdom's since law school," Barnett told me. "I was very proud to have played a small part in the honor—which the judge richly deserved."

Barnett then went to work on legislation that resulted in the federal courthouse in New Orleans being named after the judge. At the naming ceremony, Barnett was the person chosen to read the letter of congratulations from President Clinton.

To stem the criticism, Barnett let it be known that he was stepping aside as Hillary's direct counsel, but no one knew that Kendall had stepped into the breach. Williams & Connolly doesn't issue press releases. It was easy for Kendall since nobody in Washington knew what he looked like and he has no particularly distinctive characteristics. He looks as bland as a guy from Indiana is supposed to look.

In addition to representing the *Washington Post*, Kendall had worked on quite a few cases involving bankrupt savings and loan associations. When he accepted the mantle as the Clintons' personal lawyer, Kendall believed that the Whitewater investigation was indeed all about a savings and loan situation and the investment that the Clintons had made in the Whitewater land deal. Had the Clintons done anything to advantage the owners of Madison Savings & Loan in Arkansas because they were partners in this development project? Kendall was confident that this would be a snap, and on the scale of so-called presidential scandals, it seemed like pretty small potatoes.

Hillary was immediately impressed. Kendall embodied the Williams & Connolly ethic of complete and utter thoroughness. "Like all really good lawyers," she wrote, "David has the talent to transform seemingly random and disconnected facts into a persuasive narrative." However, she admitted, "reconstructing the story of Whitewater would test his skills."

The Vincent Foster files that had been in Barnett's keeping were moved into a safe in Kendall's office. His collection of records grew quickly. Kendall's experiences in Mississippi during the voting drive of 1964 had familiarized him with the culture of the southern rural county courthouse. Unlike many a New York City lawyer, Kendall loved flying into Arkansas and finding things in the stately courthouses that were located in the geographic center of every Deep South county seat. On many of the trips he picked Nicole Seligman to accompany him. She wasn't quite as comfortable in the Ozark wilds as Kendall but was anxious to learn her way around. One day, driving from Little Rock to Fort Smith, she insisted on stopping at an Arkansas "antler museum" and was fascinated by the elk, deer, and moose horns on display. She couldn't totally go native, though. Nicole bought a cappuccino maker at a Little Rock department store and then had it stored in a box at the warehouse where documents were being kept. On each visit, the cappuccino box was the first one that she and Kendall would request, so they would be caffeinated while delving through reams of paper. Kendall found his latte sipping partner more than "up to snuff," intellectually and culturally. She had worked for Kendall soon after arriving at Williams & Connolly as a summer intern in 1982, working on a libel case filed by former U.S. ambassador to Chile Nathaniel Davis. Davis had sued the makers of the movie *Missing* for $150 million. Kendall won the case for Universal Studios, but more importantly, Seligman's work as a young lawyer convinced him that she was "extraordinarily smart, energetic, and possessed of excellent judgment." Even more importantly, he said in his Indiana-speak, "Many brilliant lawyers have the personality of a root vegetable. She does not."

22.

THE HUSKY FOOTBALL STAR: NOT!

———■———

Neither Bill nor Hillary Clinton had ever been to their Whitewater Development property, so every week Kendall would arrive back at the White House to brief the Clintons on what he had found and how things were going. In those days the case was fun for David Kendall. He, least of all, expected Whitewater to get any more complicated, and to him it seemed fairly harmless. He remained confident that he could put the whole issue to rest quickly and with finality.

On one of his first such jaunts to the White House, Kendall went through the main gate on Pennsylvania Avenue, only to be spotted by Braver, who was hanging out outside the press area on the White House lawn. She was the one person in the White House press corps who *did* know what Kendall looked like. Rita didn't rat him out, but after that Kendall began using a back entrance to avoid being seen by anyone. He would represent Hillary for months before anyone else in the press corps noticed him. Despite the fact that he was a main lawyer for *Playboy*, the *National Enquirer*, and the *Washington Post*, Kendall, forty-eight, at the time, was as manic about anonymity as any lawyer in Washington could be. Some said he made Brendan Sullivan look like a publicity hound. Fully one year after he had taken the Clinton job, not a single White House beat reporter had any idea what he was doing.

In fact, his role in the case would not be reported in the national newspapers until the end of 1993, when he surfaced to negotiate the terms of a Justice Department subpoena for the business records of the Clintons' Whitewater real estate investments and his name had to appear on some court documents.

Now that he was out in public, the press began to pay some attention. The *Chicago Tribune* ran a profile of Kendall, which claimed he was a husky man with black hair who had been a football star at Wabash College. Kendall had sandy hair, was not particularly compact, and had definitely not played college football—but the *Tribune* got no request for a correction. Had Kendall seen the article, which he didn't, he would have been delighted. Kendall's best friends speculated that the inveterate practical jokester had probably supplied the misleading description himself. Kendall says he only vaguely remembers the interview but never read the published article.

Kendall's attitude was unusual in a city where lawyers and politicians are often injured in their race to get in front of a television camera first. In declining all requests by reporters to be interviewed on camera, Kendall repeated an aphorism he attributed to Edward Bennett Williams: "It's the spouting whale that gets harpooned first." Actually the phrase is a very old Norwegian expression, but Kendall says he first heard it from Williams.

Even when he went on a vacation to Turkey with buddy Chris Wallace, then a correspondent for ABC News, Kendall never mentioned a word about work. Wallace was only mildly miffed when months later he read about Kendall representing the Clintons in the paper with everybody else. Wallace knew as well as anyone that it would have been shocking if Kendall had said anything. Steven Umin, one of Kendall's partners, observed that even within the firm "there is no communication with them."

Kendall was accustomed to getting calls from reporters, but not as a news source. For weeks, when the phone rang with a Whitewater-related call from a *Washington Post* reporter, it would often be halfway through the conversation before Kendall realized he was talking to a working reporter and not a client. "What happened, did you get a subpoena?" he would ask, before realizing he had become a source and not just a news company lawyer.

While Kendall was immersed in learning the entire history of Whitewater, as only a Williams & Connolly attorney could, his main media client, the *Washington Post,* was busy submitting questions about the deal to the Clintons. Kendall advised Hillary not to answer the questions to his own client, arguing "that releasing documents to the press was a slippery slope." He would know.

Despite his reluctance to deal with an organization that he knew better than most, Hillary asked Kendall to advise government investigators "that we would provide them with all documents and cooperate with a grand jury investigation."

Hillary says she believed, contrary to Kendall's original advice, that the media would not continue to blast us for not turning over the documents to them, if the same papers were provided to the Department of Justice. So she wrote in her book.

Needless to say, the press attacks didn't stop. On December 18, 1993, still less than a year into their presidency, which had just started in January, Hillary was hosting a holiday reception at the White House when Kendall called, saying it was urgent.

"I've got to tell you about something very very ugly," Kendall began.

Hillary sat down and steeled herself for the news.

Kendall then told her about a story in a conservative magazine called the *American Spectator*. According to the article, Arkansas state troopers claimed that when they were members of Governor Clinton's security detail, they drove the president to trysts and procured women for him.

"Look, it's a lot of sleaze, but it's going to be out there," Kendall said. "You've got to be prepared."

"Is there anything anyone can do?" Hillary asked.

Kendall bestowed the advice by which he lived. "Stay calm and say nothing," he replied.

The following evening Hillary was hosting another Christmas party for friends and family. The troopers had been all over Fox News Channel that night repeating the details of David Brock's *American Spectator* story. Word was circulating that the *Los Angeles Times* was going to bring the story from the ideological fringe press into the more established news stream. From the moment the Clintons had arrived in Washington, it had been one disaster after another. Now this.

The genie behind the efforts of the *American Spectator* was none other than Brendan Sullivan's close friend Ted Olson. Nothing in America happens without the approval or imprimatur of an attorney, and the determined effort to drive Clinton from office was no exception. The owner of the ultraconservative magazine, Richard Mellon Scaife, was a billionaire who funded numerous right-wing think tanks and magazines, such as the Washington Legal Foundation and the Federalist Society, which were created to promote conservative legal projects. They were very much a conservative response to the surprisingly effective Ralph Nader organization

Public Citizen, which litigated actively against American business and for the consumer. After Clinton's inauguration in 1993, Scaife, who also owned a daily newspaper in Pittsburgh, vowed to use his influence and as much money as needed to drive Clinton from the White House. To provide the legal guidance on what his papers and organizations could do to destroy the Clintons, he had hired Olson, who, from his palatial office overlooking Connecticut Avenue a few floors above his favorite Morton's steakhouse, would enthusiastically oversee what the Clintons termed the "vast right-wing conspiracy."

Although he was no longer the Clintons' "official" lawyer, Bob Barnett had come to the White House as a party guest that night—he would have been in a position to be the only person to have known about Kendall's call the night before—and he could see that Hillary was not full of Christmas cheer. "Is there anything I can do to help?" Barnett asked.

Hillary said she had to decide how to respond by the next day and asked Barnett to come upstairs and consult with her and Bill about what to do.

Hillary wrote of the moment, "With his oversize glasses and mild features, Bob looks like everyone's favorite uncle. Now he was talking in a soothing voice, clearly trying to see whether after all that had happened this year, we had the strength for yet another struggle."

"I'm just so tired of this," Hillary bawled.

Barnett stared her square in the eyes and tried to snap her out of the sudden depression. "The president was elected and you've got to stay with this," he said. "For the country, for your family." Barnett continued, "However bad this seems, you've got to stick it out."

"I wanted to say, 'Bill's been elected, not me,'" Hillary wrote. "Intellectually I understood Bob was right and that I would have to summon whatever energy I had left. I was willing to try. But I just felt so tired. And at that moment, very much alone."

By the way, Hillary's comment about Barnett's glasses prompted him to ask his opticians, Page & Smith of New York, to come up with a smaller size—in fact, the smallest ones you can get in tortoiseshell. "My sight is not real bad," Barnett says."I just read a lot and have worn glasses since law school."

The clamor over Whitewater, and now the allegations of immoral conduct while Clinton was governor, had conservatives calling for yet another special prosecutor to be appointed. Nixon had one, Reagan had one.

Republicans now wanted a Democratic president to go through the same ordeal. Fair is fair, they argued. As author James Stewart would later define the political era, it was "blood sport." Republicans would say it had started with the absurd special prosecutorial witch hunt of Olson when he was a Reagan administration official. Now, they claimed, Olson was doing everything possible to get even. The era of tit-for-tat, while not new to Washington, was now in full swing.

A battle raged among Clinton's White House advisers about whether to appoint a special prosecutor or not. Oddly, at the time, the law providing for a special counsel made it the responsibility of the president about to be investigated to make the declaration. The leader of the pro-special-prosecutor forces inside the White House was George Stephanopoulos, the president's press aide. He believed that unless the charges and allegations were laid to rest, the president would never be able to do anything legislatively. Harold Ickes, one of the president's most overbearing political New Yorkers, agreed.

David Kendall did not. More than anyone else, he knew just how uncontrollable prosecutors could be. Once they got started, there was no telling where they would stop. On January 11, 1994, Kendall talked to Clinton on one line while the president was trying to expand NATO to include former members of the Warsaw Pact on another. "I don't know how much longer I can take this," the president croaked. "All they want to know is why we are ducking an independent investigation."

Hillary remembered more than Bill what it had been like when she and Lucchino had been on the side that was trying to harpoon President Nixon during Watergate. The image of seeing a president driven out of Washington was not theoretical to her. She had been there. Now, she hoped that one last plea from Kendall would turn the president away from a disastrous decision. The attorney complied, pointing out that the results of a special prosecutor's investigation might not be guided by the facts. He warned the president that public pressure might force an indictment that could crush the still nascent presidency. There was another old Chinese expression that Kendall believed to be all too profound and which he quoted often: "Where there is a will to prosecute, there will be evidence."

This was one argument Kendall lost. Led by Stephanopoulos, the president's political advisers urged him to go the independent counsel route and put all these "baseless" allegations behind him. Otherwise, Stephanopoulos

believed, absurd rumors of marital infidelity would dog Clinton throughout his presidency.

Surrounded by other political advisers who were sure an independent
counsel would simply make some noise and then go away, Clinton agreed
to make the request. It fell on Nussbaum and Klein to write the letter to
Attorney General Janet Reno asking that a special prosecutor be named.
A few days later Reno announced the appointment of Robert Fiske, a well-
respected, mostly nonpartisan sixty-three-year-old attorney at the New
York City law firm Davis Polk & Wardwell, to take the job.

The appointment of the independent counsel did not have the effect
that Bill Clinton hoped. Fiske's first responsibility was to lay to rest the rumors that Vince Foster's death was anything but an accident and that Rose
firm billing records had been altered or destroyed. This required that Fiske
investigate Bill's friends and Hillary's former law partners. Less than two
months later, Webb Hubbell abruptly resigned from his position as deputy attorney general at the Department of Justice. Hubbell met with
Mrs. Clinton at the White House and told her there was a misunder-
standing about his law firm's billing policies but promised that it would get
cleared up. President Clinton asked Hubbell if there was anything to rumors and allegations that he stole from his partners and clients. Hubbell
responded by lying to his friend's face, as he later admitted in his own
memoir, *Friends in High Places*. The Rose Law Firm referred the matter to
the Arkansas State Bar Association, and the evidence quickly showed that
Hubbell was a cheat and a liar. Still, to Hillary, Hubbell seemed like yet
another victim in the seemingly endless line of friends who were either
dying or having their reputations destroyed.

Arthur Liman, who had been so unctuously self-righteous about alleged
political crimes during Iran-Contra, was anxious to absolve Hubbell. He
sent the corrupt lawyer a note reminding him of Edward Bennett Williams's
famous aphorism, although speeded up from when Williams had mentioned his favorite expression to Kendall. "Washington is like Salem," Liman scrawled. "A new witch is created and burned each week."

On his last day of work at the Justice Department, the disgraced Hubbell received what he termed "a standing ovation" from employees who
were gathered in the Justice Department auditorium. "I was incredibly
touched by this show of support," Hubbell wrote. "A year before, I had come
into these people's lives as Bill Clinton's crony. Over that year I had gained

their respect, just as they had gained mine. They didn't care what problems I had back in Arkansas—I had become one of their own, and they knew that at my core, I was a good man."

Richard Nixon couldn't have said it better about Spiro Agnew. You would like to think the cheering was because a crook was leaving the Justice Department, but Hubbell probably heard it right. In Washington, scoundrels are much more admired than honest people.

There were tangible effects as well. Most of the members of the White House staff were receiving requests and subpoenas from the prosecutors. Legal bills in Washington could run up to $750 an hour in those days. Hillary felt responsible for the deluge of legal and personal misery that she, her husband, and their clueless home-state cronies had brought to the White House.

During that time, Kendall increasingly became her main source of comfort and support. She considered him a "godsend."

From the beginning of the case, Kendall advised Hillary not to read newspaper articles and not to watch television reports about the investigation or any of the related scandals. Although she did read an edited and expurgated daily "press summary," Kendall warned her "not to dwell on it."

"That's my job," he told her. "One of the reasons you hire lawyers is to have them worry for you." One of Ed Williams's favorite aphorisms had been "If one of my lawyers isn't worried, then I am worried."

Hillary's worries had cause to escalate. At a February conference of anti-Clinton obsessives a former state of Arkansas employee named Paula Jones came forward to say she was one of the women whom the troopers had spirited up to a liaison with Governor Clinton. On May 6, 1994, she filed suit alleging sexual harassment and asking for $700,000 in damages.

The prospect of a lawsuit that would carry over to the 1995–96 reelection cycle was worrisome, and White House political operatives wanted an attorney who would do a better job than the press-averse Kendall of taking their case to the public, especially the Sunday morning network talk shows. Eventually the White House turned to Robert S. Bennett, a former Washington, D.C., prosecutor, who had gotten legal notoriety as the pardon attorney for former Reagan defense secretary Caspar "Cap" Weinberger, the cabinet officer who had encouraged President Reagan to label the Soviets "the evil empire." Weinberger had been indicted in the Iran-Contra scandal for perjury and obstruction of justice after special prosecutor Lawrence Walsh discovered he had hidden some 1,700 notebooks that might have linked Reagan to the Iran-Contra conspiracy.

Before he could even be tried, however, President Reagan let Weinberger off with a full pardon. The pardon-before-even-a-trial ploy enhanced Bennett's reputation as the guy you call to kill an indictment or potentially devastating trial before it happens.

Sure enough, as Bennett would later acknowledge, his mandate was not to win the Paula Jones case but to make sure it didn't explode on the president prior to the 1996 election.

23.

THE FABULOUS BENNETT BROTHERS

———————■———————

Over time, as so often happens in law, Kendall's greatest legal opponent would not be Kenneth Starr or the special prosecutors but Bennett, who to the outside world was his co-counsel. Those on the inside quickly recognized that their simmering feud represented a vivid example of the internal feuds that continued to jolt the White House and divide it into warring camps.

Robert S. Bennett hailed from an era in Washington when routine criminal defense work was largely in the hands of a cadre of former prosecutors, mostly former deputy U.S. attorneys. His younger brother, the conservative radio commentator and author William Bennett, had served as secretary of education in the Reagan administration. President Bush in 1988 named him the federal drug czar. Bob and Bill are frequently mistaken for each other. Bob, a Democrat, often has people come up to him in airports asking how he can stand that horrible liberal brother of his. "I am the horrible liberal brother," Bob answers. Bill has to endure not only being mistaken for his liberal brother but also being frequently accosted by people who think he is Bill Parcells, the famous football coach who is his look-alike. In any event, Bill Bennett, the younger, conservative brother, is a Williams & Connolly client. His *Book of Virtues*, which sold 2.6 million copies, was represented by Bob Barnett, and at the time of its publication he was called Barnett's "most successful author" by several trade publications. Bennett was quite an expert on virtue—from both sides. After the book's incredible success, papers revealed in 2003 that he was highly attracted to high-denomination slot machines and had poured a considerable amount of the riches Barnett had gotten for him—$8 million, according to undenied published reports—right into the profit column for the Bellagio casino on the Las Vegas Strip. Bennett, who is also a Harvard Law grad, defended his "hobby" by saying he had made so much money on his books on moralizing that he had plenty of extra cash to gamble with. "*I'm* not playing with the milk money," Bill haughtily told reporters, to explain the seeming contradiction.

Bob Bennett's principal partner through the years has been Carl Rauh, whose father was the very well known cofounder of the liberal interest group Americans for Democratic Action, Joseph L. Rauh. It would have been very difficult for Bennett to be as conservative as his brother, and still be as close to Rauh as he has been for forty years, since they were both assistant U.S. attorneys.

When Bob was still practicing in his own Washington criminal defense boutique, he was an extremely popular and admired figure. Bennett worked hard, didn't care how he looked, and by all accounts was a terrific defense lawyer, just as he had been a terrific prosecutor. Bennett likes to emphasize his Brooklyn background and his record as an amateur fighter. That's the kind of personality he generated as a lawyer, the tough fighter you didn't want to get in with between the ropes. As he would later write, "I have often felt that being born in Brooklyn and having a few hundred street fights under my belt as a young man was better preparation for practicing law here than receiving law degrees from both Georgetown and Harvard."

Bennett's hall of fame moment in the courtroom had occurred in 1970 when he was prosecuting the accused murderer of a "Good Samaritan" who had offered to give the defendant a ride home and was then killed. At one point in the trial, Bennett picked up a copy of the Bible and began reading passages from the New Testament about the Good Samaritan. His opposing counsel objected, claiming that the Bible had not been admitted into evidence. The judge ruled that Bennett could use biblical expressions, but he could not read from the Bible itself. Bennett closed the Bible, set it on the table, and proceeded to recite the verses word for word by heart. That was the stuff that makes legal legends.

After three years in the U.S. attorney's office in Washington, Bennett traveled the well-trodden young-lawyer road to what he hoped was a career at Hogan & Hartson, but his freewheeling, disorganized, disheveled personality did not transfer to a fancy corporate law practice. Opposing lawyers claimed that being in a case with Bennett was actually like being in a clinch with an overweight, sweaty boxer. Bennett kept a portrait of Muhammad Ali on his wall, and one of his favorite books was David

Remnick's *King of the World: Muhammad Ali and the Rise of an American Hero.*

One colleague described his style by saying, "When he got emphatic, he took off his glasses and slammed them down on the table. When he reached over to pick up his glasses, he knocked over his trial materials. The amazing thing was that while all this was going on, he was concentrating so intently on his argument that never once did he miss a beat in what he was saying."

"Let's just say, he was a free spirit and we were a more conventional firm," said a Hogan & Hartson partner. As Edward Bennett Williams had learned decades earlier, Hogan's firm was no place for rebels.

After five years, it was clear that Bennett was not headed for a partnership. Compelled now to strike out on his own, he cofounded a small criminal defense firm that prospered for fifteen years, earning a reputation as one of Washington's best homegrown law firms. Bennett, an expert fly fisherman, did well enough to buy an expensive home in McLean, Virginia, and a summer cottage in Livingston, Montana. When the Reagan administration moved into Washington in 1980, they made an attempt to root out corruption in defense contracting. It was a trade-off: They wanted the Democratic Congress to approve massive new funding for national defense projects. Part of the strategy to sell their program was to be able to claim that Reagan was eliminating fraud, waste, and abuse from the purchasing system.

Bennett was routinely hired by both Boeing and Northrop Aviation, two wealthy defense contractors, to counter government investigations of their Defense Department contracts. Unlike Sullivan, who thought like a defense attorney, Bennett had an uncanny ability to think like a prosecutor. His clients felt that those old instincts enabled him to stay one step ahead of the opposition. It was work that elevated Bennett's reputation from a guy who could just defend drunks and murderers to someone who could handle sophisticated and complex cases for Fortune 500 companies. It also didn't hurt that Bennett played in a heralded monthly poker game with Supreme Court Justices William Rehnquist and Antonin Scalia, as well as the frustrated wannabe justice Robert Bork.

Sometimes his defense strategies seemed almost corny for a supposedly tough street fighter from Brooklyn. Once, defending a contractor against charges of defrauding the U.S. Postal Service, Bennett brought his daughter's English composition book into the courtroom to impeach a government witness who had put a deposition statement in quotes, then on the stand claimed he hadn't said those exact words, he was just paraphrasing. Bennett used the elementary school grammar book to give a lesson on what quote marks mean, adding, "I know my daughter's going to flunk English now, because I need her book for this trial." Bennett claimed that in every trial, he worked in some reference to his three daughters. "It had a real impact," said a courtroom observer. "It isn't every day that a witness is battered on cross-examination by a sixth-grade reader."

By 1989, Bennett was producing a disproportionate share of the income at his firm, so he took fourteen lawyers to become the criminal law specialists in the Washington office of a very large corporate New York law firm called Skadden, Arps, Slate, Meagher & Flom. At the time, a number of high-profile businessmen were finding themselves in criminal issues. Skadden Arps didn't want to risk referring them to criminal attorneys at rival firms, who might "use the in" to try to steal their corporate work as well. So it seemed safer to make the investment in Bennett and his group and keep all client work, from mergers and acquisitions to SEC investigations, under one roof.

To avoid the fiasco that had occurred at Hogan & Hartson, rumpled Bennett made a serious commitment to change his image. Dapper Plato Cacheris sent him the address of his tailor and made an appointment for the notoriously wrinkled Bennett to get some new clothes. Bennett junked his rumpled look and began wearing pin-striped suits and purple ties. "It's a good color for me," he mused in one interview. Still, he was the quintessential Washingtonian lawyer, but now in a New York culture. Something just didn't seem right.

The notoriety of his brother, and being mistaken for his sibling during Bill Bennett's high-profile Bush years, had made Bob Bennett hunger for more fame than his law practice currently provided. Longtime friends noted that the personality changes were immediate and unmistakable. Oddly, in the first twenty years Bennett spent at Skadden Arps, he did not try a single case in Washington, though in 2009 he did defend motor sports attorney Alan Miller in a Miami tax fraud prosecution that involved, as the principal defendant, two-time Indianapolis 500 winner Helio Castroneves. Miller was accused of helping the driver evade $5.5 million in taxes. Bennett's return to the courtroom was a success. Both Miller and Castroneves were acquitted, and a few weeks later Helio won Indy for the third time. However, most of the actual trial presentation was done by Miami's Roy Black.

Being a former assistant U.S. attorney, he did not share Brendan Sullivan's genuine and seething hatred of other prosecutors, many of whom were Bennett's close friends and former colleagues. So while Brooklyn's Boxing Bennett looked tough, rivals were hardly as scared of him as they were of the silky Rhode Island skeet-shooting champion, whom they deemed as a genuine threat to their careers. Indeed, while Bennett had a reputation as one of Washington's best defense lawyers, he could have never been hired at Williams & Connolly. With rare exceptions, the experience of being a former prosecutor was not something you necessarily wanted at the top of a résumé pile on Brendan Sullivan's desk. Rather than being a mark of criminal law experience, such a listing, so impressive to relatives, was viewed with suspicion. Could someone who had been a government prosecutor really swallow the Williams & Connolly Kool-Aid? Could he be willing to make every case not about his own client but about the conduct of the rival government attorney?

Sure, Aubrey Daniel had been a military JAG Corps guy, and Lucchino had served on the House of Representatives impeachment inquiry, but for the most part it was unusual in Washington law practice that so few of Williams's and Califano's recruits had come up by that route. Sullivan hadn't. Barnett and Craig certainly hadn't. Kendall hadn't. Neither had Barry Simon or Nicole Seligman, who was the only member of that crew born in New York City, though definitely not Brooklyn. Most defense firms in American law were comprised of former prosecutors who had gone over to the other side. Not Williams & Connolly. Its institutional antipathy to career prosecutors, in every respect, was almost unique in American legal practice.

Bennett's street-fighter persona had its appeal to certain elements in the White House, who worried that David Kendall's cerebral approach to President Clinton's defense was too genteel. Some in the White House went so far as to call him "prissy," which was not even close.

Nonetheless, Kendall's low-key style particularly grated on Deputy White House Chief of Staff Harold M. Ickes. Ickes, according to a profile of him by Judy Bachrach in *Vanity Fair*, was "admired, loathed, lusted after, denounced and feared, and that was the way he liked it." Kendall's subtle intellectualism and off-key wit simply didn't fit into a White House staff dominated by noisy New Yorkers like Ickes and Nussbaum, who shared few of Kendall's personality traits.

It was no wonder, then, that when Ickes came to Washington from

New York, he asked Bob Bennett to handle any potential legal or ethics problems that might arise for him personally. Bennett had also done work for another loud member of Clinton's Arkansas mafia, Harry Thomason. Even before the Paula Jones suit was filed, more than a month before, they had begun urging the president to hire Robert Bennett and reduce the role of Kendall. Thomason, Bennett recalled, "believed that the president's lawyer had to take off the gloves and respond to the daily allegations against him."

Thomason worried that Kendall was too preoccupied with Clinton's legal defense as opposed to his political defense. Kendall's way of trying cases didn't include making public statements about the case on the Sunday morning talk shows. Thomason told Bennett that even though Kendall might conceivably win legal dismissal of the Whitewater allegations, Clinton could still be "convicted" by the public by losing his 1996 reelection bid. Thomason said others in the White House shared his feelings that the president needed a more aggressive, politically savvy defense lawyer.

At the end of April, Ickes called Bennett and asked if he would meet with Mrs. Clinton.

According to Bennett's account, "I had never met Mrs. Clinton and was more than a little curious as to why I would be meeting with her."

After an hourlong meeting, Bennett claims, he found her to "be bright, charming and attractive, with a winning smile."

He was pretty sure that they had really hit it off.

Oddly, perhaps, Mrs. Clinton's own memoir doesn't mention that meeting, much less that they had "hit it off." In fact, it isn't until deep into her book that she even mentions Bennett's name, referring to him rather abruptly as "*Bill's* lawyer in the Jones case." In retrospect, though Bennett's memoir describes his great rapport and friendship with both the first lady and the president, the president's memoir is not that warm, either. In the 956 pages of *My Life*, Bennett only rates three brief page-mentions in the index, and one of those is a mistaken reference to U.S. Senator Robert F. Bennett of Utah.

Following the meeting with Mrs. Clinton, Bennett was courted by White House counsel Lloyd Cutler, who had replaced Nussbaum in that job. Bennett relates that Cutler said, "Bob, I want you to have a seat at the table."

Cutler repeated the complaint that Kendall would not go on the cable news and network talk shows and that the White House wanted an attorney who could respond to personal attacks, as the president did not want his press secretary or government-paid communications people detailed to that job. The Cutler meeting was followed by a visit with President Clinton, sealing the deal. Bennett offered to waive his $550-per-hour fee, but Clinton insisted that he bill in a normal fashion. To take a gift from Skadden Arps, Clinton knew, if Bennett didn't, would only cause more problems down the road. Some colleagues felt it rather remarkable that Bennett would have made such a suggestion.

Three days after Bennett's hiring, on May 6, the Paula Jones sex harassment suit was filed. Bennett used the time to try to convince Jones's attorney, Gil Davis, not to file. Bennett threatened him that it would be seen as "scurrilous and mean-spirited," but Davis probably already knew that and filed the action anyway. It was the "scurrilousness" of the suit that was one of its main attractions.

Bennett did the last thing any attorney at Williams & Connolly would do: He immediately announced that he was holding a press conference to answer the allegations in the complaint, that Paula Jones had been sexually harassed by the president while he was still governor of Arkansas.

An angry Bob glared at the army of reporters and declared the suit "tabloid trash with a legal caption on it." With that declaration, whenever reporters needed a quote, they called Bennett. In the Kendall-Bennett quote match, Bennett had scored a knockout in the first round. The reference to "tabloid trash" was not lost on Kendall. Rather it was the first punch, in a way, not just between Bennett and the right-wing attackers of Bill Clinton but between Bennett and Kendall, whose honed self-confidence Bennett saw as smug arrogance. Bennett was arrogant but not particularly smug. Kendall was proud of his affiliation with "tabloid trash," and many of his fondest recollections as an attorney were tied to experiences he had while representing the various tabloids.

In addition to publicly commenting on a legal case, Bennett's next big job was to make sure the Jones case, if it were to be tried, was not scheduled until after the 1996 presidential election. It isn't every day in Washington, or anywhere else, that lawyers admit that their entire strategy is to delay a legal case for political reasons, but that is exactly what Bennett did. "My immediate goal in the Jones case was to delay it," Bennett admitted later.

Cutler told him, "Bob, if you can delay this case until after the election, we will have won."

Bennett believed that the Paula Jones case was totally without merit and would be won at trial. The problem, however, was timing. A trial ran the risk of being bumped up into the primary or election cycle. So instead of trying the case, Bennett decided to claim presidential immunity from prosecution, citing an arcane, outdated law called the Soldiers and Sailors Relief Act. Columnists and legal authorities laughed at invoking this law, which was intended to protect active duty servicemen from lawsuits while they were serving the country. Bennett's claim that Clinton was covered by the law since he was commander in chief was not only a bad legal argument; the brief reminded Clinton's political opponents that the president had not served in the military, while many others of his generation had given their lives in South Vietnam. Bennett didn't seem to care how preposterous his brief might have sounded. He figured that by the time his most squirrelly constitutional issues ran their course through the federal court system, and ultimately the U.S. Supreme Court, it would be way past Election Day, November 1996. Meanwhile, Bennett and the White House political team would beat Paula Jones's reputation into a pulp so that no one would believe her story, and Clinton would skip happily into a second term.

On August 5, 1994, a three-judge panel replaced Whitewater special prosecutor Robert Fiske with Kenneth Starr, who by then was a partner in the Washington office of Chicago-based Kirkland & Ellis. At Kirkland & Ellis, Starr represented companies with difficult cases that were about to be argued at the Supreme Court. One of them in which Starr was deeply involved had to do with a television report that certain General Motors–made Chevy Blazers had fuel tanks that could spontaneously explode. GM hired Starr. By the time Starr was done, *Dateline NBC* had to make an on-air apology, the reporting career of *Dateline*'s Jane Pauley was tarnished, and Starr was well on his way to reversing a $100 million judgment in favor of an Atlanta couple that claimed to have been injured by the "exploding side-saddle fuel tanks." Hard to explain this to many people now, but the soon-to-be-much-maligned Starr had a great reputation with his peers at the time of his appointment. Of course, his winning career record as a Supreme Court litigator wasn't exactly hurt by the fact that, along with Olson, he had once been the top judge picker for President Reagan, who appointed three justices to the Court and elevated Rehnquist to chief justice. He particularly believed that he deserved the credit for saving the nomination of Sandra Day O'Connor, when others in the administration told President Reagan that he was not bound by a campaign pledge to appoint a woman to the court. Starr had persuaded Reagan to keep his promise, arguing that even in a campaign, promises have to be kept.

The change in prosecutors happened because the old law authorizing an independent counsel had expired, and a new procedure—allowing for a "special division" of the federal court to make the appointment—had come into being. There has always been speculation that several of the Reagan-appointed judges who ended up on the "special division" wanted a fresh look, because it appeared Fiske wasn't finding anything incriminating about Foster's death, the destruction of documents, the firing of the White House Travel Office staff, Hillary Clinton's commodity trades, or undue influence on behalf of the Clintons' banking friends in Arkansas. In 1994, those issues were what "Whitewater" was still about.

Lloyd Cutler, one of the savviest of Washington wise men, had said to Mrs. Clinton that he was unconcerned about the reauthorization of the independent counsel statute. "I'll eat my hat if Fiske is replaced," he had told Hillary.

Mrs. Clinton later reminded Cutler of his view and suggested he eat a hat composed of "natural fibers." So much for Washington's wise men.

On August 10, 1994, Bennett and Rauh asked that the Paula Jones case be dismissed on the new grounds that a sitting president is immune from a civil sex harassment suit. While that was going on, Starr announced that Hillary's Little Rock law partner Webb Hubbell had agreed to plead guilty to mail fraud and tax evasion. Hubbell, who had been Vince Foster's best friend, had stolen some $394,000 from his Rose Law Firm partners, including Hillary and Foster. The lawyer who negotiated the plea arrangement for Hubbell was John Nields, the same attorney who had represented the House of Representatives in the Iran-Contra scandal, when Brendan Sullivan had elevated the public profile of potted plants.

Susan Webber Wright, the federal judge handling the case in Little Rock, ruled that President Clinton could delay the lawsuit until after he had left the White House, whether it be 1997 or 2001. A president couldn't very well run the country and be the defendant in a long-running personal injury case of unspecified length at the same time. The judge's position made sense.

However, she ruled that the plaintiff's lawyers, Gil Davis and Joe Cammarata, could immediately begin to conduct discovery and interview witnesses to prepare for the inevitable day when the trial would be held. Neither side was particularly happy, and both sides appealed the ruling to the Eighth Circuit Court of Appeals. Ted Olson and Robert Bork, still working this "conspiracy" from behind the curtain, helped prep Davis for his argument that a president could undergo a trial while in office.

Although he would have preferred that Wright not have ruled as she did on the discovery and interview issues, Bennett was pleased that with *both* sides appealing, there would be further and longer delays.

In March 1995, Clinton appeared with the Washington press at the annual Gridiron Dinner, one of Washington's most self-absorbed affairs. "The first lady is sorry she can't be with you tonight," Clinton joked. "If you believe that, I've got some land in Arkansas I'd like to sell you." The line got hoots and hollers. President Clinton was a pretty funny guy, after all. (In truth, Clinton was not a funny person at all. The joke was written and given to him by *Saturday Night Live* writer Al Franken. Still, the papers the next morning, all of whom knew the game, pretended it was Clinton who was funny.)

On April 19, 1995, things in the country were not funny, not at all. At 11:00 A.M., a truck bomb (but not a GM Blazer) went off outside the Alfred P. Murrah Federal Office Building in Oklahoma City. The death toll was 168 people, many of them small children at a day care center in the building. Eventually two men would be arrested and charged with the crime, Timothy McVeigh and his accomplice, Terry Nichols. As any random episode in America might, the case had its tangential coincidences and connections with Williams & Connolly. The reporter who covered the tragedy for the *Washington Post*, Lois Romano, was married to former Williams & Connolly partner Sven Erik Holmes. Amazingly, Holmes, who had only been at Williams & Connolly for a few years, had managed to have President Clinton name him to be an Oklahoma U.S. district judge. Eli Jacobs's work, with plenty of help from Boren, was never done. Fortunately for Holmes, he had been assigned to the federal courthouse in Tulsa, not to the Murrah Building in Oklahoma City. McVeigh would use a local Oklahoma lawyer and eventually be executed. As a footnote, Nichols hired a former Williams & Connolly partner, Michael Tigar, who had left the firm and become a very well known anti-death-penalty advocate.

Tigar's efforts would spare Nichols from facing the same fate as McVeigh, and he is still alive, serving a life sentence. Tigar now mostly teaches law although he still takes on controversial cases from time to time.

Three days after the Oklahoma bombing, Kendall and Nicole Seligman arrived at the White House, where Kenneth Starr and his deputies were preparing to take sworn statements on Whitewater from both the president and the first lady. Kendall drilled the first lady hard. "Preparing for the interview was not something that David Kendall or I took lightly," Mrs. Clinton wrote later. "Knowing that every word I uttered would be dissected by the Office of the Independent Counsel, David insisted that I cram in prep time no matter how busy I was. I came to dread the sight of those binders because they were tangible reminders of the trivialities and minutiae I would be subjected to under oath, all of which could be used to trip me up legally."

Bill, however, was not irritated as much. Hillary had sweated through her questioning by Starr, but after Bill emerged, it was handshakes all around. Then, to Hillary's astonishment, he ordered one of the younger White House lawyers to give Starr a tour of the Lincoln Bedroom. She did not feel that Bill needed to be that hospitable to those particular guests.

While Kendall prepared to battle the special prosecutor over the Whitewater land deal, New York senator Alfonse D'Amato convened a hearing of his Senate Banking Committee centered on the events that still seemed unresolved about Vince Foster's death, particularly the removal of possibly incriminating documents from the White House in the hours and days after Foster's death.

Among those receiving a subpoena to testify was Bob Barnett. It was not a Top Ten moment of his political or legal life. There were, for sure, other lawyers in Washington who would have relished a moment like that before national television cameras, but Barnett, like Kendall and Sullivan, was not one of them. Many times, Barnett had advised his political friends and clients about how to testify at a congressional committee. Now he would have his own chance to perform in the national spotlight.

For a brief moment, it seemed everything that Barnett had worked for and built hung precariously in the balance. One wrong or indiscreet answer could conjure up an indictment for perjury, especially since he knew Ken Starr and his deputies would be watching. Testifying under oath, even if you have nothing to hide, is a harrowing prospect. Make one innocent mistake and a perjury charge looms. There was no immunity from prose-cution in this arrangement. Barnett did not have Brendan Sullivan bully-ing the committee into submission. He was a mostly friendly witness, who was only there to assure D'Amato that the Vince Foster papers had not been altered, destroyed, or hidden. Some of the flames of suspicion were being fanned by a British writer named Ambrose Evans-Pritchard, who had written an article some months earlier entitled "Doubts Linger over Clinton Aide's Suicide." The article had received widespread attention in the Scaife-run conservative press, as well as the papers owned by Austra-lian publishing magnate Rupert Murdoch and the Unification Church–run *Washington Times,* as well as on the Rush Limbaugh radio show and the entire Murdoch-owned Fox News Channel, which was merciless in its in-nuendoes about the Clintons' alleged role in Foster's death.

"One of the suspicious circumstances," Evans-Pritchard had written, "is that White House staffers removed files from Foster's office on the night of his death. Files that might have been related to the Whitewater affair." On May 1, he wrote another article widely circulated among the conspir-acy theorists, stating, "Vince Foster, the deputy White House counsel, was probably murdered and his body carried into the park as part of a staged suicide, according to a team of independent crime scene experts employed to investigate the death. . . . The private report is being taken extremely seriously by the official investigation of Kenneth Starr, accord-ing to sources close to the inquiry," he declared.

That was the cauldron of suspicion and rumor into which Barnett was stepping. If he slipped up completely and made an incorrect statement, Starr could later indict him for perjury and end his legal career. The hall-mark of prosecutors in the United States is that very often they can't prove their cases at all. So they fall back on tax charges or some minuscule mis-statement that they can wring into a face-saving or small-career-building perjury count.

In Barnett's case, there was also a worry that he could not sound evasive or sleazy. He had made himself the book agent of choice for both Republi-can and Democratic Washington. He was the unassailed puppeteer of the media, dangling by then the careers of some five hundred television and newspaper stars, many of them influential household names. Yet if Barnett had helped to hide evidence about Foster's death, or expunged something that could have been embarrassing or, worse, criminal about the Clintons'

Whitewater dealings, it would all be over for him. Barnett was extremely self-confident and not prone to worry, but his closest friends feared the old Williams adage. Would Barnett become that month's victim of a congressional burning at the stake?

It was a hot Monday morning in Washington almost exactly two years to the day after the events he had come to discuss had taken place. Barnett took his place at the witness table, next to Maggie Williams, Mrs. Clinton's chief of staff, with whom he would testify jointly. David Kendall sat directly behind him, acting as his personal attorney. The D'Amato committee's interrogator was Michael Chertoff, the former Latham & Watkins partner and future Bush homeland security director who had been detailed to D'Amato's committee as its chief counsel.

Barnett was a model of Williams & Connolly calm. In minute detail, he told the committee of arriving at the White House on July 27, of searching the boxes, of labeling and taping the boxes, and of taking them back to his office.

"We went to a room on the third floor that's a hard to define location," he testified. "It was on the front side. If you come off the elevator you turn left. If I had a map I could point it out to you."

"And you started to go through the files?" Chertoff asked.

"I wouldn't say go through the files," Barnett replied. "I opened the box. In the box were two dozen, maybe more, files. Most of them, but not all of them, were labeled. I went through the labels. The unlabeled files, as I recall, I took out and looked at to see what they were. I may have also taken one or two or more of the labeled files to look at them briefly to see what they were. But let me be clear. Everything that was in the box when I received it was back in the box when I taped it up."

The committee was getting nowhere with Barnett, so the most conservative members turned their guns on Maggie Williams. North Carolina senator Lauch Faircloth stated that he believed Williams had removed incriminating files even before Barnett arrived. Bullyingly, the North Carolinian called her a liar when she denied it and demanded that she resign her position at the White House. To be honest, Williams's memory had not been as sharp as Barnett's, and her uncertainty gave her adversaries ammunition with which to humiliate and embarrass her, which was the main point of the session—to throw some red meat to Limbaugh and his ultraconspiratorial listening audience. Congressional hearings are rarely anything more than a show. Hillary squirmed while watching at the White House as Maggie was raked over the coals again and again.

As things got testier, and D'Amato and Faircloth continued to suggest that something improper was done with the Vince Foster files, Barnett made a more impassioned defense of his own integrity.

"Let me say for the record, under oath," Barnett said, "neither the president, nor the first lady, nor Socks the cat instructed me to do anything improper with those documents." Socks, the Clinton cat, would later become a Barnett client when the Clinton pets produced a White House book of their own, *Dear Socks, Dear Buddy*. Barnett's invocation of Socks's honesty probably was not made with an eye to the future, but in Washington, you just never know.

As the hearing wound into its sixth hour, Barnett couldn't restrain his natural instincts to defend any longer. Finally, he leaned forward in his chair. "If you'll bear with me," Barnett said.

The room stilled as Barnett shed his witness role and donned the more natural cloak of Williams's defender.

"On July 20, 1993, a lot of us lost a good friend. Vincent Foster was a man I respected, worked with, admired, and saw socially. I took that loss very hard. All of us did.

"And so maybe some of the people who come before you who talk about some of the things that happened following Vincent's sad and untimely death were operating at that time in an atmosphere of grief. I don't know if you, Senator D'Amato, or Mr. Chertoff, or others here, have had the sad experience of losing a dear friend or family member. I hope you never have, I hope you never will. But this was a terrible tragedy, and it probably meant that things were done under the auspices of sadness and grief that, as we look back two and one half years now, it's hard to reconstruct.

"I must say, and I hope she doesn't fault me for this—but on the plane going to the funeral, I tried to talk to Maggie Williams. Maggie Williams was crying the entire flight. I could not talk to her."

Hillary called having to listen to those hearings "one of the hardest things I have ever done."

When it was over, most in attendance remembered not the ranting of D'Amato and Faircloth but rather the amateur actor from Waukegan's greatest speech.

24

HILLARY: THE FIRST CLIENT

———■———

Also listening to the hearing at the White House was a vivacious, newly hired White House intern, Monica Lewinsky.

By the end of 1995, it seemed like Kendall had succeeded in convincing one federal agency, the Resolution Trust Company, that the Clintons' involvement with Madison Savings & Loan was minimal. Overall, Kendall didn't see the possibility for anything criminal to come out of Whitewater, and his mood was often lighthearted. At his meeting to update Hillary, Kendall frequently brought clippings to show her from the very tabloids he represented. One that he particularly liked claimed that Hillary had given birth to an alien baby. What neither Kendall nor Hillary realized, was that on November 15, 1995, while Hillary was out of the White House taking a trip, the president was off on a little jaunt of his own, compliments of Lewinsky, although it was only to an anteroom off the Oval Office. Clinton's ten or so sojourns with Lewinsky between November 1995 and March 1997 were acts of incredible recklessness, considering the fact that the president was at that very time being sued for sexual harassment. In his book, *My Life*, Clinton curiously offers several pages of excuses and insists he was the subject of Starr's prosecutorial witch hunt. Surely, though, at the time he chose to be involved with Lewinsky, he knew that his political opponents were trying to get him.

In the first week of January 1996, the beginning of the presidential election year, a White House researcher found a set of missing Rose Law Firm records that Mrs. Clinton had previously said she could not locate. They were a summary of the work she had done for Madison S&L, while at the Little Rock firm. She said she had originally found them in August 1995 in "the book room" of the White House and that she had put them in a box and taken them to her office, only remembering them some six months later.

"Where on earth have they been?" Hillary wrote later in Alice-like prose. "What does this mean?"

Replied Kendall, "Well, the good news is we found them. The bad news is this gives the press and prosecutors the chance to go wild again."

Coincidental to this development in the Whitewater case, Hillary had written a book, sold to a publisher by Barnett, called *It Takes a Village*. On January 9, 1996, Hillary was scheduled to do a promotional interview with Barbara Walters. Barnett had personally picked Walters to handle the job. He hoped Walters would ask Hillary about the issues in the book, but he knew that by selecting her, he would get the first lady an empathetic questioner, as well as one with the biggest audience. Barnett by now had gone far beyond offering his services as a quasi-literary-agent-lawyer. He was now functioning as a full-time public relations strategist for his clients as well, frequently linking up new clients writing books with past clients who now had their own television shows, like Fox News cable host Ollie North. "I was chosen by her wonderful lawyer, Bob Barnett, to do the interview, which amazed me," Walters said in an interview later with Barnett client Tim Russert. "I never thought Hillary was going to pick me. And she did."

Unhappily for Mrs. Clinton, Walters began the interview by asking, "How did you get into this mess?"

Hillary replied, "I ask myself that every day."

The mess got worse later that same afternoon when the Eighth Circuit Court of Appeals issued a ruling completely against Robert Bennett and his client, the president. The court upheld the lower court's decision about allowing discovery in the Paula Jones case to go forward but overturned the other section that delayed the actual trial until the president had left office. It was exactly the opposite of the ruling he wanted, and it made things even worse for the president. Conversely, it was a complete win for Ted Olson and the rest of his Scaife-funded team trying so hard to unseat Clinton and pave the way for a Republican win.

Despite this embarrassing defeat, Bennett declared victory. "One very bright note was that we were getting much closer to our goal of delaying the matter until after the election," he would later write.

The court decision was followed by a subpoena from Starr ordering

Hillary to come to the federal grand jury to testify about how the Rose Law Firm billing records got lost but suddenly reappeared. Hillary was predictably distraught over this latest development, and Kendall tried to persuade Starr to let her testify in the White House or by videotape, but Starr was now under pressure from the same right-wing organizations that were prodding D'Amato. Radio host Rush Limbaugh personally ran a terror operation designed to intimidate political opponents. At his radio "orders," thousands of callers could jam a public official's phone line. Frequently that was exactly what they did, putting official Washington into a defensive crouch. Some even called in death threats. Senate Democratic Leader Tom Daschle used to say that while he never listened to the show, he could tell when his name came up, and with what intensity, by the hate calls and threats that would instantly besiege his office. Although he was the one stoking the anger, Limbaugh said he was blameless and merely provided a phone number that was part of the public record.

The Limbaugh "dittoheads," as they called themselves, were shamelessly taking credit for the Republican victory in the House in 1994 and the accompanying political ascent of Newt Gingrich. Fear of their wrath influenced Starr's insistence that the first lady come to the courthouse. Kendall then suggested they enter through a back entrance, but by then Mrs. Clinton was not comfortable having it look like she was sneaking into the building. Hillary thought it would look like she had something to hide. So she decided to walk right in the front door and not dodge the paparazzi. As she entered the building, she told Kendall, "Off to the firing squad." She apparently did well enough, however. Mrs. Clinton was never indicted, and one of the grand jurors asked her to autograph a copy of It Takes a Village. Watching in the hallway as Mrs. Clinton took out her pen, Kendall flashed to the firm's famous story about Ed Williams and Billy Graham. He knew from the amen-like smiles on the faces of the grand jurors that Mrs. Clinton had bested Starr again.

Meanwhile, the Supreme Court on June 24, 1996, agreed to hear the latest appeal of the Paula Jones case, guaranteeing that her suit would not move forward until after the election. When he heard about this, Lloyd Cutler called Bennett and proclaimed, "We won."

Bennett writes that "the President was very generous in his praise of our victory, and a great burden was lifted off the shoulders of those who were working around the clock to reelect him."

In November 1996, President Clinton defeated Republican Robert Dole and won reelection. Call this a small country, but it does seem incredible that Dole lived next to Lewinsky at the Watergate apartments and would later buy up her unit to make his larger. Well, that's Washington. Everything connects, somewhere.

It seemed that the nightmare that had been Clinton's first term was finally over. Starr's investigation was at a dead end. The Whitewater land deal investigation wasn't catching fire, and, like Fiske, Starr had inescapably come to the conclusion that Vince Foster's suicide was just a suicide. His prosecutorial strategy fell back on hoping that a plea agreement with Webb Hubbell would turn into something he could hang an indictment on, but Hubbell had neither anything substantial to give nor the desire to cause Hillary any additional discomfort. The Paula Jones case, whatever its merits, had been successfully pushed into the second term. Hillary now had good reason to believe that they were at last out of the woods, and there were no more reelections—for Bill, at least—to worry about. Nonetheless, stories about the Clintons continued to leak from what Kendall believed were partisans in Starr's office. The lawyer who rarely said a word began keeping a voluminous file on his opposing counsel and staff, who he believed having far too much to say.

One of the prime architects of Clinton policy during his first term in office had been George Stephanopoulos. He had been the most adamant aide in the White House who supported the idea that a special prosecutor would ease the pressure from the news media. By 1996, though, it was clear that his judgment on the special prosecutor had been mistaken, if not naive. "Assuming we did nothing wrong," he had told Hillary, "the best thing is for a special counsel to say so. There's an air of inevitability to this. If we don't ask for one from the attorney general, we're going to get an independent counsel from Congress."

Hillary had not forgotten George's words and was bitter that in allowing the appointment of a special prosecutor for Whitewater, she and Bill had made a horrendous mistake. The truth was that Hillary had never liked Stephanopoulos for an instant and had always questioned not only his judgment but his loyalty. In an attempt to save their reelection, Hillary had pushed for Bill to bring in a controversial political adviser, Dick Morris. Morris, who was far more conservative than Stephanopoulos or most of the advisers who had spearheaded Clinton's 1992 election, pushed

Clinton to the middle on issues like welfare reform and tax cuts. For months, Morris's place, developing Clinton political strategy, was a closely held secret. Then, in April 1995, Clinton announced Morris's new role to a shocked West Wing staff. No member of the president's team was more stunned or embittered than the idealistic Stephanopoulos. As Hillary Clinton described it, Stephanopoulos was "distraught that Bill would listen to a political turncoat like Morris and unhappy about having to compete with a rival adviser."

As Stephanopoulos plotted his White House departure, the path to private life would pass first through Barnett's office. They were old acquaintances. When Stephanopoulos was media director in the White House, he had been subpoenaed to testify about any conversations or documents he had about the Whitewater land deal. There was one in particular that looked bad, a call Stephanopoulos had made to a Treasury Department official, Josh Steiner. In that conversation, he asked indiscreetly how the administration could get Jay Stephens, then the U.S. attorney for the District of Columbia, off the president's back. Stephanopoulos knew the conversation could be "misunderstood" as if he were really asking how to thwart a lawful prosecution, which, he declared, would never be his intent.

Afraid that the Clinton White House was turning into the Nixon White House, and so quickly, Stephanopoulos called Democratic strategist James Carville for encouragement. Carville picked George up in his Land Rover, drove him around town, and finally dumped him back at the White House with some advice: "Get a lawyer. You need to talk to Bob Barnett."

On the following Saturday, Barnett agreed to meet with Stephanopoulos and give him some advice. Over a weekend lunch special of fresh fish, Barnett explained that because of Rita's position at CBS News, he was still recused and couldn't give legal help. He did give Stephanopoulos the number of Stanley Brand, a former aide to House Speaker Tip O'Neill, who was an expert in "handling" complicated investigations. As Stephanopoulos put it, "Brand specialized in cases at the intersection of politics, criminal law, and communicating in the Washington echo chamber." Brand guided Stephanopoulos through a round of questions with the special counsel, and nothing much more came of it. Still, even though Stephanopoulos's reputation was only mildly sullied, he could count on Barnett, recused or not, to put him back in good standing.

Once Stephanopoulos had left the White House, obviating his conflict problems with Rita, Barnett handled the sale of what would become Stephanopoulos's tattletale memoir. Then he would negotiate deals for the former White House aide with ABC that would eventually lead to Stephanopoulos becoming the powerful Sunday morning television successor to legendary broadcaster David Brinkley and eventually host of the *Good Morning America* show. In addition, he sold Stephanopoulos's memoir to the publishing house Little, Brown for what *Daily Variety* said was a $2.75 million advance. To the public, Barnett and Stephanopoulos denied that his book would be more than reflections on policy debates during the "political ups and downs" of his five years with the Clintons. In reality, the lure of the book would be what insights he had into the controversial presidential couple. In a way, the public explanation for the book was a cover for Barnett, who did not want to appear to be disloyal to Hillary. The first lady by now was even more furious at Stephanopoulos than ever, blaming him for a series of unflattering leaks about her to Bob Woodward of the *Washington Post*, who was yet another steady Barnett client.

Barnett would claim for years not to know that Stephanopoulos was going to criticize the first lady so explicitly in his book. In fact, Stephanopoulos's book jacket copy blames Hillary's "combative litigator instincts" for "sadly, being behind many of her husband's missteps."

"I only learned that after the book came out," Barnett told me years later. True or not, his alibi held up. He was able to succeed in creating an extremely successful career path for Stephanopoulos, with no damage to his close relationship with the first lady. Barnett, better than anyone else, had learned to walk the political tightrope. He had evolved effortlessly into the ultimate Washington zen master that Califano so clumsily had always desired to be but had never quite achieved. Barnett had arrived as Washington's indispensable advice giver, not just the successor to the Clark Cliffords and Bernard Baruchs of American politics, but arguably their equal.

2 5.

A SUMMITT AND A TRAGEDY

On January 13, 1997, Bennett arrived at the Supreme Court. Based on his past experiences in the Jones case, he would win if he won but would also win if he lost. He and the Clinton White House were quite adept at declaring victory, no matter what happened. One could guess that this would be the case again.

Bennett's argument to the Court, in a nutshell, was still that the president's time was too valuable to be spent worrying about trivialities like depositions and interrogatories. After all, Woodmont Country Club Golf Course in suburban Maryland beckoned. Okay, that wasn't part of Bennett's argument, but based on the amount of time Clinton spent there playing golf, it could have been. Clinton was also finding time, though he was too busy to give a deposition, to spend other afternoons with Lewinsky, possibly as many as a dozen. The most notable recorded episode occurred on February 28, 1997, when he stained Lewinsky's navy blue Gap dress with semen. A little more than a month later, on March 29, Clinton and Lewinsky had their final assignation, though he didn't call to tell her it was over until May 24, an event Monica recorded as "D for Dump Day."

By mid-1997, Rita was nearing the end of her tenure as the White House correspondent for CBS News. It hadn't come a day too soon for Clinton, who was convinced that Braver was "busting my chops," just to prove that her husband's relationship with the White House wasn't influencing her coverage. Barnett was relieved that his time in the penalty box was over. Before she departed the beat, though, Rita had a fortuitous meeting in the White House with University of Tennessee women's basketball coach, Pat Summitt.

On February 10, 1997, Summitt was honored at the White House as one of the country's twenty-five most influential working mothers. Female journalists who covered the White House, including Rita, were invited to sit in. Most of them, including Rita, were in fact working mothers. She and Bob had a daughter, Meredith Barnett, their only child. Summitt ended up being seated next to Rita, who had no idea who she was until each person at the dinner stood up to say her name. When Braver realized that this was the very Pat Summitt that her husband talked about all the time, Rita exclaimed, "Oh my God, my husband loves you."

The coincidental oddity of this was that Barnett was a fanatical women's basketball enthusiast and had been writing fan letters to Summitt for six years. He had a niece who played back home in Illinois. On visits to his sister's house in Glenview, Barnett would go watch the games. Sitting in the high school bleachers, he had gotten the idea that Pat Summitt could make a lot of money writing a book about her experiences as a women's basketball coach. More importantly, Barnett wanted her to write the book so that he could read more about his favorite sport. He had written her several times, but Summitt had never responded. With the legendary basketball coach now in her sights, Braver made the pitch. Summitt promised that if she won her fifth national championship that year—and she wasn't having a particularly good season—she would consider it. It was probably a polite brush-off. Her usually dominant team had already lost seven games and didn't seem to be going anywhere in 1997.

After the Lady Vols beat Old Dominion University to win her most improbable national championship, Summitt returned to Knoxville, and there was a new letter from Barnett waiting for her. He had cut out a picture from *USA Today* of Summitt screaming at her players. Her mouth was open, and he drew a cartoon bubble on the picture that said, "Oh no, not Barnett again." Despite her promise to Rita, Summitt said that while she appreciated his persistence, she was not inclined to write a book. The apocryphal story is that Barnett sent back another cartoon, this time saying, "Pat! You said."

In truth, Barnett completed the job in more of the old-fashioned Washington way, enlisting the help of powerful Tennessee politician Lamar Alexander, who before he became president of UT had just happened to be a fellow law clerk with Barnett for Judge Wisdom in New Orleans. Back in 1991, when they met at a clerks' reunion, Barnett had asked Alexander to put a good word in for him with Summitt.

He had waited six years, but persistence paid off. Summitt finally relented, under the firm stipulation that her ghost be a woman. Barnett helped Summitt hire *Washington Post* sportswriter Sally Jenkins to do the actual writing. Summitt was later quoted as saying how surprised she was that when a person reads it, Jenkins's words actually sound like "it's my voice."

Not only was the book, *Reach for the Summit*, incredibly successful, Summitt became a conduit for sending her All-American players to Williams & Connolly for representation. Some of them—such as Chamique Holdsclaw in 1999—signed with the Washington Mystics of the Women's National Basketball Association. Summitt herself became a consultant for the Mystics. Barnett let the other lawyers in his firm buy season tickets for the Redskins. He was a Mystics guy.

On May 27, 1997, after Clinton had been safely reinaugurated, the Supreme Court ruled by a 9–0 vote that the decision of the Eighth U.S. Circuit Court of Appeals had been correct: Clinton could not legally delay the Paula Jones trial, which Cutler and Bennett had already succeeded in delaying. It was as much a victory for Ted Olson as for anybody; he and Bork had prepped the anti-Clinton lawyers for their Supreme Court argument, but it was Olson's predictions and canned responses that proved to be most prescient. No one in Washington knew the Supreme Court any better than Olson, and now he had proven he could even win cases almost by remote control.

Bennett found the fact that he had lost 9–0 instead of 5–4 comforting. "With a 9–0 vote against you, I honestly think that no one could have won and there was nothing else I could have done to change the outcome," Bennett wrote. "Some cases can't be won."

On June 1, 1997, Kendall saw the article in the Sunday *New York Times Magazine* in which Starr questioned Hillary's truthfulness and suggested she still might be indicted for obstruction of justice. For Kendall, this was the smoking gun he was looking for to go on the offensive against Starr. He wrote a letter directly to Starr, accusing him of a "leak and smear" campaign. "The conduct of you and persons in your office directly and indirectly flout your obligations," Kendall wrote. Starr's deputies had developed a distinct dislike of Kendall, complaining to their boss and among themselves that he was haughty and contemptuous. To which Kendall privately told friends, "If I did anything to irritate Starr's torpedoes, I take that as praise!"

Starr's leaks continued. On June 25, 1997, the *Washington Post* reported that Starr's team was still questioning Arkansas state troopers about affairs that Clinton might have had with a variety of women, other than Gennifer Flowers, which had come up before his first successful election campaign in 1992.

There was nothing bittersweet about the summer of 1997 at Williams & Connolly. The tension levels were already astronomical, and each partner was up to his neck in litigation, politics, awkward media requests, and unfortunate personal tragedies.

While Whitewater continued to play out, Califano's old protégé Richard Cooper worked tirelessly on behalf of tobacco industry clients, heading for an inevitable showdown at the U.S. Supreme Court over whether the Food and Drug Administration had the legitimate authority to regulate nicotine. Cooper, the brilliant former *Harvard Law Review* editor, who had been briefly wooed away by Califano to become general counsel of the FDA, was hired by the R. J. Reynolds and Brown & Williamson tobacco companies to fight efforts by the FDA and by the surgeon general to classify and regulate tobacco as a drug. When Califano heard that his former protégé, a Rhodes Scholar and a former clerk to liberal Supreme Court Justice William J. Brennan Jr., was continuing to sell his considerable legal talents and FDA experience to the tobacco industry, he was distraught. By now Joe was one of the nation's most identifiable antismoking zealots. He had left the active practice of law and was running the National Center for Addiction and Substance Abuse. He says he called and beseeched Cooper not to represent the tobacco clients, but Cooper said that representing clients, even evil ones, was what the firm did, and would always do.

Cooper was hardly a lone wolf in devoting his life to the cause of smoking. The tobacco industry had shamelessly bought up the services of nearly all of Washington's top firms, particularly Covington & Burling, and Arnold & Porter, two of the three largest. Hogan & Hartson was the best known major Washington firm that did not represent tobacco companies. Cooper took the position that only Congress can pass laws about controlling nicotine. As one of the largest contributors in the nation to the campaign coffers of members of Congress, to say nothing of employing armies of lobbyists and public relations people, Big Tobacco had little to fear from Congress. In the way that casinos fueled the economy of Las Vegas, tobacco was a financial engine that provided a handsome lifestyle for many in Washington. However, while they could count most members of Congress

in their pockets, the tobacco companies were scared to death of a truly au-
tonomous FDA, the agency that Cooper, as a former general counsel,
knew better than most. Congress was easily bought off with smoky campaign contributions, but if somebody at the FDA took money from tobacco companies, that somebody could go to jail.

Like many of the partners at the law firm, Cooper had a brilliant and
successful spouse, Judith Areen. For a random group of professional men,
their marriages were almost as remarkable as anything else they did. All
were married to strong, brilliant, successful career women. David and
Anne Kendall; Greg and Derry Craig; Brendan and Lila Sullivan, also an
attorney; Jay Monahan and Katie Couric; Bob Barnett and Rita Braver.
Lucchino, who fostered the playboy image, was the only one of this group
who had not been married while at the firm.

Yale Law graduate Areen was a law professor and ethics expert at
Georgetown University and later became the dean of the law school. She
sat as a board member of WorldCom, a corrupt telephone company whose
founder, Bernie Ebbers, would later go to jail for fraud. Areen was left as
one of ten board members who had to come up with $18 million out of
their own pockets for failing to protect investors while Ebbers ripped off
shareholders. So nobody's perfect. As much as the Craigs and the Ken-
dalls, though perhaps not as much as the Barnetts, Cooper and Areen
constituted a true Washington power couple.

It was not any surprise that two people who most likely had the highest
combined IQ score of any married couple in Washington would also have
a brilliant and talented seventeen-year-old son, Benjamin Eric Cooper. Ben
was the third of their four children, about to enter his senior year at
Georgetown Day School. He had been selected to the school's prestigious
It's Academic team, and he mentored inner-city children in both scholas-
tics and basketball.

On August 11, 1997, Richard Cooper was one of several tobacco industry lawyers who traveled to the U.S. Circuit Court of Appeals in Richmond to argue about the FDA's authority to regulate tobacco products,
which it had unilaterally asserted in 1996. One of Cooper's co-counsel was
the original special prosecutor in the Whitewater case, Robert Fiske.
Among Cooper's other, myriad co-counsel, also representing Brown &
Williamson, was Kenneth Starr. Despite his no-smoking, no-drinking,
no-dancing rural Texas upbringing, Starr was comfortable moving on

from fighting presidential peccadilloes to fighting to make the world safe for smokers. So, apparently, was Cooper.

The following day, August 12, teenaged Ben had gone to a Washington scientific research center called the Carnegie Center for Terrestrial Magnetism, where he was studying the origins of life on our planet. The research institute was located across the street from Temple Sinai Synagogue, on the edge of Washington's sprawling Rock Creek Park. At first glance the sign suggested a center for the study of "extraterrestrials." The institute was actually a place where serious geophysical science was studied, and Ben had wrapped up his research for the day and was headed home in his light blue Plymouth Acclaim when the accident happened.

In the driver's seat of a massive 57,000-pound dump trunk that afternoon was sixty-one-year-old Willis Curry. In June 1996, Curry had been convicted of speeding. In July 1996, he was caught speeding in his dump truck again. Then again, and again, until it was four speeding citations. He also had tickets for failing to obey signs and in November 1996 had been convicted of "backing without caution."

In less than five months, Curry had gathered seven convictions and lost twenty-five driving points, but no judge had yet taken away his license, which was, after all, his livelihood. No judge wanted to deprive him of being able to make his living.

Just a month before that miserably hot day in August, Curry crossed the median strip of a road in a Maryland county outside of Washington and hit a car. This time, his license was revoked for six months, but his driving privileges for the purpose of work were restored. Since he showed up for work most of the time, Curry was considered a good employee, even if he did wreck the company trucks. They had insurance.

Curry claimed that he was going the speed limit on August 12 when he lost control of his vehicle at the intersection near the synagogue and ran through a red light. "I was pulling the emergency brake, but it got soft on me, it got softer and I pumped 'em again and it went to the floor."

He couldn't stop. All he could do was try to swerve the truck to avoid a Cadillac at the intersection, where Ben Cooper in his Plymouth was waiting for the light to turn. The 57,000 pounds of truck and rocks and sand swerved away from the Cadillac and collapsed directly on top of Ben, crushing him to death instantly. Willis Curry walked away from the accident, but the enormity of the death of such a talented and blessed young man was hard to take. Later evidence would show that the brakes of the truck were worn to their metal rivets and the brake drums were cracked. For the next month, about thirty partners at Williams & Connolly held a morning memorial service each day for their partner's son. A dozen years later, the accident still haunts the firm, and eyes tear up at its mention.

In May 1998, Curry was convicted of involuntary manslaughter and sentenced to serve ten to thirty years in prison for his role in the accident. "I would rather this happen to me than what happened to him," Curry told the judge on sentencing. "I am very sorry, I didn't go out there to hurt anyone." He seemed genuinely remorseful.

A year and a half later, on August 4, 1999, Cooper and Areen agreed to a $4.6 million out-of-court settlement from the hauling firm that loaded and owned Curry's truck, as well as from the excavation company that loaded the truck on the day of the accident.

Judith and Richard turned their son's death into a crusade to reform local laws concerning construction trucks. With the settlement money they established a foundation in their son's honor. Said Cooper, "The focus should not be on us, the focus should be on the industry because that's where changes can be made to improve public safety. We filed the lawsuit because we want Ben to be remembered for good things—for contributions to worthy institutions."

The Ben Cooper Foundation would sponsor an annual event to raise money for genuinely good causes from the Coopers' well-heeled friends. Through it all, Richard Cooper continued to work defending the tobacco industry against regulations that most believed would result in fewer children and adults dying of lung cancer. On December 1, 1999, Cooper was chosen from a vast array of possible attorneys to present the tobacco industry's position before the U.S. Supreme Court. The FDA had claimed since 1996 that nicotine was a drug. Therefore, the agency's argument went, tobacco was responsible for four hundred thousand deaths per year, and therefore the FDA had an obligation to regulate the sale and delivery of tobacco products.

Cooper's rather novel rejoinder to the agency he once represented was to claim that the FDA existed to regulate and monitor the ill effects of products that had health benefits, such as the drugs that people take to make them well. There was never intent, Cooper argued, for the FDA to regulate products like cigarettes that had no health benefits at all. The FDA's mandate was to make sure that products are safe, and since cigarettes are hardly safe and no longer claim to have health benefits, Cooper said, they could not be regulated by the FDA without a specific mandate from legislation passed by Congress. If the FDA were to assume responsibility for regulating cigarettes, it would have no choice but to ban them. "FDA's assertion of jurisdiction here is lawless," Cooper claimed, "and however admirable its intentions, . . . it is setting aside established principles of law."

Though it seemed like sophistry to antismoking groups, on March 21, 2000, in a 5–4 decision, the Supreme Court agreed. Sandra Day O'Connor, who owed her appointment to tobacco industry attorney Ken Starr, wrote the majority opinion. During argument, she had asked the government's attorney whether the agency could also regulate horror films "because so many people go to them to get scared and get their adrenaline pumping."

For Califano, Cooper's passion for the protobacco argument was as hard to fathom as O'Connor's tortured analogy. "Finally, I gave up trying to talk to him about it," Califano said.

26.

PRICKED BY A HATPIN

———————■———————

B ack in Little Rock, Susan Webber Wright set the trial date in the
Paula Jones case for May 27, 1998. A pretrial deposition of the president was scheduled for January 17. A list of possible witnesses at the trial
included the name of Monica Lewinsky, who had been chatty about her
relationship with the president with a friend named Linda Tripp, who in
turn had found her way to Ken Starr's lawyers. Bennett conducted what
he termed "careful due diligence" as to Monica Lewinsky before the president's deposition but decided Clinton had done nothing untoward, not
even given her a kiss. Bennett had no idea that Clinton had left voice mail
messages on Lewinsky's tape machine, words that could be construed to
assume that he wanted to coordinate their stories. On January 7, Lewinsky
filed an affidavit with the court declaring, "I have never had a sexual relationship with the President." The same day, a Capitol Hill newspaper reported that Braver had given up the White House beat, allowing Barnett
to go back into the business of defending the Clintons.

On January 16, Starr's prosecutors trapped Lewinsky in a hotel room at
the Ritz-Carlton, where she was given the opportunity to be a cooperating
witness and asked to participate in "consensual monitoring," as Starr
would later describe it. "We described it to her at a high level of generality,"
he said. In other words, Starr had her dead to rights for perjury.

The president's deposition the next day was taken in an eleventh-floor
conference room at Skadden Arps, just a few hundred yards from the
White House, across the street from the Treasury Building. The conference room is renowned for its spectacular view of the Washington Monument and the National Mall area and was hardly a perfect setting to talk
about blow jobs, but such was the insanity that had captured the nation's

capital in the final months of the twentieth century. The president took a seat at the head of the table, and Judge Wright was several chairs away to his left. To the president's right were Paula Jones and her attorneys. No one seemed to realize how odd this all was.

Bennett presented the Monica Lewinsky affidavit and, he writes in his memoir, "Judge Wright allowed only a few questions about it."

In fact, Clinton had been asked more than a hundred separate questions about Lewinsky, many of them so loaded with details that Bennett and his partner Mitch Ettinger at one point looked at each other in amazement. One of the questions, in particular, involved whether or not the president had given Lewinsky the gift of a hatpin. It should have been clear to Bennett that the deposition was too full of surprises and specifics for him to allow his client to continue. If there was ever a moment where a perjury trap was obvious, this was it.

Despite the reality of the situation, Bennett later wrote, "We all felt the deposition was uneventful and that the questioning of the President was so imprecise that the Jones lawyers failed in their efforts."

When it was over, Bennett complimented the president on doing an excellent job. Clinton delighted his attorney by asking him to ride back to the White House with him. While Bennett says he was thrilled to be sitting next to a president in a limousine, Clinton was not happy at all. After arriving back at the White House, he complained to Hillary that the whole procedure had been a "farce" and wanted to cancel plans they had to go out to dinner. It was an uncharacteristically foul mood for the usually buoyant Clinton. The president had a foreboding of what was to come and a more realistic appraisal of the disaster that had just ensued. Bennett, however, seemed to be clueless. He told White House staffer Sidney Blumenthal, "They didn't lay a glove on him. On a scale of one to ten, it was a fifteen."

Unbeknownst to both the president and Bennett, though it should have been obvious, Starr had received his own information about the relationship between Lewinsky and the president. Starr had obtained taped conversations between Lewinsky and Linda Tripp. Eager to learn what the president might say about the relationship in the deposition, Starr had quietly gone to a friendly GOP-appointed federal judge and received authority to expand his investigation beyond the simple real estate deal and investigate possible perjury and obstruction of justice by President Clinton.

Four days later, on January 21, 1998, the president couldn't sleep, and he shook Hillary early to give her some news. He told Hillary that there were reports about to be published that he had had an affair with a White House intern and, worse, that he had instructed her to file a false affidavit with Judge Wright's court. Starr's investigation, he said, had now moved from Whitewater and Vince Foster into an inquiry about sex and lies in the White House. The president assured the first lady that he had merely spent some time with Lewinsky giving her job and career advice.

Later that day, Hillary was taking a train to Baltimore for a gathering at Goucher College when Kendall called. Kendall had learned that Starr was commencing a "full court press" to prove that the president had lied in his deposition when he testified he had not really known Lewinsky. Kendall told her to hunker down. He warned her that Starr intended to subpoena every employee and family member who might know something about Lewinsky's relationship with the president. When she was asked by reporters upon arrival in Baltimore if she believed her husband's adamant denials, she simply replied, "Absolutely."

On January 26, the president denied a relationship in a news briefing where he coldly said he had "never had sex with that woman, Miss Lewinsky." The next day, Hillary was scheduled to appear on the *Today* show, but Katie Couric had to cancel. Jay Monahan, her "painter," had died of colon cancer just a few days before, on January 24, 1998.

Hillary worried that she would be too strident in her criticism of Starr with Matt Lauer, who had taken over the interview. By now, Kendall felt there was no reason for any lawyerly restraint. He was convinced that Starr was yet another prosecutor who was out of control. He had predicted it from the beginning. Now, in his mind, there was nothing Hillary could say or do that would be too strong.

Hillary denied that her husband had done anything improper and attributed the assaults on the administration to Ted Olson's "vast right-wing conspiracy." There was "a politically motivated prosecutor who is allied with the right-wing opponents of my husband . . . looking at every telephone call we've made, every check we've ever written, scratching for dirt, intimidating witnesses, doing everything possible to try to make some accusation against my husband," she told Lauer's audience.

The first person she called after the interview was Kendall. Hillary told him that she had spent the entire interview thinking about what he might be saying at each moment.

"I heard your words of wisdom ringing in my ear," she said.

"And which words of incredible wisdom were you hearing?" Kendall replied.

"Screw 'em," Hillary said.

"It's an old Quaker expression," Kendall replied. "Except we say it, 'Screw thee.'"

While Kendall continued to deal with Lewinsky and Whitewater, Bennett decided the string had run out on the Paula Jones case. With the election over, there was no reason for any more delays, so he really had nothing to do. Bennett's evaluation that Paula's case was weak proved to be true, and the judge was willing to dismiss the complaint without it ever going to a jury. However, rather than endure further appeals—and his appeal record in this case had not really been so good—Bennett advised Clinton to pay Jones $850,000 in exchange for dropping all further appeals and putting an end to the sorry and embarrassing saga. In his memoir, Clinton wrote, "I hated to do it because I had won a clear victory," but he was just too busy, he said, to "spend five more minutes on Paula Jones." Besides, it wasn't going to be Clinton's money anyway. He had to borrow from a Hillary trust fund and against an insurance policy to come up with the money. Having his wife in effect pay for his extramarital dalliance was a nice touch.

After four and a half years the Paula Jones case was over, but the furor over the Monica Lewinsky liaison was just beginning. Armed with legal wiretaps and taped conversations from Linda Tripp, and with plenty of pressure points with which to force Lewinsky to testify against a president she loved, Starr had negotiated a deal: He would not prosecute Lewinsky for filing a false affidavit if she would reveal all the details of her relationship with the president. As her attorney, she hired Plato Cacheris, whose expertise was in handling femme fatales, as he had in the Oliver North case. Plato was the smoothest of operators when it came to working *with* a special prosecutor, as opposed to working against one.

Up until August 1998, Hillary clung to her story that the charges against her husband were the result of the vast conspiracy. Kendall, though, was beginning to learn otherwise. As close as Kendall and Hillary had become, the realization that the president had lied to his wife, and the country, stretched Kendall's Indiana-grounded imagination. Somebody had to break the news to Hillary, and Barnett volunteered to perform that most unpleasant task.

Barnett went through the White House gate on Friday night, August 14, and was ushered into the second-floor Yellow Oval Room and seated on a gorgeous crimson armchair under a French Empire chandelier. It was the very same room where on December 7, 1941, President Roosevelt had learned of the attack on Pearl Harbor.

Barnett's news was a little less majestic, as Hillary wrote in her memoir.

"How are you holding up?" he began.

"I'm just sorry all of us have to endure this," Hillary said.

"What if"—Barnett paused—"there's more to this than you know?"

"I wouldn't believe anything Starr said or did based on my own experience."

"But you have to face the fact that something about this might be true."

Replied Hillary, "Look, Bob. My husband may have his faults, but he has never lied to me."

Through his owl-like lenses, Barnett stared at her in some amazement. He had delivered his warning; there was nothing more for him to say.

The next morning, Clinton told Hillary the truth about his relationship with Lewinsky, as he would have to tell it to Ken Starr in a videotaped deposition on the following Monday.

On August 17, the date of the president's deposition, Kendall consented to a videotaping of the proceeding, in case a juror couldn't be there. Some of the president's political advisers suggested that Clinton speak to the nation first, then do the deposition, but Kendall said such an unusual move would only give Starr more ammunition, not less.

Clinton had not yet told anyone on his staff or in his cabinet about his relationship with Lewinsky. As outside attorneys, Kendall and Nicole Seligman were the only two people with whom Clinton had confidence that he could speak freely. He had been criticized for lying to his cabinet officials and friends about the affair with Lewinsky, but had he told them, it could have been them as well as himself in legal jeopardy. So while some later complained that their friend and leader had lied, he had actually done each individual a big favor. Without the lawyer-client privilege, they would run the risk of being subpoenaed by Starr to testify about their conversations. Then they would have to worry about a perjury charge for even an innocent mistake or faulty recollection. They would have had to hire a lawyer to answer Starr's queries. At $750 per hour, that can add up.

By now Clinton had learned that Starr had the semen sample from Lewinsky's blue dress. Confronted with that reality by Kendall, he finally had to come to grips with how to admit it, first to Starr and then to the American people. He wanted to phrase it his way, and not give the cable news army, most of whom had their jobs because of Bob Barnett, a sound bite that they could play over and over again. Kendall advised the president not to use the words "oral sex." He was definitely not to say the words "phone sex." Instead Kendall gave Clinton a lesson in euphemisms, telling him to say "inappropriate intimate contact" and "inappropriate sexual banter." From years of editing the stories in the *National Enquirer*, Kendall knew how to kill a headline, as well as how to write one. Kendall, the secret caretaker of the nation's tabloid "trash," also had a unique perspective on what was going to happen to the videotape. Starr's deputies would leak it at the first opportunity. Clinton would be foolish to think that anything Starr promised would be confidential would in fact be so. He should fully expect that anything and everything would be leaked, despite assurances to the contrary. Like all the other lawyers at Williams & Connolly, Kendall and Seligman were masters of war-gaming the process. They could predict exactly what questions would be asked. Because of the unique nature of the inquisition, Kendall's advice was to speak over the heads of the prosecutors, right out to the American people, in front of whom Kendall was sure the videotape would eventually land.

At 12:30 P.M. on August 17, Starr arrived at the White House. Fifteen minutes before the president's deposition was to begin, Kendall pulled Starr aside for a ten-minute talk in the White House library. Starr alluded to a newspaper story that talked about how much respect Kendall had for his adversary. "You know all those nice things I was quoted saying about you?" Kendall said with a smile. "I didn't say them." Kendall suspected that the comments had been attributed to him by White House political operatives who thought Starr might be softened up by kinder words than Kendall himself would speak.

Kendall then let Starr know that the president planned to make some admissions but that he would not besmirch the office of the presidency by describing "privacy-invading" details. "We'll give you what you need, but if you try to go further, I'll fight you to the knife, both in the room and publicly," Kendall told Starr. The reference to the "knife" surprised both men. Kendall didn't know how the phrase popped into his lexicon, but it illustrated the intensity of the combat. Kendall was later criticized for the phrase, when Starr's deputies began asserting that Kendall had used language "threatening" the special prosecutor, although Starr, who knew Kendall well, hadn't immediately taken it that way. Kendall claimed later that the words had just popped into his head and were not preplanned. "They were most assuredly not a physical threat," he said. In fact, it was more like standard operating procedure for any Williams & Connolly lawyer. Even one not as overtly bullying as, say, Bob Bennett, was a lawyer always well armed.

Starr brought six of his lawyers into the room. In addition to Kendall and Seligman, the newest in a long line of White House counsels, Charles Ruff, who had been a longtime partner at Covington & Burling, was there. In the 1960s, Ruff, a graduate of Swarthmore and Columbia University Law School, had won a Ford Foundation grant to teach law at a school in Liberia. One evening he was bitten by a mysterious bug and the next morning couldn't move his legs. Ruff never recovered. For the next forty years, he would be compelled to use a wheelchair, but it became so much a part of him that nobody really noticed or ever considered him handicapped. Many started calling Ruff "Ironside" when the Raymond Burr show of the same name became popular. He took it in good humor, especially around the poker table, where he was regarded as one of the best seven card stud players in his social set.

The interview began with an annoying lecture for the president from Starr's deputy independent counsel, Solomon L. Wisenberg. Then the stage was turned over to Robert Bittman, whose father, William Bittman, had been one of Washington's most illustrious defense lawyers during the Watergate hearings, as the lawyer for the swashbuckling Watergate burglar and novelist E. Howard Hunt. Just as interestingly, he had been the attorney in the famous acquittal of Labor Secretary Raymond Donovan, in the case where Donovan's comment about his reputation became the most memorable moment. In yet another famous episode, Bittman, as a prosecutor, had bested Edward Bennett Williams several times, including the conviction of LBJ aide Bobby Baker for fraud and tax evasion. Bittman was remembered after that case for having to follow Williams in what many believed was one of the most impassioned and brilliant closing arguments of the great defense lawyer's career. Bittman sauntered up to the jury and was silent for a moment. Then he said, "You have just heard the greatest argument by the greatest lawyer in the world." Pause. "All I have are the facts." Baker was convicted.

That was Bill Bittman the father. This was the son.

"Were you physically intimate with Monica Lewinsky?" Bittman asked.

Clinton put on his glasses and pulled out a paper with the precise language Kendall and Seligman had given him to use.

"When I was alone with Ms. Lewinsky on certain occasions in early 1996 and once in early 1997, I engaged in conduct that was wrong. These encounters did not consist of sexual intercourse. They did not constitute sexual relations as I understood them to be defined at my January seventeenth deposition. This is all I will say about the specifics of these particular matters."

For Ruff the admission was startling. He had not been in the solarium with Seligman and Kendall.

"What about Robert Bennett's claim that there 'is' no sex of any kind in any manner, shape, or form?" asked Wisenberg. "That was an utterly false statement. Isn't that correct?"

Clinton, going off the cuff, provided the press and television media with what would be the biggest sound bite from the hearing.

"It depends what the meaning of the word 'is' is," Clinton replied.

For nearly three hours, three Starr deputies (Starr, who never even met Monica Lewinsky, never asked a question) tried to get Clinton to say something for which they could later indict him for perjury. Finding some picayune ancillary crime, when they couldn't prove anything real, was the favorite game of prosecutors in America. They elicited a denial from Clinton that he had groped a White House visitor named Kathleen Willey, hoping to later indict him on her unprovable claim that he had.

The prosecutors had agreed to interrogate the president for no more than three hours. With twelve minutes to go, Kendall put the prosecutors on the clock. In a bizarre stretch of questions, they spent the time trying to prove that Clinton's necktie was a secret signal of solidarity to Monica. Even Clinton had to laugh at the absurdity. Having run out the clock with silliness, the hapless Starr deputies asked to extend the session, but

Kendall wasn't about to let that happen. The deposition ended, and Clinton went to his office to work on the speech he planned to give that night about his testimony to the nation. Once again, he sought advice from Hillary and Kendall as to how aggressive to be in his remarks.

In his speech following the testimony, Kendall urged Clinton to attack the prosecutors. Hillary agreed with Kendall but was also characteristically diffident. "It's your speech, say what you want," she told the president.

It was the central tenet of the Williams & Connolly practice that one never stops attacking. Clinton had learned that by now, and his post-deposition speech was Ed Williams from the grave.

"The fact that these questions were being asked in a politically inspired lawsuit, which has since been dismissed, was a consideration, too. In addition I had real and serious concerns about an independent counsel investigation that began with private business dealings twenty years ago, dealings, I might add, about which an independent federal agency found no evidence of any wrongdoing. The independent counsel investigation moved on to my staff and friends, then into my private life. And now this investigation itself is under investigation," he declared.

Following the speech, the Clintons decided to see if they could follow through on a previously planned visit to Martha's Vineyard. Hillary was under pressure from women's groups to put up a show of indignation at her treatment by her husband. After the Gennifer Flowers episode and everything else, it was clear that she didn't put a high value on Bill's fidelity. Her repeated public protestations that "Bill had never lied to me" have to be taken with a grain of salt. If she really believes that, President Obama may want to reconsider whether she should be in a room alone with Vladimir Putin.

When Clinton arrived in Martha's Vineyard, he began calling political supporters, or public officials that he hoped were still political supporters. Among those was Patrick Leahy, the ranking Democrat on the House Judiciary Committee. Leahy was back on his family farm celebrating his twenty-fifth wedding anniversary at the time, and his tolerance for Clinton's antics was running low. Leahy said, "Don't even look for sympathy. You're going to have to be damn sure your testimony has been honest before the grand jury. People will be very critical of Starr, but they aren't going to excuse your conduct one iota just because of Starr's misuse of office."

Leahy offered the president his standard piece of advice: He should consider bringing Greg Craig onto his defense team. Greg had once again left Williams & Connolly, this time to work at the State Department for Secretary of State Madeleine Albright. "We're like a bus to him," one partner said derisively. "He gets on and off."

The president received a similar call of recommendation from Senator Kennedy. White House Chief of Staff John Podesta had several conversations with Craig, but the lawyer was strangely noncommittal. Most of his colleagues in town would have leaped at a chance to be so close to cameras.

On September 7, Kendall wrote Starr a letter complaining that the lurid details of the Starr report were already saturating the media.

The case that was supposed to have long been over was now entering its most cricial and dangerous phase. What was euphemistically termed "Whitewater" would now span the entire eight years of the Clinton presidency. On September 9, 1998, Starr issued his report, concluding that the president of the United States had lied under oath. He submitted it to the House of Representatives for a possible impeachment. The strategy of Bob Bennett and Lloyd Cutler, to allow the president to testify after the election was safely over, now threatened Clinton with being the first president since Andrew Johnson in 1868 to be impeached (Nixon had resigned from office before a vote of the full House of Representatives on his fate). Bennett had gotten him past the 1996 election, but the danger that Kendall had always predicted, what would happen afterward, still loomed. Nixon, after his resignation, had a home in San Clemente to go back to. Bill's physical departure would be much more problematic. Once the helicopter was in the air, and he had given his final wave, where would he go? He had no casa at Santa Barbara, no ranch in Texas, not even a peanut farm in Georgia. Unlike his multidomiciled wealthy predecessors, Clinton wasn't dealing with mere political survival anymore; he was in a fight for his life, his family, and even his living quarters.

Despite the fact that there was no shortage of lawyers on the president's team, Clinton decided to call Craig on September 12, as the heat from the impeachment referral intensified. Craig was having dinner on his back porch in northwest Washington when the phone rang. It was President Clinton. "Greg, can you come on down to the White House?" Clinton asked.

"You mean right now?" Craig asked.

"Yes," Clinton replied, "now."

So Craig said good night to his dinner guests and drove down to the White House. Having gone to school with Clinton, Craig had never been one to believe that he was wholly innocent, first of the Paula Jones accusations and later of the Lewinsky rumors. When Clinton had first gotten involved in politics, Craig was skeptical that his buddy could overcome a history of womanizing. Craig's Yale friends had always known that when it came to women, Clinton was "out of control." Looking at the relative intelligence and character of the two men, one of whom Allard Lowenstein had predicted would be president, it was hard to see where Clinton was the better man. Clinton, though, had done the one smart thing politically. He had gone home to Arkansas and run for office. Craig had come back to Washington, where political careers end but do not begin.

That evening, Craig arrived at the White House and was escorted to the second floor. For nearly two hours the two old acquaintances talked, and Clinton asked if Craig would help him.

Looking into the eyes of the once likable student he had first met at a Yale seminar in 1971, Craig could barely believe what he saw. "He was a man in deep trouble, personally, emotionally. You could tell it. He is usually a strong man, and I think part of the turmoil on his face and in the way he addressed the issue was that he felt out of control. He seemed almost helpless.

"Clinton knew he was in trouble," Craig recalled to the *Vineyard Gazette*. "The relationship inside the Clinton household was very strained. He had trouble with his cabinet. He was in trouble with his staff. He had misled everyone about what happened."

Craig said he would have to talk it over with Derry. "I'd like to help you," Craig said to his onetime tenant, "but I've got to tell you I, too, am absolutely livid about what you did."

While Craig mulled his next move, White House political operatives decided to put the whole cast of presidential lawyers on the Sunday morning talk shows. Ruff, a reluctant Kendall, and others were shipped off for television duty. None of them was as smooth, handsome, or photogenic as Craig. Ruff looked grumpy and put-upon; Kendall's absolute dislike of publicity shone through the screen.

Craig meanwhile began visiting the players in the White House, trying to soothe any possible personal resentments. Ruff figured he could use all the help he could get. Kendall was in rock solid with Hillary Clinton but was not unhappy to have another layer of lawyer between himself and Bill. If anybody was going to step in, he preferred his partner over someone like Bennett, with whom he simply could not get along.

Craig had decided he was not going to come cheaply. "I wasn't enthusiastic about this enterprise," he confided, "but when a classmate says he is in trouble, you feel personal loyalty to that relationship."

He insisted on an office near the president and having the ability to call or meet with him on a one-on-one basis whenever he needed to. Much to Ruff's chagrin, Podesta acceded to Craig's requests. When Craig's appointment was announced by the White House, he was designated as the "quarterback" of the president's defense team. A decade later, if you ask Greg what his title was in the Clinton defense, he still says "quarterback."

Craig started his new position on September 15. He had acquired a lot of friends in the Senate from his five years with Kennedy. He called one of the best of them, Kent Conrad from North Dakota. Conrad told him, "You're about three days away from a delegation of senior Democrats coming up there to ask the president to resign," he said.

Conrad's words were a shock. "I had no sense of the apocalyptic aspect of this matter," Craig said.

The president's taped address to the public would be aired just six days after Craig's hiring, on September 21, and still the only people who knew what was on it—other than Starr's team—were Kendall, Seligman, and Ruff, and none of them was talking.

Starr's investigation of President Clinton, according to Kendall's count, had cost the U.S. taxpayers $45 million, consumed the time of seventy-eight FBI agents, and used twenty-eight high-powered attorneys and an undisclosed number of private investigators. His own firm's bill was approaching $10 million. Finally the case—like Clinton's term in office—was coming to an end, one way or the other.

On November 19, 1998, the House Judiciary Committee convened to begin hearings on what to do. Starr was the sole witness for the prosecution.

Kendall had won thirty minutes from House Judiciary Committee chairman Henry Hyde to rebut the opening argument in the impeachment case against Bill Clinton. "It's a daunting exercise," Kendall conceded. "But let me begin with the simple but powerful truth that nothing in this overkill of an investigation amounts to a justification for the impeachment of the President of the United States." Then the long-awaited clash between Starr and Kendall began.

"How are you, David?" Starr asked.

"I'm very well, Ken."

Kendall then began to extract some rather remarkable admissions. Starr acknowledged that he had never actually met Monica Lewinsky.

"You have never exchanged words with Ms. Lewinsky, have you?" Kendall asked.

Replied Starr, "That's correct. The answer is yes. I have not had the occasion to meet or otherwise to look her in the eye myself."

"The same is true for her mother?"

"Yes, that is true as well. That is true," Starr said.

The conversation continued with Starr admitting, witness by witness, that he had never met or interrogated any of the principals in the Clinton impeachment case, not presidential secretary Betty Currie nor White House Chief of Staff John Podesta. "I was not actually present for any of the depositions themselves, including of Secret Service officers," Starr said.

"Mr. Starr, I bring this out not to cast aspersions or question your use of time, but . . . you are not a fact witness. Is that correct?"

"There are a number of facts I can testify to," Starr sputtered, adamant that the decision to proceed with the impeachment referral was made by the collective wisdom of his staff, and not at the insistence of Olson and the vast right-wing conspiracy.

The hearing ended with Starr looking foolish, but it was all a pointless exercise. Fully embarrassing the president—and the country they claimed to love—was a strategy the Republicans were not going to abandon.

Craig and Kendall's immediate goal was to persuade the House and the public to skip impeachment and merely censure the president. However, on December 12, 1998, the Republican-controlled House voted to send articles of impeachment to the Senate for trial. It would now be up to a team of "House managers" to persuade the Senate to convict Clinton. The Senate trial would need more than just Ken Starr to state the prosecution case. Yet how could the distinguished Senate have witnesses about oral sex and stained dresses? It was quite a dilemma, one that repressed Republican leaders like Trent Lott did not welcome. Privately Lott, with his less than positive physical appreciation of Mrs. Clinton, didn't blame Bill as much as his out-of-control former colleagues from the House of Representatives.

The trial began on January 7, 1999, with a debate over whether the Senate should call witnesses or not. Senator Ted Stevens opposed granting the House's request for real witnesses. "We'll look goofy," he complained. Stevens may have been many things in Washington, but hypocrite was not one of them. Stevens played politics the old-fashioned LBJ way, steering as much cash as he could to his home state of Alaska. You wouldn't find him, like some of his ham-fisted colleagues, bitching about earmarks and corruption, though. Such pious blather from people like his holier-than-thou colleague John McCain made Stevens's skin crawl.

On January 19, Charles Ruff wheeled into the well of the Senate to open up the president's defense. The next morning, January 20, Craig discussed the perjury charges, labeling them as vague, false, and not corroborated. Assistant White House Counsel Cheryl Mills went third, and then it was Kendall's turn. Finally Dale Bumpers, the former senator from Arkansas and a colorful orator in the style of nineteenth-century senators like Henry Clay, delivered a stem-winder.

Robert Byrd walked up to shake hands with Bumpers, and he patted Craig and Cheryl Mills on the back. "You did a good job for your client," he said. Byrd then proposed a motion that the impeachment be dismissed, but it was voted down.

On January 26, Kendall fought a motion that would give the House three witnesses whose testimony would be taken first in videotaped depositions. Kendall said, "First they filed the charges, which have been spoon-fed by Mr. Starr. Then they don't bother to check these out, they take them at face value, and now they finally want to talk to witnesses ... The House managers are like the character in *David Copperfield*, Mr. Micawber, who was always hoping that something would turn up." Growing up in rural Indiana without a strong television signal, Kendall had been one of those rare kids whose favorite author was Dickens.

Among the senators judging Clinton were North Carolina's John Edwards and South Carolina's Strom Thurmond. In a blaze of publicity, Edwards would later be revealed to have had an affair while his loyal wife was suffering from cancer. Thurmond came to acknowledge that while advocating segregation and the superiority of the white race for decades, he had fathered at least one child out of a relationship with the daughter of an

African American house servant back in South Carolina. Edward Kennedy had driven a young woman to a watery death while he was drunk but had managed not only to avoid prison until his death but to maintain his "lion of the Senate" status. The Republican senator from Idaho, Larry Craig, habituated airport restrooms looking for quick companionship. Another Republican having affairs was Nevada senator John Ensign. They were just a few of the Senate "judges" that we would come to know something about.

On February 6, it was Nicole Seligman's turn. The House managers, Seligman said, "have distorted, they have omitted, and they have created a profoundly erroneous impression." She said that Starr failed to turn over exculpatory evidence. Ruff was the final speaker, and then the long, embarrassing, and ultimately depressing saga was nearly over.

On February 12, an unseasonably warm seventy-four-degree day in Washington, the Senate acquitted Clinton on both perjury and obstruction of justice. Bill Clinton would not become the first president in American history to be expelled from office by the Congress. Kendall, Seligman, and Craig accompanied the president back to the Oval Office. They expected Clinton to sigh a breath of relief and to be effusive in his thanks. Instead, he seemed interested only in the politics of it all, particularly the fissures in the Republican Party that the whole episode had disclosed. "We got five Republican votes," Clinton crowed. "That's not bad!"

One of those five Republicans was Alaska's Ted Stevens.

27.

ELIÁN

———■———

Two months later, on April 14, a farewell party was held in the White House for Greg Craig. He collected Derry's artwork and returned to Williams & Connolly, where Kendall, Seligman, and Barnett were waiting. Like everyone who had been involved in the Clinton defense team, except perhaps for Bennett, Craig could bask in the glow of having won that year's biggest case. His career had begun by defending the person who had shot a president, but now he had achieved true legal stardom by defending a president against a political party that hoped to shoot him down, though thankfully not literally as Hinckley had. Sullivan liked to look around the office and see how his colleagues, one by one, were getting the cases of their lives. Before Clinton could even exit the field, Craig would be back in the news again. During the summer months, Kendall tried a long vacation—an inveterate traveler, he hadn't taken one for years—but in the fall, everyone seemed to be back and ready to go again.

Brendan Sullivan was spared the direct aggravation of Whitewater, but not the general mood of scandal that hung over the Clinton administration. For those who wondered where *he* was while all this went on, Sullivan was negotiating with a different special prosecutor over charges that his client, Housing and Urban Development Secretary Henry Cisneros, had lied to the FBI during his cabinet secretary background check about money he had given to a girlfriend.

On December 12, 1997, Cisneros was charged with eighteen counts of obstruction of justice and perjury for allegedly paying a secret girlfriend not to reveal details of their relationship after he was named to his government post. While the prosecution claimed the sums amounted to hush money, others thought so little of the allegations—he could have been giving her cash for any reason—that they said hiring Sullivan was like "engaging a howitzer to swat a gnat." More than a month later the girl-friend, Linda Jones, also known as Linda Medlar, pleaded guilty to twenty-eight counts of fraud and admitted to lying about buying a house with the money that Cisneros had given her. She was promised a sentence of no more than three and a half years in prison if she would testify against Cisneros in a trial that was supposed to begin in November 1999. Prosecutors had obtained some thirty-three tapes in which Cisneros discussed with her how he hoped to cover up their long-term affair and still win the job as HUD secretary, but Sullivan and Barry Simon forced Jones to acknowledge that she had altered and edited the supposedly incriminating tapes in an effort to blackmail Cisneros herself. During Cisneros's pretrial hearing in June 1999, Sullivan cross-examined Linda, exposing her as a habitual liar whose testimony could not be believed. When Sullivan was done, her usefulness as a federal witness was obliterated.

On September 7, 1999, Sullivan put an end to the Cisneros prosecution, having him plead guilty to a single misdemeanor in exchange for no jail time, a $10,000 fine, and a promise that the onetime mayor of San Antonio would not be barred from seeking public office again in the future. He called the Cisneros plea one of his only exceptions in his long career to his rule of never pleading a case out. Before he did, Sullivan had an ironclad agreement that the very favorable terms of the plea could not be undone.

Even though Cisneros's case seemed over, the special prosecutor, a Republican lawyer from Indiana named David M. Barrett, proceeded to keep his office open for what eventually totaled eleven years, spending $21 million on his investigation, even though there was really nothing more to investigate. When he had been appointed, officials at the Justice Department had expected Barrett to take about two months to figure out whether Cisneros had lied or not. To find out what Barrett was doing for over a decade, the government's General Accounting Office had to launch its own costly investigation into the special investigator. According to Neil Lewis of the New York Times, the GAO never found any malfeasance on the part of Barrett as to how the $21 million was spent—but neither, wrote Lewis, did it discover why the money was spent, except that Barrett believed that if he just had a little more time, and a little more money, even after the plea bargain, he could still nail Cisneros on a new tax count. He never did, but not for lack of trying. As Starr has shown and Olson had personally learned the hard way, once a special prosecutor gets started, there isn't much that can stop him.

Although Cisneros walked free, his ex-girlfriend had been sentenced in March 1998 to three and a half years in prison for concealing information about receiving $185,000 from Cisneros in exchange for not talking about their two-decades-long affair. That was the hush money that he paid but was never punished for. In the plea bargain deal, she agreed to take a light sentence in exchange for testifying about the relationship with Cisneros. In the deal with Cisneros, she allegedly took money from him to *not* talk about their relationship. Only one of the two arrangements was criminal. Henry had the most expensive and experienced defense lawyer in the country. Linda had been principally advised by two public defenders from Lubbock, Texas.

On Thanksgiving, November 25, 1999, as Cisneros counted his blessings, three fisherman found an inner tube floating in the Florida Straits. Inside the inner tube was a six-year-old-boy, Elián González. His mother, Elizabet Brotons, had died at sea with eleven others attempting to flee Cuba, and he was placed by U.S. officials in the custody of a great-uncle who lived in Miami, Lázaro González. Immediately Elián, and ultimately Greg Craig, found himself at the center of an international controversy that pitted the needs and wishes of a poverty-stricken Cuban family against the passionate desires and grand dreams of the Cuban exile community in South Florida.

Cuban Americans had spent decades vilifying Fidel Castro and his repressive Communist regime, so the idea that little Elián could be shipped from his hard-won life of freedom back to Castro's Caribbean gulag was unthinkable for many people. On the other hand, here were conservatives who had argued consistently through the decade of the 1990s for family values. Here was a young boy whose father lived in Cuba and wanted him to come home. He had not even known that his ex-wife had taken the boy out of the country—and even in the United States taking a child away from a divorced but adoring parent would be considered more an act of kidnapping than one of heroism.

In politics, unfortunately, principles—even lip service to the sacred family—are easily and quickly abandoned when it becomes useful. That is one of the immutable rules of Washington. Miami, too, apparently.

The major players all claimed to have the interest of the young boy at heart, but there is no escaping the reality that people on both sides would sometimes put him second to their political goals. On the one side was the Cuban community. To some extent they were invested in their own propaganda. When Cuba had been run by an avaricious dictator, Fulgencio Batista, aided and abetted by mob figures like Meyer Lansky and Lucky Luciano, nobody seemed to mind. Wealthy Cubans didn't complain then about their bad government, nor about the abject poverty and repression of the Cuban peasants. After he was overthrown by Castro, Batista went into the life insurance business in Spain, where he died of a heart attack in 1973.

Nonetheless, as a political issue, Cuba had become one of those "third rails" of American politics, the way Social Security is often described. Anyone who dared to suggest that the United States normalize relations with Cuba was just asking for political oblivion. Hardly a politician existed who could stand up to that political pressure. Castro was the devil and that was the end of it.

However, there were powerful forces in America who quietly, very quietly, longed for the day when Cuba would become a trading partner and ally of the United States. The diplomatic and political history of Cuba had become one of the real tragedies of the age, considering what Cuba could have been. During the economic boom of the 1990s and early 2000s, a free Cuba could have become one of the wealthiest and most attractive nations on earth, an international mecca of travel and tourism. Havana could well have had its own Major League Baseball club; it would have been a far more perfect location than Miami, where support for the Florida Marlins was so poor that owner John Henry was looking for a new partner with whom to invest in a more loved team, like the Boston Red Sox.

Among the companies with the biggest interest in making overtures to Castro was Archer Daniels Midland, the "Supermarket to the World," which had been represented by Williams & Connolly in a long-running and complicated price-fixing case (and sponsored the ABC Sunday morning news program that Barnett rarely missed). ADM had dreams of opening agricultural facilities in Cuba. The most prominent figure on ADM's board of directors was Brian Mulroney, the former prime minister of Canada. A leading advocate of the North American Free Trade Agreement, Mulroney left office in 1993 and joined the Montreal-based law firm Ogilvy Renault, which advertises itself as "home to Canada's foremost international trade practice," and it boasts that "our lawyers have acted in more international trade proceedings" than any other Canadian firm. The leader of the practice is Mulroney. In addition, the firm roster boasts both the former Canadian ambassador to the United Nations and the former Canadian ambassador to the United States. All are now making millions of dollars from the trade policies they put in place while in office. The practice of ex-politicians walking through the revolving door from public service did not stop at the U.S. border.

It was thus no surprise when Archer Daniels Midland officials began to work behind the scenes to bring Greg Craig into the Elián González case. ADM's retired chairman, Dwayne Andreas, had long cultivated ties to the National Council of Churches, a liberal theological organization. He was a major donor to Florida's Barry University, where his wife, Inez, had been chairwoman of the Board of Trustees. The law school at Barry is named the Dwayne O. Andreas School of Law. The business school is named the D. Inez Andreas School of Business. The original locale for negotiations between opposing sides in the Elián conflict was, coincidentally, Barry University. For months no progress was made, and it appeared that time was on the side of Elián staying in Miami.

Finally Senator Patrick Leahy advised the coordinator for the National Council of Churches, Joan Brown Campbell, "I think you need a lawyer. I know one who can do it and would do it. His name: Gregory Craig." The National Council of Churches agreed to pony up the money to hire him, some of it from ADM contributions to their organization. Craig knew from his experiences with Castro a decade earlier that it would take the Cuban premier's cooperation and political skill to break the deadlock. There were only a handful of lawyers in the United States who had personal experience negotiating with Castro. Greg was the one who knew him best. He didn't need much convincing to take the case. "I was already there on the issue of father and son," he said, "and I thought I could make a difference."

He also knew that possession was nine tenths of the law. Every minute that Elián lived in Miami with his relatives made it that much harder for him ever to be reunited with his father. Craig had to find some way to get Juan Miguel González, the forgotten father of the story, into Miami and to change the momentum of the incident. For that to happen, Greg knew that he would once again need Fidel.

Craig was dancing a dangerous tightrope of negotiation. For Elián to be reunited with Juan Miguel, the American people would have to see the father in the flesh—they needed to be assured that he was not a Communist monster. On the other hand, for Castro to let Juan Miguel come to the States, he needed to be absolutely convinced that Juan Miguel would not bolt, demand political asylum, or otherwise embarrass the Cuban government.

On April 25, Craig flew to Cuba and was ushered into Castro's presidential sanctum. Juan Miguel had already been moved from Cardenas, his home two hours outside of Havana, to an apartment where he could be made quickly available to Castro, if needed.

After his first visit with Castro, Craig announced, "I think all that has happened tonight is that the president of Cuba has said there is no Cuban government impediment to him coming and remaining here as long as it takes to exhaust the appeals, if by coming he can take custody of Elián.

"There are two players," Craig said. "The relatives in Miami have said they won't release Elián. And the INS and the government of the United States have not said, 'If you come we will arrange for you to have custody.' Those two hurdles have not been overcome. The conversations that are going on in Miami hold the key. What I want to do is to set Juan Miguel free. I want the father to make a decision uncoerced from Havana, uncoerced from Miami, uncoerced by the press, independently and freely to make a decision where and how he wants to raise his family. That's all I'm concerned about."

The next morning Craig met with Castro again and assured him, as only he could, that he would not let him be embarrassed. Then, having convinced Castro to let Juan Miguel come to America, he had to persuade the father that this was necessary. Juan Miguel, just thirty-one, was not accustomed to the spotlight. Curiously, when the INS officer in Havana first interviewed him, Juan Miguel asked that his own parents be allowed to accompany him. His reluctance to exhibit more maturity himself was frustrating to Craig. One of Juan Miguel's uncles, who was urging his nephew to press his claim more forcefully, said that Juan Miguel did not trust the United States and that he was "fearful" and "confused."

When Craig got to the villa where the Cuban government had moved Juan Miguel, he had to negotiate in a different way. "We can't wait any longer," Craig pleaded with urgency. "If we don't go now, we may never get him back."

Craig showed Juan Miguel a noncommittal but optimistic letter he had from the American Immigration and Naturalization Service promising to "begin the process of transferring Elián to his father's care." He also carried a letter from Leahy, who had previously given Craig his promise that if Juan Miguel came to America "he would not be left waiting" to obtain custody of his son.

Silma Dimmel, who ran the small INS office in Havana, later wrote in the official report that Juan Miguel "did not appear at all nervous or intimidated." Although Juan Miguel asked to be interviewed in the presence of his own parents, he did not seem "in any way influenced by some unknown person or persons." She said that Juan Miguel had paid more than the legally required child support and provided extra food and clothes for his son and ex-wife. Elián spent more nights with Juan Miguel than with his mother, in part because she lived in a tiny single room and he had his own apartment. He certainly seemed to have been loved by both of his separated parents, she believed.

After four hours of conversation, Craig returned to his hotel room not sure what was going to happen.

Juan Miguel had to be in Washington by 9:30 A.M. to make the next negotiating session between INS officials and the representatives of the Miami relatives who wanted to keep Elián. Castro, always concerned about appearances, still didn't like the image of Craig and Juan Miguel traveling together to the United States. "It looks like a rescue mission," he complained to Craig.

"I don't care what it looks like," Craig said. "I want Juan Miguel to come to the U.S. now. Now is the time." Craig suggested that they go separately, just so it was soon.

"Let's do it that way," Castro proclaimed, satisfied. Craig looked over at Juan Miguel. He flashed Craig a thumbs-up. Castro then personally put Juan Miguel on a Cuban-government-owned private plane headed for the United States. Although there had been talk of having him accompanied by all of Elián's classmates and friends from home, the only Cubans with Juan Miguel were his new wife and new baby boy. Castro had only Craig's word that Juan Miguel would not embarrass him by defecting or asking for political asylum. Once Juan Miguel arrived at Dulles Airport, it didn't seem likely that the United States would send him home without his son, although the family-values-oriented Cuban exile community was prepared to raise $2 million if Juan Miguel would walk away from his boy.

The Cuban exile community had not counted on Craig succeeding in his gambit, and now the Williams & Connolly attorney had successfully turned the issue not to *whether* Elián would be turned over but to when and, just as importantly, how. The relatives announced that while they could not stop the government's taking Elián, they would not be seen in Miami handing him over, either. That meant one thing: The INS would have to come in and take him. Before Attorney General Janet Reno would order that Elián be taken into custody, though, she wanted to meet with Juan Miguel herself. It was interesting that the most emotional moment of Reno's term in office would involve Miami, the very city in which she had been the state's attorney.

On the way over in the car, Craig said to Juan Miguel, "You are meeting with the highest law enforcement officials in the land. It is an entirely private meeting. If you have any concerns or questions, feel free to raise them. Feel free to ask them for anything you or your family could want." The intent of his comments was to glean from Juan Miguel if he had even the slightest thought of defecting or asking for asylum. Craig was certain that he didn't. "If he wanted to stay in this country," he says, "he could have asked." In fact, it was the last thing Juan Miguel wanted.

On Friday morning, Janet Reno met with Juan Miguel, his wife, and their infant in her office. There were no Cuban officials present, and if Juan Miguel had wanted to seek asylum, this was the place to speak up. Instead, Juan Miguel again made it clear that he wanted to return to Cuba with his son. Reno seemed emotionally affected by the encounter and promised that he would get his son back. The attorney general and Elián's father then embraced. "All you needed to do was listen to him and look at him and see how much he loved that little boy," Reno, who had no children of her own, said later.

The lawyers for Elián's great-uncle Lázaro had demanded that a team of outside psychiatrists be appointed to determine if Elián should return to Cuba. The attorney general topped them by appointing her own team—two psychiatrists and a psychologist—to advise on the best way of turning over the boy to his father. Their answer was: right away, and with the support of all his family. That, however, would have been too simple for the Miami relatives, who couldn't be seen by their rabid neighbors turning him over to a life of enslavement. Instead, on April 22, 2000, armed INS agents went into the home and, in a confused scene that produced hours of cable fodder for the anti-Castro Cubans, removed the boy into their own custody. Craig says he did not know of the raid in advance but had suspected it after INS agents called to ask if Elián had any allergies and what his blood type was.

Elián was then put into the care of his father and Craig. Until all the appeals by the relatives ran out, Elián and his father lived the good life at Rosedale, an 1,100-acre government-owned villa outside of Washington. On the morning that they were to leave, Juan Miguel ordered his son to put on a freshly ironed pair of khaki slacks. Elián refused, plopped into a chair, grabbed the remote, and changed the channel from CNN to the Cartoon Network.

Craig, who has five children of his own, started laughing. They then flew back to Cuba, where they were met at the plane by a Soviet-built Lada sedan and driven off into the subtropical evening. Elián was back in Cuba, it seemed, for good—no longer an icon in a fading political cause or a pawn between nations, just a little boy. A few months later Craig quietly flew back to Cuba for Elián's seventh birthday party, which Castro also attended.

28.

PARDON US

———————◼———————

By the fall of 2000, the Clinton years were clattering to an end. Coming into the White House, they were probably the least wealthy people to ever occupy the Oval Office. Bill and Hillary had never even so much as owned a house together. Bill's salary as governor of Arkansas was just $15,000 a year, the lowest pay for a chief executive in any U.S. state. Although Paula Jones had originally sought only $700,000 in damages in her sex harassment case against Clinton, Robert Bennett had somehow managed to end up promising $850,000, which the Clintons had to largely borrow, to make it go away.

As Clinton had gotten poorer over the years, though, Williams & Connolly became wealthier and wealthier. In the ten years from 1991 to 2001, average per-partner profits had spiked from $750,000 to well over $1 million. Once one of the smaller "boutique" firms in Washington, it was now well on its way to employing more than two hundred lawyers, most of them billing at the highest rates in Washington. Rainmaking partners like Brendan Sullivan and Bob Barnett were earning more than $2 million a year, a sum that would climb throughout the succeeding decades.

In addition to the immediate need to pay Paula Jones, Clinton was committed to paying Bennett's legal bills as well as those of Kendall, Seligman, and Barnett. Craig had been hired by the White House, and his fees were taken care of by the White House legal budget. The total amount that Clinton owed to Williams & Connolly—for nearly seven years of top-drawer wall-to-wall legal service—was conservatively estimated at $9 million to $10 million.

With the Whitewater-impeachment craziness over, Nicole Seligman finally broke up with Eli Jacobs and at once became the most eligible single woman in Washington. At the White House Correspondents Dinner in 2000, former White House counsel Joel Klein noticed that Bob Bennett had been assigned to sit next to Seligman at the dinner. During Whitewater, Klein had noticed her but appropriately kept his distance. Now, with his own dinner companion not nearly as interesting, he swapped his place card for Bennett's. When Bennett caught him in the act and growled, the divorced Klein explained, "You're married. I'm single. She's beautiful." Seven months later, Klein and Seligman were married. They would soon thereafter move to New York, Klein taking the CEO job of the American division of the German publishing conglomerate Bertelsmann AG, while Seligman became general counsel for Sony Corporation. Klein later left Bertelsmann to become New York City's chancellor of education.

In November, the presidential election was held. Williams & Connolly still seemed more invested in the retiring Clintons than in the Gores. Barnett was using his well-honed debate skills to help Hillary win her U.S. Senate race in New York against Republican opponent Rick Lazio. Somehow playing a lowly congressman like Lazio seemed beneath Barnett. When it came time to hire attorneys to try to win the deadlocked election in the U.S. Supreme Court, Al Gore went with Harvard professor Laurence Tribe and New York–based litigator David Boies. Even though both received a majority of the votes cast in their respective election contests, Hillary won; Gore lost.

Of course, whether Gore really won or lost was not only the subject of an HBO special but a matter of partisan debate. The vice president certainly got the most votes, but in 2000 it was finally Ted Olson's turn to win something. After unsuccessfully doing all he and Ken Starr could to get Clinton impeached and thus damage the Democratic Party for 2000, Olson now set about to undo the clear popular-vote result. While his vivacious attorney-wife, Barbara, managed vote-counting operations on the ground in Tallahassee, Olson directed the legal arguments, eventually convincing the justices—several of whom he had literally gotten placed on the Court—that there was no need to count the votes, nor to consider the intent of the voters when they cast their ballots. So much for the lip service President G. W. Bush and his supporters would later pay (in his administration's foreign policy) to "democracy."

Nobody could say that Bill Clinton was sad about how the 2000 election turned out. He and Gore were already barely speaking by the time of the election, and the Clintons were already maneuvering to put Hillary in the White House in either 2004 or 2008. Having Gore out of the way just made it easier.

For Ted Olson, it was a tragic period. On his sixty-first birthday, in 2001, his Barbara, who had worked as hard as he had, or harder, to put Bush in the White House, was a passenger aboard the American Airlines Boeing 757 that was flown by terrorists into the Pentagon outside of Washington. She was on her cell phone to Ted when the plane exploded.

It was a few days before Christmas in 2000 that Clinton sat down to ponder what would be the final and perhaps most controversial actions of his presidency, the traditional end-of-term pardons.

The most controversial would be the pardon that Clinton bestowed upon Marc Rich, a businessman who had been indicted by the Justice Department after falsely valuing the price of certain oil transactions in order to reduce his tax liability. His case had been around since the early 1980s, when employees began complaining about his shady deals to federal prosecutors in New York. Rich's most prominent criminal attorney in the United States had been Edward Bennett Williams. It was while Williams was negotiating a plea bargain with the government that Rich began preparing to flee to Switzerland. After U.S. Attorney Rudolph Giuliani handed up a fifty-six-page, fifty-one-count indictment, Rich refused to come back to the United States and took asylum in the Swiss village of Zug, surrounded by expensive works of art and a luxurious lifestyle.

Although his company would later plead guilty to thirty-eight counts of tax evasion, Rich's exile enabled him to fall under the Williams & Connolly umbrella as yet another obviously guilty person who had never served a day in jail. Even so, this was not the way Williams & Connolly really liked to do it.

In his memoir, *My Life*, Clinton comes up with numerous rationales for why Marc Rich deserved a pardon, none of which, of course, had anything to do with Rich's ex-wife, Denise, having been a major campaign contributor to the Clintons. "I made the decision based on the merits," Clinton insisted. If Rich was so innocent, many wondered, why didn't he let Edward Bennett Williams persuade a jury of that?

Exactly how someone who had fled the U.S. justice system rather than confront whatever the charges were in open court could be exonerated based on the "merits" is rather hard to fathom. Rich had gamed the system, using his ill-gotten gains, and somehow managed to beat it. To almost everyone in America, except for Clinton, the Rich pardon was the ultimate outrage of Clinton's presidency.

Marc Rich constituted one of Williams & Connolly's oldest pieces of outstanding business, and Bill Clinton did owe Williams & Connolly nearly $10 million. True to his name, Rich would have gladly paid that for his pardon. Clinton, however, and Williams & Connolly insist that the president's debts had nothing to do with any of his decisions.

Another controversial Clinton pardon was for Susan Rosenberg and Linda Sue Evans. In the mid-1980s, they had been involved in the robbery of a Brink's truck, in which two New York state troopers and a Brink's security guard had been murdered. They had cast their crimes in political terms, which apparently, they felt, made it OK to kill someone.

According to the prosecutor in the case, Rosenberg's defense was "brazen." She told the court, "When we were first captured we said, we're caught, we're not defeated, long live the armed struggle." Her defiant attitude played a major role in the judge's decision to give her a fifty-eight-year sentence.

Nevertheless, Clinton commuted Rosenberg's sentence, as well as that of co-conspirator Linda Sue Evans, who had gotten forty years. The principal pardon attorney for Rosenberg was Howard Gutman, a partner at Williams & Connolly and one of Greg Craig's best friends and most reliable colleagues on cases involving South America.

Then there was the curious pardon of John Mark Deutch. Almost a footnote to CIA history, Deutch was the last director of the CIA before Clinton named Eli Jacobs's friend George Tenet to the post in 1996. Deutch got in trouble after he began downloading classified CIA documents to his personal unsecured laptop computer. Deutch hadn't actually even been charged with a crime by the time the matter came up to Clinton, but just in case, he had hired Terrence O'Donnell, the Republican Williams & Connolly partner most connected to the incoming Bush administration. O'Donnell's task was to make sure that the Justice Department policy of the Clinton administration, which was *not* to charge him with any crimes, remained government policy. As it turned out, what might happen to Deutch in the transition turned out to be a needless concern. Clinton pardoned Deutch in advance of the Bush administration coming into power, on the very last day of his presidency.

While the Clinton impeachment saga was taking place, Clinton's secretary of housing and urban development, Henry Cisneros, had pleaded guilty to one misdemeanor count of lying to FBI investigators during the background check he had to provide before he could be named to the Clinton cabinet. He was fined $10,000 for the crime but not given any jail time. As if the fine wasn't light enough, he got a presidential pardon on top of it. His attorneys were still Brendan Sullivan and Barry Simon.

One of his few friends that Clinton didn't pardon was his wife's law partner Webb Hubbell. Hubbell's crimes were considerably underwhelming, compared to the bombers, international fugitives, and cabinet officials who did get favorable consideration. Webb had actually gone through the judicial system, rather than flee the country, and he certainly hadn't killed a police officer or stolen government secrets—but he was represented by Sullivan's old nemesis, John Nields.

Of course, it could have been a coincidence that so many Williams & Connolly clients got pardons. At the time, though, there was no certainty that Bill Clinton would ever be able to pay Williams & Connolly in dollars. Logically, people thought that he would have money again, but nobody knew how much. Still, even if he never paid Williams & Connolly a dime of his monumental legal fees, he had pretty much cleared the decks of their key cases. He could leave the White House believing that what they had gotten was more than fair, even though Williams & Connolly always expected its fees would be paid in the conventional way, which they later were.

A short time after she had been sworn in as a U.S. senator in New York, Hillary was asked in a television appearance about her role in the presidential pardons.

"You know, I did not have any role in the pardons that were granted or not granted," she said warily. "Oh, you know, as I have said in the past, when it became apparent around Christmas that people knew that the president was considering pardons, there were many, many people who spoke to me, or, you know, asked me to pass on information to the White House Counsel's Office, and they, along with the president, made the decisions."

On page 942 of *My Life*, the former president contradicts his wife, saying that Hillary—and Kendall—did play a role in advocating pardons for particular people, especially for Webb Hubbell. Needless to say, David Kendall also has no comment about any role he would have played in greasing the Williams & Connolly pardon agenda. In the book's acknowledgments, Clinton reveals that Kendall read and approved the manuscript, so one would have to assume that if Bill Clinton was mistaken, Kendall would have noticed it.

29.

GOLDIN PARACHUTES

———————■———————

Following the disputed presidential election of 2000, the crush of Clinton aides and cabinet members fleeing from government to private enterprise sounded more like the tinkle of an old cash register to Bob Barnett. Methodically he matched government officials up with new jobs and negotiated their new deals. Health and Human Services Secretary Donna Shalala, for example, went to the University of Miami, where she became the new chancellor.

Barnett had things covered both coming and going. He placed former NASA administrator Daniel Goldin in a new job as president of Boston University. Barnett's contract with the university would have made Goldin one of the highest-paid university presidents in the country. It included a retirement plan worth more than $1 million, life insurance valued at three times his annual pay, and a furnished house with a small staff and a car and driver. The deal also included more unusual perks for a university president, like first-class travel for him and his wife and $10,000 a year worth of advice on financial planning. As with his negotiations with publishers, trustees would later say that Barnett exercised his customary Svengali-like power, convincing the board that privileges and pay that no college had *ever* agreed to were perfectly reasonable.

However, before Goldin could even begin work, sanity began to return to the minds of the university trustees who had approved the much too lucrative deal. One day before he was to begin his job at BU, Barnett extracted from the school an agreement to pay Goldin $1.8 million—*not* to come to work. Apparently, members of the board had begun to feel threatened by Goldin's volatile temperament and his plan for sweeping changes at the school. Before hiring him, they hadn't bothered to even contemplate an interview he had given in 1998 in which he had self-analyzed himself.

"Basically, I'm a volatile person," Goldin had said. "Every minute, I've got to manage my emotional control. Some people are born to be level. I fight every day of my life to be level, and I'm not allowed the luxury of blowing up. But occasionally I do."

Washingtonians familiar with Goldin's personality had been amused back in 1999 when he met his match—Arizona senator John McCain, customarily known around Capitol Hill as "Senator Hothead." After a $125 million space probe crashed on Mars because of a NASA screwup, McCain, then chairman of the Senate Commerce Committee, called Goldin to his senatorial hideaway. There he proceeded to scream at and curse Goldin for what seemed to aides like an unusually long period of time, even for McCain. When the senator was done, he pitched Goldin out of the office.

While Goldin regrouped in the hallway, he was suddenly summoned back to speak to McCain, ostensibly to apologize—but when Goldin returned, McCain lost it again, and a second rant ensued without Goldin ever getting a word in edgewise. When he did try to answer, McCain interrupted and ejected him for the second time in an hour.

The collapse of the deal with Boston University was humiliating for Goldin, but not for Barnett. He saw it as simply another opportunity. "Mr. Goldin and I are very pleased that this matter has been resolved amicably," Barnett said. "Mr. Goldin has some exciting opportunities that he will now pursue." Barnett eventually helped him start a high-tech aerospace business in San Diego.

Barnett also got double work out of former Clinton treasury secretary Larry Summers. After the 2000 election, Barnett handled the negotiations for Summers to become the president of Harvard University. He managed an unprecedented contract that allowed Summers to make money on outside consulting duties while he still worked at Harvard. When Summers was forced out as president in 2006 for allegedly making remarks questioning the ability of women to comprehend math and science, Barnett stepped in to handle the severance package as well as to help Summers procure a position with the D. E. Shaw Group, a New York–based hedge fund. Summers would make $5.2 million from the hedge fund, and his new speaking package allowed him to receive as much as $135,000 for a single talk. That record-breaking fee was paid by the New York investment bank Goldman Sachs, which had benefited from Summers's tenure as secretary of the treasury and would be in a position to benefit again from his subsequent elevation to economic czar in the Obama administration—despite predictions that his supposedly sexist remarks disqualified him for public office. The Barnett "Trans-Washington Highway," in and out of government, had paid off for Summers. After losing the Harvard presidency, he ended up more powerful and wealthier.

There is an old saying in Washington that there is nothing so popular as a vacancy, and the turn from one administration to the next is like Christmas in D.C.

There was, of course, the matter of the Clintons themselves. They were limping out of office with some $10 million in personal debt and their reputations, at least the president's, in tatters. Hillary had managed to escape with some modicum of dignity and had already parlayed that into a U.S. Senate seat from New York. Elected on November 7, 2000, Hillary became the first first lady to win a Senate election while living in the White House.

First, Barnett sold Mrs. Clinton's memoir, which would be published under the title *Living History*, to Scribner. He began contacting publishers while Mrs. Clinton was still the first lady, and her husband still the president, in the fall of 2000. Publishers were interested, many being of the mind that first-lady books are more honest and more popular with readers than the stodgier accounts of their husbands. Presidents tend to write as if they are Olympian gods, while first ladies are more inclined to want to settle scores, as was the case with Nancy Reagan's book, *My Turn*. Barnett had the nation's top book editors come one at a time to meet and talk to Mrs. Clinton. It was a delicate dance. Everyone wanted an assurance that she was going to reveal how she felt about her husband's affair with Monica, but no one wanted to come right out and bring that up. Standing or sitting constantly by her side, notebook in hand, Barnett had prepared Hillary for the possible Kabuki dance. So they spoke in code, with her assuring them that she would write an "honest" yet dignified book. According to David Kirkpatrick in the *New York Times*, publishers concluded that she would write "an inspirational survivor's story, focused on her emotions and inner life rather than on the details of the goings-on inside the White House." In mid-December 2000, she eventually agreed to an advance in excess of $8 million. She was said to be disappointed that the sum failed to break the record, set by Pope John Paul II for *Crossing the Threshold of Hope*.

Senators are generally banned from accepting outside income; however, the rules exclude book earnings, as long as the amount received from the book is "usual and customary." Only one senator raised a question about whether the advance was "customary." That was the perpetual curmudgeon McCain, who rudely asked that the contract be reviewed by the Senate Ethics Committee. His Senate rival for hotheadedness, Alaska's Ted Stevens, offered no such objection.

Barnett did not begin shopping the president's memoir until he had left the White House. He still had some sticky legal business that David Kendall continued to handle. It was clear by now that if Clinton hadn't violated any federal laws, he had certainly run afoul of the lawyers' code of ethics, as silly as that could be. Down in Arkansas, in the last act of the impeachment drama, Judge Wright stripped Clinton of his law license and forced him to reimburse her $1,202 in travel costs, money she had spent to go to the deposition where he lied. Clinton was also tied up defending his controversial pardons, and Barnett felt that giving the anger over that time to subside might bring him some extra millions.

Not being president gave Clinton a lot more time to spend writing, and Barnett sold Bill's memoir in August 2001 to Alfred A. Knopf for $10 million. Now the Clinton family—richer cumulatively by at least $18 million—would at last be able to pay their Williams & Connolly legal bills. There was again much debate about whether Clinton beat out the pope for the number one spot in the advance race. Although the pope had received $8.5 million, Clinton claimed to a friend that, adjusted for inflation, he had gotten slightly more than the Holy Father. Blood sport in Washington had turned into very profitable "booksport." Only in Washington were egos so large that so many felt comfortable measuring themselves favorably against John Paul II.

Barnett became the key player in resuscitating the lives and reputations of both Clintons. For all the crazy unethical things Bill had done in the White House, large numbers of the American people, reflected in polls, had fallen in love with the sinner, largely because in the end, he had won.

One idea that initially intrigued Clinton was to host his own television talk show, one that would be a cross between *Oprah* and *Nightline*, combining talk on a couch with intelligent, serious discussions of world affairs. The project got far enough along that both CBS and King World, the daytime television syndicator, had extensive talks about how the revenues might be divided, where the show might air, and what the target audience would be. To Clinton's network of crass Hollywood friends, it seemed like a terrific deal. Something about it offended Barnett's sense of presidential decorum, though. Barnett no more wanted to be a party to having Clinton destroy presidential dignity than Larry Lucchino had wanted to ruin the traditions of baseball.

Lucchino had long ago given up trying cases and certainly no longer billed by the hour, but with the sale of the Orioles to Peter Angelos, Lucchino was left without a team to operate. Angelos, a Baltimore personal injury lawyer, made some overtures that could sound to the naive like Lucchino could continue to run the team, but Larry was not born in the back of a hay truck. He had been there when Ed Williams had made similar false entreaties to Jerry Hoffberger.

The perfect job for Lucchino in baseball would have been to become the commissioner. With his love and attention to baseball history and traditions, Lucchino was just what the game needed. Ironically, in the eyes of the rapacious owners, that was what made him a liability. Given a choice between the additional television revenue of playing a World Series game on a cold Sunday night or paying homage to the grand tradition of delightful afternoon games in the fall, Lucchino would have been inclined to play in the sunlight. More significantly, Allan "Bud" Selig, who had been acting commissioner since 1992—and done everything possible to ruin the game with innovations like interleague play and interminable seasons that lasted into frigid nights in early November—wasn't going anywhere. Selig had been a major player in the sale of the Orioles to Eli Jacobs, and Lucchino was hardly of a mind to challenge somebody who had been a key ally and benefactor over the years. The rough game played by Williams & Connolly partners often involved destroying enemies but not knifing your friends.

For many years, Lucchino had been pals with Tom Werner, a television producer who had made millions by developing and then syndicating *The Cosby Show*. After the death of Williams & Connolly partner Jay Monahan, Werner had become Katie Couric's boyfriend. Also a baseball fan, Werner purchased controlling interest in the National League's San Diego Padres from Joan Kroc, the widow of McDonald's owner Ray Kroc, who had been the sole and original owner of the Padres.

Werner's interest in the Padres faded after some discouraging fights with the city of San Diego over how and where to build a new stadium. In 1994, he sold the team to businessman John Moores. The timing was fortuitous for Lucchino, and the lure of living in Southern California appealed to every playboy instinct in his body. With his Orioles money, Lucchino bought 10 percent of the Padres and was named by Moores as the president and CEO. He bought a beautiful home in La Jolla, and he asked his friend the marketing genius Jay Emmett to serve on the team's board of directors.

For Moores, Lucchino was the missing piece in the Padres ownership. The outstanding issue with regard to the team was building a new park. The team had a good general manager and some fine players, like outfielder Tony Gwynn, a good friend of Cal Ripken's; they shared the same agent and had both heeded his advice to stay in one baseball town their entire careers. Moores felt he didn't need Larry as much for baseball decisions as he did for his expertise and experience in dealing with local government and getting the new stadium built.

"Larry's résumé said Camden Yards," Moores commented. "Then I realized it said Camden Yards forty-three times." Werner's failure had been his inexperience in dealing with Byzantine municipal politics, and that was the one thing Larry knew better than anyone.

The Padres had experienced the worst record, the worst attendance, and the worst revenue in the National League. Trying to instill some of the old pride of the Baltimore Orioles into the lackluster team, Lucchino invited his PR director, Charles Steinberg, and Steinberg's annual summer helper-intern, Theo Epstein, to California. He also wanted fans to know that the new ownership was bold. One of his first steps as club president was to engineer a twelve-player trade. Among those he brought to the Padres were Steve Finley, a former Orioles center fielder, and Ken Caminiti, a hard-hitting outfielder. Caminiti became an outspoken critic of Lucchino, claiming, "He has no people skills. He's the money man. He'll do anything for money. Larry puts a damper on things. A lot of people are unhappy."

A few seasons after making those remarks, Caminiti, who had been the National League's Most Valuable Player in 1996, admitted that he was addicted to both steroids and cocaine. The "selfless" player who claimed Lucchino would do "anything for money" died of a drug overdose at age forty-one in 2004.

Both Steinberg and Epstein heeded the call, left the Orioles, and came west. Epstein still had a year left at Yale, but he agreed to come work for the Padres in 1995; his job would include organizing the wedding and birthday announcements on the Padres scoreboard. The following year, Epstein's portfolio expanded to writing and handing out press notes, as well as operating the radar gun that measured the speed of the pitches. The year after that, 1997, Epstein finally got his driver's license at the age of twenty-three, and at Lucchino's suggestion he enrolled at the University of San Diego Law School. According to an account of their relationship by Dan Shaughnessy in *Reversing the Curse*, Epstein traded tickets to the games in exchange for detailed notes of the classes he missed.

The decision to go to law school nearly had the unintended effect of ending Epstein's baseball career. He proved to be such a good law firm prospect that Ted Olson's prestigious firm, Gibson, Dunn & Crutcher, offered him $140,000 a year to become an associate in its Orange County office. The Padres' general manager, Kevin Towers, countered with $80,000 a year if Theo would stay with the club.

Amazingly, in 1998, Lucchino's fourth year at the helm of the Padres, the usually hapless team made it to the World Series. Lucchino had turned them around by bringing in all-star pitcher Kevin Brown and ace relief pitcher Trevor Hoffman. The Padres had the greatest season in their history, winning 98 games. They were dispatched in four games by the New York Yankees, but nobody much cared. There were only a few storied franchises in baseball history, and the Padres weren't one of them.

Much of Lucchino's work was on development of the new downtown stadium, which would open in 2004 as Petco Field. Most people assumed that because in Baltimore Lucchino had been the father of the retro American baseball stadium, this would be the case in San Diego as well. Instead, in creating the drawings for San Diego's new park, Lucchino came up with a whole new design and plan, one that he felt reflected the character and history of San Diego. He threatened to fine any member of the Padre organization who called what they were building a "stadium" five dollars.

Back in Pittsburgh, Forbes had been a "field." Its replacement, Three Rivers Stadium, was an architectural blight that Lucchino struggled every day of his life to forget. "There is something intimate and traditional and irregular about ballparks that doesn't exist when you talk about stadiums," he told the *Princeton Review* one day.

Finally, in 1998, San Diego voters approved Lucchino's plan to build in a twenty-six-acre area of the city called East Village. Along with the park, Lucchino revitalized the district with space for expensive hotels, restaurants, and bars. The $453 million stadium was made of natural sandstone and stucco and blended into the hills that surrounded the city. As he had at Camden Yards, he saved architectural features of the neighborhood. There was no warehouse, but he did use the four-story redbrick Western Metal Supply Company building which had been built in 1909. Its southeastern corner became the new park's left field foul pole. Lucchino named one 2.7-acre grassy section "the Park at the Park." Children could play in a sandy beach area while their parents munched barbecue named after the Padres' first great pitcher, Randy Jones.

For the ten years until the World Series victory, Larry had maintained his partnership with his firm, even though he rarely visited his office in Washington anymore. Some suspected that it was to maintain the continuity of his health insurance. Others who knew him better sensed that something deeper and more psychological was at work. Wherever he had gone in baseball he had kept a photograph of Ed Williams on his desk, right there with Rose and Dominic. The idea of not being a partner at Williams & Connolly was frightening to him, and he needed that connection as much as anything in his life. In 1998, however, through no fault of Larry's, Williams & Connolly found itself the subject of a malpractice suit, filed against the firm by former client Michael Viner and his wife, Deborah, who ran a publishing house called Dove Entertainment. Dove published racy novels and soft porn and had made a lot of money with books about the O. J. Simpson case. In 1997, Viner had decided to sell his business. He hired TV host Maury Povich's brother David, a partner at Williams & Connolly, to oversee the case. Povich, in turn, assigned a junior attorney, Charles Sweet, to handle the transaction. Viner and his wife were not happy with the results and claimed that some key clauses had been left out; they filed suit in Los Angeles alleging that Williams & Connolly's "poor job" had cost them millions. The fact that Viner's suit was filed in California was considered a huge advantage to the plaintiffs, and a jury awarded Viner and his wife $13,291,532 in damages, one of the largest legal malpractice verdicts of the year.

Williams & Connolly did not have nearly the recognition or scare quality in a California court that it would have had if the suit had been filed in Washington. Ordinarily Williams & Connolly would have challenged the venue and tried to get the verdict reversed on jurisdictional grounds—the firm would have a hook into whoever the local judge was—but the fact that Larry was residing in California and was still a firm partner had opened the legal door for Viner to legitimately sue on his home turf. To make sure this never happened again, the firm's partners asked Larry to finally resign from his partner's status, which he did. (The firm eventually appealed on other grounds, and some years later the award was overturned by the California State Supreme Court.) In fact, Larry became not a firm partner in name only. He still kept Williams's picture on his office desk and communicated regularly with the lawyers back home. Larry never mentioned to even his closest friends that his partnership had been terminated.

After the 2001 baseball season, conflicts between Lucchino and Padres owner John Moores prompted Larry to leave San Diego. Acccording to local newspaper accounts, Lucchino was distraught after the FBI began investigating gifts from the team to a San Diego city councilwoman. No charges were ever brought, and the investigation was dropped, but Lucchino was disturbed that the team owners would even contemplate something that dangerous. His own famous temper was unleashed. Moores claimed to be stunned at the intensity of Larry's anger. "To save my soul, I don't understand how people can change their opinions that quickly," he told a San Diego newspaper.

Once again, Larry was a lawyer without a team. Rumors abounded that he would try to buy his hometown Pirates from the Galbreath family; or that he would come back to Washington to run the new club there.

But Larry was, if anything, a romantic when it came to baseball. He knew as early as October 2000 that the Boston Red Sox were coming up for sale. Their longtime owner, Tom Yawkey, had died in 1976, and the Yawkey Trust, which controlled the shares in the team, had announced that they intended to sell the Red Sox to local Boston people who understood both the team and its fans. Their pick would be made in conjunction with Commissioner Selig and a majority of the owners.

Throughout Larry's baseball career, the idea that a Williams & Connolly partner could own the Red Sox, one of baseball's most storied franchises, loomed like a dream. Sure, the Pirates might have been Larry's favorite team growing up, but the Red Sox had been New Englander Ed Williams's. Larry remembered that many of their late-night drinking sessions had ended with Williams wishing that it wasn't the Orioles he owned but the Red Sox. Lucchino still remembered him saying, "I'd give up both the Redskins and the Orioles for the Red Sox. Now that's a franchise."

By November 21, 2001, the executors of the Yawkey Trust had winnowed the candidates down to six, with the leading prospect being the group headed by Charles Dolan, the owner of Cablevision Systems. The founder of Home Box Office before it was sold to Time Warner, Dolan had substantial interests in sports properties including Madison Square Garden in New York. His son owned the New York Rangers of the National Hockey League, as well as the New York Knicks of the NBA. In short, he didn't seem exactly suited to the profile of the local owner for whom the trust and the baseball commissioner were searching.

What almost all the groups had in common was their plan to abandon historic but tiny Fenway Park and move to a bigger new field on a picturesque site near the Charles River. Larry, the native Pittsburgher, was the one candidate for ownership most certain to save Boston's baseball landmark. Because of Fenway Park's role in his battle against cancer, he had his own reasons for feeling something special about it. He believed that when he was ill, thoughts and dreams of Fenway had somehow helped keep him alive. Now, he would do what he could to save the fabled park.

Larry, though doing better than most of his ex-partners, didn't have the kind of supermoney it takes to buy a professional sports team, and neither did Tom Werner anymore, even with the syndicated success of *Cosby* and his other notable hit, *Mork & Mindy.* As Selig sifted through the Red Sox offers, Larry and Tom arranged to meet in New Haven for the annual Yale-Brown football game. While Yale and Brown battled in the Yale Bowl, Lucchino answered a cell phone call from John Henry, the owner of the Florida Marlins. Miami had proven to be a terrible place for Major League Baseball, and after they had won a World Series, the former owner, Wayne Huizenga, had sold off all the team's players, then sold the team itself to John Henry. Miami suffered in part from what made Washington a bad baseball city. It had too many people who had come there from somewhere else and had no fan base of its own. Also, to the extent it was a sports town, in the same way that Washington belonged to the Redskins, Miami was more in thrall to the powerful Dolphins of the NFL. The "summer game," as elegant writer Roger Angell had called baseball, was hardly suitable for sweltering Miami, and the city fathers had no inclination to pay for an air-conditioned domed stadium.

Discouraged, Henry had already decided to sell the Marlins and was in negotiations to buy the Angels. However, when those talks hit a snag one

Saturday afternoon, he called Lucchino to see how things were going with the Boston deal.

"We're dialing for dollars," Lucchino replied.

Henry asked if Lucchino needed an investor, making the point that he only wanted to invest if he could also have control. "If I can be the control person, I'll fund this thing," Henry said.

"Let me talk to Tom," Lucchino said, and with that the ownership triumvirate of Werner, Lucchino, and Henry was formed. They then got a commitment for an additional $75 million from the *New York Times*, which had bought the *Boston Globe* newspaper in 1993 and was looking to boost its image with New Englanders.

Shortly before Christmas in 2001, Selig announced that Lucchino's ownership group had won the bidding war for the team. On March 1, 2002, the new ownership group was introduced to the Red Sox faithful at City of Palms Park in Fort Myers, where the team spent spring training. How did it actually come to pass? No one has ever fully put that together, though not for lack of trying.

In *Red Sox Century*, authors Glenn Stout and Richard Johnson explained, or didn't explain, it this way: "Someday somebody should write a book detailing the process of the Red Sox sale, but that probably won't happen until certain parties are given immunity, others are placed in the witness protection program, and there are more than a few deathbed confessions. The whole thing reeked."

Be that as it may, the sale price totaled $700 million, and it brought the buyers not just the Red Sox but the valuable New England Sports Network as well. "We didn't just buy a baseball team," Lucchino explained.

"A third World Series in a third ballpark," Lucchino, the younger brother who always needed to prove himself, mused. "That would be nice. I could then face my old teachers and classmates from Allderdice with a sense of satisfaction." One would have thought that two World Series rings would have been enough, but Lucchino was driven to prove himself to his boyhood friends, many of whom he continued to keep in touch with and even entertained at his La Jolla mansion.

In November 2002, just a year after the fortuitous call at the Yale-Brown game, Lucchino found himself firmly in charge of the day-to-day operations of a legendary team that had not won a World Series in eighty-six years. Just as he had brought the spirit of the Orioles to San Diego, Lucchino now sought to transport that winning provenance to Boston. Unlike the Padres of a decade earlier, the players were happy. Red Sox outfielder Johnny Damon observed, "The new guys were cooler than Justin Timberlake. Larry Lucchino was the baseball guru, the negotiator, the guy who knows how baseball players think." A couple of years later Damon, after a dispute about the length of his contract, left the Red Sox and joined the Yankees.

Although stoking public interest in the Red Sox is not that much of a challenge, Lucchino displayed himself as a fan-oriented owner. He came with a slogan—WAAF, We Are All Fans—and throughout his tenure as club president would wander around the stadium directing fans to their seats or even handing out programs. Some thought it was ironic that Lucchino, the guy who was associated with building new baseball parks, declared that Fenway Park would remain where it was. Instead of moving the park, Lucchino used his experience dealing with city and county officials to expand the stadium by blocking off streets and making tweaks that saved the great park from the wrecking ball.

Nothing Lucchino would do was more inspiring to Red Sox fans than his decision to treat the pursuit of a World Series for the Red Sox in the same manner that any Williams & Connolly lawyer would pursue victory in the courtroom. The self-image of any firm attorney was to be a member of a band of marauders, taunting the enemy, pitching hand grenades from behind trees. Lucchino had always thought that if he had been asked to design the new headquarters for Williams & Connolly, it wouldn't have been a square corporate building with Italian marble and fancy moldings. "If I had built the new building," Lucchino opined, "it would have looked like a Marine Corps barracks, because that is the closest analogy to what we were—we were to litigation what the marines were to battle."

One of the first steps in any battle, Lucchino had been taught, was to identify and demonize the enemy. It was the way things were done in Washington, if not in Massachusetts, as Reagan had mastered years earlier.

One of the first pitchers that Lucchino tried to sign for the new Red Sox team was a Cuban hurler, José Contreras, who at the age of thirty-one had moved from Cuba to Nicaragua and made himself available to play in the gringo major leagues. The Red Sox made a determined bid to sign Contreras, but near the end of 2002, he signed a four-year contract with the Yankees for $32 million. Asked for comment after hearing that the Yankees had won the Contreras sweepstakes, Lucchino told *New York Times* reporter Murray Chass, "The evil empire extends its tentacles even into Latin America."

Steinbrenner, who in 1974 had pled guilty to two counts of making illegal campaign contributions to Nixon, remembered his experiences with the young prosecutor. "Larry has always been a whiner," he said pointedly.

If Lucchino had quickly gotten under Steinbrenner's skin, that was exactly the effect he was looking for. Deliberately getting under an opponent's skin was a quintessential Williams & Connolly strategy. "I made it a New Year's resolution not to respond to George's personal attacks and gross mischaracterizations of my record," Larry said, "but I may underline those dates when the 'empire' visits Fenway Park."

Lucchino's task of finding a general manager for his new Boston Red Sox began with an attempt to hire Billy Beane, the general manager of the Oakland A's, who had been turned into a legend in a bestselling sports book by Michael Lewis called *Moneyball*. Beane was a statistics protégé of Bill James, whose "sabremetrics" approach to evaluating players revolutionized both the real game as well as the statistically oriented fantasy leagues. To help lure Beane, he hired Bill James as a consultant to the team, the way that in litigation he would have hired an expert witness to go over the trial documents. With the A's, Beane had directed the team to the playoffs three years in a row, a success rate largely attributed to his acumen in finding undervalued and discarded players for a club that was not one of the wealthier ones in the league. Lucchino put on a full-court press, offering Beane $2.5 million a year. Red Sox partner Tom Werner had his girlfriend, Katie Couric, call Beane's wife after discovering that she was a huge fan of the *Today* show. At the last minute, though, Beane backed out, telling the new Red Sox owners that he would "burn out" working in Boston. Some sports columnists took that to mean that he would burn out working for the hypercharged Lucchino. Larry was insulted. "That's a red herring and a false issue," he said.

Larry wasn't going to sit around and grieve. He still had his entourage.

When Beane turned the job down, Lucchino decided to offer it to Theo Epstein, who accepted and thus became the youngest general manager, twenty-eight, in the history of baseball. Lucchino's departure from the Padres had been acrimonious enough that John Moores did not at first want to give Lucchino permission to talk to his employees. After Lucchino began making jokes about "freeing Epstein," Moores sheepishly relented.

On March 24, 2002, Epstein was cleared to leave the Padres and join the Red Sox. He revealed that from the very beginning his goal had always been to come home to run the Red Sox. "I just never expected it to happen this quickly," he told writer Seth Mnookin for his book *Feeding the Monster*.

In parochial Boston, Epstein was a popular selection. He had attended high school there and played on the Brookline High baseball team. His father was a well-known professor at Boston University and an author. Neither Epstein nor any of his living relatives had ever seen the Red Sox win the World Series. Few people who lived in Boston really believed that they ever would. Whether there was a "Curse of the Bambino" or not, the Red Sox had not won a pennant since trading Babe Ruth to the Yankees. That most Bostonians believed in the curse was what made it real.

Certainly the 2003 season didn't do much to help Boston's lack of self-esteem. As usual, the team got right up to the edge of the American League championship. Then a fatal mistake was made. The grounds crew was under pressure to get the field prepared for the World Series, if they beat the Yankees in the final game of the playoffs. Lucchino had become a wildly superstitious person. His hatred of Friday the thirteenth was legendary across the league. Not only had Edward Bennett Williams died on Friday the thirteenth, Lucchino had been diagnosed with cancer on that day. As Jay Emmett would say, "Hey, don't even get him started with the Friday the thirteenth."

Lucchino watched in horror as the grounds crew began drawing World Series logos on the playing field. His calls to the head of the crew to stop were not heeded. If they were going to be ready for Game One of the World Series, he was told, the logos needed to be drawn. Lucchino was unable to stop them. Needless to say, the Red Sox were beaten on an eleventh-inning home run by Yankee third baseman Aaron Boone.

The 2004 season did not start very well for the Red Sox. They were on the verge of besting the New York Yankees in a duel for the services of Texas Rangers hitting star Alex Rodriguez. (Neither team knew that A-Rod's beefy batting stats were partially the result of illegal bodybuilding drugs.) Lucchino also brought in Curt Schilling, who had pitched for the Orioles for three seasons in the Eli Jacobs era. Years before, Lucchino had traded him to the Houston Astros just before he got good, in one of the worst baseball trades ever made. Bringing him back after twelve years in the National League gave Lucchino some sort of redemption, a do-over.

On the other hand, nothing Lucchino did was criticized more than his unsuccessful attempt to bring A-Rod to the Sox. It had seemed that a deal to trade star Manny Ramirez to the Texas Rangers was a foregone conclusion. The only hitch was that the Red Sox wanted to renegotiate certain aspects of A-Rod's massive contract with the Rangers, one that literally had guaranteed him as much money as the team seemed to be worth. The contract negotiation brought the players' union into the situation, as the union had a contractual right to approve or disapprove salary negotiations. By most press accounts, Lucchino's scorched-earth negotiating style clashed with players' union president Gene Orza, who ultimately would not approve what he perceived to be a cut in Rodriguez's pay. The two sides came to an impasse, and Lucchino canceled the talks and let Rodriguez stay with the Texas Rangers. There was an unfortunate side effect, though. The negotiation also destroyed the team's relationship with its own star shortstop, Nomar Garciaparra, who would have been traded had the Rodriguez deal closed. He was one of the most popular players in Boston, and his unhappiness and ultimate trade to the Chicago Cubs were blamed on Lucchino's insensitivity to his concerns during the A-Rod negotiations.

Then Aaron Boone, the very same player who had hit the winning home run in the 2003 playoff series to doom the Red Sox and send the Yankees to the World Series yet again, hurt his knee in a pickup basketball game. This left the Yankees with no third baseman. Alex Rodriguez was a shortstop, and Steinbrenner saw an opportunity to get a good player and humiliate Lucchino at the same time. He was not about to let that pass. After obtaining a promise from A-Rod that he would play the hot corner and not threaten popular all-star Derek Jeter at short, Steinbrenner agreed to send his star second baseman, Alfonso Soriano, to the Rangers in exchange for A-Rod, and to do it without any significant change to A-Rod's existing contract. The union quickly approved the trade. It seemed that in a heartbeat A-Rod had gone from certainly being a Red Sox to becoming a hated Yankee.

ESPN baseball commentator Peter Gammons blamed Lucchino's Williams & Connolly–litigator personna for blowing the deal for Boston. The *Boston Globe* also attacked Larry for the fiasco, saying his "temperament and hubris" were responsible for the failed negotiations. The reviews of the unsuccessful A-Rod trade read like those in the legal journals after the first conviction of Niels Hoyvald. Wrote one sportswriter, "Those people had A-Rod locked up and locked away before Christmas. That deal was done . . . but somehow, someway, Boston blew it." History, however, would come to judge the Yankees experience with A-Rod differently. Rodriguez became known as a player who often failed to deliver for the Yankees in key World Series situations. Then, worse, it would be revealed that he had lied to the public and the fans about his pattern of steroid use. In retrospect, the Red Sox may have been better off without him.

Of course, no one knew at the time how the A-Rod deal would turn out. As Lucchino's public image suffered, Theo Epstein, the local Brookline grad, was becoming regarded as a godlike figure who comparatively speaking could do no wrong. Nor did Epstein himself do anything to contradict the opinions of the sportswriters and the fans. He gave every impression of agreeing with the criticisms of Lucchino, that Larry's meddling and combative attitude had hurt the trade discussions for Rodriguez. Loyalty was the very least that Lucchino felt he deserved from his longtime ward, but he wasn't getting any. When his suspicions that Theo was giving off-the-record comments about the controversy to sportswriters were confirmed, Lucchino was genuinely wounded.

Lucchino's own loyalty to Ed Williams had been full, complete, and total. Something was amiss here. Pop psychologists like to think that as Larry had been the son Ed Williams always wanted, Theo must have been the son that Larry would have wanted. Nothing could have been further from the truth. Religious differences aside (they would certainly never go to mass together), Lucchino and Epstein shared none of the paternal feelings that had existed when Lucchino was the younger man in his relationship with Ed Williams.

The perceived betrayal was not something that Larry would easily get over. Later, when the Red Sox traded Nomar Garciaparra to the Chicago Cubs, many fans once again blamed Lucchino. Epstein let it be known that he had consented to the deal only under pressure. Owner John Henry told the papers, "No matter what happens, Larry is the one who gets blamed." In a strange turnabout to the A-Rod situation, when Lucchino felt Epstein was undercutting him, now Epstein felt Lucchino was trying to blame him for the Garciaparra fiasco.

Lucchino did not appreciate the comparisons, and yet he couldn't miss the reality of how the personality clashes, and the way the public evaluated them, mirrored many of the things that happened in the last days of Edward

Bennett Williams's life, particularly his resentment when Brendan Sullivan had begun to eclipse him as the world's toughest litigator. Perhaps Theo was not the young Lucchino, but Larry had very much become the embodiment of Williams—if without the mood-o-meter, which some of his employees might have found just as useful as the young associates at Williams & Connolly had in the 1970s.

As New Yorkers crowed over their good fortune, Lucchino's lifelong hatred of the Yankees threatened to turn into an obsession. Larry had been fifteen when the Pirates played the Yankees in the 1960 World Series. That was the historic series where Bill Mazeroski's ninth-inning home run won it for the Pirates in the seventh game. Larry had listened to the blast on his transistor radio. As for most Pittsburgh kids of his generation, the Maz homer on October 13, 1960, had remained his most indelible childhood baseball memory. The fan who caught the Maz homer later returned the ball to the Pirates in exchange for two cases of beer. At the time, Ted Szafranksi, now a high school basketball coach in Illinois, was thirteen years old.

The three-game series that Lucchino had penciled in against the "empire," which began on June 1, 2004, did not go so well. It was before the Garciaparra trade, and the star was sulking badly. The Yankees won three straight games in Boston that weekend.

Following the departure of Garciaparra, though, the team caught fire. By the end of the 2004 season, the Red Sox had qualified for the American League playoff season as a wild card team. In the first round of the playoffs, they dusted off the California Angels in three straight games, setting up a rematch of the 2003 American League championship against A-Rod, Steinbrenner, Jeter, and the rest of the "evil empire."

It would prove to be one of the most exciting playoff series in the history of baseball, with the Red Sox losing the first three games and then winning four straight. This time there were no premature celebrations either in the owners' box or painted on the field. That was not the Williams & Connolly way. It almost seemed anticlimactic when they then beat the St. Louis Cardinals to bring the world championship to Boston for the first time in eighty-six years. Real or not, the curse had been broken. One of the greatest records of frustration in baseball history had ended. It had just taken a Williams & Connolly partner to figure out how to do it.

30.

BOOK SPORT IN D.C.

———■———

By the middle of 2007, as the Democratic primaries gained steam, Barnett had also locked up the representation of virtually all the Democratic candidates for president, including both Hillary Clinton and former vice-presidential candidate John Edwards—and his cancer-battling wife, Elizabeth, as well. Proving the publisher's adage that the wives' books sell better than the husbands', sales of Elizabeth's first book totaled 103,000 copies and made the *New York Times* bestseller list. John's first book, which used a different agent and got only a modest advance, sold only 35,000 copies, prompting Simon & Schuster, which held the option for a second Edwards book, to pass on a sequel. Edwards then retained Barnett to handle his proposal for a coffee table book about famous people and their first homes. The idea was lame, and if anyone other than John Edwards had suggested it, or Barnett represented it, the proposal would have gone nowhere, just as it had been declared a dumb idea at Simon & Schuster. However, when Barnett appeared on the scene, and when Edwards's presidential poll numbers for 2008 began rising, suddenly the idea sounded better. A publishing company owned by conservative media baron Rupert Murdoch awarded Edwards $900,000 for the book. Murdoch would only recover a small portion of that sum, but perhaps he viewed it as an insurance policy, just in case Edwards did become president. At worst, Edwards figured to become attorney general, which is also not a bad position with which to have influence, if you own an international communications empire with antitrust concerns.

Had Edwards not left the Senate after just one term, this one might have gotten the attention of the chamber's ethics committee, which had the right to determine whether an advance was reasonable or not. Since Edwards was just a likely president or vice president, he was free to take whatever outsized advance the head of News Corporation, which included conservative Fox News, was willing to offer. Before news of the advance became public, Edwards had been an outspoken critic of the fact that his Democratic primary opponent, Hillary Clinton, had accepted $20,000 in campaign contributions from Murdoch employees. The details of Barnett's deal for Edwards with Murdoch were revealed by the Murdoch-owned *New York Post* in a headline that read, "Edwards in a Biz Hate & Switch." The story revealed that while $500,000 would be the advance, the amount applied against royalties that the book might earn (and it would never earn that much), Barnett squeezed out of Murdoch an astounding $300,000 in money for personal expenses and a promise of $120,000 for publicity. According to book industry sources, *Home: The Blueprint of Our Lives* sold about the same number of copies as Edwards's first book and not close to what was needed for the book to break even at $29.95 per copy. For Edwards it was a good deal. Murdoch absorbed the loss. In addition to the money Barnett had won for him—some of which prosecutors later came to believe was funneled to a girlfriend who was the mother of their child— Edwards used the $120,000 publicity budget to fund an eighteen-city tour that miraculously, and this was probably no coincidence, landed him at venues that were almost all in key early primary states such as New Hampshire, Iowa, and South Carolina.

Frequently Barnett's book clients could act as loss leaders for the firm, as Williams & Connolly would be likely to pick up the work if litigation ensued from something they had written. More likely, the authors would call Barnett for legal advice that he could refer out to younger lawyers to work on. Everyone at the firm was amused when word got out that Edwards had called to see if the firm would help him sue the *National Enquirer* for libel, as a result of their stories about the girlfriend and their "love child." The firm could hardly sue its longtime client, but one senior partner admits that they did investigate Edwards's claims. "We looked into it and decided everything they had written was true," the partner admitted. For both of the two reasons, client conflict and bad case, Barnett referred Edwards to Neil Eggleston, the onetime deputy to John Nields on the Iran-Contra committee, who is now a criminal defense attorney with the Washington office of Debevoise & Plimpton.

Among Barnett's other clients in the Democratic Party were Al Gore, Howard Dean, Madeleine Albright, Bill Richardson, and Joe Lieberman.

Whereas in the past Barnett could turn on a network news broadcast and realize that he represented all the talent, the sponsors, and the network, now he could watch a presidential debate and take comfort in representing all the candidates, all the questioners, and sometimes the university or organization acting as host. There was also a good chance that he had been involved in the debate prep for at least one candidate.

Out in the America that is increasingly getting its news from cable television, the notion that the same attorney promoting Hillary and Edwards was also lining up Richard and Lynne Cheney, Laura and Jenna Bush, and even former George W. Bush press secretary Ari Fleisher should be a little dumbfounding. His work was not only about books, either. When George Bush confidante Karen Hughes was hired to be an adviser to the president while she was still employed by the Republican National Committee, she asked Barnett to review her arrangement and issue an opinion on whether that was both legal and ethical.

Wander around the atmosphere of the big political dinners where politicians, journalists, and lobbyists wine and dine and laugh together, and it quickly becomes apparent that most of what happens here is nothing more than a big show designed to entertain and sometimes baffle the folks back home in Greenville, Mississippi. To a large extent, partisanship is just part of that show. In Washington anyone can be a friend, and your bitter enemies are just as often as not people who belong to your own party or share your ideology. The guys hosting the faux fights on television news shows, like Wolf Blitzer and Christiane Amanpour of CNN or Oliver North of Fox News or George Will of all television all the time—they all are or have been clients of Barnett as well. Like the mock political battles of lovers James Carville and Mary Matalin, most of what people see in Washington is simply staged, more like professional wrestling than a semilegitimate boxing match. Geraldine Ferraro had come to appreciate that fact many years before. When Barnett sold the memoirs for defeated Supreme Court selection Robert Bork, his efforts on Bork's behalf were extraordinary. Bork not only represented a political philosophy 180 degrees away from Barnett but had helped mastermind, with Olson, a campaign to drive Hillary and Bill from office. In West Virginia this might have been cause for a family feud. *You're doing what?* In Washington it was simply business as usual. Barnett did more than represent Bork's book. He hired a political demographer to do studies on where Bork's book would sell best. He then arranged a publicity tour that started Bork in those areas of strength to drive up the sales figures. Only at the end of the process did Bork enter the potentially hostile eastern markets where he was not so popular.

When "Second Lady" Lynne Cheney called Barnett in a panic in 2004, Democrat or not, he was there to help. Years before, Cheney had written a racy political novel called *Sisters* that included scenes in brothels and made mention of attempted rapes and lesbian love affairs. The publisher who owned the rights to the work decided to reprint it after Cheney became the wife of the vice president, hoping that her new fame would now boost sales beyond what they had been years ago. Being that it was an election year, Vice President Cheney was not happy. His campaign advisers worried that people might extrapolate from the book that Mrs. Cheney and even the vice president were not the anti-gay-marriage prudes that many conservatives wished them to be. Nobody knows exactly what Barnett said to the proprietors of New American Library—he denied legal action was threatened—but suffice it to say the reprint never saw the light of day. After the 2004 election was safely in hand, Barnett sold *Now It's My Turn: A Daughter's Chronicle of Political Life*, which includes an account of the 2004 political campaign, written by the Cheneys' openly gay daughter, Mary Cheney. He rarely missed an opportunity to sell every aspect of a politician's life—books by children, mothers, and almost always, as with Socks, the family pet.

Barnett's relationship with the Cheneys was already one of the more vexing ones for his friends to explain. but it got complicated in the fall of 2007, when Lynne Cheney's new book *Blue Skies, No Fences* was released. As part of the launch, Barnett helped arrange for her to be interviewed on CBS's *Sunday Morning* by Rita. Although Braver acknowledged in her piece that her husband had represented Cheney in getting a publisher, media critics still scoffed at the propriety of Braver boosting the stock of one of her husband's best-known clients. Wrote one, "I'm appalled. Braver's husband helped publish this book. How nice that she has a network at her disposal to help him with his advertising."

A spokesperson for CBS defended the choice of Braver, saying that since Barnett was paid a fee "up front," he had no financial stake in Cheney's success. Perhaps—but after Dick Cheney left office in 2009, the overly powerful vice president hired Barnett to sell his memoir, expected to be the bestselling vice-presidential account of all time. It was noteworthy that prior to the announcement he was putting a book up for auction, Cheney began to appear on an apparently endless cycle of interviews in which he attacked President Obama's terrorism policies. Talking heads speculated about why Cheney, who had not been all that chatty while he was in office, had suddenly surfaced with such furor. Could it all have been a plan to boost interest in the book? It was not the kind of question that Barnett would respond to, but insiders in Washington thought they already knew the answer. After Cheney signed to write his memoirs, he suddenly appeared less frequently, telling questioners that now they would have to buy his book to find out what happened in the Bush-Cheney White House.

In the fall of 2004, Barnett began negotiating to sell the memoirs of former CIA director George Tenet, who to a large extent owed his longevity in the position to the firm's old friend Eli Jacobs, though the book made no mention of him. Tenet eventually agreed to a $4.5 million advance against royalties, a sum four times greater than the cumulative pay he received as CIA director for more than ten years. Tenet, however, was not as overjoyed as one might think. According to press reports, after shopping the proposal to twelve publishers, Barnett had to diplomatically explain to a slightly disappointed Tenet that his book had failed by half a million dollars to get as much as the $5 million that Tommy Franks, the commander of operations in the first Iraqi war, got for *his* book. At least Tenet wasn't comparing his value to the pope's, though he probably didn't lack the ego to do so.

In May 2006, Barnett successfully sold the memoir of Alan Greenspan, who had been chairman of the Federal Reserve Board and was considered the ultimate financial guru before he was replaced by Princeton economist Ben Bernanke. Barnett also negotiated Greenspan's employment contract with the bond company and economic consultants PIMCO. He claimed that Greenspan "received more offers than any client I've ever represented, other than Bill Clinton. Alan Greenspan is the Roger Clemens of the world economy, and every team seems to want to have him pitching for them." A few months after Barnett made those comments, Roger Clemens hired a lawyer at Covington & Burling to represent him in connection with a congressional investigation into steroid use. Clemens's testimony was so self-defeating and obviously untruthful that it sparked an investigation into whether he should be indicted for perjury. Meanwhile Greenspan, who supposedly knows more about money than any other living human, said he would rely on Barnett to examine the small print of his contracts and his speaking engagement deals.

By the end of 2007, Bob had gone global. He landed the representation of former British prime minister Tony Blair. Not only did he arrange a book contract, he negotiated Blair's retainer agreement as an adviser to both J.P. Morgan and Zurich Financial Services. Barnett became a confidante of Blair, arranging a speech in China for which Blair was paid £240,000. As he had for Hillary and Bill when they went to China, Barnett acted as Blair's advance man for the speech and the rest of his international lecture circuit. London's *Evening Standard Magazine* noted, "Barnett has raised the negotiation of these golden hello contracts to a new art form."

In a manner of speaking, it is the representation of Barnett all by itself that boosts his clients' value. If he will represent you, you must be somebody. It seems that business leaders and publishers believe that someone who's important enough to have Barnett for an agent-attorney is important enough to get at least twice what he or she is worth for advice, speeches, or books.

By now, the only client seemingly beyond his reach is the queen of England, but Barnett still hopes that if he could break down Pat Summitt, the queen is not out of the question. Years ago his driving ambition was to convince Joe DiMaggio to write an autobiography, but he was never able to convince the shy Yankee Clipper to reveal his secrets. With DiMaggio's death, the queen has become his obsession. Clinton had led to Blair, and Blair might lead to the queen. So far it hasn't happened, but from Washington to London, it is now almost a foregone conclusion that if the queen ever writes a book, Barnett will be the one to broker it.

Then there was the Karl Rove book, which allegedly got half of what Rove expected and didn't even bring him close to the pope. It finally went, after several major houses had turned it down, to Mary Matalin, who had become a publisher with her own imprint called Threshold at Simon & Schuster. Barnett had now been selling books for so long for media figures that some of them had gone into the book business themselves and would purchase books from Barnett even when nobody else would. This truly closed the circle of Barnett's power and influence. He now could represent the author, the interviewer, the publisher, the reviewers, and the networks like ABC and CBS, whose bookers selected how much time and space to give authors on national television.

In 2008, Arkansas writer John Brummett began a story about Bob Barnett by saying, "There's this lawyer in Washington who pretty much runs everything in that incestuous little company town where they do public service for personal profit. His name is Robert Barnett."

Since Barnett almost never appears on television, only a privileged few in Washington, and almost no one outside of it, could have picked his mug out of a police lineup. Yet the customers continued to come. First Laura Bush, then her husband, George W. Bush. Then Barnett was approached to handle the sale of Sarah Palin's memoir. Publishers love books by the women who stand next to politicians, but Sarah Palin would offer the best of many worlds, from the adventure aspects of a woman living a rugged life in Alaska to her complicated motherhood and her daughter's unwed pregnancy to her strained relationship with John McCain, all wrapped around her increasingly rock star status with the fanatic book-buying Republican right. As bizarre as it seemed to those who had known this former beauty queen back at the University of Idaho, Palin snagged one of the biggest book advances in history for someone who had never held national office or been the head of a major religion. Not more than a year after A. B. Culvahouse had flown to Juneau to check her out, his initial judgment had proven to be accurate. He had told McCain that "Sarah Palin fills the room." Now her ghostwriter's book was going to fill the rooms of millions of adoring fans. It was hard to figure. Barnett was already calculating. First there would be Sarah. Then he could sell the wise sayings of the First Dude. There would, of course, have to be a book by the jilted daughter, possibly a morality tale of the dangers associated with teen pregnancy and motherhood. Palin's contretemps with David Letterman, over a supposed joke about her daughters, was classic Barnett. While the rest of the cable television universe obsessed about the Letterman-Palin "feud," Barnett could contemplate what the well-publicized dispute would add to the sales price of her memoir. Both the publisher of Palin's book and the Fox Network that continued to overly obsess on the Letterman jab were owned by Rupert Murdoch's News Corporation.

Barnett was more than happy to do whatever he could for the new queen of the Republican right. He wouldn't have to wait until 2012 to make his first president, though. He could claim that in 2008, although in *Revenge of the Nerds* fashion, the Pi Lambda Phi frat boy ended up winning the presidency—but with the wrong candidate.

31.

BARACK ATAH ILLINOIS

■

In 2004, the voters of Illinois elected Barack Obama, formerly a mere state legislator, to succeed Peter Fitzgerald as their United States senator. The son of a Kenyan scholar and a white mother from Kansas who died young, Obama did not have the typical pedigree of a member of the Senate, usually an all-white club filled with self-employed millionaires. If there is one thing that characterizes those who succeed in a democracy, it is being self-employed. The vast numbers of people who are employees have neither the wealth, the time, nor the personal freedom to seek elective office. Thus positions from the county courthouse level to the state legislatures and especially national office are filled with people who own their own real estate companies, their own law offices, their own stores or shops—or those who inherited their name recognition and money from a parent, such as Lisa Murkowski, Chris Dodd, Ted Kennedy, George Bush, or dozens of other politicians lucky enough to have careers handed to them on a silver platter so they can lecture incessantly to voters about the value of hard work.

Barack Obama did not have that luxury, nor in any way had life been fed him on a silver spoon. However, he had gotten at least one unexpected break in his career. While he was in law school, a New York City–based book agent who works on percentage, Jane Dystel, had noticed an article about his success and his unusual personal history in the *New York Times*. His story had first come to light in February 1990 when the Associated Press reported his election as the first black president of the *Harvard Law Review*. Obama was a twenty-eight-year-old second-year law student at the time. "He has not," the wire service reported, "ruled out a future in politics."

Dystel was often on the lookout for little nuggets that might turn into books, and she contacted Obama and persuaded him to write a memoir of his life experiences. As she told the *New York Post*, "We talked. He was attractive, charismatic, passionate about public service. I told him there was a story here." Obama said he was too busy with law school to do it before graduation, but he gave Dystel permission to go ahead and get him a deal.

"I liked his authoritative voice," Dystel said. "He was so focused. Mature, really together, already sure of himself and not your typical kid. No question whatsoever that he was going someplace. I told him, 'If ever an African American becomes president of the United States in my lifetime, it's going to be you.' I could tell this wasn't the first time he had heard this."

Obama's first contract was with Poseidon Press, and when he failed to deliver a manuscript on time, Dystel bagged him a second contract and a $40,000 advance from Times Books. The original proposal highlighted a book about race relations. Obama kept postponing the project until he had a job as a teacher at the University of Chicago, and once he started writing, he felt increasingly drawn to his own personal story, much to the delight of his agent and editors. As Obama would write in the introduction to what was titled *Dreams from My Father*, the manuscript was ultimately about "a boy's search for his father and through that a search for a workable meaning for his life as a black American."

Henry Ferris, the editor at Times Books, was impressed with the cleanness of the manuscript, although some sections needed to be cut back. Nonetheless, Obama says he felt an intense amount of pressure to finish. He disappeared to Bali in Indonesia to get the necessary solitude. He later said he wanted to contemplate what he was saying without telephones and without the pressures of family members, who had gotten as nervous as he was about what he might reveal about them. The book was released to the public in the summer of 1995 and sold about nine thousand copies in hardcover.

Obama's election to the Senate came shortly after his stirring nationally televised keynote address at the 2004 Democratic National Convention. The speech and his election victory heightened interest in his remarkable personal story, and Dystel had quickly gone to work to get the book reissued with a new preface for an increasingly larger audience. Obama's keynote address drove potential buyers to find out about the book, and Barnes & Noble became besieged with orders, causing it to order twenty thousand copies. Before even hitting the shelves, the reissue had made the list of the top fifty books at Amazon, the online bookseller.

Dystel quickly moved to capitalize on Obama's newfound fame and the popularity of *Dreams from My Father*. She went to work with Crown Books to sign him to a three-book package. The first was to be about his "spiritual convictions" that led him to victory in the Illinois Senate race; the second would be a book about his life aimed at children, especially African American children, that would capitalize on his "Yes, you can" message. The third book was not defined, but there was plenty of time for that.

It had the potential to be one of the biggest deals of Dystel's career.

Since Jane Dystel has been my own agent since 1988, my retelling of this story could probably be seen as yet another one of those Washington coincidences. I can't say what happened next; it wouldn't have been appropriate for me to ask. Until last year when I saw Obama's book jacket on the wall of her office, I didn't know she had represented him.

Instead, here's what the *New York Post*'s Cindy Adams, whom I don't know and have never met, wrote about it, "Go back maybe fifteen years. New York literary agent Jane Dystel reads he's *Harvard Law Review*'s first black president. She reaches out. She suggests a book. Nobody knows him, so nobody cares. She hustles and finally pushes *Dreams from My Father* onto a publisher. The deal somehow becomes undone and she's obliged to peddle the manuscript twice. Its subsequent sales prove minimal.

"Fade in, fade out. The guy's moving. He gets noticed. Gets the star spot at the Democratic National Convention. Gets elected senator from Illinois. His book gets reissued. Now it's selling. Before the election, this brand-new nova and his longtime agent execute an agreement to do more deals. Dystel nails contracts for two future Obama books. One's *What I Believe*—his philosophies, stuff he lives by. The other is, so far, undefined.

"However, Barack Obama now realizes who he is. He now understands where he is. He never gets around to signing with the publisher. Too busy. He's doing interviews, signing autographs. On TV. Campaigning. Climbing. He'll handle this as soon as he can.

"Meanwhile, what he was handling was a switch to the Clintons' book agent, attorney Robert Barnett."

The *New York Times*, in a May 2008 article, had a more succinct description. "He untethered himself from his longtime literary agent in favor of Robert B. Barnett," wrote reporter Janny Scott.

When Crown Books made the announcement of the three-book deal with Obama, the press release credited Dystel but added that it had been "negotiated and concluded by Robert B. Barnett of Williams & Connolly."

Asked about it later, Obama said, "It really had more to do with the fact that by the time *The Audacity of Hope* was written, I was going to be in Washington and was obviously now very high profile."

Well-known editor Peter Osnos was quoted in newspaper stories about the deal as saying Obama's actions were "disloyal but not unusual."

When the dust and the settlement negotiations had settled between Barnett and Dystel, Obama had landed a $1.9 million advance. This deal at least turned into a bargain for the publisher. *Dreams from My Father* and *The Audacity of Hope* have sold millions of copies and earned the Obamas more than $6 million, $2.7 million in 2008 alone, when he ran for president.

Among the most enthusiastic of Obama's new legion of readers was Greg Craig. The old friend of Hillary and Bill's had been introduced to Obama at the home of another Clinton friend, Vernon Jordan, in 2003 at a fund-raiser held to support Obama's candidacy for the Senate. Craig was skeptical. He told Jordan that he wasn't that inclined to support every state senator who wanted to be a United States senator.

Jordan replied, "No, you don't have to give him any money. Just come over, we need some bodies."

Craig was introduced to both Barack and his wife, Michelle. "I was very impressed," Craig admitted, and he decided to give Obama some money anyway. Then he went home and started calling friends from Chicago and telling them to "look him up."

After Obama won the U.S. Senate seat, Craig decided to invest in his book. "I was blown away by it," Craig said. "I thought it was a huge literary achievement. I learned a lot about my own life just reading about his."

As the 2008 presidential primary season dawned, the Clintons had pretty much taken it as a given that Craig would once again be working on their team. Craig now had other ideas, though, and when a friend poked him during an Obama speech and said, "I haven't heard anyone like that since Bobby Kennedy," Craig knew that he was hooked. He called Obama and told him to "sign me up." Craig joined Obama's foreign policy advisory team, but his friendship and utility expanded far beyond eggheaded discussions of strategic relationships. As the Washington insider most knowledgeable on New England politics, Craig volunteered to write a precise and methodical guide to how Obama could do well in the 2008 New Hampshire primary.

Hillary was shaken by the news that her Yale classmate was endorsing a Harvard guy, apparently forgetting that Craig had also been a Harvard undergrad. Craig had gone much deeper than simply endorsing an opponent. He had quickly become an integral and key member of Obama's inner circle. Even worse, Craig encouraged Ted Kennedy and his niece Caroline to endorse Obama, which many who followed the campaign considered the most significant turning point of the primary battle. As the presidential debates began, Craig was eager to help Obama deal with Hillary, who was still then the front-runner for the nomination. He was able to use his long and intimate knowledge of both the Clintons to prepare Obama for the live debate sessions. It was roughly akin to a traded football player handing his old team's playbook over to his new coach.

Nor was Craig reticent about criticizing his old friends, despite the autographed picture on his wall from Bill that read, "To Greg: We struck the right pose—and you struck the right chords! Thanks, Bill Clinton 2/99."

It was ironic that in some sense this cascade of disloyalty had all been sparked by Barnett agreeing to help Obama with his book. One had to wonder in retrospect what the stoic Hillary had thought of it all. It was Barnett who advised Hillary on what to say about her husband's racial jabs at Obama, which he had been flinging ever since the South Carolina primary. Barnett had stood beside Hillary for nearly twenty years. He had been her ultimate male confidante, in some ways more so than a husband whom she couldn't trust any farther than she could throw a lamp. In her first debate with Rick Lazio, Barnett had delivered his usual virtuoso performance, although one might well argue that at this point in his career, it was a little like Shakespearean actor John Gielgud playing the part of the porter instead of Macbeth—and as in a Shakespearean tragedy, it was his queen who ended up getting the knife. He had tried to save her. Or was it his knife? Shakespeare is not always easy to follow.

As Hillary's campaign bitterly imploded in the Obama onslaught of 2008, Barnett implored her campaign aides, many of them his clients, to regroup for her cause.

"I have held my tongue for weeks," he beseeched them in a striking e-mail—striking because Barnett did not often send mass e-mails, or get his hands dirty in the nitty-gritty of politics—but, he said the infighting among her aides "makes me sick."

He continued, "This circular firing squad that is occurring is unprofessional, unconscionable, and unacceptable. I know each and every one of you to be better than this. It must stop.

"We are failing our donors who have put their time and money on the line, the voters who have put their future and their trust in us. The young people who look to grown-ups for leadership—and have commented to me how disappointed they are. Ourselves by making us look unprofessional and foolish. And most importantly our candidate to whom we owe our attention, our loyalty, and our best.

"My message is simple—STOP IT."

Later he admitted that the childish infighting never did stop. The same "grown-ups," like Harold Ickes, who had nearly destroyed the Bill Clinton presidency had now done their job on Hillary. Her campaign would go from bad to worse after Barnett's note, and eventually she would be forced reluctantly to concede the presidential nomination that at one time seemed hers for the taking.

Barnett could not control his friends on the Hillary Clinton campaign staff, but he never dared to dissuade Greg Craig, who seemed on a mission to destroy Hillary's political future. As the Obama campaign took shape, Craig became an outspoken critic of Hillary's foreign policy experience and emerged as a leading contender to be secretary of state after Obama got the nomination. Craig was qualified. He had been Ted Kennedy's foreign policy adviser; he had twice worked in the State Department; he had become one of Washington's leading experts on the geopolitics of the western hemisphere. Instead, Obama named Hillary as the secretary of state but gave Craig the powerful consolation prize of White House counsel, a job Craig had actually turned down in 1996 when Clinton had offered it to him. Craig's friends were initially stunned. Hillary seemed to have been rewarded, with Craig taking the less visible position.

At first, though, Craig appeared to get the last laugh, as Williams & Connolly partners most often do. In the close physical proximity of the White House, compared to Hillary's suite in Foggy Bottom, some blocks away, Craig ended up with the influential role of picking Obama's first Supreme Court appointment, helping to revise the administration's policy on torture and confinement of terrorists, and working effectively to change U.S. policy toward Cuba in the post-Fidel era. Before too many months of Obama's presidency had elapsed, two of Craig's former Williams & Connolly partners, one of them his closest collaborator at the firm, had been named to plush ambassadorships in Belgium and Denmark. Other former associates and partners littered the landscape of the new government. Former Williams & Connolly lawyers held such positions as chief counsel to the vice president; general counsel of the Department of Energy; director of Western Hemisphere Affairs at the National Security Council; and deputy general counsel at the Department of Defense.

Craig didn't have to worry about getting angry phone calls about meddling in foreign affairs from the State Department, either. Hillary and Greg had months before effectively stopped speaking to each other, though the new secretary of state and her still bitter followers waged a noisy war against Craig through pro-Clinton columnists at the *Washington Post* and the *New York Times*.

Eventually the infighting at the White House and the State Department took its toll on Greg. During the summer, the death of his mentor and, in many ways, his sponsor, Senator Edward Kennedy, hurt his bargaining position. In the fall of 2009, loyalty not being one of President Obama's strong suits (as Dystel had also learned, the hard way), Craig announced he would leave the administration and join the Washington office of Skadden Arps, which needed a new Washington guru after Bob Bennett left to return to Hogan & Hartson.

32.

DUELING HOTHEADS

—————■—————

In the fall of 2006, the law was closing in on one of America's longest-serving and most powerful United States senators. For forty years, Alaska, the nation's least densely populated state, had been represented by irascible Ted Stevens, the powerful chairman or alternately cochairman of the Senate Appropriations Committee for two decades. If New York's Senator Alphonse D'Amato had once been known as "Senator Pothole," Stevens's nickname was "Senator Earmark." The end goal of both Republicans, whose party constantly ranted about too much federal spending, was to spend as much money as possible in their own states. After all, that's what they felt voters in their state had sent them to Washington to accomplish. When Republican presidential candidate John McCain criticized the wasteful "bridge to nowhere" in his 2008 race against Obama, it was Ted Stevens's pet project that he was constantly blistering.

Stevens was well known for his volcanic temper, which frequently exploded on the floor of the U.S. Senate, giving cable producers and local Alaskan television stations great 11:00 P.M. news footage. Stevens's personal motto was "To hell with politics. Just do what is right for Alaska." His favorite necktie sported a portrait of his imaginary alter ego, the Incredible Hulk. As one of the few Republicans to vote against the impeachment of President Clinton, Stevens proved that while he was many things, a hypocrite was not one of them.

Colleagues called him a "mad penguin," and many after meeting him for the first time hoped that would be their last encounter. In fact, Stevens was much more complex than the comic book imagery that his tie conjured up. Texas Senator Kay Bailey Hutchison called him "all bark and no bite." Kansas colleague Pat Roberts claimed that "under this great gruff facade" was a "passionate, caring, wise" man. As chairman of the committee that authorized federal spending, Stevens had no qualms about dividing up the spoils for his fellow senators, especially for the bills most important to them around reelection times. What was refreshing about Stevens, in a town full of calculated falsity, was that he made no excuses for what he did or how he did it. Loyalty was a trait that had gotten many politicians in trouble, and Stevens had that quality in abundance. He never reneged on a deal, no matter how bad it might look in the newspapers. His colleague Larry Craig, once arrested in a Minneapolis airport for allegedly misbehaving in a men's room, was impressed that "Uncle Ted," as he called him, even had his own airport in Anchorage named after him. "I thought, oh my God, Ted's got an airport. That's neat," Craig had once declared on the Senate floor, oblivious to the irony. West Virginia Senator Robert Byrd also held Stevens's legislative skills in awe. "May all the roads that you have built, Ted, rise up to meet you," he once said.

Stevens, who had held his office since 1968, showed no signs that he would ever retire. The election of 2008, despite his yeoman's service to his constituents, figured to be his toughest yet. His opponent was a very attractive up-and-coming mayor of Anchorage, Mark Begich, who seemed to have a great political future, and 2008 was not a great year for Republicans overall.

For many years, one of Stevens's closest friends and political supporters in Alaska was businessman Bill Allen. His company, VECO, was in the oil services business. On occasion Allen spread out to other enterprises, such as trying to win a contract to build and privately operate a federal prison in Alaska. He paid careful attention to what was happening in Washington, and it was no secret that Allen counted on Stevens to steer and support federal projects that would benefit him and the Alaskan oil and gas business in general. This was no different than what most of the other ninety-eight senators (sans McCain) would attempt to do for their own state businesses and especially for their campaign contributors.

Over the years Stevens had performed various legislative favors for his friend, once even calling World Bank officials to make sure that the government of Pakistan compensated Allen in a timely manner for his share of a pipeline that had been constructed there. The fact that Allen had such a powerful pal, who wasn't afraid to flaunt their connection, enhanced his businesses. There was certainly nothing hidden about their personal or professional relationship.

Around 2000, Allen decided to help Stevens renovate his Alaskan "chalet" in the resort town of Girdwood off the Chickaloon Bay. When the work, which included adding a story to the house, was done, Stevens sent Allen a note, dated October 6, 2002, which read, "When I think of the many ways in which you make my life easier and more enjoyable, I lose count. Thanks for all the work on the Chalet. You owe me a bill—remember Torricelli, my friend. Friendship is one thing—compliance with these ethics rules is entirely different . . . it just has to be done right."

Allen, however, never did send the senator a bill, and that, as they say, was where the trouble started.

Flush with oil revenues, a Wild West libertarian mentality, and a powerful Republican Party that controlled most of the key state and national offices, Alaska politics was rife with political corruption, bribes, extortion, and backscratching. Starting in 2002, the FBI became determined to stop political corruption in Alaska and began investigating payoffs and bribes from Bill Allen and his company to various political officials and legislators, largely intended by Allen to stymie tax increases that were opposed by the oil drilling industry. As Allen was one of Stevens's best friends from back home, if not his very best, it seemed logical for prosecutors to speculate that Stevens could have been a recipient of Allen's bribes. Among the Alaska legislators that the FBI was particularly watching was Stevens's son Ben, who was a state senator and seemed to be his father's logical heir apparent. Supporting the efforts of the government reformers was the attractive mayor of Wasilla, Sarah Palin. Her ultimately successful primary challenge for governor against establishment candidate Frank Murkowski was viewed with horror by Stevens's friends and family. In the midst of her 2006 gubernatorial campaign, she got what she termed a "threatening" call from the young Stevens, who told her, "You're running against me, my dad, and the whole Republican Party."

In late August 2006, the FBI raided various offices of the Alaska State Senate and House of Representatives, carting off reams of documents related to payoffs by VECO to legislators. Some of the lawmakers were so brazen, they had printed up T-shirts and hats identifying themselves as members of the "corrupt bastards club." The FBI search warrant gave the investigators permission to seize anything with that logo.

On the day of the raid itself, Allen quickly reached Stevens, saying he had been trying to get hold of Ben, whose state capital office had been sacked by the FBI, but couldn't reach him.

"Hey, Ted," he said, "I've been trying to get ahold of Ben. I can't get ahold of him. And the FBI got a warrant and searched my house and the office."

"For what?" Stevens asked.

"Trying to figure out, you know, what kind of, you know, what he has done for us," Allen replied.

"I see," Stevens answered. "Okay."

Allen said, "They asked me what I done on your house."

"Yeah?" said Stevens.

Allen went on, "And I said, well he's paid for everything, and you know you don't need this problem again, Ted, but that's what they are talking to me about, and I just told 'em, I wouldn't talk to them."

Following the first round of raids, the FBI appeared at Stevens's chalet and began taking pictures of the renovations, as well as certain objects in and around the property. In public comments, the investigators said that Stevens was not a target of their investigation. That wasn't completely true, or even true at all.

In September, Stevens talked to Allen again, urging him to "keep your heart going, 'cause we got a fight out there ahead of us. And we are going to win it because we didn't do anything wrong. You've got a right to spend all the money you got to support the party you believe in. The question is whether you did something illegal and I don't think you did."

But while Stevens framed the question to speculate whether Allen "did something illegal," he wasn't taking any chances. There were a host of familiar attorneys who plowed the grounds of the U.S. Senate. Many of them were lawyers who had once worked at the Senate and popped up with some regularity representing senators in ethics investigations or the occasional paternity suit. Bob Bennett was the most prominent of that group. His expertise in killing indictments and making deals before they ever became public was his main calling card.

Stevens was not about to entertain the thought of copping a plea to any charge that might come his way. He was determined not just to defy the FBI but to run for reelection in 2008 and to win.

Among others, Stevens consulted his best friend in Washington, Hawaii Democrat Senator Daniel Inouye. Representing the two newest states in the union, Inouye and Stevens were both World War II war heroes who had served their states virtually since their admission. They had served together on the Senate Appropriations Committee, alternating as chairman over the years but working together in such a way that Congress rarely noticed which one had the gavel. Stevens had been an enthusiastic supporter in the 1980s when Inouye asked him to cosponsor the Japanese-American Restitution Bill. True to form, Stevens made sure that in addition to compensating sixty thousand Americans of Japanese descent wronged during World War II, funds were inserted for native Alaskans, principally Aleuts, who lost property during the war as well. Stevens's bipartisan support for the measure helped persuade President Reagan to sign it into law.

Inouye remembered that Sullivan had gotten Ollie North off and figured he could accomplish miracles for anybody.

At the time when Stevens's troubles had begun to escalate, Sullivan's fortunes and reputation had reached new levels for a Washington-based lawyer.

In the 1970s and 1980s, it would have been almost unheard of for proud New Yorkers to hire a Washington attorney to get them out of trouble. The great firms of the world were supposedly all based in New York: Dewey Ballantine; Winthrop Stimson; Milbank Tweed; Sullivan & Cromwell; Davis Polk & Wardwell.

Few large cities had a more dismal legal reputation than Washington, where lawyers were considered mere fixers or dull regulatory attorneys who pounded the beige hallways of dreadful commissions that decided trucking rules or countered changes in energy policy at horrific places with names like the Federal Energy Regulatory Commission.

The emergence of Sullivan on the national stage had almost single-handedly changed that image. In 2002, he was chosen by a collection of state attorney generals to pursue an antitrust case against Microsoft Corporation. During the entire case Sullivan never referred to Microsoft founder Bill Gates by his name but only in the seemingly evil incarnation of "the chairman." His opponent in that case was Chicago attorney Dan Webb, who had been a constant yin to Sullivan's yang over the decades. In 1998, Webb had opposed Sullivan in a fight over the estate of Redskins owner Jack Kent Cooke. Webb had claimed that the billionaire's two-time Bolivian wife, Marlene Ramallo Cooke, had deserted and abandoned her husband while he was alive. Webb also claimed that she stole four hundred items that did not belong to her, including his briefcase and wallet. Sullivan pushed back, countering that Cooke had bullied her into signing a premarital agreement and describing him as a psychological predator who constantly tracked her whereabouts. Sullivan also threatened to reveal tapes of Cooke making ethnic remarks about African Americans and Jews, which if played in court would be damaging to his memory. Marlene eventually settled for $20 million.

In the Iran-Contra hearings, Webb had been the assistant to the special prosecutor who had interrogated North during the trial of Admiral John Poindexter, the National Security Council director who was accused of shredding documents and obstructing justice.

Webb, who was as perpetually youthful looking as Sullivan was not, had been harsh with North during five hours of testimony, claiming that during the Iran-Contra hearings, North had "lied through his teeth . . . lies . . . lies . . . lies." Sullivan had not been pleased, until the verdict came in that basically exonerated his client. He was the one who liked to blister witnesses, and he didn't always appreciate it when someone else tried to play his game.

In 2004, Sullivan was hired by New York Stock Exchange chairman Dick Grasso to represent him against charges by State Attorney General Eliot Spitzer that Grasso had received $188 million in excessive compensation. The report, compiled by Webb, called Grasso's package "far from reasonable," pointing out that Grasso was making more money than executives at many for-profit Wall Street firms, while the New York Stock Exchange was then chartered and taxed as a nonprofit organization.

Based on Webb's report, Spitzer sued Grasso in 2004, contending that the $188 million Grasso had received was exorbitant and in violation of New York's "not-for-profit compensation law," which states that executives at nonprofits must receive only "reasonable" compensation. The suit against Grasso claimed that by accepting the pay package—and by putting friends on the board of the Exchange—Grasso had violated and manipulated the law.

Sullivan's strategy was to paint Grasso as the hero who had kept the capitalist system operating after a terrorist attack, a towering figure of 9/11, just as Sullivan had painted Oliver North as a military hero with a chest full of glittering medals. On the surface no two clients could have seemed less alike. One was short, bald, and Italian; the other was a handsome Virginian of normal height. Nevertheless, to Sullivan, Grasso, like North, could be portrayed as an honorable man who had been wronged and hung out to dry by the very people that had approved his pay. It was in large part the steep odds against Grasso that made the case so appealing. Grasso, like North, now had to face the full weight and fury of the government by himself. One of the most subtle and defining elements of Sullivan's various representations was that while he did not talk to or cooperate with reporters, he had a keen sense of how to present his client in the most favorable way for public consumption. According to Chris Wallace, now with Fox television, Sullivan appeared as a guest on a television discussion in 1993 to talk about the role of a defense lawyer in society. Wallace said Sullivan told him that it was the only time he had ever voluntarily appeared on television, and by all accounts it was also the last. Sullivan says he only appeared as a personal favor to Wallace, who had just started a new job at Fox and wanted to show he could lure guests that no one else could. Sullivan insists that he gave away no secrets and spoke only in meaningless generalities. "I would never talk about tactics," he said. "I don't want the government or anyone else to know what I think."

When Spitzer insisted Grasso voluntarily return his compensation, lesser men and their attorneys would have compromised. Said Sullivan, "Mr. Grasso has no intention of returning any portion of his compensation to the Exchange. If the Exchange believes it has a valid claim, it should file it rather than conducting a campaign through the press and intermediaries in an attempt to pressure Mr. Grasso." Then Sullivan and his partner Gerson Zweifach threatened to sue the New York Stock Exchange for another $50 million that Grasso felt he was still owed.

The state of New York blinked. In July 2008, an appellate court ruled that Grasso was entitled to keep all of the $188 million that was at issue. The state backed down and promised no further appeals, enabling Grasso to keep most of the money. Sullivan and Zweifach collected $25 million to $30 million in fees, which Grasso said he was happy to pay. As for New York state's lead prosecutor, Eliot Spitzer? After becoming governor of New York, he was discovered in a room with a prostitute in Washington's Mayflower Hotel. Spitzer resigned his office in humiliation. He thus joined a long list of government lawmen who seem to self-destruct for no logical reason during and after their bouts with Brendan Sullivan.

Among Sullivan's most satisfying clients were three of the suspended Duke University lacrosse players who had been pursued unjustly by a North Carolina state prosecutor run amuck. The result of that was that the disgraced former prosecutor ended up serving twenty-four hours in jail for criminal contempt and losing his law license. The students, who had been falsely accused of sexual assault, went free and filed a $30 million lawsuit against the city of Durham, where Duke is located. Sullivan characteristically made it a requirement of any settlement that the Durham Police Department set up an ombudsman to rein in police and prosecutorial misconduct.

33.

HALF-BAKED ALASKA

———————————

When Stevens, himself a former prosecuting attorney, had gotten word that he was under investigation, he quickly realized his strategic options. He could hire Bob Bennett, who could almost certainly work out a deal that would promise to spare Stevens from any jail time; or he could signal the Justice Department, by whom he hired, that they were in for a battle with a couple of pit bulls. A former staffer for Stevens, however, had known one of the Duke University lacrosse students and had seen the job that Sullivan had done on that case. He strongly urged that his former boss hire Sullivan, correctly perceiving early that a strategy of attacking the prosecutors, perhaps for political motivations, might be Stevens's best legal and political option. If he could persuade the voters that he was the victim of a political witchhunt, that might mitigate the damage to his reelection campaign.

Despite how busy and in demand he was, Sullivan would always find time for a case like Stevens's. This was what he lived for, and he gave Stevens his standard speech, warning him that while he had so far done nothing wrong, the prosecution would try to catch him in a lie or a tax violation—it was standard practice. Stevens wanted to know if he could still spend time with his friend. Sullivan said he could, as long as he didn't do it in a way that looked suspicious; if you go to a restaurant and sit in a corner and whisper, he said, government lawyers could later claim you and Allen were coordinating or concocting a story. Sullivan reminded Stevens about the Martha Stewart prosecution. When the government couldn't prove that Stewart had engaged in any unlawful insider trading, they had fallen back on a charge that she lied to an FBI agent. Stewart ended up spending five months in prison. Sullivan made no secret of his contempt for prosecutorial tactics even to a senator whose political party's mantra had always been to support and appoint judges who allowed and approved wide prosecutorial latitude.

"They say we should have no problem, we can meet, you know, have dinner or whatnot," Stevens told Allen. "But we should not look like we're going to try to keep things from the world. And he said we ought to really lay low right now because this grand jury is meeting. And if they got wind that if it looked like we were going to try to do, you know, what they call obstruct justice, they could call us before the grand jury on a different thing altogether."

Stevens added, "You've got to keep a mental attitude that these guys can't really hurt us. You know they're not going to shoot us. It's not Iraq. What the hell? The worst that can be done, the worst that can happen to us is we round up a bunch of legal fees and might lose and we might have to pay a fine, might have to serve a little time in jail. I hope to Christ it never comes to that. So I'm going to go right through my life and keep doing what I think is right."

Allen, though, was in a much different situation than Stevens. He had committed crimes, and he had already complicated things by lying to investigators. Not in a position of strength, he hired a completely different type of attorney. He chose Bob Bundy, who was the former U.S. attorney in Alaska and a career prosecutor. Bundy was in the mold of other ex-prosecutors turned defense attorneys. He did not believe that Bill Allen could beat the government and convinced his client that the best and easiest path was cooperation.

Allen hated the idea of ratting out his best friend. Like many Americans, he had the concept of not being a "tattletale" ingrained in him at an early age. He hated the idea that once you get older, the government can say that you have to. The demand that he would turn state's evidence in a federal prosecution of Stevens for accepting his gifts filled him with sleepless nights and nausea, but prosecutors, joined by his attorney, said it was his only way of getting a lighter sentence for himself. Already, under Bundy's counsel and direction, Allen's testimony and statements to the FBI had been used to convict several bribed members of the Alaska legislature, including a former speaker of the house and a onetime chief of staff to an Alaskan governor. Turning against Ted required a higher degree of will, though, one that Allen was not sure he possessed.

The turning point for Bill Allen came when the federal prosecution team from Washington, after landing at Ted Stevens International Airport in Anchorage, came to deliver a stern message. They had learned that Allen's son Mark had paid a $2,000 bribe to an Alaskan state legislator on August 18, 2003. The handover had taken place in a South Anchorage restaurant. After learning of the incident, Allen had called his son to ask if it was true. According to Allen, Mark replied, "Yes, Dad, I did."

Mark had never even really wanted to be in the oil supply business with his father—he was a horse-racing enthusiast who liked to buy and sell Thoroughbreds, some of which he trained at the ranch he owned in New Mexico, and he had actually sold some shares in horse partnerships to Stevens from time to time, though they hadn't amounted to much—but Bill had wanted Mark around to help with the business. Mark had claimed that the bribe was well meant. It was in the course of his talk with the legislator that she started complaining about money. Mark took that as a cue and handed her $2,000, as she would later testify in her own pleading. Mark would later claim that he didn't go to the meeting with the intent to offer a bribe, but she was so pitiful, he handed it over.

With his son's misdeed as their cudgel, the Justice Department lawyers put the pressure on Allen to cooperate. As Bill would later testify under oath, he felt pressured "to help them get the guys I bribed, and if I did that, they wouldn't mess with my kids."

Allen asked them to steer clear not only of his own son but Stevens's son as well. "Let's keep the kids out of it," Allen had told them. On that, the government stayed true to its word. Neither of the two men's sons was ever charged with a crime, and Mark was specifically given immunity from any prosecution as part of his father's plea deal with the government.

With Stevens now officially involved in the investigation, the lead on the case had shifted from the prosecutors in Alaska to a special anticorruption section of the U.S. Department of Justice called the Public Integrity Section.

Stevens had never been a person averse to using the power and influence of his office to accomplish seemingly difficult or impossible tasks for constituents. A few of his colleagues knew the story about how with one phone call Stevens had managed to have a military aircraft fly a sick Alaskan civilian to Washington so that she could get medical care available only at nearby Johns Hopkins University Hospital. When the woman recovered but needed to stay near her doctors, Stevens found her a job on Capitol Hill. There were hundreds of such examples of his largesse, which frequently cut through Washington red tape and just got things done. Stevens didn't advertise such things, not because he didn't want to get into trouble but because he hated to damage his gruff "Hulk" image.

Stevens couldn't have been, his personality and tenacity aside, an easier target for prosecutors looking to make an example of someone.

When federal investigators went to his home in Girdwood, Alaska, it was full of "gifts." As one might imagine, if they knew anything about Ted Stevens, these so-called gifts were not reported on his financial disclosure statements. He was not the kind of person who cared much about filling out forms. That, of course, was where modern-day federal prosecutors really excelled.

Nor was it any accident that the investigation of Stevens began rolling after McCain had nailed down the Republican presidential nomination. He was a person that the Public Integrity Section had always been anxious to please, and now that he stood on the verge of wrapping up the Republican presidential nomination, that was even more true. McCain had used the same influence, with the same set of federal prosecutors, to demand action against corrupt lobbyist Jack Abramoff, whom McCain detested, largely for personal reasons. As odious as some of the things Abramoff had done and written in e-mails were, his providing of meals and golf outings were standard practice for Washington lobbyists, just as Stevens's actions were simply an extreme example of what happens in Washington every day, like it or not. The sentencing judge in Abramoff's case had been Ellen Huvelle, who after law school at Boston College had become a partner at Williams & Connolly. She had been appointed to the federal bench by President Clinton in 1999, shortly after the firm had successfully defended him against impeachment.

Abramoff had been unlucky. Before he could get around to hiring a lawyer, Williams & Connolly had been hired by another party in his case, meaning the firm couldn't represent him, though he did ask. Abramoff then chose Washington veteran Abbe Lowell, who steered him into a cooperative posture with prosecutors and an eventual "plea bargain" that sent Abramoff to federal prison. There is a saying in poker that if you look around a table and don't see a "fish," it's you. Although Abramoff supposedly was going to testify against other "big fish," for the most part he ended up being his own large catch.

McCain also reveled in the idea of picking Palin, the Stevens family rival, to be his vice-presidential candidate. As he was finally moving up the political ladder, McCain wasn't averse to sticking it to his fast-falling rival one last time.

The lead prosecutor in both the Abramoff and the Stevens cases was Brenda Morris. It would be hard to describe any African American lawyer more qualified and more perfect for the role of a federal prosecutor in Washington, a place where, fairly or not, the racial composition of a jury was always on people's minds. A graduate of the University of Southern California and Howard University Law School, Morris had joined the Department of Justice in 1991. She worked in the Public Integrity Section for thirteen years before being promoted to deputy chief for litigation in 2004, in charge of a unit of thirty other attorneys. Morris was also widely respected as a teacher and professor of law at Georgetown University, as well as being a principal instructor of other federal attorneys at their never-ending training sessions. Attractive, articulate, professional, experienced, and an unassailably brilliant woman, Brenda Morris made a nice target for Brendan Sullivan. Anything less would have been beneath him.

To her credit, Morris tried to avoid a direct confrontation with Stevens and Sullivan. She offered Stevens the opportunity to plead guilty to a single count of failing to report gifts that he had received on his federal financial disclosure reports. If Stevens would just plead guilty, which would make it impossible for him to continue running for reelection, Morris would spare the eighty-five-year-old Senate titan from any jail time. Also, it would have gotten her section off the hook for never being able to establish that any real crime had occurred. She received the same curt reply that Eliot Spitzer had gotten. The "negotiations" did not last long. Sullivan wanted Stevens to have his trial, and to have an opportunity to be acquitted of the charges before Election Day. He reminded her that he did not, as a rule, plead his clients guilty. With the "plea negotiations" having fallen through, Morris had to move to Plan B.

Thus the indictment against Stevens was filed with the court on July 29, 2008.

The charges fell far short of what a Senate lion like Stevens was entitled to expect. With all the posturing and newspaper headlines, one would have thought that the Alaskan would be felled for stealing a Boeing 767 or maybe a jet fighter. Sullivan could barely believe this indictment was serious. At the heart of the allegations was the charge that Stevens had failed to report repair work on his house. Then there was the massage chair, a stained glass window, the Christmas lights, and the barbecue grill. There was some other stuff, but for the most part the case was underwhelming. There were no allegations of bribery and no mention of the benefits Allen and his company might have received in exchange for the chair and the grill.

Another allegation involved the value of a sled dog named Keely that had been given to Stevens. Stevens had listed Keely's worth as $250. Morris claimed it was worth $1,000. The government spent more money getting testimony from dog breeders about the value of huskies than the dog itself was worth.

The paltry allegations were perhaps worthy of the chairman of a county commission somewhere like Sunflower County, Mississippi, which I once covered as a newspaper reporter. Stevens felt personally insulted that this was the best the government could come up with. To him the prized "gifts" were mostly junk. "I didn't want any of that stuff," Stevens told me.

Just as prosecutors often charge someone with a tax offense because they can't prove theft, Stevens was charged with failure to honestly fill out some forms because they weren't certain that accepting a massage chair and a grill constituted a real bribe. Nor could they identify a specific quid pro quo, if it was a bribe. Ordinarily the publicity value of their allegations would have bludgeoned a defendant into a confession on a small charge, but hiring Brendan Sullivan ended the chances of that. The government's main miscalculation was that it could humiliate and embarrass Stevens into a quick settlement. He was immune to embarrassment, however. His noisy Senate career and scoundrel's reputation were an open book.

Ordinarily in the case of high-profile defendants, it takes almost a year for such cases to actually get to trial. However, under the "speedy trial" language of the U.S. Constitution, every criminal defendant has a right to trial within sixty days of being charged. Ordinarily it's the defendant's lawyers who drag things out. That was often the strategy of Bob Bennett, the one he had pursued in the Clinton case. Why not try to postpone the trial until Stevens's election? Sullivan felt that negative press reports would make Stevens seem guilty. Although there is a widespread myth of an anti-law-enforcement media, in fact, reporters and cable producers are often more than willing to believe defendants guilty before trial and to assume that anyone charged is guilty. Sullivan agreed with Stevens that it was best to have the verdict in before the general election. Sullivan was also happy with a change of pace. His most immediate jury trial experience prior to the Stevens case, on behalf of corporate executive Walter Forbes, had lasted a total of five years. It also involved three separate trials. Forbes was eventually convicted, and became Sullivan's first client in decades to go behind bars.

The one thing the government could claim was a star witness: Bill Allen. By the time the Stevens case came up for trial, the Feds' corruption net had snared seven separate convictions, including that of a former Alaska speaker of the house, an elected member of the legislature, a former chief of staff to the Alaska governor; and an Alaskan lobbyist. Both Allen and a VECO vice president, Richard L. Smith, had pleaded guilty in May 2007 to paying $400,000 in bribes around the state.

Despite the flimsiness of the indictment against Stevens, Senator McCain, by now the Republican presidential candidate, was among the first to call for his old rival to resign as senator and to cease his campaign for reelection.

The judge in the case, Emmet Sullivan (no relation to Brendan), acceded to the request for the trial to start immediately and pledged to accommodate Stevens by doing everything he could to get a verdict before Election Day. This included postponing an important trial by star animal activist lawyer Katherine Meyer, alleging mistreatment of circus elephants by the Ringling Brothers Circus.

Asking that the case be resolved before Election Day did not stop Brendan Sullivan from filing his accustomed pile of motions and requests to inundate the prosecution with paperwork. Among the most significant requests was to move the trial to Alaska, where Stevens could be judged by his constituents, but logically where the alleged bribes had occurred. Morris countered successfully that the crime had not occurred in Alaska, because the only criminal acts alleged were the failure to disclose the gifts on the forms. "The Girdwood residence is not the scene of the crime," Morris declared. "It is rather the subject of some of the defendant's false statements." Judge Sullivan kept the trial in Washington and scheduled jury selection on September 22, 2008.

On August 14, Morris handed to Sullivan some hundred thousand pieces of paper that buttressed the government's claims that Stevens had let his friend give him a chair and a grill and had underpaid for some of the work Allen's people did on Stevens's house. Washington pundits hoped that Morris could find more, anything, something that was commensurate with the power and status of Ted Stevens. Surely there was more to this than Keely, the sled dog. On the other hand, the big nothing that the government had accumulated was buttressed with stacks and stacks of paper, the one thing Washington lawyers were good at producing. In addition, Morris produced 450 hours of wiretaps. At Sullivan's hourly lawyer's rate, you could say that was about $4.5 million worth of surveillance, and it would eventually cost Stevens that much in legal fees for Sullivan and his team—which sometimes numbered as many as thirteen younger associates—to review them all.

The reams of materials were turned over to the defendant largely because of a 1963 Supreme Court ruling called *Brady v. Maryland*, which established the principle that a criminal defendant had the right to see and prepare rebuttal for the evidence that was going to be used against him. Up until then, trials could be more like *Perry Mason*. Witnesses or testimony could appear almost out of nowhere. The Supreme Court had decided that while this made excellent television, it was bad law.

Among those who publicly expressed doubt about the speedy-trial request was the old delayer, Bob Bennett. He told the lawyers' trade paper *Legal Times* that the bad speedy-trial decision was made by Stevens. "Lawyers get blamed all the time for the decisions of their client," Bennett said, ostensibly coming to the defense of Sullivan.

Stevens wasn't making the decisions, though. Like all of Sullivan's other clients, he had early on been read the rules: If I were a senator; you could tell me how to get my bill passed and signed, but this is my chamber, and if you want to get out of this, you listen to me.

If the conventional wisdom was that a speedy trial benefited the prosecution, those wise people didn't understand Brendan Sullivan and his style of practice. Jeffrey Kindler, who had gone on to become the chairman and chief executive officer of Pfizer, clearly remembered the time when as a young lawyer he had been sent to the courthouse to review documents while Sullivan appeared before the judge upstairs. Hour after hour passed, and Kindler worked like a slave in a basement room in the courthouse, reading and taking notes. Eventually he noticed that the building was being closed and that no one he recognized was around anymore. Kindler went upstairs to the courtroom and discovered that everyone was gone, but no one had come down to get him or tell him what had happened. By the time he returned to the offices, Kindler had talked himself into a fury. He wondered how he could allow himself to be treated that way, and he stormed into Sullivan's office to demand an explanation. Eventually Sullivan looked up with a bemused smile and said that while he had won a postponement of the trial, allowing him to return early in the day, he had not forgotten Kindler at all. There still would be a trial one day, he said, and he didn't want the prosecution to think that just because there was a delay Williams & Connolly would be taking any kind of a breather. Every trial was a war, Sullivan said. The side that won the war was the side that outprepared, outarmed, and outfoxed the other.

Sullivan could be confident that, speedy trial or not, he would be as up on the facts and as familiar with the documents as Morris, despite her having access to them for many, many, more months than he did, which was supposed to account for her strategic advantage.

Sullivan was not only interested in the hundred thousand documents that Morris had provided the Stevens defense. He was just as curious about what the prosecution hadn't given him, and he did occasionally make observations about the watermarks, just in case that happened again. Sullivan never started a trial with a high opinion of the honesty of federal prosecutors. In private conversations he sometimes referred to government attorneys with the same respect he gave World War II–era storm troopers. He had seen them make up and re-create documents as if they were authentic. He had seen them withhold evidence. He had seen them suborn or deliberately bring in perjured testimony from their witnesses, while threatening opposing witnesses with jail time if they lied. These were all things that happen in the court system almost every day, but there were few defense lawyers in the country who made that the major element of their practice. Most of his peers would have spent the next few months looking for inconsistencies in the documents that had been provided. Sullivan would devote *his* time looking for that one document that the prosecution was hiding—that one exculpatory piece of paper that Brenda Morris didn't want him to see or find.

The government's star witness was going to be Allen. According to the story Sullivan got from Senator Stevens, he would have paid for the renovations, but Allen had never sent him a bill. The October 6, 2002, memo from Stevens to Allen had asked that he be sent a bill. So why hadn't a bill been sent?

According to the theory of the prosecution case, Allen had been advised by a close friend of Stevens not to take the note seriously. Allen, to be as cooperative and helpful as possible in reducing his own sentence, was now telling prosecutors about a conversation he had with a man named Bob Persons. Persons ran a restaurant in Girdwood and frequently looked after Stevens's house when the senator was in Washington. Allen was now claiming that Persons told him that Stevens's note was a "cover your ass" memo, and that he was not to send a bill.

The trial began on September 25, 2008. Morris told jurors in her opening statement that Stevens had used VECO as his own personal handyman service. "You'll learn that the defendant never paid VECO a dime for the work on the chalet," she said. "Not a penny."

Sullivan answered that Allen had never said what the cost of the project would be. As for the so-called gifts like the grill and the Christmas lights, Stevens "didn't want these things, he didn't ask for these things," Sullivan said. "He never once hid anything." Later Sullivan questioned whether anyone would even consider the items as belonging to Stevens. He said that as far as the senator was concerned, they were Allen's items that he had just left at Stevens's house.

Even as he delivered his three-hour opening statement to the jury, Sullivan was sure something was missing. He began searching through an April 2008 federal deposition of Allen. In all the material that was sent to him, he couldn't find where Stevens had been asked about the discussion with Bob Persons. Surely, Sullivan figured, it had to have come up in that deposition. He read and reread it. There was no question about the conversation. When the trial recessed, of course, most of the prosecutors, and indeed most of the defense attorneys, piled out of the courtroom for lunch, which usually lasted a couple of hours until the trial resumed at 2:00 P.M.

Sullivan was not among the lunchers, he did not run the gamut of reporters and onlookers in the hallway outside. Slight, white-haired, and looking every bit of his sixty-seven years, he read through his folders of depositions and statements. Others took lunch breaks; Sullivan rarely did. Some may claim that in their jobs not a minute is wasted, but most who say that at least eat. Not Brendan Sullivan. No wonder he is so slender.

On October 22, 2008, Allen had taken the stand and testified about his conversation with Persons, but Sullivan had by now requested an unredacted complete copy of the April interview that Allen had given to the

FBI. When it arrived, he discovered that Allen had been asked about the conversation with Persons, and the businessman had replied that no such conversation had taken place. The papers with those comments had not been among the hundred thousand pieces that he had been given.

Sullivan was in a blind rage. He had also found handwritten notes from the interview in which Allen had stated that he believed that if the senator had been sent a bill he would have paid it.

In a dramatic display outside the hearing of the jury, Sullivan pitched prosecution documents in the air. He accused Morris of the worst kind of prosecutorial misconduct and wailed that she had deliberately withheld exculpatory documents that could have been used in his opening argument. Now it was too late, he said. Morris tried to stand toe-to-toe with Sullivan. "He called me out, Judge," Morris complained. "All I am hearing from Mr. Sullivan is a lot of noise."

The judge reprimanded Morris and said he, like Brendan Sullivan, was having trouble with "confidence that the Public Integrity Section has public integrity."

At that, Morris acknowledged that she had made a "serious mistake" by not handing all the papers over to Stevens's defense team. "We admit we made a gross error," she said, "but there is no harm to the defendant."

Just as worrisome to Sullivan was the government's treatment of a possible witness, Robert "Rocky" Williams, who had overseen much of the work at Stevens's Alaska home in 2001. Originally scheduled to be a government witness, Williams, who was suffering from liver disease and would die before the end of the year, was subjected to several mock examinations. Trials are not question-and-answer sessions where one is looking for information; they are more like plays with the questions and answers scripted in advance, something that Geraldine Ferraro had learned about debates years ago. When Williams failed to provide the answers that the government prosecutors were looking for, they concocted a story that he was too sick to testify, rather than admit that his testimony stood to be counterproductive. The government needed to prove that the work on Stevens's home was valued over a certain threshold that required it to be reported on the Senate disclosure forms. Williams undercut their case by saying his work wasn't worth nearly as much as the prosecution had estimated. Morris's team also submitted erroneous time logs to the jury, even though attorneys knew that for seven of the weeks Williams was supposed to be working on Stevens's house, he was actually visiting family members in Oregon.

"This is a search for truth," the judge declared in outrage. Later, however, Judge Sullivan's fervor was weakened again when during Allen's testimony he thought he saw Bob Bundy making hand signals to the witness from the front row of the spectators' gallery. "I couldn't believe what I was seeing," Judge Sullivan said. "That's borderline obstruction of justice." The Stevens prosecutors, who themselves were later accused of obstructing justice, came to the defense of the lawyer, calling him a "stellar" attorney. Brenda Morris blamed Brendan Sullivan for the fracas and called it a scurrilous attempt to stir up trouble in the case and "smear" yet another attorney, besides herself.

The irony was that Stevens was being prosecuted for failing to honestly disclose things of value that he had received. In pursuing Stevens, the prosecutors had established their own pattern of not disclosing things of value to Stevens that they had received in their investigation and were under a duty to reveal. It seemed the perfect paradigm for a slippery city in which rules, statements, opinions, philosophy, and votes change each and every day, depending on whose party is in power that day and what the daily focus groups report.

By October 9 of the speedy trial, Sullivan was ready to wrap up what had become one of the shortest "celebrated" trials in history. First, though, there was one last Stevens friend that he wanted to call as a character witness. That was Daniel Inouye.

Like Stevens, Inouye was now over eighty years old. Stevens reigned as Alaska's longest-serving senator; Inouye was Hawaii's longest-serving senator. Inouye had come to the Senate in 1963, Stevens in 1968.

As Sullivan stood to question Inouye as a friendly witness, both knew what they had meant to each other. In an odd twist of circumstance, there were some who could make the argument that Inouye had saved the firm. It was his exchange with Sullivan, some twenty-one-and-a-half years earlier, that had prompted Sullivan's most memorable legal retort, the potted plant line. That single line had made Sullivan a national figure and enabled Williams & Connolly to forge on, more powerful than ever. For all his vaunted concentration, Sullivan could barely avoid the flashback to that moment in the great caucus room of the Senate—but he didn't let anyone know it.

Inouye was called as the first defense witness for Stevens. He was the man Stevens's daughter called "Uncle Dan," and, Inouye noted, he was proud of it. "I have never known Ted Stevens to lie," Inouye said. "His word is good enough to take to the bank."

Despite the best efforts of the defense, the jury still voted to convict Stevens, even though one of the jurors had fled the scene so as not to miss the Breeders Cup horse races in California that year. She told the judge that her father had died. The Stevens trial may have been the political trial of the year, but at least one juror kept it in perspective. The remaining jurors—and the alternate who replaced the racetrack enthusiast—voted to put Stevens in prison for his sins. The jury had never been privy to the discussions about evidence or been able to glean from the judge that there had been misconduct. Judge Sullivan wanted to get a verdict first, one that would set up a reversal by the appeals court. Otherwise he might have had to sit through the entire trial a second time, which no one really wanted.

McCain was among the first to blast the newly convicted Stevens, saying the verdict proved that he "had broken his trust with the American people." Palin, a notorious bandwagon jumper, also leaped at the chance to condemn Stevens. "I had hoped that Senator Stevens would take the opportunity to do the statesman-like thing and erase the cloud," she said. "He has not done so. Alaskans are grateful for his decades of public service, but the time has come for him to step aside."

Stevens would not step aside, however, and very nearly retained his seat, despite the conviction. His reelection count against a popular mayor of Anchorage went late into the night and next day before it became clear that Stevens was beaten. The news anchors and those that abide by the Washington tradition of going with the front-runners assumed Sullivan had lost. Like the magazine reporters who thought Niels Hoyvald was going to prison, they were wrong.

Sullivan was disappointed but not surprised at the jury verdict. An elderly, white, curmudgeonly U.S. senator was not the most popular defendant to bring before a jury in the District of Columbia in 2008, after a series of congressional scandals that had left many people thinking all politicians were crooks anyway. Most of the battles over evidence and prosecutorial misconduct had taken place outside the hearing of the jury.

Besides, technically the jury was correct. Stevens had not reported these "gifts" on his financial disclosure forms. That was simply a fact. They couldn't help it if the financial disclosure forms were silly. Sullivan had rolled the dice with the early trial but had come up short. The guilty verdict and the Palin attack on his candidacy almost certainly made up the margin of difference that cost him his supposedly safe Republican seat in a razor-thin election.

Sullivan believed he already had a long laundry list of sins that Brenda Morris and her team had committed, but the holy grail of prosecutorial misconduct was found in the form of a whistle-blowing FBI agent from Alaska, who was willing to write a letter to the attorney general complaining that agents were allegedly the ones accepting gifts and favors from sources. The whistle-blower was close enough to the investigation that he had been in the room on August 30, 2006, when agents persuaded Allen to turn state's witness.

For Sullivan, the letter from the agent was the smoking gun. He confirmed that information was withheld from the defense, not inadvertently but deliberately, because the testimony would have contradicted the prosecution's narrative.

Ordinarily, Sullivan would have used all this as grounds for appeal, but the Stevens case, as far as he was concerned, was still on a fast track. Stevens, after all, was not a young man. So instead of filing his appeal papers first, Sullivan submitted a letter of complaint to the new attorney general, Eric Holder. He cited a letter from the FBI "whistle-blower" saying that another agent, while investigating Stevens's gifts, was getting "too close" to witnesses and taking "things of value" from them.

Thus, before Stevens would even be sentenced, Holder decided to personally investigate the allegation by Brendan Sullivan that prosecutors had withheld evidence, squirreled away witnesses, and generally violated accepted rules of legal combat. He quickly concluded that it was all true and asked Judge Sullivan to dismiss the case, an almost unprecedented result after a high-profile conviction. Indeed, the result was far better than even winning a lower court appeal. Holder's decision was absolutely final.

Ted Stevens marched out free, except for the nearly $4 million he still owed Brendan Sullivan in legal fees. Fortunately for him, however, Senate rules allow a member formally accused of taking gifts to accept cash gifts up to $10,000 per contributor to pay legal bills.

As a footnote, Bill Allen's decision to testify against Stevens and put this whole process in motion had been sparked by his desire to save his tough cowboy son Mark from jail. Mark had never really wanted to live in Alaska, but his father had wanted him and his two brothers as partners. In spite of the criminal charges swirling around them, the Allens were able to sell VECO's assets for $380 million to a Colorado construction and engineering firm. Mark's share of ownership brought him $30 million, which he took back to his ranch in Roswell, New Mexico, as far away from trouble as he could get. There, Allen met a veterinarian named Leonard Blach, and they decided to buy an undersized three-year-old Thoroughbred racehorse who had won some big races in Canada the previous year. Had Allen been tagged with any kind of a criminal record, under New Mexico law, he would not have been able to race the horse. With no impediments, Allen and Blach paid $400,000 for the stakes-winning gelding. Four months later, Mine That Bird, as he was named, won the Kentucky Derby and its million-dollar purse at odds of 50–1. When Allen and raffish trainer Bennie "Chip" Woolley went to Baltimore for the Preakness, they were met at the Baltimore city line by a police escort. Allen joked that this was the first time he had gone into a town where the police were leading, not chasing.

Had Stevens not been indicted and gotten crosswise with the Allens, he might well have become an investing partner in Mine That Bird. The $250,000 worth of so-called gifts and repairs, costing close to $5 million in total legal fees, lost him a shot at standing in the Kentucky Derby winner's circle, probably cost him reelection to the Senate, and forced the proud senator to endure being the butt of jokes and insults on television and the Internet for over a year. "This was the worst experience of my life," Stevens grumbled to me after it was all over. "You have no idea."

Just as Stevens had emerged a net loser, so had the government. The Justice Department spent millions of dollars and thousands of hours on a case that ultimately went worse than nowhere. After throwing out the conviction, Judge Sullivan announced that he was appointing a special prosecutor to investigate the conduct of Brenda Morris, as well as that of her colleagues, in the case. When last seen, Morris was on her way to Hogan & Hartson, to see if *she* could find a lawyer.

How the cost of a chair, a grill, some Christmas lights, and a sled dog could escalate! In pursuit of justice, the federal government had spent upwards of $15 million on the case and gotten nothing from it, except for now having to pay even more money for the legal bills to defend its own attorneys.

34.

AFTERWORD

———————■———————

In the aftermath of the Stevens case, much like that of the Omni tax fraud dismissal years earlier, Williams & Connolly did not suffer from any shortage of detractors. Ruining the lives and careers of hardworking, relatively young, mostly underpaid career prosecutors did not seem to everyone to be an inevitable result of a trial. To critics, lawyers from Williams & Connolly didn't seem satisfied with merely winning their cases; they would, as even someone as civilized as David Kendall had once expressed it, fight every case "to the knife." Anyone between their client and acquittal stood in jeopardy. The careers of judges, higher-office-seeking attorney generals, prosecutors, and independent counsels often dangled on the precipice while the likes of Sullivan, Simon, Lucchino, Seligman, Kendall, or Craig whittled relentlessly away. This was not gentlemanly conduct but life-or-death combat. In my life as a newspaper reporter, covering trials, I would often see prosecutors, defense attorneys, and sometimes even the judge sitting in chambers while awaiting a verdict, laughing, smiling, telling jokes, while the defendant sat alone in the courtroom with a bailiff or guard. I always wondered what the accused must think, hearing his lawyer laughing it up with the district attorney. That isn't something that Williams & Connolly defendants ever hear. Their trials rarely end with the two competing battalions cordially shaking hands and wishing each other well, and often the verdict isn't the end but the beginning of when things start to really get interesting.

Williams & Connolly partners are not going to win any popularity contests. Greg Craig was not at the White House for two months before other staffers were rattled by his self-confident and can-do style and ultimately sent him packing. Lucchino, while masterminding the winning of the World Series, still lagged behind Theo Epstein in the love department among both fellow owners and fans. Sullivan, Simon, and even Kendall all have a way of irritating opponents. Bob Barnett has alienated the universe of book agents by disrupting their long-standing business model while capturing a disproportionate share of prominent political and media clients and their many million-dollar deals. Their arrogance is something that many people just don't like. Their success—new lawyers start at close to $270,000 a year, and partners make close to $3-4 million—simply makes it worse.

Yet that dislike plays right into their hands. The Williams & Connolly track record in itself is often enough to prompt opponents to ultimately offer favorable settlements to save their own careers. The mantra of modern criminal law is that many defendants would rather plead guilty to something they *didn't* do than fight state and federal prosecutors who have unlimited time, money, and resources, to say nothing of unfettered favorable access to newspaper and television reporters anxious to declare an indicted person guilty after the first press conference. Williams & Connolly is consistently the one opponent that the government hasn't been able to overwhelm.

Yet even while its best-known attorneys fight government, others infiltrate it. In the Republican administrations, lawyers like John Vardaman and Terrence O'Donnell helped draft and define governmental policies. In Democratic administrations, Barnett, Kendall, and Craig are omnipresent advisers and counselors. In Barnett's case, his overarching relationships with presidents, vice presidents, secretaries of state, senators, political advisers, ex-officeholders, university presidents, first ladies, and even presidential pets is so far-reaching that it spins all previous definitions of Washington "power player" on their head. In the world of business, Williams & Connolly alums spread out to run or help direct the biggest drug company, the largest defense contractors, the important private accounting firms, the most prominent electronics companies, the most influential sports leagues, the law departments of the country's most important educational institutions, and even the government's most important legal agency. Twenty-two years after the death of Edward Bennett Williams, the firm that bears his name is richer and bigger than ever, and it still clings to his iconoclastic values and aphorisms about how law should be practiced—and it isn't the chummy club way.

That Williams & Connolly had survived and prospered on its own terms seemed to be what mattered most to its partners. They were, Brendan Sullivan would always remind the new recruits, the elite—a band of lawyer marines, the way soldiers were portrayed in 1940s movies: polished, professional, clever, brave, always victorious, and taking no prisoners and frequently no credit.

Among American law firms, Williams & Connolly—with its one office, its one-for-all attitude, and its unique don't-poach-the-rivals policy—is the anachronism that proves the folly of its clumsy PR- and consultant-driven competitors. To many, American law firms have become the protectors of modern corporate greed and willing and malleable partners eager to play ball with federal and state prosecutors who consider their jobs a sport. Today, when those giant law firms get into trouble themselves, it is almost always the very law firm that so many of them despise, Williams & Connolly, that *they* call to get them out of trouble.

In the continuing contest that is modern American law, Williams & Connolly is the unrivaled master of the game.

BIBLIOGRAPHY

——■——

Abramson, Jill. "Taxpayers 2, U.S. 0: Sharp Detectives Score in 'Omni.'" *Legal Times*, June 16, 1986.

Adams, Cindy. "Barack's Dreams Beyond His Agent's." *New York Post*, Nov. 10, 2004.

Ahrens, Frank. "Post Co. Names Weymouth Media Chief and Publisher." *Washington Post*, Feb. 8, 2008.

Amidon, Jim. "Thirty Minutes with David Kendall." *Wabash Magazine*, Fall/ Winter 2001.

Apuzzo, Matt. "Stevens Lawyers Question FBI Authority." Associated Press, Aug. 14, 2008.

Arnold, Martin. "Making Books: Is the Agent Really Needed?" *New York Times*, Jan. 15, 1998.

Baker, Billy. "The Guy Who Gets Things Done: Dr. Lee Nadler." *Boston Globe*, June 9, 2008.

Baker, Peter. *The Breach: Inside the Impeachment and Trial of William Jefferson Clinton*. New York: Scribner, 2000.

Bendavid, Naftali. "Calm Crusader Kendall Might Be White House's Greatest Legal Asset." *Chicago Tribune*, March 19, 1999.

———. "GOP Targets Lawyer for Elian's Dad." *Chicago Tribune*, April 23, 2000.

Bennett, Robert S. *In the Ring: The Trials of a Washington Lawyer*. New York: Crown Publishers, 2008.

Berry, Attila. "Closing In on $200K: Williams & Connolly Boosts First-Year Numbers to $180,000. Are Bigger Numbers on the Way?" *Legal Times*, Dec. 24, 2007.

Bloomberg News. "WorldCom Claims Settled: Company Directors Will Pay Investors from Their Own Pockets." March 19, 2005.

Blumenthal, Sidney. *The Clinton Wars*. New York: Farrar, Straus and Giroux, 2003.

Bolstad, Erika. "Inouye Tells Jury He Has 'Absolute Faith' in Stevens." *Anchorage Daily News*, Oct. 9, 2008.

———. "Stevens Legal Defense Bill Tops $1 Million." *Anchorage Daily News*, May 15, 2009.

Brelis, Matthew. "Book Propels Kitty Dukakis into Limelight Once Again." *Boston Globe*, July 29, 1990.

Brennan, Tom. "Courting Success: Son of Big-Time D.C. Lawyer Makes Pitch for the Big Leagues." *Calgary Sun*, May 21, 2000.

Briggs, Michael. "Rosty to Get a New Lawyer; Bennett Leaves Case by 'Mutual Decision.'" *Chicago Sun-Times*, June 3, 1994.

Brill, Steven. *The Teamsters*. New York: Simon & Schuster, 1978.

Broder, John. "For Elian's Father, a Lawyer with Ties to Clinton." *New York Times*, April 4, 2000.

Brummett, John. "Book Broker to the Rescue." *Las Vegas Review-Journal*, June 29, 2008.

Buder, Leonard. "Ex-Beechnut Chief Seeks Probation." *New York Times*, June 7, 1988.

Califano, Joseph A. *Inside: A Public and Private Life*. New York: Public Affairs, 2004.

Canepa, Nick. "Lucchino's Impact on Baseball Felt from One Coast to Another." *San Diego Union-Tribune*, June 27, 2007.

Caplan, Lincoln. "The Insanity Defense." *New Yorker*, July 2, 1984.

Carlen, Linda. "Into the Mouths of Babes." *New England Business Journal*, March 1989.

Carmody, John. "Chris Wallace to ABC News; Leaves NBC for Spot on Primetime Hour." *Washington Post*, Dec. 7, 1988.

Chass, Murray. "Lucchino: Just a Soul Who's Misunderstood." *New York Times*, Nov. 20, 2005.

Clines, Francis X. "Clintons' Counsel Keeps His Own." *New York Times*, May 31, 1997.

Clinton, Bill. *My Life*. New York: Alfred A. Knopf, 2004.

Clinton, Hillary Rodham. *Living History*. New York: Simon & Schuster, 2003.

Clymer, Adam. *Edward M. Kennedy, A Biography*. New York: William Morrow, 1999.

Cockerham, Sean. "Palin Signs Deal to Write Book for HarperCollins by 2012." *Anchorage Daily News*, May 12, 2009.

Cockerham, Sean, and Erika Bolstad. "McCain, Palin Urge Stevens to Quit." *Anchorage Daily News*, Oct. 29, 2008.

Cohen, Lester. *Frank Hogan Remembered*. Washington: Hogan & Hartson, 1985.

Cohen, Richard M., and Jules Witcover. *A Heartbeat Away: The Investigation and Resignation of Vice President Spiro T. Agnew*. New York: Viking, 1974.

Contreras, Joseph. "A Little Boy Goes Home." *Newsweek*, July 10, 2000.

Cornelius, Maria. "Lawyer's Persistence Finally Nets Book Deal with Summitt." *Knoxville News-Sentinel*, March 15, 1998.

Couric, Emily. *The Trial Lawyers: The Nation's Top Litigators Tell How They Win*. St. Martin's Press, 1988.

Crerar, Pippa. "Blair Hires U.S. Lawyer over Book." *Evening Standard* (London), Aug. 17, 2007.

Damon, Johnny. *Idiot: Beating "the Curse" and Enjoying the Game of Life*. New York: Crown Publishers, 2005.

Daniel, Aubrey. "The Judgment of Peers: The My Lai Inquiry." *Washington Post*, July 1, 1979.

Dart, Bob. "New Defense Team Members to Go Head-to-Head with Congress." *Palm Beach Post*, Sept. 16, 1998.

Davies, Frank. "Attorney Recounts Drama in Elian Saga." *Miami Herald*, July 1, 2000.

Denniston, Lyle. "Justices Skeptical of Tobacco Restriction; FDA Plan Questioned at High Court Hearing." *Baltimore Sun*, Dec. 2, 1999.

Doyle, Paul. "New Fenway, Little by Little." *Hartford Courant*, Feb. 9, 2006.

Eisele, Al. "Got a Killer Idea for a Book? Bob Barnett May Be Interested." *Hill*, Oct. 23, 1996.

Eisenberg, John. *From 33rd Street to Camden Yards: An Oral History of the Baltimore Orioles*. Lincolnwood, Ill.: Contemporary Books, 2001.

Eisler, Kim Isaac. "Greg Craig's A-List." *Washingtonian*, July 1, 2000.

———. "Sen. Ted Stevens Hires Super-Lawyer Brendan Sullivan." *Washingtonian*, July 1, 2007.

Enda, Jodi. "Clinton Bolsters His Defense Team: A State Department Official Was Named 'Quarterback.'" *Philadelphia Inquirer*, Sept. 16, 1998.

Fehr, Stephen. "Truck Driver in Fatality Has Many Tickets: License Revoked in July, Then Restored." *Washington Post*, Aug. 14, 1997.

———. "U.S. Shuts Down Truck Firm Linked to Crash." *Washington Post*, Sept. 27, 1997.

Ferraro, Geraldine. *Ferraro: My Story*. Evanston, Ill.: Northwestern University Press, 2004.

Finder, Chuck. "Curse Buster? Pittsburgh Native Larry Lucchino Tries to End the Suffering of Red Sox Nation." *Pittsburgh Post-Gazette*, May 5, 2002.

Fisher, Marc. "Legal Titan Edward Bennett Williams Dies: Famed D.C. Lawyer-Politician Owned Redskins, Then Orioles." *Washington Post*, Aug. 14, 1988.

Fleming, Michael. "Stephanopoulos in $2.75 Mil Book Deal." *Daily Variety*, Dec. 17, 1996.

Fraley, Gerry. "Radically Shaping the Future; Camden Yards Set a Standard Others in Baseball Emulated." *Rocky Mountain News*, June 8, 2007.

Frank, T. A. "Look Who's Hitched: The Secret Lives of Washington's Power Couples." *Washington Monthly*, May 1, 2007.

Fujiwara, Toyoaki. "Young Team Ready to Retool Sony." *Nikkei Weekly*, Nov. 14, 2005.

Fuller, Vincent. "*United States v. John W. Hinckley Jr.*" *Loyola of Los Angeles Law Review*, Jan. 2000.

Geewax, Marilyn. "Father and Son Reunited: Away from Hubbub, Boy Spends Day with Family." *Atlanta Journal-Constitution*, April 23, 2000.

Graff, Christopher. "Gregory Craig's Vermont Connections." Associated Press, Dec. 15, 1998.

Graham, Katharine. *Personal History*. New York: Alfred A. Knopf, 1997.

Gutlon, Jerry M. *It Was Never About the Babe: The Red Sox, Racism, Mismanagement, and the Curse of the Bambino*. New York: Skyhorse Publishing, 2009.

Halberstam, David. *The Best and the Brightest*. New York: Random House, 1972.

Henneberger, Melinda. "Clinton Case Is Risky for His Legal Adviser, Too." *New York Times*, Aug. 16, 1998.

Holland, John. "Lawyer Takes Tough Cases: Gregory Craig Has Defended John Hinckley, President Clinton and Is Fighting for Juan Miguel Gonzalez—Elian's Dad." *Orlando Sentinel*, April 7, 2000.

Hubbell, Webb. *Friends in High Places*. New York: William Morrow, 1997.

Hutchinson, Dennis J. *The Man Who Once Was Whizzer White*. New York: Free Press, 1998.

Inouye, Daniel, and Lee Hamilton. *Report of the Congressional Committees Investigating the Iran-Contra Affair.* Washington: U.S. Government Printing Office, 1987.

"Inside the Shadowy Empire of Eli Jacobs," *Business Week*, Nov. 18, 1991.

Jermanok, Stephen. "Dreamy New Field Enlivens Old-Town Side of San Diego." *Boston Globe*, June 6, 2004.

Johnson, Carrie. "Cendant's Ex-Chair Convicted in Fraud; Landmark Probe Spanned Eight Years." *Washington Post*, Nov. 1, 2006.

———. "Their Own Defense; D.C.'s Clubby Attorneys Keep Corporate Work in the Flock." *Washington Post*, June 18, 2007.

Johnson, Carrie, and Brooke A. Masters. "KPMG Hires Federal Judge; Firm Facing Investigation, Civil Charges." *Washington Post*, Jan. 21, 2005.

Junkin, Tim. *Bloodsworth.* Chapel Hill, N.C.: Algonquin Books of Chapel Hill, 2005.

Kalman, Laura. *Abe Fortas: A Biography.* New Haven: Yale University Press, 1990.

Kirkpatrick, David. "The Kingpin of Washington Book Deals." *New York Times*, Dec. 11, 2000.

———. "Publisher Will Pay Clinton over $10 Million for Book." *New York Times*, Aug. 7, 2001.

Krim, Jonathan. "For Rivals, a Change of Venue; Microsoft Case Puts Familiar Opponents in Unfamiliar Territory." *Washington Post*, April 15, 2002.

Kutler, Stanley. *The Wars of Watergate: The Last Crisis of Richard Nixon.* New York: Alfred A. Knopf, 1990.

Lawrence, B. H. "The Passing of Power at Williams & Connolly." *Washington Post*, Sept. 19, 1988.

Lemann, Nicholas. "Worlds Apart: Obama, McCain, and the Future of Foreign Policy." *New Yorker*, Oct. 13, 2008.

Lewis, Neil. "Judge Berates Prosecutors in Trial of Senator." *New York Times*, Oct. 2, 2008.

———. "Law Business? That's Entertainment." *New York Times*, Oct. 14, 1985.

Locy, Toni. "Cisneros's Ex-Mistress Pleads Guilty." *Washington Post*, Jan. 16, 1998.

Loth, Renee. "Aides to Kitty Dukakis Silent on Speaking Tour." *Boston Globe*, Jan. 11, 1989.

Loverro, Thom. "Lucchino's Little Engine." *Washington Times*, Oct. 17, 2007.

Low, Peter W., Jeffries, John C., Jr., and Richard J. Bonnie. *The Trial of John W.*

Hinckley: A Case Study in the Insanity Defense. Mineola, N.Y.: Foundation Press, 1986.

MacFarquhar, Larissa. "Ms. Kennedy Regrets." *New Yorker,* Feb. 2, 2009.

Malone, Julia, and Mike Williams. "Costs Piling Up in Fight over Elian." *Austin American-Statesman,* April 30, 2000.

Marcus, Ruth. "The Lawyer's Lawyer; Counsel Nicole Seligman, Williams & Connolly's Early Riser." *Washington Post,* Aug. 17, 1998.

Martin, Gary. "Cisneros Lawyer Defended Col. North, My Lai Officer." *San Antonio Express-News,* Jan. 14, 1998.

Mauer, Richard. "FBI Whistleblower Alleges Stevens Trial Misconduct." *Anchorage Daily News,* Dec. 12, 2008.

Mauer, Richard, and Erika Bolstad. Stevens' Lawyers Accuse Prosecution of Smear Tactics. *Anchorage Daily News,* August 25, 2008.

McCartney, Laton. *The Teapot Dome Scandal: How Big Oil Bought the Harding White House and Tried to Steal the Country.* New York: Random House, 2008.

McFarlane, Robert. *Special Trust.* New York: Cadell & Davies, 1994.

Melder, Keith. *City of Magnificent Intentions.* Washington: Intac, 2001.

Miller, Bill. "Cisneros Accuser Admits Lying to Prosecutors." *Washington Post,* June 27, 1999.

Moore, W. John. "Agent for the Literati and Glitterati." *Washington Post,* March 6, 1993.

———. "High Court Apprenticeship: Richard M. Cooper." *National Journal,* March 18, 1989.

Muret, Don. "Camden Yards Turns 15, Still Inspires Other Parks." *Washington Business Journal,* April 16, 2007.

North, Oliver. *Under Fire: An American Story.* New York HarperCollins, 1991.

O'Brien, Tim. "Brendan Sullivan Bombs in Brooklyn: Maybe His Client Needed a Potted Plant." *American Lawyer,* Sept. 1988.

O'Connell, Brian. "New Sheriff in Town at Pfizer." *Biopharm International,* Sept. 2006.

Oei, Lilly. "Sony Names Seligman Top Legal Eagle." *Daily Variety,* Sept. 7, 2001.

Packer, George. "The Choice: The Clinton-Obama Battle Reveals Two Very Different Ideas of the Presidency." *New Yorker,* Jan. 28, 2008.

Palmer, Ann Therese. "D.C. Law: There's Lots of Hollywood in a Top Washington Practice." *Chicago Tribune*, Jan. 17, 1993.

Ponder, Jon. "Rove's Book Sold for Half of What He Expected—and Buyer was Mary Matalin." *Pensito Review*, Dec. 22, 2007.

Providence Journal-Bulletin. "Brendan V. Sullivan Sr." Obituary, May 26, 1996.

Queenan, Joe. "Juice Men: Ethics and the Beech-Nut Sentences." *Barron's*, June 20, 1988.

Quigley, Eileen. "U.S. Says Case Sends a Message to Corporate America: Ex-Beech-Nut Officials Get Prison Terms." *Los Angeles Times*, June 17, 1988.

Saperstein, Saundra. "Burch Hits Back at Political Critics of Carcich Plea." *Washington Post*, May 26, 1978.

———. "Father Carcich: A New Life; Father Carcich Builds a New Life in North Carolina Parish." *Washington Post*, July 16, 1981.

Schlesinger, Arthur M., Jr. *Journals: 1952–2000.* New York: Penguin Press, 2007.

Scott, Janny. "The Story of Obama, Written by Obama." *New York Times*, May 18, 2008.

Secord, Richard. *Honored and Betrayed: Irangate, Covert Affairs, and the Secret War in Laos.* New York: John Wiley and Sons, 1992.

Segal, David. "Washington Hearsay . . . Williams & Connolly Loses Verdict in Lawsuit by Hollywood Dealmaker." *Washington Post*, Oct. 11, 1999.

Shapiro, Leonard. "Vardaman Makes His Case on the Senior Circuit." *Washington Post*, Oct. 28, 2005.

Shaugnessy, Dan. *Reversing the Curse: Inside the* 2004 *Boston Red Sox.* Boston: Houghton Mifflin, 2005.

Slevin, Peter. "Trucker Convicted in Death of Student; Manslaughter Verdict Called a Compromise." *Washington Post*, May 19, 1998.

———. "Youth Killed by Dump Truck Will Have a Legacy of Reform: Parents to Donate $4.6 Million Settlement, Seek Safety Standards." *Washington Post*, Aug. 4, 1999.

Starr, Mark. "Reversing the Curse." *Newsweek*, April 19, 2004.

Streitfeld, David. "James Baker Signs Book Deal; Putnam Wins Bidding War for Statesman's Memoirs." *Washington Post*, Feb. 5, 1993.

Stephanopoulos, George. *All Too Human: A Political Education.* Boston: Little, Brown, 1999.

Stolberg, Sheryl Gay. "For a Power Lawyer, A New High-Wire Act." *New York Times,* Jan. 17, 2009.

Stone, Peter H. "No Tears for Tobacco Lawyers." *National Journal,* July 19, 1997.

Strauss, Valerie. "A Rebellion at Georgetown Law; Students, Faculty and Alumni Work to Fight Dean's Ouster." *Washington Post,* April 16, 1998.

Summers, Anthony. *The Arrogance of Power: The Secret World of Richard Nixon.* New York: Viking, 2000.

Stewart, James B. *Blood Sport: The President and His Adversaries.* Simon & Schuster, 1996.

———. *The Partners: Inside America's Most Powerful Law Firms.* New York: Simon & Schuster, 1983.

Taylor, Stuart. "Closing Arguments Are Made in Washington Post Libel Trial." New York Times, July 28, 1982.

Thomas, Evan. *The Man to See: Edward Bennett Williams.* New York: Simon & Schuster, 1991.

Thomas, Landon, Jr. "There, in Grasso's Corner, Is That Oliver North?" *New York Times,* May 23, 2004.

Thomas, Landon, Jr., and Jenny Anderson. "Report Details Huge Pay Deal Grasso Set Up." *New York Times,* Feb. 3, 2005.

Toobin, Jeffrey. *Opening Arguments: A Young Lawyer's First Case.* Rev. ed. New York: Penguin Books, 1992.

———. A Vast Conspiracy. New York: Random House, 1999.

Torry, Saundra. "Williams Eulogized at Mass as a Man of Stalwart Faith." *Washington Post,* Aug. 17, 1988.

Trueheart, Charles. "Washington: The Book; A Reader's Guide to the Literature of Power." *Washington Post,* June 4, 1989.

Van Voorhis, Scott. "Hub's Just Wild About Larry." *Boston Herald,* Oct. 31, 2004.

Von Drehle, David. *Among the Lowest of the Dead: The Culture of Death Row.* New York: Times Books, 1995.

Walsh, Lawrence E. *Firewall: The Iran-Contra Conspiracy and Cover-up.* New York: W. W. Norton, 1997.

Weeks, Linton. "Hillary Clinton Seals $8 Million Book Deal." *Washington Post,* Dec. 16, 2000.

———. "Low-Key Lawyer Takes Center Stage." *Washington Post,* Feb. 11, 1998.

Weintraub, Arlene. "The Lawyer Is in at Pfizer; Jeffrey Kindler's Ascent Reflects the New Challenges Drugmakers Face." *Business Week,* Aug. 3, 2006.

Wittes, Benjamin. *Starr: A Reassessment.* New Haven: Yale University Press, 2002.

Woodward, Bob. *Shadow: Five Presidents and the Legacy of Watergate.* New York: Simon & Schuster, 1999.

Zane, J. Peder, and Rob Christensen. "Murdoch Surprises Publishers by Buying Edwards Book for $900,000." *Raleigh News & Observer,* Aug. 11, 2007.

INDEX

———■———

EBW stands for Edward Bennett Williams.
W&C stands for Williams & Connolly.

ABC, 172, 207, 234
Abramoff, Jack, 25, 28, 288
Abrams, Elliot, 128
Abramson, Jill, xii
Acheson, Dean, 10–11, 44
Adams, Cindy, 272
Adams, Ken, xii
African Americans, in politics, 47
agents, literary, 116–17
Agger, Carolyn, 48
Agnew, Spiro, 26, 58–60, 61
Agriculture Department (USDA), 8
Alaska
    "bridge to nowhere," 277
    political corruption alleged in,
        279–80, 286, 291
Alaska natives, 281
Albright, Madeleine, 225, 264
Alexander, Lamar, 209
Alexander the Great (movie), 39
Al Fayed, Mohamed, 5
Allen, Bill
    and renovation on Ted Stevens's
        chalet, 278–80
    failure to send Stevens a bill, 279,
        293–95
    pressured to cooperate with
        prosecutors, 285–87, 291,
        298–99

Allen, George, 76, 77
Allen, James, 103
Allen, Mark, 287, 299
Allen, Steve, 104
Al Shiraa newspaper, 124–25
Amanpour, Christiane, 265
American justice system, importance
    of money in, 84
The American Lawyer, ix, 5, 146–47
American Spectator, 182
America Online, 25
Ames, Aldrich, 9
Andreas, Dwayne, 235
Andreas, Inez, 235
Angell, Roger, 255
Angelos, Peter, 250
apple juice, in baby food, 144
Archer Daniels Midland, 52, 172,
    234
Areen, Judith, 212–14
Arkansas
    Kendall's explorations of, 179
    state trooper allegations
        ("Troopergate"), 182, 186, 211
Arlington National Cemetery, 46
Army-McCarthy hearings, 137
Arnold, Tom, 166
Arnold & Porter, 48–49, 69, 70,
    211

associates, 36–37
  pay of, 170
Atlantic Monthly, 116
Atlas Club, 37–38
AT&T, 17

Babby, Lon, 33
baby food scandal, 144–49
Bachrach, Judy, 192
Baker, Bobby, 47, 222–23
Baker, Howard, Jr., 106, 127, 158
  bio and career of, 19–24
  and Watergate, 61
Baker, James, 173
Baker, Joy, 20, 106
Baker Donelson, 21
Baltimore, Md., 118–19
Baltimore Colts, 118
Baltimore Orioles
  EBW ownership of, 151
  losing seasons, 155–56
  Lucchino's leadership of, 121–23,
    157–62, 250
  plan for new stadium, 118–19,
    161–62, 251, 253
  popularity of, 78–79
  stars of, 171
Baltimore Sun, 106
Bantam Books, 116
Baptists, 18
Barnett, Bernard, 86, 88
Barnett, Meredith, 209
Barnett, Robert (grandfather of
    Robert Bruce Barnett), 86
Barnett, Robert Bruce
  bio and career, 86–90
  book agent role, ix, 49, 123, 188, 199,
    206–7, 248–49, 263–69, 272–74,
    301
  clerks for White, 95–96
  clients of, 5, 27, 28
  as Clintons' personal attorney, 164, 216
  consoles Hillary over Whitewater
    woes, 183, 220

as debate coach, 112–17, 155–56,
    163–64, 241
  earnings of, 240
  growing success of, 124
  helps Hillary Clinton's Senate race,
    241
  interviews with, xi
  job agency of, 33, 171–74, 246–48
  law background of, 192
  mentioned, 212
  political influence of, 301
  in the presidential election of 2008,
    274–75
  public relations role, 203, 249–50,
    268
  testimony to Senate Banking
    Committee on Whitewater,
    198–201
  and the Vincent Foster affair, 175–78
  in W&C management, 171
  in W&C "State Department," 103–5
  work style, 103–5
Barr, Roseanne, 166
Barrett, David M., 232
Barry, Bill, 170
Barry University, 235
Baruch, Bernard, 207
baseball, 118, 161–62, 250–62
  commissioner of, 250
  players' union, 260
Bass, Mike, 77
Bates, Joe, 82
Batista, Fulgencio, 234
Bay of Pigs invasion, 45, 111–12
Bazelon, David, 167
Beall, George, 59
Beane, Billy, 258
Bear Stearns, 29
Beathard, Bobby, 77
Beckwith, David, xii
Beech-Nut (original company), 144
Beech-Nut Nutrition, 144–46
Beggs, James, 131–32
Begich, Mark, 278

Belnick, Mark, 135, 143
Ben Cooper Foundation, 214
Bennett, Robert F. (Senator, Utah), 193
Bennett, Robert S.
  bio and career, 188–97
  legal bills owed by Clinton, 240
  mentioned, 276
  and the Paula Jones case, 203–4, 208, 210, 216–17, 219, 223, 225, 227, 240, 290
  reputation as defense lawyer, 186, 280, 285, 292
  sometimes mistaken for older brother William Bennett, 188
Bennett, William, 188–89
Berkowitz, Sean, 29
Berlin, Isaiah, 94
Berman, Michael, 112
Bernanke, Ben, 267
Bertelsmann AG, 241
The Best and the Brightest (Halberstam), 46
"bet the company case," 124
Biden, Joe, 22–23, 26
Bilbo, Theodore, 7
Billard, Mary, xii
billing
  double, 9–10
  by the hour, 50
bipartisanship, 24–25
Bittman, Robert, 222–23
Bittman, William, 222–23
Blach, Leonard, 299
Black, Hugo, x, 173
Black, Roy, 169–70, 191
Black, Walter, 108–9
BlackBerry, 9
Blair, Tony, xi, 5, 268
Blitzer, Wolf, 5, 177, 265
Blood Feud (TV movie), 39
Blumenthal, Sidney, 217
Boeing, 190
Boggs, Hale, 20
Boggs, Thomas Hale, Jr., 20, 24

Boies, David, 241
book contracts, 115–17, 156, 173–74, 263–69
Boone, Aaron, 259, 260
Boren, David L., 157, 158–59, 197
Borgnine, Ernest, 39
Bork, Robert
  book contract of, 265–66
  failed Supreme Court nomination, 22–24
  and the anti-Clinton effort, 197, 210
  mentioned, 190
  on Nixon staff, 62
Boston, Mass., 120–21
Boston Globe, 256, 260
Boston Red Sox, xi, 254–62
  Lucchino's admiration of, 121
  Lucchino's purchase of, 4
  World Series pursuit for, 257–62
Boston University, 246–47
Boynton, Rob, xii
Bradlee, Ben, 37, 151, 152
Bradley, Bill, 72–73, 155
Brady, James, 81
Brady v. Maryland, 292
Brand, Stanley, 206
Braver, Rita, 88–90, 105, 163, 171, 172, 176–78, 180, 206, 208, 212, 216, 266
Brennan, William J., Jr., 16, 17, 65, 147, 167
Brewster, Kingman, 68
bribes alleged, 287
"bridge to nowhere," 277
Brierton, David, 99
Brill, Steven, xii, 39
Brinkley, David, 152, 172, 207
Brock, David, 182
brokerage companies, 29–30
Brotons, Elizabet, 233
Brown, Kevin, 252
Brown & Williamson, 211, 212
Broyhill, Joel, 43

Brummett, John, 269
Bruton, James, 168
Buchwald, Art, 60, 152
Bull Durham (movie), 136
Bumpers, Dale, 229
Bundy, Bob, 286, 296
Burch, Francis, 107
Burger, Warren, 16, 109
Burnett, Carol, 164
Burning Tree Country Club, 41
Burr, Raymond, 222
Burton, Richard, 39
Bush, Barbara, 114, 172
Bush, George Herbert Walker
    administration, 24–25, 188
    Barnett's impersonation of, in debate
        preparation, 163–64
    in presidential election of 1988, 155
    in presidential election of 1992,
        172–73
    Supreme Court picks, 16–17
    as vice-presidential candidate, 113–15
Bush, George W., 5, 14, 19, 25, 29,
    159–60, 173, 241–42, 269, 270
    administration, 29, 128
Bush, Jenna, 265
Bush, Laura, 5, 265, 269
Business Week, 158
Butterfield, Alexander, 61–62, 74
Byrd, Robert, 229, 278

Cablevision Systems, 255
Cacheris, Plato, 8–10, 127, 191, 219
Calder, Alexander, 70
Califano, Joseph A.
    antismoking crusade, 65–66, 211, 215
    bio and career, 44
    in the Carter Cabinet, 65–66
    hirings by, 58, 75, 76, 103–4, 192
    joins W&C in leading role, 50,
        58–59, 70–71
    new firm founded by, 80
    and the peace movement, 68–69
    political background, 44–49

and the Reagan transition, 81
and Watergate, 61–63
Califano, Mark, 58
Califano, Ross & Heineman, 66
California Angels, 262
Calley, William, 50–52
Cambodia, 68–69
Camden Yards, Baltimore, 161–62, 251,
    253
Caminiti, Ken, 251
Cammarata, Joe, 197
campaign money, 112
Campbell, Joan Brown, 235
cancer, 119–22, 152–53
capital punishment, 95–100
Capitol, U.S., 7
Capra, Frank, 113
Carcich, Guido John, 106–7
Carlisle, Olga, 80
Carnegie Center for Terrestrial
        Magnetism, 213
Carter, Hodding, III, xii
Carter, Jimmy, 65, 80–81, 84, 103–4
    administration, 45, 65–66, 80–81,
        144
Carville, James, 173–74, 206, 265
Case, Steve, 25–26
Cassidy & Associates, 135
Castle Bank, 105
Castro, Fidel, 111–12, 233, 235–37
Castroneves, Helio, 191
Catholics
    in legal field, 44
    in politics, 44–45
CBS, 26, 249
CBS Evening News, 55, 176
CBS News, 163, 206, 208
Central America, 127
Chaney, James, 92, 93
Chase, Nicholas, 37–38, 50
Chass, Murray, 258
Cheney, Lynne, 173, 265
    new book by (in 2007), 266
    Sisters, 266

Cheney, Mary, 266
Cheney, Richard, 133, 160, 173, 265, 266
  memoir proposal by, 266–67
Chertoff, Michael, 200
Chevy Blazers, 195
Chicago Tribune, 172–73, 180–81
China
  Clinton's visit to, 268
  trade with, 25
Chineson, Joel, xii
Christopher, Warren, 19, 25
Chu, Morgan, 15
Church, Frank, 69
Churchill, Winston, 120
CIA, 9, 158–59, 243
Cisneros, Henry, 231–33, 244
City of Palms Park, Fort Myers, Fla., 256
civil rights movement, 91–94
Clay, Henry, 229
Clemens, Roger, 267
clients
  conflicts in representing, 64–65
  defense of, 130, 154–55
  high-profile, 142
  warnings to, from their attorneys, on how to handle themselves in the justice process, 133, 285, 292
Clifford, Clark, 66, 207
Clinton, Bill
  anger at Gore, 241–42
  Arkansas state trooper allegations, 182
  attorneys of, 5
  defense of, as president, 183
  deposition in Paula Jones case, 198, 216–17, 221–24
  and Dick Morris, 206
  disbarred in Arkansas, post-presidency, 249
  disgraced and in debt, post-presidency, 248–49
  finances of, 240

impeachment ordeal, 192–94, 198, 210, 216–30, 277
  lack of time of, to address the Paula Jones case, 208
  legal bills owed by, 240, 244, 249
  and Lewinsky, 9, 15, 202, 208
  Lewinsky liaison admitted, 220
  Martha's Vineyard visit, 224
  meets Hillary, 70
  memoir by (*My Life*), 193, 202, 242, 244–45, 249
  mentioned, 178
  pardons, end-of-term, 242–45, 249
  and the Paula Jones case, 194
  political rise, 70–71, 75, 163–64
  popularity and success of, post-presidency, 249–50
  in the presidential election of 2008, 274
  prophecy that he would become president, 68
  reticence of interviewees about, xi
  in school, 73
  special prosecutor appointment debate, 184–87
  Starr's pursuit of, 216–28
  television talk show proposal, 249–50
  visit to China, 268
  "what the meaning of the word 'is' is," 223
  Whitewater investigation, 17
  and the Whitewater land development, 180
  womanizing trait, 226
Clinton, Bill, administration, 159, 175–88
  attorneys in, 19
  closing days of, 240–41
  end-of-term pardons, 242–45, 249
  feuds within, 188
  media coverage of, 171
  members of, leaving for private enterprise, 246–48
  transition team, 24–25

troubles of, 175–88, 231
W&C partners in, 164
Clinton, Hillary
and Barnett, 163–64
and Bennett, 193
and Bill Clinton's end-of-term
pardons, 244
during Bill's first months in office,
and appointments, 175–78
book contracts of, 263, 265
book *It Takes a Village*, 203
elected Senator from New York, 241,
248
Kendall's representation of, xi, 5,
180–86, 210, 226
learns of Lewinsky allegation, 217,
218–20
memoir by (*Living History*), 193, 248
mentioned, 264
in the Obama administration, 275–76
in the presidential election of 2008,
241, 273–75
and Rose Law Firm missing records,
201, 203–4
schooling of, 73
and Stephanopolous, 205–7
in the Watergate investigation, 74–75
CNN, 265
Coca-Cola, 69
Cohen, Richard, 59
Cohen, Steve, 68
the Colonnade apartments,
Washington, D.C., 112
Common Cause, 68
Communists, suspected, 38–39
compensation, excessive, 282–83
Conconi, Chuck, xii
Confrontation (yacht), 153
Congressional Country Club, 37
congressional hearings
perjury trap danger at, 198–201
restraints on attorneys during, 137,
141
Connally, John, 63–64, 151

Connolly, Paul, 49, 50, 65, 153
Conrad, Kent, 227
conscientious objectors, 70
construction trucks, safety issue, 214
Conte Hernandez, Ramon, 111–12
Contras, 125–26, 127
Contreras, José, 257
Cooke, Jack Kent, 75–76, 78, 151,
281–82
Cooper, Benjamin Eric, 212–14
Cooper, John Sherman, 69
Cooper, Richard M., 59, 65, 76, 211–15
Cooper-Church Amendment, 69
Corey, Irwin, 104
Costello, Frank, 38, 164
Costner, Kevin, 123, 136
counterintelligence, 159
Couric, Katie, 5, 26, 171, 173, 212, 218,
250, 258
Courtesy Motors, 104
Covington & Burling, 10–11, 36, 41, 211
Cox, Archibald, 62
Cox, Christopher, 29–30
Craig, Bill, 67, 80
Craig, Gregory
in Agnew affair, 59
bio and career, 67–69, 73–75
clients of, 80
comings and goings of, from W&C,
79
in Cuba, 111–12
defense of Clinton in impeachment
battle, 225–30
defense style, 300
early acquaintance with the Clintons,
70–71
and the Elián González affair, 235–39
growing success of, 105, 124
and the Hinckley case, 82–85
interviews with, x
joins W&C, 49, 66
law background of, 192
leaves Clinton employ, 231
legal bills owed by Clinton, 240

Craig, Gregory (*continued*)
    mentioned, 212, 243
    in the Obama administration, 275–76
    political influence of, 301
    in the presidential election of 2008,
      273–75
    and Ted Kennedy, 168–70
    as White House counsel, 3–4, 5
Craig, Larry, 230, 278
Craig, Lois, 80
Cranston, Alan, 55
criminal defense, 50, 188
Cronkite, Walter, 55–56, 129
cruel and unusual punishment, 96
Cruise, Tom, 13
Cuba
    Bay of Pigs prisoner release, 111–12
    demonization of, in American
      politics, 234
    Elián González affair, 233–39
    escapes from, by sea, 233
    wish to normalize relations with,
      234–35
Cuban exile community, in Miami,
    233–34, 238–39
Culvahouse, Arthur B., Jr. ("A. B."),
    20–25, 26–28, 29, 30, 45, 61, 106,
    127, 269
Culvahouse, Arthur B. (father of A. B.
    Culvahouse, Jr.), 20
A Current Affair, 170
Currie, Betty, 228
Curry, Willis, 213–14
Cutler, Lloyd, 193–96, 204, 210, 225

Dale, Billy, 175
D'Amato, Alfonse, 198–201, 204, 277
Damon, Johnny, 257
Damon, Matt, 52
Dana-Farber Cancer Institute, Boston,
    120–21
Daniel, Aubrey M., III, 50–52, 58, 192
Danzig, Richard, 95
Darrow, Clarence, 34

Daschle, Tom, 204
Dateline NBC, 195
Davis, Gil, 194, 197
Davis, James W., 44
Davis, Nathaniel, 179
Davis Polk & Wardwell, 281
Dean, Howard, 264
death, fighting it, as selfish (EBW), 152
death penalty, 95–100
debates
    presidential, 116–17, 155, 274
    vice-presidential, 113–15
Debevoise & Plimpton, 264
DeCell, Ken, xii
defendants
    assumed by media to be guilty, 290
    plead guilty rather than face
      unlimited prosecution, 301
Defense Appropriations Bill, 125
defense attorneys
    former prosecutors as, 286
    role in society, 283
    in Washington politics, 128
defense contracting, 190
Delahanty, Thomas, 81
democracy, 270
Democratic National Committee, 50,
    60, 63, 151, 163
Democratic National Convention of
    2004, 271
Democrats
    and bipartisanship, 24–25
    in Washington, D.C., 112
    Williams & Connolly ties with, 173
De Niro, Robert, 84
Denman & Goddard, 9
Department of Defense, 190
deregulation, 30
D. E. Shaw Group, 247
Deutch, John Mark, 243
Dewey, Thomas E., 44–45
Dewey Ballantine, 44–45, 281
Diana, Princess, 5
Dickens, Charles, 229

Dick the Bruiser, 104
DiMaggio, Joe, 268
Dimmel, Silma, 237
Disney, Walt, 153
dittoheads, 204
DLA Piper, 7
Doar, John, 75
document review, in the Stevens case,
    291–95
Dodd, Chris, 270
dogs, police, 142
Doheny, Edward L., 35
Dolan, Charles, 255
Dole, Robert, 106, 114, 205
Donaldson, Sam, 171
Donaldson, William, 29
Donovan, Raymond, 8, 35, 222
double billing, 9–10
Douglas, Paul, 92
Dove Entertainment, 253
Dreams from My Father (Obama), 271
Dukakis, Kitty, 156
Dukakis, Michael, 155–56
Duke University, lacrosse players
    accused at, 284–85
Duke Zeibert's Restaurant,
    Washington, D.C., 118
Dunleavy, Steve, 170
Dunne, Thomas, ix
Durham, N.C., Police Department,
    284
Dystel, Jane, ix, 270–73

Ebbers, Bernie, 212
Edelson, Nona, xii
Edward, Elizabeth, 263
Edward Bennett Williams Building,
    12–13
Edward Bennett Williams for the Defense
    (Robert Pack), 13
Edwards, John
    book contracts of, 263–64, 265
    girlfriend and love child of, 229, 264
Edwards, Kevin, 152

Eggleston, Neil, 264
Eisenhower, Dwight, 16, 17
Elizabeth II, Queen of England, if she
    ever writes a book, who her agent
    will be, 268
Emmett, Jay, 119, 121, 251, 259
Enron, 28–29
Ensign, John, 230
Environmental Protection Agency
    (EPA), 77, 109
Epstein, Theo, 161, 251–52, 258–59,
    261–62, 300
Ervin, Sam, 61, 63
Ettinger, Mitch, 217
Evans, Linda Sue, 243
Evans-Pritchard, Ambrose, 199
Evening Standard Magazine, 268
Examiner (tabloid), 165
ex-presidents, books by, 248
Exxon, 11
Exxon Valdez oil spill, 11

Faircloth, Lauch, 200–201
Fall, Albert, 35
family values, and the Elián González
    affair, 233
FBI, 9, 105, 279–80, 298
Federal Express, 21, 24
Federalist Society, 182
Federal Reserve Board, 267
Feffer, Gerald, 168
Fenway Park, Boston, 121, 255, 257
Ferraro, Geraldine
    book by, 115–16
    observations of, 134, 265
    as vice-presidential candidate, 27,
    112–16
Ferrer, José, 39
Ferris, Henry, 271
Field of Dreams (movie), 123
Fifth Amendment, 130, 133
Finch, Robert, 62
Finley, Steve, 251
The Firm (movie), 13

"The Firm That Runs the World," x
first ladies, books by, 248
Fisch, Alan, xii
Fisher, Alice, 29
Fiske, Robert, 185, 195–96, 212
Fitzgerald, Ella, 158
Fitzgerald, Peter, 270
Fitzwater, Marlin, 173
Fleisher, Ari, 265
Florida, election recount of 2000,
    241–42
Florida Marlins, 255
Flowers, Gennifer, 211, 224
Food and Drug Administration (FDA),
    8, 65, 145–46, 211–15
Forbes, Walter, 291
Forbes Field, Pittsburgh, 118, 252
Ford, Gerald, 106
Ford, Henry, 153
forms, failure to honestly fill out, as
    crime, 290
Fortas, Abe, 48–49
Fortensky, Larry, 165–66
Ft. Myers, Florida, xi
Foster, Jodie, 82–85
Foster, Vincent, 175–79, 185, 196,
    198–201
Fox News, 19, 182, 199, 264, 265, 269
Franken, Al, 197
Franks, Tommy, 267
Freiwald, Aaron, xii
Friday the thirteenth, 153, 259
Fried, Frank, Harris, Shriver &
    Jacobson, 10, 160
The Front Page (movie), 167
Fuller, Vincent, 82–85
Furman v. Georgia, 95–96

Gammons, Peter, 260
Garciaparra, Nomar, 260, 261, 262
Gardner, Fred, 54
Gardner, John, 67, 68–69
Garvin, Glenn, xii
gasoline, price of, 26

Gates, Bill, 281
gay marriage, 266
General Accounting Office (GAO),
    232
General Motors, 105, 195
Gentile, Richard Lee, 54
Georgetown University, 53, 56
Georgetown University Medical Center,
    119, 152
George Washington University, 18
ghostwriters, 156
Giancana, Sam, 38
Gibson, Dunn & Crutcher, 14, 15,
    18–19, 26, 33, 109, 252
Gielgud, John, 274
gifts, disclosure of, 288, 298
Gill, Brendan, 79
Gingrich, Newt, 204
Girdwood, off the Chickaloon Bay,
    Alaska, 279
Gish, Lillian, 34
Giuliani, Rudolph, 28, 83, 113, 242
Globe (tabloid), 165
Going Rogue (Palin), 27
Goldberg, Arthur, 48, 67
Goldberg v. Kelly, 65
Goldin, Daniel, 246–47
Goldman Sachs, 247
Goldwater, Barry, 26
González, Elián, 112, 233–39
González, Juan Miguel, 235–39
González, Lázaro, 233, 238
Goodell, Charles, 55
Goodman, Andrew, 91–93
Good Morning America, 207
Good Samaritan trial, 189
Gordon, Richard Alan, 56–57
Gore, Al
    book contracts, 264
    and the Internet, 25
    loss of 2000 election, 241–42
    staff of, 19
Gorgeous George, 104
Gould, Milton, 151

Graham, Bill (son of Katharine Graham), 50, 165
Graham, Billy, 64, 204
Graham, Bob, 97
Graham, Katharine, 41–42, 47–48, 49, 151
Graham, Philip, 41–42, 97
Grasso, Dick, 3, 282–83
Gray, Boyden, 16
Green, Allen I., 58–60, 61
Green, Tom, 127–28
Greenberg Traurig, 28
Greenspan, Alan, 5, 267–68
Greenville, Mississippi, 265
Greider, Bill, 116
Gridiron Dinner, 197
Grisham, John, 13
guilty, pleading, rather than face unlimited prosecution, 301
gun control, 81
Gutman, Howard, 243
Gwynn, Tony, 251

Haig, Alexander, 46, 62, 81
Halberstam, David, 46
Haldeman, Bob, 62
Hall, Fawn, 8, 125, 127, 132
Hamilton, Lee, 133–34
Hanssen, Robert, 9
Harding administration, 34–35
Harding College, 18
Hard Times, 54–55
Harper & Row, 117
Harrington, John, 121
Harrison, William Henry, 176
Harvard Law Review, 270
Harvard Law School, 131, 167, 270
Harvard University, 247
Harvard University Medical School, 120
hatpin question of Clinton, 217
Hausfeld, Michael, 11–12
Hawk missiles, 125
Hayes, Helen, 34
Height of Buildings Act, 7

Heineman, Ben, 65
Helmsley, Leona, 32, 168
Henry, John, xii, 255–56, 261
Hinckley, John W., Jr., 2, 81–85
Hinckley, John W. (father), 82, 83
history, keeping memories for (diaries, tapes), 115
Hoffa, Jimmy, 39–40, 82, 146
Hoffberger, Jerold, 78, 250
Hoffman, Richard, 4
Hoffman, Trevor, 252
Hogan, Frank, 34–35
Hogan & Hartson, 7, 34–37, 60, 189–90, 211, 276, 299
Holder, Eric, 2, 298
Holdsclaw, Chamique, 210
Holmes, Sven Erik, 4, 159, 160, 197
Holocaust, 11
Hoover, J. Edgar, 39
hornbooks, 167
hostages, in Lebanon, 124–25
House of Representatives
    Judiciary Committee, 227–28
    Nixon Impeachment Inquiry, 71, 74
    Republican control of (1994), 25
    Task Force on Capital Markets, 30
    Un-American Activities Committee (HUAC), 38–39
Howrey & Simon, 135, 143
Hoyvald, Niels, 144–49
Hubbell, Webb, 175, 185–86, 196, 244–45
Hughes, Karen, 265
Huizenga, Wayne, 255
Hume, Brit, 142, 177
Humphrey, Hubert, 16
Hunt, E. Howard, 222
Hunt, Richard, 12–13
Hutchison, Kay Bailey, 277
Huvelle, Ellen, 288
Hyde, Henry, 227

Ickes, Harold, 184, 192–93, 275
Illinois, politics in, 270

Immigration and Naturalization Service (INS), 236, 238–39
impeachment, 74, 225
The Informant! (movie), 52
Inouye, Daniel, 133, 138–39, 140–41, 280–81, 296–97
insanity defense, 82–85
insider trading, 285
Internet, 25
Iran, weapon sales to, 124–26, 137
Iran-Contra scandal, 21, 124–43, 150, 186–87, 282
  criminal phase of, 153–54
  W&C gets a publicity boost from, 153
IRS, 107–9, 168
Israel, 137, 145

Jacobs, Eli, xii, 157–60, 197, 240, 243, 250, 267
Jacobsen, Jake, 63–64
James, Bill, 258
Japan, 24
Japanese-American Restitution Bill, 281
Jaworski, Leon, 62
Jenkins, Sally, 210
Jeter, Derek, 260
JM Family Enterprises, 105, 172
John Paul II, Pope, book by, 248, 249
Johnson, Andrew, 225
Johnson, Carrie, 29
Johnson, Lady Bird, 46
Johnson, Lyndon B., 43, 46–48, 62
  administration, 67
Johnson, Richard, 256
Jones, Linda (Linda Medlar), 231–33
Jones, Paula
  allegation and suit of, 186–87
  Bennett's handling of case, 203–4, 208, 210, 216–17, 219, 223, 225, 227, 240, 290
  case, 193, 194–97, 203–4, 208, 210, 216–17, 219

  deposition in case, 198, 216–17, 221–24
  out of court settlement of case, 219, 240
  question of truth of the allegation, 226
Jones, Randy, 253
Jordan, Vernon, 273
journalism, ethics of, 177
July 2 Cases, 96
Jurgensen, Sonny, 76, 150
Justice Department
  Criminal Tax Fraud Division, 107–9
  Office of Legal Counsel, 109
  Public Integrity Section, 287, 289, 295
justice system, American, importance of money in, 84

Kagan, Elena, 4
Kaplansky, Zeev, 145
Keely, a sled dog, 290
Kelley, Paul X., 135
Kendall, David
  bio and career, 91–102
  clients of, 5, 16, 17, 164–66
  and the Clinton end-of-term pardons, 244–45
  in Clinton's defense against impeachment charges, 192–94, 198, 210, 218–30
  as Clintons' personal lawyer, 178–88, 202–5, 249
  defense style, 300, 301
  and Robert Bennett, 188
  growing success of, 124
  idealism of, 103
  interviews with, ix, xi
  "the Kendall exception," 98
  legal bills owed by Clinton, 240
  mentioned, 212
  studiousness of, 73
  in W&C management, 171
  in the Whitewater case, 200

Kennedy, Caroline, 131, 132, 274
Kennedy, Edward (Ted), 111–12,
    168–70, 225, 230, 270, 274
Kennedy, John F., 44–46, 64, 111,
    169
Kennedy, Robert, 39–40, 46, 146, 170,
    273
Kennedy family, 70, 169
    hijinks of, earning fees for W&C,
    169–70
Kentucky Derby, 299
Kerlow, Eleanor, xii
Kilmer, Billy, 76
Kindler, Jeffrey, x, 4, 165, 167–68,
    292–93
King, Larry, 84
King, Martin Luther, 46
King World, 249
Kirkland & Ellis, 17, 195
Kirkpatrick, David, 248
Kitman, Marvin, 177
Klain, Ron, 19, 24, 25–26
Klein, Edward, xii
Klein, Joel, 176, 185, 241
Korologos, Tom, 23
Kroc, Joan, 250
Kroc, Ray, 250
Ku Klux Klan, 93

Lader, Linda, 163
Lader, Philip, 163–64
Lansky, Meyer, 234
lateral hires, not practiced by W&C,
    32, 36–37, 98
Latham & Watkins, 14, 26, 29–30,
    33
Latin America, 111–12, 169
Lauer, Matt, 218
law firms
    ideological labels of, 19
    New York and Washington, D.C.,
        compared, 280–81
    partners and associates, 32
    self-promotion of, 30–32

viewed by public as protective of
    corporations and compliant with
    prosecutors, 302
lawyers
    anonymity of some, 180–81
    ethics of, 148, 249
    holding press conferences, 194
    jokes about, 21–22
    loyalty to their firms, 32–33
    not revered in small towns, 94
    publicity seeking of some, 181, 194
Laybourne, Geraldine, 102
Laybourne, Larry, 101–2
Laybourne (Kendall), Anne, 100–102,
    212
Lazio, Rick, 241, 274
Leahy, Patrick, 80, 224–25, 235, 237
Lebanon, 124
lecture fees, 247
Legal Times, ix, 135
Lehrman, Lewis, 157
Leno, Jay, 22, 143
Letterman, David, 269
leverage (ratio of associates to partners),
    36
leveraged buyouts, 159
Lewinsky, Monica
    affair with Clinton, 15, 202, 208
    apartment in Washington, 205
    blue dress of, 221
    defended by Cacheris, 8–9
    Starr never met, 228
    trapped by Starr, 216–23
    question of truth of the allegation, 226
Lewis, Michael, 258
Lewis, Neil, 31, 232
libel cases, 164–68, 264
Liberace, 166
LiCari, Jerome, 144–45
Liddy, G. Gordon, 60
Lieberman, Joseph, 158, 264
Liman, Arthur, 135–36, 139–43, 185
Limbaugh, Rush, 199, 200, 204
Limpert, John, xii

Lincoln, Abraham, 7
literary agents, 116–17
Lithgow, John, 67
Livorsi, Frank, 147
lobbyists, 8
Los Angeles, Calif., 14
Los Angeles Times, 182
Lott, Trent, 74, 228–29
Louis, Joe, 40
Lowell, Abbe, 288
Lowenstein, Allard, 68, 83, 226
loyalty, 32–33, 273, 276, 278
Lucchino, Dominic, 72, 253
Lucchino, Frank, 72, 119
Lucchino, Larry
    bio and career, 72–79
    cancer episode, 119–23, 152–53
    defense style, 300
    growing success of, 124
    interviews with, ix, xi, xii
    maintains partnership in W&C
        but is finally asked to resign,
        253–54
    mentioned, 192, 212
    psychology of, especially re: EBW,
        261–62
    sports ownership of, x, 4, 6, 118–23,
        157–62, 250–62
    superstitiousness of, 259
    in the Watergate affair, 184
    as W&C star, 105
    in W&C "War Department," 104
Lucchino, Rose, 72–73, 253
Luciano, Charles "Lucky," 37, 39, 234
Lyons, Jim, xii

MacFarlane, Robert, 137
Madison Savings & Loan, 179, 202
Madison Square Garden, New York,
    255
Madoff, Bernard, 29–30
Mafia, 38
    as clients, 50
Major League Baseball, 158

Maloney, Andrew J., 148
malpractice suits, 253–54
The Man to See (Evan Thomas), 13, 34
March on Washington (1963), 46
Marcus, Ruth, 132
Marine Corps, 134–35
Maris, Roger, 120
Marshall, Thurgood, 131
Martin, Suzanne, 151
Martindale-Hubbell Law Directory, 7
Marty (movie), 39
Matalin, Mary, 173–74, 268
Mazeroski, Bill, 72, 262
McCain, John
    feud with Stevens, 229, 277, 288, 291,
        297
    in presidential election of 2008,
        26–28, 30, 269, 288
    questions Hillary's book contract,
        249
    temper of, 247
McCarthy, Joseph, 38–39, 137
McCarthy, Tim, 81
McClellan, John L., 39
McCord, James, 60
McDonald's, 168, 172, 250
McFarlane, Robert, 125–26
McMillan, John L., 43
McNamara, Robert, 45, 46, 67
McVeigh, Timothy, 197
media, defendants assumed to be guilty
    by, 290
media practice, 171–72
Medlar, Linda, 231–33
Meese, Ed, 125–27, 130
Meet the Press, 5
Memorex, 157–58
Memorial Stadium, Baltimore, 118,
    158
Mendell, Alice Jean, 18
Mercer, Anne, 170
Methodist Church, 18
Metropolitan Club, Washington, D.C.,
    xi, 6, 36

Meyer, Katherine, 291
Miami, Florida, 233–34, 255
Miami Dolphins, 255
Microsoft, 281
migrant workers, 69
Milbank Tweed, 281
Milken, Michael, 135, 142, 158
milk industry lobby, 63–64
Miller, Alan, 191
Miller, Judith, 4
Miller, William, 26
millionaires, Senate composed of,
   270
Mills, Cheryl, 229
Mine That Bird (Thoroughbred horse),
   299
Minute Maid, 69
Missing (movie), 179
Mississippi Summer Project, 91–94
Mitchell, Andrea, 171, 177
Mitchell, Chad (Trio), 87
Mitchell, John, 135
Mnookin, Seth, 259
Mobil Oil Company, 16
Monahan, Jay, 171, 212, 218, 250
Mondale, Walter, 69, 103–4, 112–15
Moneyball (Lewis), 258
Montero-Duque, Ricardo Miguel,
   111–12
Moores, John, 250–51, 254, 258
Moran, Jim, 104–5
Morris, Brenda, 289, 291–96, 298–99
Morris, Dick, 205–6
Mr. Smith Goes to Washington, 113
MSNBC, 19
Mudge Rose, 135
Muhammad Ali, 189–90
Mulroney, Brian, 234
Murdoch, Rupert, 199, 263–64, 269
Murkowski, Frank, 279
Murkowski, Lisa, 270
Murphy, Eddie, 166
Mussina, Mike, 153
My Lai Massacre, 50–52

NAACP Legal Defense and
   Educational Fund, 93, 95–98
Nader, Ralph, 27, 182
Nadler, Lee, 120–21
NASA, 247
National Basketball Association, 33
National Center for Addiction and
   Substance Abuse, 211
National Council of Churches, 235
National Enquirer, 5, 13, 164–68, 221,
   264
National Labor Relations Act, 69
National Security Agency, 125
National Security Council, 124–26
native Alaskans, 281
Negroes, in politics, 47
Nelson, Edward, xii
Nestlé, 145–46
New American Library, 266
Newberg, Esther, 116
New England Sports Network, 256
News Corporation, 263–64
Newsday, 177
New York
   law firms, 281
   lawyers from, ill success in
      Washington, 192
New York Knicks, 255
New York Post, 264, 271, 272
New York Rangers, 255
New York Stock Exchange, 282–83
The New York Times, 31, 55, 210, 232,
   248, 257, 272
   article about Obama, 270
   bestseller list of, 263
   and the Boston Red Sox acquisition,
      256
New York Yankees, 60, 257–61, 262
Nicaragua, 125–26, 127–28
Nichols, Terry, 197–98
Nicklaus, Jack, 173
nicotine, 211
Nields, John, 135–39, 143, 196,
   244

Nields, The, Katryna and Nerissa
(singing group), 143
9/11 terrorist attack, 242, 282
Nixon, Richard
impeachment question, 71, 74,
225
mistakes made by, 22
pardons Calley, 51–52
political rise, 44
resigns presidency, 63, 74
special prosecutors of, 183
and vice president Agnew, 26, 59
in the Watergate affair, 19, 61–63,
184
Nixon, Richard, administration, 48, 58,
62, 69
taping system, 61–63, 74
Noriega, Manuel, 169
North, Betsy, 132, 136
North, Oliver
host of TV show, 203, 265
in Iran-Contra hearings, 124–43,
282
leaving the White House with secret
documents, 8
personality, 150
political aspirations, 150
on trial, 153–55, 282
Northrop Aviation, 190
not-for-profit compensation law, 282
Noyes, Derry, 70, 74
Noyes, Eliot, 70
Noyes (Craig), Derry, 79, 212, 226
Nussbaum, Bernard, 74, 175–76, 185,
192, 193

Oakland A's, 258
Obama, Barack
bio and career, 270–76
books by, ix, 271–74
Illinois Senate campaign, 273–74
loyalty component of, 273, 276
in the presidential election of 2008,
273–75

terrorism policies of, attacked by
Cheney, 267
Obama, Barack, administration, 248,
275–76
staffers from W&C, 4
Obama, Michelle, 273
O'Brien, Tim, 147
obstruction of justice, 231
O'Connor, Sandra Day, 196, 215
O'Donnell, Terrence, 173, 243, 301
Ogilvy Renault, 234–35
oil drilling industry, 279
Oklahoma City truck bombing, 197–98
Oliver North Legal Defense Fund,
141–42
Olson, Barbara, 241–42
Olson, Ted
and the anti-Clinton effort, 182–84,
197, 203, 210, 218
bio and career, 14–15
clients of, 127
and the presidential election of 2000,
19, 241–42
and the presidential election of 2008,
28
and Supreme Court justice picks, 18,
30, 195
and special prosecutor investigation
of EPA refusal to supply
documents, 109–10
and tort reform, 23–24
O'Melveny & Myers, 7, 14, 19, 20–21,
24–25, 26, 28–29, 33
Omni International, 107–9
O'Neill, Tip, 81, 206
Orange County, California, bankruptcy,
30
organized crime, 113
Oriole Park, Baltimore, 161–62
Ortega, Daniel, 127
Orza, Gene, 260
Osnos, Peter, 273
Oxford University, 94
Ozarks, 179

Pack, Robert, 13
Page & Smith opticians, 183
Palin, Sarah
    attacks Sen. Ted Stevens, 297
    book proposal, 5, 269
    bucks the Alaska establishment,
      279
    as vice-presidential candidate, 26–28,
      113
    why chosen as McCain's VP, 288
Palmer, Jim, 78, 171
Panama, 169
Parcells, Bill, 188
pardons, presidential, 242–45
partisanship, staged (a la professional
    wrestling), 265–66
partners, 36–37
Patton Boggs, 24
Paul, Weiss, Rifkind, Wharton &
    Garrison, 135, 143
Pauley, Jane, 195
Pearson, Drew, 17, 38
Pentagon, reorganization of, 45–46
Pepperdine University Law School,
    17–18
perjury, 198–201, 217, 223, 231
Perot, Ross, 130
Persons, Bob, 294
Petco Field, San Diego, 252
Peters, Hank, 122
Peterson, Peter, 157
Pfizer, 168
photocopying, cost of, 10
PIMCO, 267
Pitt, Harvey, 29
Pittsburgh, Pa., 118, 252
Pittsburgh Pirates, 254, 262
Platt, Thomas C., 148
plea bargains, 288
pleading guilty, 60, 192, 232, 289, 301
Podesta, John, 225, 227, 228
Poindexter, John, 125–26, 128, 133, 140,
    282
Policzer, Milt, xii

politicians, wealth of, facilitating career,
    270
politics, as theater, 114, 265–66
Pope, Generoso, 164–65
Postal Regulatory Commission, 101
"potted plant" remark, Sullivan's, 141
Povich, David, 253
Powell, Boog, 161
presidential election of 1976, 65, 104, 106
presidential election of 1980, 163
presidential election of 1984, 116–17,
    163
presidential election of 1988, 112–15,
    155–56, 163
presidential election of 1992, 163–64,
    172–74
presidential election of 1996, 205
presidential election of 2000, 19
    election recount, 241–42
presidential election of 2008, 26–30,
    263–64, 269, 273–75, 288
presidential immunity, 195, 196
Presidio army base, San Francisco,
    anti-Vietnam War sit-in protesters
    at (the Presidio 27), 52, 54
privacy, 156
pro bono, 141
Project Haven, 105
Project Purse Strings, 69
prosecutions, million dollar cost of, 227,
    232–33, 299
prosecutors
    attacking them for misconduct, as
      W&C defense strategy, 106–9,
      285, 300
    hatred and contempt for, 285–86
    misconduct of, 293–99, 301
    perjury trap used by, 223
    run amuck, 284
    self-destructing, after meeting with
      Brendan Sullivan, 283–84
    suspicion of, at W&C, 192
    who become defense lawyers, 188,
      192, 286

Public Citizen, 183
public office holders, payoff to, after
    leaving office, 21

Quayle, Dan, 159–60, 173
Quayle, Marilyn, 173
Queen of England, if she ever writes a
    book, who her agent will be, 268
Quinn, Msgr. W. Louis, 152

rainmakers, 172, 240
Ramallo, Marlene, 282
Ramirez, Manny, 260
Rather, Dan, 126, 176
Rauh, Carl, 189, 196
Rauh, Joseph L., 189
Rayburn, Sam, 7
Reagan, Nancy, 30, 82, 126
    memoir (*My Turn*), 248
Reagan, Ronald
    assassination attempt, 2, 81–85
    and the Iran-Contra scandal, 21–22,
        125–26, 130, 186–87
    memory lapses and Alzheimer's
        disease, 126, 130
    mentioned, 281
    political rise of, 15
    presidential election of 1984, 115,
        116–17
    special prosecutor of, 183
    Supreme Court justice picks,
        195–96
Reagan administration, 30, 116–17, 190
    attorneys in, 14, 109
    first appointments by, 81–85
Recount (HBO movie), 19
Reeves, Richard, 134
Regan, Donald, 116
Regardie's magazine, 152
Registrato, Joe, xii
Rehnquist, William, 190, 195
Remnick, David, 190
Renaissance Weekend, 163–64, 176
Reno, Janet, 175, 185, 238

Republican National Committee, 81,
    265
Republican Party, Transition Office, 81
Republicans
    in Alaska politics, 279
    and bipartisanship, 24–25
    and Clinton's impeachment, 228, 230
    and federal spending, 277
    House victory in 1994, 25, 204
    in Washington, D.C., 112
    W&C ties with, 173
reputation, 35
    getting it back, 155
Resolution Trust Company, 202
Resor, Stanley, 55
Rich, Denise, 242
Rich, Marc, 242–43
Richardson, Bill, 264
right-wing organizations, 183, 203–4,
    218
Riley, Richard, 163, 164
Ringling Brothers Circus, 291
Ripken, Cal, Jr., 78–79, 122–23, 171, 251
R. J. Reynolds, 211
Robb, Chuck, 50
Roberts, Pat, 277
Robinson, Brooks, 78, 171
Roche, Thomas, 149
Rodham, Hillary, 68, 70–71
Rodriguez, Alex, 259–61
Roe v. Wade, 95
Rogers, William P., 41
Rogers & Wells, 41, 164
Romano, Lois, 160, 197
Roosevelt, Franklin D., 45
Roosevelt, Theodore, 34
Rosedale villa, outside Washington, 239
Rose Law Firm, Little Rock, 175, 185,
    196
    Hillary Clinton's missing records
        from, 202–3
Rosenberg, Susan, 243
Rove, Karl, 268
Rudman, Warren, 16, 133, 135, 143

Ruff, Charles, 222, 223, 226–27, 229, 230
Russert, Tim, 5, 203
Ruth, Babe, 161, 259

Sabonjian, Robert, 86–87
St. Gabriel's Cemetery, Potomac, Maryland, 153
St. Louis Cardinals, 262
San Diego, East Village neighborhood, 252–53
San Diego Padres, 250–54, 256–59
   stadium for, 251–53
Sandinistas, 127
Sarasohn, Judy, xii
savings and loan associations, 178–79
Scaife, Richard Mellon, 182–83, 199
Scalia, Antonin, 190
Schilling, Curt, 259
Schlossberg, Edwin, 132
Schwarzenegger, Arnold, 160
Schwarzer, William, 80
Schwerner, Michael, 92, 93
"scorched earth" philosophy, 129, 154–55
Scott, Janny, 272
Secord, Richard, 127–28
Securities and Exchange Commission (SEC), 29–30
   Enforcement Division, 29
securities industry, deregulation, 30
segregation, 43
Seidenberg, Faith, 92
self-employed millionaires, Senate composed of, 270
Selig, Allan "Bud," 158, 250, 254–56
Seligman, Nicole
   bio and career, 131–32
   business success of, 4
   in Clinton impeachment episode, 198, 227, 230
   as Clinton's lawyer, 220
   connections to Kennedy family, 169
   defense style, 300

law background of, 192
lawyering skill of, 179
legal bills owed by Clinton, 240–41
socializing of, 160
Seligman, Stephanie, 131, 176
Senate
   Appropriations Committee, 277, 281
   Banking Committee, 198–201
   in Clinton impeachment trial, 228–30
   composed of self-employed millionaires, 270
   Ethics Committee, 249, 263, 280
   Judiciary Committee, 22–23
"Senator Earmark," 277
"Senator Pothole," 277
senators
   doing favors for constituents, 287–88
   ethics of, 229–30
   gifts to, to pay legal bills, 298
   outside income not allowed, excluding book contracts, 248–49
   seniority system, 24
   southern, 24
September 11, 2001, terrorist attack, 242, 282
sex, Bill Clinton coached in euphemisms in talking about, 221
Shakespearean tragedy, 274
Shalala, Donna, 246
Shapiro, Ron, 123
Shark Tank, ix
Shaughnessy, Dan, 252
Shoemaker, Willie, 17
shredding, 125
Shriver, Bobby, 160
Shriver, Eunice, 160
Shriver, Maria, 160
Shriver, Sargent, 160
Shultz, George, 126
Siegel, Benjamin, 20
Simon, Barry
   aggressive style of, 108–9, 131, 146–48

Simon, Barry (*continued*)
  defense of Cisneros, 232, 244
  defense style, 300, 301
  law background of, 192
  meets North, 150
Simon, William, 78
Simpson, O. J., 30, 169, 253
Simpson, Thacher & Bartlett, 44
Sinatra, Frank, 107, 168
Sirhan, Sirhan, 170
Sirica, John, 36, 60
Sisters (L. Cheney), 266
Skadden, Arps, Slate, Meagher & Flom,
  191, 216, 276
Skilling, Jeffrey, 28–29
Skolnik, Barney, 59
slip-and-fall lawsuits, 23–24
Smith, Jean Kennedy, 169
Smith, Richard L., 291
Smith, Steven, 169
Smith, William French, 14, 15, 17, 109,
  125
Smith, William Kennedy, 169–70
Smurfs and Hogs, 150
Snelling, Richard, 67
Socks the cat, 201, 266
Soldiers and Sailors Relief Act, 195
solicitor general, 16
Solzhenitsyn, Alexsandr, 80
Soriano, Alfonso, 260
Sotomayor, Sonia, 4
Souter, David, 16–17
Southeast Toyota, 104, 105
southern senators, 24
Spacey, Kevin, 19
speaking fees, 247
special prosecutors
  of Cisneros, 232–33
  of Clinton, 183–87, 195–96, 205
  of Iran-Contra scandal, 130
  of Nixon, 183
  runaway, 109–10, 232–33
Specter, Arlen, 23
speedy trial, right to, 290, 292

Spencer, Susan, 176, 177
Spenkelink, John, 96–100
Spitzer, Eliot, 282–83
Spring Hill College, Alabama, 152
Squibb, 144
stadiums, sports, 118–19, 161–62, 251,
  252
  named "stadiums" or "fields," 252
Stahl, Lesley, 90
Starr, Kenneth
  bio and career of, 15–18
  clients of, 212
  in Clinton deposition, 198–99
  and Clinton impeachment, 216–28,
    230
  at House Judiciary Committee
    hearing, 227–28
  in law firms on staff, 14
  leaks of, in Clinton case, 210–11, 221,
    225
  never met Monica Lewinsky, by own
    admission, 228
  in Reagan administration, 109
  right-wing pressure on, 203–4
  as special prosecutor, 195–96, 205
  Supreme Court connections, 30, 215
Starr Report, 225
state attorneys general, case against
  Microsoft, 281
state's evidence, 286
Stein, David, 112
Steinberg, Charles, 251
Steinbrenner, George, 60, 258, 260
Steiner, Josh, 206
Stephanopoulos, George, 184, 205–7
Stephens, Jay, 206
Stevens, Ben, 279–80, 287
Stevens, Catherine, 1
Stevens, Ted
  evidence in trial of, some hundred
    thousand pieces of paper, 291–95
  gifts received by, not disclosed on
    financial disclosure statements,
    288, 298

indictment of, triviality of items on, 289–90
political career of, 277–81
reelection campaign of 2008, 289, 297
renovation of his "chalet," 279–80
trial of, 31–32, 285–99
trial of voided and case dismissed, 1, 297–98
voted not to impeach Clinton, 229
Stewart, James, 184
Stewart, Jimmy, 73
Stewart, Martha, 285
Stockman, David, 116–17
Stout, Glenn, 256
Students for a Democratic Society (SDS), 68
subprime housing crisis, 30
Sullivan, Brendan
  bio and career, 52–57
  business brought in by, 50
  called "Solomon" by EBW, 57, 118
  clients don't go to prison, 147
  defense of Cisneros, 231–33, 244
  defense of North, 127–43
  defense of Stevens, 1, 281–84, 285–98
  defense of various other cases, 106–10, 146–49
  defense style, 31–32, 300, 301
  earnings of, 240
  growing success of, 124
  interviews with, ix, x
  in Iran-Contra scandal, 127–43
  joins W&C, 58–60
  leadership of W&C after EBW's death, 153–55, 302
  mentioned, 212
  "not a potted plant," 141
  pallbearer for EBW, 152
  pictures in office of, 153–54
  policy not to plead a client guilty, 60, 192, 232, 289
  policy not to trust the government, 60

  superstar status of, after North case, 150, 262
  in W&C management, 171
  as W&C star, 105
  in W&C "War Department," 104, 120
Sullivan, Brendan, III, 153
Sullivan, Ed, 104
Sullivan, Emmet, 2, 291, 295–99
Sullivan, Lila, 212
Sullivan, Sharon, 167–68
Sullivan & Cromwell, 281
Summers, Larry, 247–48
Summitt, Pat, 208–10, 268
Sunflower County, Mississippi, 290
Sununu, John, 16
Supreme Court
  clerks of, 95
  Clinton-Jones decision, 208, 210
  Florida recount decision, in the presidential election of 2000, 241
  ideological changes of members after arriving on the bench, 16
  nominations to, 3, 18, 22–23, 30, 195–96
  prospective members of, 16
Sweeney, Dennis, 83
Sweet, Charles, 253
Swiss banks, 11
Szafranksi, Ted, 262
Szymankiewicz, Joe, 97

Tanner, Jim, 33
tax evasion alleged, 168
tax fraud alleged, 191
Taxi Driver (movie), 84
Taylor, Elizabeth, 165–66, 167–68
Teapot Dome scandal, 34–35
Tenet, George, 159, 243, 267
terrorism, Cheney on, 267
Texas Rangers, 260
Thomas, Evan, 13, 34, 41, 141, 151, 152
Thomas, Helen, 27
Thomason, Harry, 193

Three Rivers Stadium, Pittsburgh, 252
Thurmond, Strom, 74, 229
Tigar, Michael, 197–98
Timberlake, Justin, 257
Time-Life Books, 101
Time magazine, 10–11, 101
Times Books, 271
tobacco industry, 11, 65–66, 211–15
Tolkien, J. R. R., 94
Torricelli, Robert, 279
tort reform, 23
Towers, Kevin, 252
Toyotas, 172
transition teams, 25
"Trans-Washington Highway" (Barnett's), 248
trial, as warfare, 293
Tribe, Laurence, 241
trickle-down economics, 116
Trimble, Elizabeth, 108–9
Tripp, Linda, 216, 217
truck safety, 214
Truman, Harry, 45
    administration, 139

Umin, Steven, 181
underworld, 38
Unification Church, 199
United States
    democracy in, 270
    justice system, importance of money in, 84
Universal Juice, 144
Universal Studios, 179
University of Chicago Law School, 88
University of Miami, 246
University of Pittsburgh Law School, 118
University of Richmond School of Law, 52
University of San Diego Law School, 252
University of Southern California, 35

University of Virginia, 56
university trustees, 246
USDA, 8
use immunity, 133–34

Valenti, Jack, 64, 152
Vance, Cyrus, 44–46, 65, 104
Vanity Fair, 192
Vardaman, Jack, 173, 301
vast right-wing conspiracy, 183, 218
VECO, 278, 291, 294, 299
Venable, 7
vetting of newspaper stories, 165
vice-presidential candidates, 26–28, 112–16
Vietnam War, 51, 53–56, 129
    protests against, 67–69
Viner, Deborah, 253
Viner, Michael, 253–54
Vinson & Elkins, 20–22, 28, 33, 64
Virginia, 43
Virginia Military Institute, 15
Von Drehle, David, 98

Wachtell, Lipton, Rosen & Katz, 131, 176
Wallace, Chris, 5, 181, 283
Wall Streeters, lack of success in Washington, D.C., 135
The Wall Street Journal, xi, 177
Walsh, Lawrence E., 130–31, 133, 150, 154, 187
Walters, Barbara, 203
war crimes, 51
Warren, Earl, 16, 17
Warren Court, 3
Washington, D.C.
    architecture of, 7, 12
    a bad baseball city, 255
    a company town in the business of government, 269
    congressional commissioner, rule of, 43, 47
    law firms of, 280

old Greyhound station, 11
party preferences of, 80–81, 112
permanent government of (Nader), 27
presidential/mayoral rule of, 47–48
resentment of, 27
Washington, Walter, 48
Washington and Lee University, 56
Washington Evening Star, 48
Washingtonian, ix, x, xi, xii, 19
Washington Legal Foundation, 182
Washington Mystics, 210
Washington Post, xii, 4, 5, 16, 28–29, 37, 41, 47, 49, 59, 60, 63, 98, 106, 124, 132, 151, 153, 160, 165, 181, 197, 207, 210
Washington Redskins, 75–78, 150, 151, 255
Washington Times, 199
Watergate affair, 19, 60–63, 74, 184
hearings (1970s), 19–20
Watergate apartments, Washington, D.C., 112, 205
Webb, Dan, 281–83
Webb, Robin, 41–42
Weekly World News (tabloid), 165, 166
Weinberger, Caspar, 186–87
Weiner, Larry, 87
Welch, Joseph, 137
Werner, Tom, 250–51, 255–56, 258
Weymouth, Katharine, 4, 165
whistle-blowers, 145, 298
White, Byron, 90, 91, 95–96, 103, 135
White House Travel Office, 175
Whitewater Development land dealings, 17, 176, 180
"Whitewater" investigation, 179, 180–81, 193, 196, 198, 206
cost of, 227
Wilder, Thornton, 87
Will, George, 5, 113, 171, 265
Willey, Kathleen, 223
Williams, Connolly & Califano, 49
new hires by Califano, 75

Williams, Dorothy (daughter of Frank Hogan), 35
Williams, Edward Bennett
bio and career, 34–42, 60
books about, 13
cancer of, 121–23, 124, 152
cases, 135, 137, 164
conflict of interest accusations, 151
at daughter's marriage, when he was very ill, 152
death and funeral of, 152–53
defense of John Connally, 63–65
defense of Hinckley, 82
enduring influence on practice of law at W&C, x, 301
and evangelist Billy Graham, 64, 204
and financier Marc Rich, 242
five disciples of, xi
friend of Katharine Graham, 47–49
hiring by, 50–52, 56–57, 58, 70, 192
"I'm about to see true power," 152
and the Iran-Contra scandal, 141–42
jealous of other lawyers' stardom (e.g., Sullivan), 150, 261–62
loses the Bobby Baker case, 222
mood-o-meter of, 76
nobody is "the next," 154
philosophy, that life is a contest, 122
pictures in office of, 153
political power of, 151–52, 163
preparedness for trial, 114
press coverage, 151
prevents Califano from recruiting W&C partners for the Carter administration, 65
refusal to admit defeat, 35, 40
sayings of, 152, 181, 185, 186
scorched earth philosophy, 129
sports ownerships of, 75–79, 118–19, 161, 250, 254
Williams, Maggie, 176, 200–201
Williams, Robert "Rocky," 295–96
Williams, Ted, 52

Williams, Tony, 34
Williams & Connolly
  alumni of, joining government or
    business, x, 301
  an anachronism among law firms,
    302
  Califano removes himself from, 65
  client defense comes first philosophy,
    155
  clients don't go to jail philosophy, 130,
    154–55
  clients for whom Clinton issued
    presidential pardons, 242–45
  criticisms of, 300
  former prosecutors not hired by,
    192
  future of, after death of EBW, 124,
    153
  game-changing Iran-Contra case,
    124, 153–54
  hired by other law firms to defend
    them, 28, 302
  hiring of attorneys, 50
  "if the case was winnable, they
    wouldn't hire us" belief, 41
  informal atmosphere and
    administration, 50
  lateral partners not accepted by, 32,
    170–71
  legal bills owed to, by Clinton, 240,
    244
  loyalty of its lawyers to the firm,
    32–33
  mail received by, 142
  malpractice suit against, 253–54
  masters of the game, 302
  military analogy, 120, 129, 257–58,
    302
  not overawed by government
    prosecutors, 301
  not popular with other lawyers,
    300–301
  and the Obama administration, 276
  offices of, 13, 257
  partners' marriages to successful
    career women, 212
  power of, in government and
    business, 33, 301
  press coverage of, ix
  profits and wealth of, 240
  public relations not practiced by,
    31–32, 33, 194
  rainmakers at, 240
  reporters not talked to, 13, 31
  scorched earth tactics (the scorpion
    defense), 154–55
  size of, 240
  uniqueness among law firms, 302
  "War Department" and "State
    Department" wings of, 104
  as a white guys' club, 131
Winston & Strawn, 7
Winthrop Stimson, 281
Wisdom, Bonnie, 89
Wisdom, John Minor, 88–89, 178,
  209
Wisenberg, Solomon L., 222
Witcover, Jules, 59
Wolff, Paul, 164–66
women's basketball, 209
Woodmont Country Club Golf Course,
  208
Woodward, Bob, 5, 60, 86, 127, 207
Woolley, Bennie "Chip," 299
WorldCom, 212
World Series, 250, 257
Wright, Susan Webber, 196–97, 216–17,
  249

Yale Club, New York City, 23–24
Yale University Law School, 73, 95
Yawkey, Tom, 254
Yawkey Trust, 254–55
Young Democrats, 18

Zaccaro, John, 112–13, 135
Zacharias, Steve, 87
Zweifach, Gerson, 167, 283